Evangelical
Missiological
Society
Series

no.17

MISSIONS from the MAJORITY WORLD:

PROGRESS, CHALLENGES, and CASE STUDIES

OTHER TITLES AND EDITORS IN THE EMS SERIES

Missions from the Majority World:
Progress, Challenges, and Case Studies
Copyright © 2009 by Evangelical Missiological Society

Published by
William Carey Library
1605 E. Elizabeth Street
Pasadena, CA 91104
www.missionbooks.org

Naomi Bradley, editorial manager
Johanna Deming and Rose Lee-Norman, assistant editors
Hugh Pindur, graphic designer

William Carey Library is a ministry of the
U.S. Center for World Mission
Pasadena, CA USA
www.uscwm.org

Printed in the United States
13 12 11 10 09   5 4 3 2 1 CH

Library of Congress Cataloging-in-Publication Data

Missions from the majority world : progress, challenges, and case studies /
Enoch Wan and Michael Pocock, editors.
p. cm. -- (Evangelical Missiological Society series ; no. 17)
Includes bibliographical references.
ISBN 978-0-87808-019-9
1. Missions. I. Wan, Enoch Yee-nock. II. Pocock, Michael, 1942-
BV2070.M579 2009
266--dc22
2009029014

Evangelical
Missiological
Society
Series

no.**17**

MISSIONS from the MAJORITY WORLD:

PROGRESS, CHALLENGES, and CASE STUDIES

ENOCH WAN and MICHAEL POCOCK, editors

WILLIAM CAREY
LIBRARY

About EMS

WWW.EMSWEB.ORG

The Evangelical Missiological Society is a professional organization with more than 350 members comprised of missiologists, mission administrators, teachers, pastors with strategic missiological interests, and students of missiology. EMS exists to advance the cause of world evangelization. We do this through study and evaluation of mission concepts and strategies from a biblical perspective with a view to commending sound mission theory and practice to churches, mission agencies, and schools of missionary training around the world. We hold an annual national conference and eight regional meetings held throughout the U.S.A. and Canada.

DEDICATION

In grateful memory of Ralph D. Winter, founder of the U.S. Center for World Mission and member and former vice president of the Southwest Region of the Evangelical Missiological Society. His fellowship and passion for the unreached peoples of the world gave prophetic missionary direction to us all.

EDITORIAL COMMENT

The editors accept responsibility for any grammatical awkwardness in the papers presented in this volume. The genius of this book is that it represents the thinking of many majority world writers. We ask the readers for patience with occasional lapses in the use of standard English. We are listening appreciatively to the voices of brothers and sisters who live the reality of missions from the majority world.

ACKNOWLEDGMENTS

The editors wish to express their appreciation for the tireless assistance of Rose Ann Hopwood, Coy D. Stark and to Kelley Mathews for assistance in editing this manuscript.

CONTENTS

INTRODUCTION

Enoch Wan

This volume is titled *Missions from the Majority World: Progress, Challenges, and Case Studies*,[1] and this introduction first gives a brief overview of the key concept "majority world" and related terms. Then follow explanations of why the focus is on majority world and what are the underlying assumptions and anticipated outcomes of this volume. Finally, the introduction outlines the organization of this volume and offers helpful tips for maximizing its use.

"MAJORITY WORLD" AND RELATED TERMS

The several terms related to "majority world" include "third world," "developing countries" or "under-developed countries," and "the south" and "global south."

---

1   On the case study method in missions, see the two titles below:
    Paul G. and Frances F. Hiebert (Author), *Case Studies in Missions*. Baker, 1987. The book is out of print, and a digital version is available for free download at www.GlobalMissiology.org "resource links" section.
    Alan Neely, *Christian Mission: A Case Study Approach* (American Society of Missiology Series). Orbis, N.Y., 1995.

The term "third world"[2] was used commonly during the Cold War era in reference to the part of the world that was neither of the first (i.e. Western democracies) nor the second world (the Soviet Union and its allies). But the Cold War has long since passed, and the term "third world" is now passé. Some scholars still use it in reference to countries that are technologically and economically less advanced. However, with the dynamic forces of globalization, urbanization, and politically sensitive speech, "third world" is no longer a helpful label, for it precludes the social and cultural wealth of many countries.

The terms "developing countries" and "under-developed countries" have strong negative connotations of lagging behind technologically and economically. Such terms nowadays are considered stereotypical and inappropriate. They focus negatively on what some countries lack in comparison to economically wealthy countries. The geographically oriented terms "the south" and "global south" are inadequate in reference to countries of economic standing and geographical location (counter-examples include Albania, Australia, Japan, and Mongolia).

"Majority world" is the term of choice for this volume, for it is a descriptive label highlighting the fact that countries within this category are populated by the majority of humankind demographically. The term lacks any negative connotation or judgmental evaluation.

---

2   For references on the term "third world," see A. R. Kasdan, *The Third World: A New Focus for Development* (1973); E. Hermassi, *The Third World Reassessed* (1980); H. A. Reitsma and J. M. Kleinpenning, *The Third World in Perspective* (1985); J. Cole, Development and Underdevelopment (1987). Michael Quinion (2005-02-26). "First, Second, and Third Worlds" (html). World Wide Words. http://www.worldwidewords.org/qa/qa-wor3.htm. Retrieved on 2009-05-22.

EMS 2008:
MISSIONS FROM THE MAJORITY WORLD

In September 2008, EMS celebrated its national conference in conjunction with The Mission Exchange (formerly EFMA) and CrossGlobal Link (formerly IFMA) at the North American Mission Leaders Conference (Triennial 2008). The theme for the annual conference was "Mission Initiatives from the Majority World Churches," and the presentation schedule featured many outstanding papers on the theme.

Well before this conference, Philip Jenkins[3] had highlighted the shift of Christianity from the West to the South and East. Other scholars, such as Andrew Walls[4] and Lamin Sanneh,[5] had convincingly proposed that lessons can be learned from missionary experiences outside of the West. This was the underlying assumption for the annual theme of EMS 2008, both at regional and national levels. The editors of this volume, Enoch Wan and Michael Pocock, served as the EMS 2008 conference program committee and operated with the same assumption in article selection. The outcome of the conference and the resulting volume, number 17 in the EMS series, is presented in the chapters that follow. This volume shows the progress and challenges of Missions from the

---

3   Philip Jenkins' *The Next Christendom: The Coming of Global Christianity – The Coming of Global Christianity*. Oxford University Press. 2002.

4   See Andrew Walls, "World Christianity, the Missionary Movement and the Ugly American," in *World Order and Religion*, edited by Wade Clark Roof, Albany, State University of New York Press, 1991.
       Also Andrew Walls, "Structural Problems in Mission Studies," *International Bulletin of Missionary Research*, vol. 15, no. 4, October 1991.

5   Lamin Sanneh in "Global Christianity and the Re-education of the West," in *The Christian Century*, July 19-16, 1995, pp. 715-718, stated well, "Edinburgh scholar Andrew Walls has argued that the shift of the numerical bulk of Christians from Europe and North America to Asia, Africa, Latin America and other areas outside the Northern Hemisphere has had more than demographic significance."

Majority WORLD and illustrates by case studies from Asia, Africa, and Latin America.

VOLUME 17 ORGANIZATION

Volume 17 is organized into six parts. Part 1, "Global Overview," features four chapters covering broad aspects of missions from the majority world:

- A Newer Missions Paradigm and the Growth of Missions from the Majority World;

- Seven Essentials of Majority World Emerging Mission Movements;

- Global Mission Partnership: Missiological Reflections After Ten Years of Experience; and

- In Through the Back Door: Reaching the Majority World in North America.

After the global overview, our focus narrows to regional aspects of Missions from the Majority WORLD. Seven chapters (Parts 2-4) look at issues in Asia, Africa and Latin America. Part 5, "Issues of Concern to Majority World Missions," features three chapters covering topics such as the use of narrative in missions movements from the majority world.

In Part 6, three case studies show the progress and challenges of missions from the majority world. Contributors include missionaries from the West and practitioners from the majority world, providing diversity of perspective.

These case studies are Christian responses to the trend of movement of people at a global scale in the 21st Century.[6] It is worth noting that the Lausanne Committee for World Evangelization (LCWE) has recognized the significance of the new paradigm of "diaspora mission" by appointing Dr. Sadiri Joy Tira as senior associate for diasporas. The LCWE also has designated one evening of the 2010 program of Lausanne III to feature diaspora missions.

Thus, of special interest in Volume 17 are the concepts of "reaching to" and "reaching through" people on the move (e.g. Mongolian migrant workers, scattered Tibetan Buddhists). Key articles covering these concepts are as follows:

- In Through the Back Door: Reaching the Majority World in North America (page 75);

- University Bible Fellowship: What Happens When Missionaries from Korea Descend on North American College Campuses? (page 121);

- Majority World Harvest Among Tibetan Buddhists: Historical Review, Ethnographic Overview, and Dynamic Development (page 151);

- Migrant Workers' Churches as Welcoming, Sending and Recruiting Entities: A Case Study of Mongolian Migrant Workers' Churches in Korea (page 371); and

- The Filipino Experience in Diaspora Missions: A Case Study of Mission Initiatives from the Majority World Churches (page 387).

---

6   For more on "diaspora missiology," see Enoch Wan, "Diaspora Missiology," *Occasional Bulletin of EMS,* Spring 2007, and organizations such as the Institute of Diaspora Studies (IDS-Asia in Manila and IDS-Korea in Seoul).

Maximizing Use of Volume 17

For use as a text or reference for seminary or Bible college students, the introduction and Part 1 will be essential for foundational understanding. Instructors might let students from various regions of the majority world conduct research on their countries of origin and then report their research findings as case studies of life-experience and living illustration. Discussion questions can be generated from the conclusion of each chapter, encouraging further reflection on issues raised.

Conclusion

The significance of this volume lies in the fact that it represents a current and growing phenomenon in world missions. The churches from the whole world are joined in the effort to reach the whole world. Although it has been documented that Western missionaries serving outside their countries still comprise the majority of world missions workers, the growth rate of majority world missionaries far outpaces that of the West.[7] In recent years, while Western missionary forces are shrinking in numbers and possibly in influence, Missions from the Majority WORLD have proliferated, bringing amazing progress and some challenges.

This volume represents the thinking of 11 majority world mission scholars and 10 Westerners with lengthy experience in the missionary enterprise. The editors trust that this volume will assist missionaries, agencies, local churches, and students preparing for missions.

---

7   Michael Jaffarian. "Are There More Non-Western Than Western Missionaries?", *International Bulletin of Missionary Research,*, Vol. 28, No. 3, July 2004.

CONTRIBUTORS

HOWARD BRANT is a third-generation missionary who grew up in Ethiopia. He and his wife, Jo-Ann, have served with SIM in Ethiopia, Ghana, India, and internationally. They are currently based in Nairobi, Kenya. In his current role as Champion for New Initiatives in Mission (emerging missions), he lectures, advocates, and seeks to advance the cause of emerging mission movements from all parts of the world. He is a strong advocate for kingdom diversity within missions like SIM. Howard received a D.Miss. from Trinity Evangelical Divinity School.

MEG CROSSMAN, director emeritus of PathWays Partnership, edited the *PathWays to Global Understanding* and *PathLight* curricula. An active missions mobilizer for 20 years, she helped produce more than 100 classes in Arizona and served on the boards of Caleb Project and Frontiers. Meg's background includes 10 years of prison ministry; living in Japan and Egypt; and short-term ministry in China, Mexico, India, and the Navajo reservation. A U.S. citizen, Meg holds a B.A. in English from the University of Arizona.

JULIO GUARNERI was born in Mexico City. He has served several churches in Texas as youth minister, minister of education, church planter, and pastor for a total of 25 years. Julio holds an M.A. from

Southwestern Baptist Theological Seminary and is currently pursuing a Ph.D. in leadership studies at Dallas Baptist University. Julio is pastor of Iglesia Bautista Getsemani in Fort Worth.

STEVE (HEUNG CHAN) KIM was born in Korea and has served 32 years in Latin America (Paraguay, Argentina, and Brazil). He currently serves as a missionary in Argentina and is founder of Barnabas Ministry, a sending agency from majority world to majority world. Steve received his Ph.D. with a major in missions from Southwestern Baptist Theological Seminary.

TESILIMI ADEREMI (REMI) LAWANSON, a Christian convert from Islam, obtained his Ph.D. in intercultural studies from Fuller Theological Seminary. He served as pioneer executive director for the Association of Evangelicals in Africa's Stewardship and Accountability Commission, as well as the foreign mission director for the Foursquare Church–Nigeria. As a bi-vocational mission administrator, Remi also worked in investment banking and actuarial services. He currently serves as an adjunct faculty member for Fuller Theological Seminary, Azusa Pacific University, and Biola University.

MYUNGHEE LEE was born and raised in South Korea. She earned her M.Div. from International Theological Seminary and Th.M. in Old Testament from Calvin Theological Seminary. She currently is writing her dissertation for the Ph.D. in intercultural studies at Trinity Evangelical Divinity School. Myunghee served as a missionary to India from 1996-1997, affiliated with the Presbyterian Church in Korea (Hapdong). She also has served as a teaching pastor and missions pastor in several churches in Korea and the United States.

Contributors

FOHLE LYGUNDA LI-M is the founding executive director of the Centre Missionnaire au Coeur d'Afrique (Mission Center in the Heart of Africa), based in the Democratic Republic of Congo. His ministry mobilizes churches for mission and trains and sends out African missionaries. He teaches mission and leadership in several African seminaries and is the author of *Initiation aux defis de la mission dans le contexte africain,* a textbook on mission in African contexts. Fohle received a D.Min. from Asbury Theological Seminary. He lives in Kinshasa, Democratic Republic of Congo.

JOEL MATTHEWS has been working in development in West Africa with SIM International since 1991. He directed an integrated development project in Niger, and he lectures on community development at Daystar University, Kenya. His M.A. thesis (2002) at the University of Wales focused on transformational development, and he is pursuing a P.h.D. in intercultural studies at Fuller Theological Seminary.

A. SCOTT MOREAU served 14 years on staff with Campus Crusade for Christ, including 10 years in Africa. He taught science at Ntonjeni Swazi National High School and missions at the Nairobi International School of Theology. In 1991, Scott joined the Intercultural Studies Department at Wheaton College, where he currently serves as professor. In 2000, he became managing editor of the Network for Strategic Missions Knowledge Base, a Web-based database on missions. Scott became the editor of *Evangelical Missions Quarterly* in 2001.

DAVID OLESON, a native of Washington state, holds an M.Div. from Fuller Theological Seminary and is currently enrolled in the D.Miss. program at Western Theological Seminary. He spent 25 years in Asia with the Assemblies of God World Missions, serving in the Marshall Islands, Philippines, Tibet, and India. For the past 10 years, David has been the coordinator for the intercultural studies and missions programs at Northwest University.

TIMOTHY KIHO PARK is director of Korean studies and associate professor of Asian mission at Fuller Theological Seminary School of Intercultural Studies. As an Asian missiologist, he has extensive experience in cross-cultural church planting and theological education. He serves as director of the Institute for Asian Mission, president of Asian Society of Missiology, and president of EAST-WEST Center for Missions Research & Development. A native of Korea, Timothy holds a Ph.D. in intercultural studies from Fuller Theological Seminary.

J. D. PAYNE is a national missionary with the North American Mission Board and associate professor of church planting and evangelism at The Southern Baptist Theological Seminary. A U.S. native, he has pastored churches and served with church-planting teams in the United States. He is the founder of Northamericanmissions.org, a Web-based resource, and the author of *Missional House Churches*, *The Barnabas Factors*, and *Discovering Church Planting*. He holds a Ph. D. in evangelism and church growth from The Southern Baptist Theological Seminary.

MICHAEL POCOCK, a native of England, spent his formative years in the United States. He pastored a diverse church in Chicago and served with TEAM as a missionary in Venezuela and later as mobilization director. He currently serves as senior professor and chairman of world missions and intercultural studies at Dallas Theological Seminary and as chairman of Evergreen Family Friendship Services/China. Mike holds a D.Miss. from Trinity Evangelical Divinity School and has researched and written on multicultural churches and the impact of global migration on missions.

SERGIO A. RAMOS was born in Mexico. He served as a director for Tarrant Baptist Association, leading churches in community ministries, and is currently a director for Buckner Children and Family Services. He gives leadership to multiple collaborations with churches, organizations, and institutions in the United States. Sergio obtained his M.A. from

Southwestern Baptist Theological Seminary and is currently pursuing a Ph.D. in leadership studies at Dallas Baptist University.

DOUGLAS L. RUTT, a native of Minnesota state, holds a Ph.D. from Concordia Theological Seminary. He served as a missionary and theological educator in Guatemala, as a parish pastor in southern Minnesota, and as area secretary for Latin America/Caribbean for World Missions of the Lutheran Church–Missouri Synod. At Concordia, he has served as an associate professor of pastoral ministry and missions, supervisor of the Ph.D. in missiology program, and now as dean for distance learning. Douglas is the chairman of the board of Lutheran Bible Translators.

JOSEPH L. SCHAFER is an associate professor of statistics at The Pennsylvania State University. He has been a member of University Bible Fellowship since 1982.

ROBERT STRAUSS is president of Worldview Resource Group, an organization that provides training in worldview analysis and expositional storytelling in support of emerging mission movements from the majority world. He works as an intercultural consultant in India and South America. Robert received his D.Miss. from Biola University School of Intercultural Studies. An affiliate faculty member at Regis University, he is the *pro tem* executive director of the Rocky Mountain Local Group of the Society for Intercultural Education Training and Research (SIETAR).

ANDRE TALLA is a pastor and educator in Cameroon. Over the past 20 years, he has developed an integrated ministry that includes training Christian workers (African Academy of Christian Leadership), planting churches, and directing believers in continuous outreach to the unreached in Cameroon and other French-speaking areas of Africa.

He heads an association of 250 churches and maintains a very practical training program that produces 100 new workers each year.

SADIRI JOY TIRA holds a D.Miss. from Western Seminary and a D.Min. in intercultural studies from Reformed Theological Seminary. Born and raised in the Philippines, Joy now serves as the international coordinator for the Filipino International Network (FIN) and as senior associate for diasporas for the Lausanne Committee for World Evangelization (LCWE).

ENOCH WAN serves as director of both the D.Miss. program and Institute of Diaspora Studies at Western Seminary. He is founder and editor of the multilingual online journal www.GlobalMissiology.org, president of the Evangelical Missiological Society, vice president of Great Commission Center International, member of LCWE-Diasporas Leadership Team, and advisor to FIN. He is contributing editor to *Cultural Encounters*, *Great Commission Bi-Monthly*, and *Asia Pacific Journal of Intercultural Studies*.

MARK YOON came from Korea to the United States in 1976 as a missionary with the University Bible Fellowship. After ministering to college students on Chicago-area campuses for 30 years, he moved to Boston in 2007 and currently serves there as a campus minister at Boston University. He holds a Ph.D. in philosophy of education from Loyola University–Chicago.

1. A NEWER MISSIONS PARADIGM AND THE GROWTH OF MISSIONS FROM THE MAJORITY WORLD

Steve (Heung Chan) Kim

INTRODUCTION

The growth of the majority world is surprising. In lands where numerous missionaries have worked for many years without results, God is moving in amazing ways. During the colonial era, missionaries served in the majority world, sometimes with and sometimes without the help of the colonial rulers; they had success in some areas but in others did not have many results. Several strategies were used to reach those lands. Among those, the most effective in term of conversion was the forced conversion, especially in Latin America, where vast lands were reached. However, the theological background that brought the *exploradores* produced nominal and formal religion characterized by a minimum level of spiritual commitment. Another effective strategy was the Three-Self Formula, which was applied successfully in some areas but failed in others. Now, at the beginning of the 21st century, many missionaries are talking about the Partnership strategy. This strategy, like other strategies, has both positive and negative aspects.

The Growth of the Majority World Church

One of the most surprising changes studied recently is the growth of non-Western Christianity. Contrary to the negative and pessimistic views that Christianity is shrinking, the church is actually growing, but this growth is happening in the majority world countries. Nevertheless, secular commentators such as Samuel P. Huntington have given a negative view of the future of Christianity. Besides his emphasis that the source of conflict in the new century world will be primarily cultural rather than ideological or economic, Huntington predicts that Islam will, in the end, overcome Christianity. According to Huntington, Christianity spreads by conversion, but Islam spreads especially by demographic increases, which will make Islam the predominant world religion. By the year 2025, Muslims will probable account for 30 percent of world's population.[1]

However, Huntington's prediction did not take into account the growing number of Christians in the majority world. Philip Jenkins, looking more globally, predicted that in 2050 the proportion of Christians to Muslims will be three for two. In fact, he predicted that Christianity will be the next leading religion rather than Islam. In addition, he mentioned that Huntington's prediction took into account only the

---

1 Samuel P. Huntington, *The Clash of Civilizations and the Remaking of World Order* (New York: Simon and Schuster, 1996) 65-66; Philip Jenkins, *The Next Christendom* (New York: Oxford University Press, 2007), 5; Marty Shaw, Jr. and Enoch Wan, "The Future of Globalizing: What the Literature Suggests" [on-line]; accessed 12 April 2004; available from http://www.globalmissiology.org/english/docs_html/featured /shaw_and_wan_future_of_globalizing_missions.html; Internet.

Western Christian world and did not consider the explosive increase of Christianity in the majority world.[2]

Because of this growth of Christianity in the southern hemisphere, several scholars have commented that the shift in Christianity has taken root.[3] Kenyan scholar John Mbiti believes that the centers of Christianity will be in the nations of the southern hemisphere and are no "longer in Geneva, Rome, Athens, Paris, London . . . New York, but Kinshasa, Buenos Aires, Addis Adaba, and Manila."[4] Christianity is going well, and it is expanding, but more to the south of the equator. This expansion to the south will make the church look more to this area, and it will have more weight for the future of Christianity. Philip Jenkins, in a very optimistic prediction, says that the liberal churches will decline and that the main growth trend lies in the majority world. Jenkins also observes that Pentecostalism, the main force for this trend, is expanding very quickly— in 2050, he predicts, there will be as many Pentecostals as Hindus and twice the number of Buddhists.[5]

Another phenomenon tied to the growth of majority world Christianity is the increasing number of missionaries being sent out from this part of the world. Missions are the result of this growth or could even be the reason for this growth. Countries from the majority world have received several waves of missionaries, but now they are the sending nations. Even though there are many unreached people groups, many of these nations, rather than receiving missionaries, have became more mature and started sending missionaries to foreign lands.

---

2   Jenkins, *The Next Christendom*, 5.

3   Kwame Bediako, *Christianity in Africa* (Edinburgh: Edinburgh University Press, 1995), viii, 154; Jenkins, *The Next Christendom*, 2; Lamin Sanneh, *Whose Religion Is Christianity?* (Grand Rapids: W. B. Eerdmands, 2003).

4   John S. Mbiti, "Theological Impotence and the Universality of the Church," *Mission Trends No.3,* ed. Gerald H. Anderson and Thomas F. Stransky, (Grand Rapids: Eerdmans, 1976), 9-10.

5   Jenkins, *The Next Christendom*, 9.

The Spread of Christianity in the Majority World

Christianity was predominantly Western at the end of the 19th century—Europe and North American were the places where most of the Christians lived. David Barrett, in the *World Christian Encyclopedia*, states that, in 1900, 80% of the Christian population came from Western lands, and also one third of the population were Christians. The spirit of that time was so high that they thought that the "Evangelization of the World in This Generation" was possible.[6] It was the time when "Christian" meant primarily white Europeans or Americans. That is one of the reasons why Christianity was tied to the Western cultures. However, this proportion shrank during the course of the century. Sixty years later, in 1960, the Christian population of Western nations diminished to 58%. This tendency continued, and in 1990 this number had fallen to 38%. Now it is predicted that in 2025 only 20 percent of Christians will be from Europe and that this number will include Protestants as well as Catholics. The 20th century saw a massive growth of Christians in the majority world and large diminution in the Western World.[7]

Patrick Johnston's statistics show that the proportion of non-Western Christians has grown steadily. In 1900, 16.7% of Christians were part of the non-Western world. This tendency grew to 35.6% in 1960,

---

6   David B. Barrett, George T. Kurian, and Todd M. Johnson, *World Christian Encyclopedia*, 2nd ed., vol. 1 (New York: Oxford University Press, 2001), 3-23; Donald E. Miller, "Emergent Patterns of Congregational Life and Leadership in the Developing World: Personal Reflections from a Research Odyssey," Duke Divinity School, *Pulpit and Pew Research Reports*, no. 3 (Winter 2003): 5. John R. Mott wrote a book expressing the high spirit of his time: John R. Mott, *The Evangelization of the World in This Generation* (New York: Student Volunteer Movement for Foreign Missions, 1901).

7   Patrick Johnstone, *Operation World* (Grand Rapids: Zondervan, 1993), 25; Stan Guthrie, *Missions in the Third Millennium: Key Trends for the 21st Century* (Waynesboro, GA: Paternoster Press, 2000), 133-34; Jenkins, *The New Christendom*, 2; Barrett, Kurian, and Johnson, *World Christian Encyclopedia*, 5.

reaching 59.4% in 2000. According to Johnstone, Christianity is now "truly a global religion once more—a status it lost twelve centuries ago."[8] The pendulum has swung from the West to the majority world. Michael Pocock says that the reason for these differences is not only that Western peoples are leaving Christianity but also that the growth has taken place outside the West; in some sections of the world, the expansion of Christianity has been explosive.[9] Thus, if this tendency continues—and it probably will—the majority world will become the Christian world's majority.

Also, Philip Jenkins optimistically states that by 2025 the number of Christians worldwide will reach 2.6 billion—including 595 million in Africa, 623 million in Latin America, and 498 million in Asia. The Christian population of Europe would be around 513 million. Africa and Latin America together would then comprise more than 50% of the world's Christian population. This trend, as Jenkins commented, would make the phrase "a white Christian" sound like an oxymoron. And, when one asks what type of theology the majority of Christians will have, the theological weight will go to the nations south of the equator, since Christianity is growing there and leaving its fingerprints on the theology of the church.[10]

If one looks for the number and location of Christians in the world, one can track the "center of gravity," the place where all Christians can be divided by half, whether the north section or the south section, in the East or the West. This "center of gravity" will identify the main

---

8   Johnstone and Mandryk, *Operation World*, 5.
9   Michael Pocock, Gailyn Van Rheenen, and Douglas McConnell, *The Changing Face of World Missions* (Grand Rapids: Baker Academic, 2005), 134.
10   Jenkins, *The Next Christendom*, 2-3. In fact, Jenkins suggested that because of the numerical growth of the South, the reading of Scripture will be more "literal and fundamentalist," since most of Christians hold this view in the Majority World. See also: Philip Jenkins, *The New Faces of Christianity: Believing the Bible in the Global South* (New York: Oxford University Press, 2006), 2-7.

geographic point of the growing number of Christians. Charting the movement of this "center of gravity" reveals the demographic growth of the church throughout the history of Christianity. Starting from AD 33, the year most agree marked the beginnings of Christianity, the center began to move from Jerusalem to the north and west. Later on, the center point started to go to the west and south. Todd M. Johnson observes that in 1970 this "center of gravity" changed direction and started to go to the east and south. This change of direction shows that Christianity became more oriented to the south and east and that the growth is occuring in those countries that are close to this point.[11]

Africa

From the genesis of the church, Africa was part of it. Acts 2 mentions Africans accepting the Christian faith. Acts 8:26-39 is about the conversion of the Ethiopian eunuch through Philip. Also, Simeon the Niger and Lucius of Cyrene, personages that have African background, appear in Acts 13:1-3. In the patristic era, Augustine of Hippo and Tertullian of North Africa put their mark on Christian history. Africa has always been on the heart of God, and He has continued working in these lands.[12]

Africa was the place where the colonial powers planted the gospel along with political and cultural dominion. Many Africans have seen the gospel in Western clothes and accompanied by European power. Lamin Sanneh, a professor at Yale and Harvard, says that despite the problems that came with the colonial era of Christianity in Africa, several factors led to the extraordinary growth of Christianity in Africa. One of those

---

11   Todd M. Johnson and Sun Young Chung, "Tracking Global Christianity's Statistical Centre of Gravity, AD 33-AD 2100," *International Review of Mission* 93 (April 2004): 166-68.

12   Pocock, Van Rheenen, and McConnell, *The Changing Face*, 135. Andrew F. Walls, *The Cross-Cultural Process in Christian History* (Maryknoll, NY: Orbis Books, 2002) 86-87.

factors is the end of the colonial era and the expansion of nationalism. This end of colonial power removed a major stumbling block to the spread of the gospel. Another factor in this growth is the translation of the Scripture in vernacular language these translations have brought cultural renovation and allowed Africans to see Christianity as part of their own identity. The third factor is the Africans themselves—they led the expansion without foreign compromise and bondage. The last factor that Sanneh mentions is a theological one—the continuing use of the indigenous name for God, which allows certain degrees of compatibility with the gospel.[13] It was the establishment of native African churches with their national and indigenous forms of worship and theology that brought this tremendous growth in the Sub-Saharan region, making it predominantly Christian.[14]

The growth of African churches is amazing. In 1900, 9.2% of the population was Christian (around 10 million), but this number increased to 45% in 1990 (around 276 million). The number of evangelicals has grown from 1.9% of the population in 1900 to 13.2% in 1990. This increase is so extraordinary that one could say that Africa is "turning to Christianity."[15] As early as 1970, David Barrett predicted that because of the growth of Christianity in Africa, Christianity will become a non-Western religion.[16]

Andrew Walls, professor of history at Edinburgh University, wrote that "African Christianity is undoubtedly an African religion ... it is not a

13   Lamin Sanneh, *Whose Religion Is Christianity? The Gospel Beyond the West* (Grand Rapids: Eerdmans, 2003), 18-19, 41-42.
14   Alister E. McGrath, *The Future of Christianity* (Malden, MA: Blackwell Publishers, 2002), 32-33.
15   Patrick Johnstone, *Operation World: The Day-by-Day Guide To Praying For The World* (Grand Rapids: Zondervan, 1993, 36-37). Pocock, Van Rheenen, and McConnell, *The Changing Face*, 134-35. Barrett, Kurian, and Johnson, *The World Encyclopedia*, 13.
16   David Barrett, "AD 2000: 350 Million Christians in Africa," *International Review of Mission* 59 (January 1970): 39-54.

pale copy of an institution existing somewhere else ... Africa may be the theatre in which some of the determinative new directions in Christian thought and activity are being taken."[17] He also notes: "What happens within the African Churches in the next generation will determine the whole shape of church history for centuries to come; what sort of theology is most characteristic of the Christianity of the twenty-first century may well depend on what has happened in the minds of African Christians in the interim."[18]

He adds, "We have to regard African Christianity as potentially the *representative* Christianity of the twenty-first century."[19] Despite problems like syncretism, with its growing Christian population Africa will affect Christianity in a major way.

Latin America

The Roman Catholic Church is the stronghold in Latin America. Most Latinos believe in the Virgin Mary and follow the Pope; however, the growth of Protestantism has been a surprising phenomenon. In 1900, 90.1% were Roman Catholic, and 1.4% were Protestant. The proportion of Protestants grew, and in 1970, the proportion was 88.4% Catholic to 4.4% Protestant. By 1990 the proportion had changed to 88.9% Catholic to 9.1% Protestant. In 2000, the figures were 88.8% Catholic (461,220,001 population) to 9.3% Protestant (48,131,716). David Barrett projects that in 2025 the proportion will be 87.0% Catholic (606,059,020) to 10.9% Protestant (76,191,140).[20]

---

17   Walls, *The Cross-Cultural Process in Christian History*, 119.
18   Arthur F. Walls, "Towards an Understanding of Africa's Place in Christian History," in *Religion in a Pluralistic Society*, ed. J. S. Pobee (Leiden: E. J. Brill, 1976), 183.
19   Walls, *The Cross-Cultural Process in Christian History*, 85. Italics from the author.
20   Barrett, Kurian, and Johnson, *World Christian Encyclopedia*, 14.

Latin America is a place where forced conversions took place—the gospel brought by the Spaniards and Portuguese came with the sword of conquest. When the Europeans found the New World, they applied what they did with the Muslims in their land: conversion or death. The lust for gold and power also was tied to the conquest of the new land. Even though they encountered some large kingdoms, the native civilizations were not powerful enough in a military sense to withstand the Europeans, and their religion spread rapidly. Because of the nature of Roman Catholic theology of that time or because of the urgency to conquer and subjugate the native people, the result of the missionary efforts was nominalism. Actually, although Catholicism remains very strong, most Catholics are nominally religious, without a strong commitment to Christ.[21]

Because of this nominalism that spread throughout Latin America or because of the strong commitment of the Catholic Church to maintain their status quo and help the elite of the community, many Latinos have decided to change their religion. Especially the poor and marginalized have embraced the religion that offered "prosperity and happiness"— Pentecostalism. Liberation theology reached the elite scholars, but Latin America Protestantism reached the forgotten masses of people. However, as happened in Latin America, Pentecostalism also affected other parts of the world, especially Africa. Despite the problems of the prosperity gospel it offers, Pentecostalism has expanded, touching and affecting all Protestant denominations and the Catholic Church in Latin America as well.[22]

The growth of Protestantism prompted several scholars to question if this tendency will make Latin America Protestant. David Stoll, with his book *Is Latin America Turning Protestant?*, asked this question and

---

21 Pocock, *The Changing Face of World Missions*, 141.
22 Ibid, 145-46.

concluded with an open question.[23] The theology of liberation that reached the academic level and was much discussed in academic life did not reach the poor. It was more an intellectual exercise rather than help in resolving the problem of the poor or outcast, even though the idea was to resolve the problems of those people. On the other hand, the *evangélicos* or Protestants, especially those from the Pentecostal churches, reached the masses by preaching an experiential religion and helped them to fulfill their lives and achieve their goals.[24]

Asia

In most continents of the world, Christianity is the majority religion; however, there is one exception: Asia, the most populated and geographically the largest continent. In Asia, Christians are not numerous in terms of proportion, but in terms of Christian individuals, the number is considerable.[25] In 1900 Christians represented 2.3% of the total population in Asia. This proportion grew to 7.8% of the population, or 248,728,290, in 1990. The proportion has grown to 8.5% in 2000, and it has been predicted that by 2025 it will be 9.8% of the population, or 464,800,100 people.[26]

Asia is the continent that represents the 10/40 Window, the most populated region of the world, where the religions of Islam, Hinduism, and Buddhism are very strong. Asia has so many differences and problems that to put all these nations together in a single block is difficult. The

---

23 David Stoll, *Is Latin America Turning Protestant? The Politics of Evangelical Growth* (Berkeley, CA: University of California Press, 1990), 331. Another is David Martin, Tongues of Fire: The Explosion of Protestantism in Latin America (Oxford, UK: Blackwell, 1990).

24 McGrath, *The Future of Christianity*, 36-39.

25 Proportionally 76% of worlds Christians are now in the 10/40 Window. David J. Cho, "Perspectives of Distinctive Missionary Motives in Asia" in *New Global Partnership for World Mission*, ed., Timothy K Park (Institute for Asia Mission, 2004), 12-13.

26 Barrett, Kurian, and Jonhson, *World Christian Encyclopedia*, 13.

unfinished task of global evangelization can be seen everywhere in Asia. The Arab world poses a big challenge along with China with its population and numbers of non-religious people. Also, India's caste system and traditionalism make it very difficult to penetrate with the gospel. For many reasons, therefore, this continent is the last and biggest challenge for the church. However, there are some sections of Asia with a high proportion of Christians, like the Philippines or Korea.[27]

THE MISSIONARY MOVEMENT IN THE MAJORITY WORLD

The growth of the church in the majority world had a vitality that formed several mission association involvements. An example of this is the Nigeria Evangelical Mission Association (NEMA). Organized in 1982, this mission association has 90 missionary agencies and more than 3,800 missionaries in 38 nations. In addition, the Indian Mission Associations connect around 200 national mission agencies. In Latin America, COMMIBAM has formed an association of 26 nations in a missionary movement.[28]

The missions associations that have come out of the majority world are characterized by: (1) a local base for the mission churches and a direct relationship between the missionary and the church that sent him. (2) A main focus on church planting and evangelism. (3) Long-term commitments from the missionaries. (4) Growth of the mission-ary force, in contrast to the decreasing number of missionaries sent from the West. (5) The South-South relationship, the contact between

---

27 Johnstone, *Operation World*, 41.
28 David D. Ruiz, "The Two Thirds World Church," Lausanne Occasional Paper No. 44 (paper presented at Lausanne Committee for World Evangelization, 29 September to 5 October 2004. Pattaya, Thailand) [on-line]; accessed 20 March 2007; avail-able from http://www.lausanne.org/documents/2004forum/LOP44_IG15.pdf; Internet.

majority world countries in mission has ideological proximity, which helps to expand missions. However, not all mission associations from the majority world shine bright; some weaknesses need to be resolved. For example, the financial involvement from churches to missionaries is not strong or continuous. Many missionaries came from countries with great harvest and have felt frustrated with having to sow while seeing so little harvest. Another problem is that many of the missionaries are sent to the same culture and to people with similar languages, with little emphasis on reaching people with far different languages and in distant countries.[29]

While missionary movements from the majority world started early, the beginning of the Western churches' awareness of this majority missionary movement has been relatively recent—around 1970 and 1980. Authors Larry Pate and Lawrence Keyes were touched by the movement and brought awareness to the church. They predict that this movement will spread and grow. They said that that if this tendency continues, the missionaries from the majority world will outnumber the Western missionaries. While this movement was growing slowly, the collapse of the Soviet Union and the opening of mission opportunities there made the Western church more open to this movement.[30]

As Keyes and Pate have noted, the movement of missionaries from the majority world is not new—the new thing is the awareness of this movement. The first serious study of this movement took place in 1972 at Fuller Theological Seminary. Under Dr. Peter Wagner's guidance, Peter Larson, Edward Pentecost, and James Wong studied the majority world mission agencies, and they discovered that there existed 210 mis-

---

29 Ruiz, "The Two Thirds World Church."
30 Larry Keyes and Larry Pate, "Two-Thirds Missions: The Next One Hundred Years," *Missiology: An International Review* 21 (1993): 187-206; Shaw, "The Future of Globalizing Missions: What the Literature Suggests"; Vinay Samuel and Christ Sugden, "Mission Agencies as Multinationals," *International Bulletin of Missionary Research* 7, no. 4 (October 1983): 152-55.

sionaries' societies that had sent 3,404 missionaries to the world. Later on, Keyes did another research project and found out that this missionary movement had grown from 3,404 missionaries in 1972 to 13,000 in 1980 and from 210 missionary agencies in 1972 to 743 agencies in 1980. Additional research was conducted by Pate in 1988, by which time the number of majority missionaries had increased to 35,924 serving in 118 countries among 2,425 people groups. The number of mission agencies had reached 1,094. Because of this growth, Pate predicts that the number of missionaries from the majority world will surpass the number of missionaries from the Western countries.[31]

The reasons for the growth and the impact of this movement are several. One of the reasons is that majority world missionaries can travel to countries that are close to their own but difficult for missionaries from the Western countries to enter. Another reason is that the majority world missionaries are culturally closer to the target group of unreached people and therefore can identify with them more readily. The financial need can be also an important factor, since the missionaries can generally live on the same economic level as the target group, even though the financial support from the majority world is not constant. However, not everything is easy for them. There are several problems and difficulties, one of which is the lack of adequate missionary training—many of them go without it. Consequently, many of them make the same mistakes that the Western missionaries did.[32]

In 1990, according to the research from Larry D. Pate, 157 Protestant missionaries from the majority world were sent by non-Western mission agencies, and 2,727 were sent by Western missionary agencies. So, at the end of 1990, majority world missionaries comprised 35.6% of the total number of Protestant missionaries in the world. From 1980 to 1990, the percentage of majority world missionaries had an average

31   Keyes, "Two-Thirds Missions," 188-90.
32   Ibid, 191.

annual increase of 13.3%; numerically, there were 32,919 missionaries in 1990, 248% more than a decade earlier. During the same period of time, the Western missionary force grew 0.4% annually, or 48% from 1980 to 1990. These figures show that the number of non-Western missionaries is growing more than five times faster than the number of Western missionaries. This is why Pate projected in 1991 that by 2000 the "number of Two-Thirds missionaries would overtake the number of Western missionaries sometime in 1998. By 2000 . . . [the numbers] would make the non-Western missionary force 55.5 percent of the total Protestant missionaries."[33]

FORCED CONVERSIONS

On September 12, 2006, Pope Benedict XVI gave a lecture at the University of Regensburg in Bavaria, Germany. The title of his lecture was "Faith, Reason, and the University—Memories and Reflections." The point of his lecture was that God is *logos* or reason and that acting with reason, one can be in harmony with the nature of God. He stressed that religion and violence do not go together but religion and reason do. The problem was that in his lecture he mentioned a dialogue between Byzantine emperor Manuel II Paleologus and a Persian scholar. In this dialogue the emperor argues against the use of violence for conversion. Pope Benedict mentioned that Muhammad spread his faith through the sword and violence. This dialogue has prompted great protests and opposition from the Muslims, who argue that it was blasphemous of Muhammad and depicted him wrongly. According to the Pope, he only cited this dialogue, but the Muslims did not accept his position.[34]

---

33   Larry D. Pate, "The Changing Balance in Global Mission," *International Bulletin of Missionary Research* 15, no. 2 (April 1991): 58-59.

34   Samir Khalil Samir, "Church-Islam Dialogue: The Path Starts from Regensburg's Pope" [on-line]; accessed 16 January 2007; available from http://www. asianews.it/index.php?l=en&art=8242&size=A; Internet; Jimmy Atkinson, "Debate Regarding Pope's Islam Quotes Blown Out of Proportion" [on-line]; accessed 11

The lecture by the Pope and his comments raise the question of forced conversion and violence. Even though violence and forced conversion seem only part of the Muslim religion, from the Christian side, one cannot forget what has happened in history. There have been several attempts by the proponents of Christ's love to force conversions through violence. The Crusades are one of the prime examples of what happens when violence is chosen rather than love. Violence, forced conversions, nominalism, syncretism, mass conversions—these seem to characterize other religions rather than the religion of love and grace. However, Christians cannot negate the fact that violence has also been part of the history of Christianity.

One of the examples of this type of violence and forced conversion is the conquest of Latin America. From the genesis of Christianity in Latin America, violence and forced conversions have been part of its history. The Christian people who came to conquer the land brought their theology by force with swords. The method was very effective in terms of numerical growth. While the Protestants were fighting each other and trying to survive in their struggle with theology and Catholic opposition, the Catholics of Spain and Portugal gained the most fantastic expansion in Christian history. According to Justo González, "It was the most fantastic expansion in all the history of Christianity."[35]

On the other hand, one of the intriguing questions that arise for evangelical Christians is the great number of nominal Christians in Latin America. The nations having the most Roman Catholic believers are also the countries where there are the most nominal Roman Catholics, many of whom do not know what they believe or why they are Catholic. The Roman Catholic Church, which is responsible for resolving this

October 2006; available from http://thepopeblog.blogspot.com/2006/09/debate-regarding-popes-islam-quotes.html; Internet.

35   Justo L. González, *Historia de las Misiones* (Buenos Aires, Argentina: La Aurora, 1970), 140. Translated by the writer.

problem, has not resolved this lack of spiritual knowledge and faith. Even though the numbers of Protestants are growing, the main religion in Latin America is still Roman Catholicism. The Catholics make the great proportion of the population, and their influence is very strong in society.

THE HISTORICAL CONQUEST OF LATIN AMERICA

One aspect of the conquest of New Spain is the time frame of the conquest. The 16th century was an important time period since it was the period of formation and foundation of what later would be Latin America. During this period the native American elements and their Spanish counterparts clashed and formed a new element. The native peoples had their own religion and cultural background, as did the Spaniards with their rich Catholic and Iberian background; these would clash and form new elements. Moreover, this period saw the formation of missionary methodology when the foundation and organization of the modern church started to develop. The Spaniards expanded both geographically and missiologically, not only spreading from the Iberian coast to the entire world but also bringing about the "spiritual conquest of New Spain."[36]

At the Conference of Edinburgh in 1910, there was a belief that Latin America was Christian and there was not a necessity to do missions there. Later on, this misconception was challenged by Protestants. Protestant

---

36   Robert Ricard, *The Spiritual Conquest of Mexico* (Los Angeles, CA: University of California Press, 1966), 3-4.

writers like W. Stanley Rycroft,[37] John Mackay,[38] and Samuel Escobar,[39] as well as ecumenical Protestants such as José Miguez Bonino,[40] saw the failure of the Roman Catholic missions in Latin America. Catholic missionary work did not produce spiritual fruit; it promoted institutional conversion rather than personal conversion.

This criticism is leveled not only by Protestants but also by Catholics themselves. For example, the situation of Catholicism in Latin America was addressed at the Chimbote conference in Lima, Peru, in 1953. The delegates claimed that the state of Catholics in Latin America is "*solo de nombre*, that is, nominal Catholics." They do not practice their religion and do not show their religion in their daily life. [41]

Moreover, the Catholic Church in Latin America has recognized the need for the start of a new evangelization of Latin America. Catholic leaders see the need for a "profound restoration in order to approach the full Christian ideal, today still quite distant."[42] They do not mention the word failure, but they say that there is a need for Catholicism to be rekindled. There is a vast land, where evangelization is needed among Indians, students, and intellectuals; there are several groups of people whom the Catholic faith has not reached. Besides the belief that Latin America is Christian, Catholics have several concerns

---

37   W. Stanley Rycroft, *Religion and Faith in Latin America* (Philadelphia: The Westminster Press, 1958).

38   John Mackay, *The Other Spanish Christ* (New York: The Macmillan Company, 1933).

39   Samuel Escobar, *Changing Tides. Latin America and World Mission Today* (Maryknoll, NY: Orbis Books, 2002).

40   José M. Bonino, "Historia y Misión" in *Protestantismo y Liberalismo en América Latin* (San José, Costa Rica: DEI, 1983).

41   William J. Coleman, *Latin-American Catholicism: A Self-Evaluation* (Maryknoll, NY: Maryknoll Publications, 1958), 20, 33.

42   Coleman, *Latin America Catholicism*, 33.

about Christianity there and speak of the necessity of pursuing a "new evangelization."[43]

The Argentinean Protestant Miguel Bonino adds: "Latin America never was 'Christian'... What took place here was a colossal transplantation, the basic ecclesiastical structures, disciplines, and ministries were brought wholesale from Spain, and were expected to function as a Christian order."[44] Angelyn Dries holds the same position: "The southern hemisphere was, therefore, not to be seen as a 'mission' country but as an extension of Spanish Catholicism in an American setting."[45] The Catholicism that Spain brought from Europe to Latin America was superficial, and it continues that way until now.

The liberation theologians, besides their radical calling for political and social reforms, saw the weakness of the Latin America Catholicism. Starting from their pastoral concerns, they worried that the Catholic Church made great numbers of "Christians" but not conversions. They baptized all people, but Christianity did not have deep roots in the continent.[46] Even sociologists say that the church was not effectively planted, nor did evangelism really take place. The church used political methods to control society in times of crisis, rather than being a moral

---

43   John Eagleson and Philip Scharper, eds., *Puebla and Beyond: Documentation and Commentary*, trans. John Drury (Maryknoll, NY: Orbis Books, 1979), 172; Segundo Galilea, *Evangelización en América Latina* (Quito, Ecuador: CELAM-IPLA, 1969); idem, *La Responsabilidad Misionera en América Latina* (Bogotá, Colombia: Ediciones Paulinas, 1981).

44   Miguel Bonino, "Latin America," in *The Prospects of Christianity Throughout the World*, ed. M. Searle Bates and Wilhelm Pauck (New York: Charles Scribner's Sons, 1964), 168.

45   Angelyn Dries, *The Missionary Movement in American Catholic History* (Maryknoll, NY: Orbis Books, 1998), 98-99.

46   Juan Luis Segundo, *De la Sociedad a la Teología*, (Buenos Aires, Argentina: Ed. Carlos Lohlé, 1970), 34-44; Escobar, *Changing* Tides, 39-40; Gustavo Gutiérrez, *Lineas Pastorales de la Iglesia en América Latina* (Lima: CEP, 1970), 16-17; idem, "Notes for a Theology of Liberation," in *The Roman Catholic Church in Latin America*, ed. Jorge I. Dominguez (New York: Garland Publishing, Inc., 1994), 17-19. Gustavo Gutierrez is against the sacramental view of salvation.

authority. They did not root faith in the people, and the people did not live their beliefs in their daily lives.[47]

These negative views are materialized when one see the theology of Roman Catholicism. The Roman Catholics' missionary objective is to plant a Catholic church rather than to convert individuals. This idea came from the middle ages, when there was "baptism *en masse*, by force," with little instruction before the baptism.[48] This position changed after Vatican II; however, the ideas remain prevalent in the actual Roman Catholic missionary efforts.[49] Some, even among the Catholics, have questioned this view. However, in Latin America, Catholicism succeeded at the institutional level. Catholics were successful in planting churches but failed in converting people.[50] For this type of theology the conquest of Latin America is a great achievement; however, from the pietistic

---

47   Ivan Vallier, *Catholicism, Social Control, and Modernization* (Buenos Aires, Argentina: Amorrortu Editores, 1970), 72-78; Escobar, *Changing Tides*, 40-41.

48   The mission activities in Asian countries have differed from those in Latin America in that they have incorporated more of an inculturation process. Missionary efforts start within the cultural setting of the people—there was a dialogue with that culture to discern and understand and finally to reach the people with the message. This approach was very different from that applied in Latin America, where political and economical conquests were the dominant factors. See Stephen B. Bevans and Roger P. Schroeder, *Constants in Context* (Maryknoll, NY: Orbis Books, 2004), 201-03.

49   Escobar, *Changing Tides*, 36, 38; Ricard, *La Conquista Espiritual de Mexico*, 21. There are the preconciliar church (before Vatican II) and the postconciliar church (after Vatican II).The Roman Catholic Church was rejuvenated after Vatican II.

50   There are several differences between the Protestant and Catholic works Latin America. Protestants have had a strong missionary movement that spread in Latin America, but despite the great number of individual conversions, they lack a strong ecclesiastical presence. Also, they do not have unified institutional presence. Another interesting difference is that from the beginning, the authority of the Catholic Church provided an element of dependence on foreign forces—since they lacked priests to fulfill the different ecclesiastical duties, church leaders came mostly from Europe or America. In contrast, the Protestants, since they gave authority to the lay people, did not lack church leadership. See C. R. Boxer, *The Church Militant and Iberian Expansion 1440-1770* (London: The Johns Hopkins University Press, 1978), 14-30; Escobar, *Changing Tides*, 39, 72-73; Segundo, *De la Sociedad a la Teología*, 11-28.

Protestant point of view, it is a huge failure. There was not individual conversion; there was only conversion at the institutional level.

THE THREE-SELF FORMULAS

The term "Three-Self Formula," also called "Indigenous Church-planting," refers to the strategy of implementing self-support, self-propagation, and self-government. Henry Venn (1796–1873) of the Church Missionary Society and Rufus Anderson (1796–1880) of the American Board started to use these terms and ideas. The idea is to implement churches that could be native and propagate themselves. Venn and Anderson started training nationals to hand over the churches to them as soon as possible. The church is indigenous when the church is self-governing. That means that a community of believers ministers among themselves and resolves their own problems without the necessity of foreign help. The indigenous church has to be self-supporting since providing foreign funds to pay the salary of the leader has proved counter-productive. The church also needs to be self-propagating; the community surrounding the church can be reached by that church. Indigenous churches have to be responsible in organization, finances, and evangelization.[51]

IMPLEMENTATION IN KOREA AND NEVIUS' PLAN

In 1890 a group of beginning missionaries in Korea sent a letter inviting Nevius to instruct them in the missionary method that he proposed in China. This method, even though it did not gain popularity in China, was accepted unanimously among missionaries in Korea. Nevius went

---

51   Charles H. Kraft and Tom N. Wisley, eds., *Readings in Dynamic Indigeneity* (Pasadena, CA: William Carey Library, 1980), xxvii.

to Korea and instructed the missionaries in the method and it became the policy of the mission in Korea. Nevius introduced the method, but the implementation was made by a few missionaries, who were just beginning their work. These pioneer missionaries included Horace G. Underwood and S. A. Moffett. Underwood was the missionary who formally opened the Protestant mission in Korea. He and his fellow companions, after careful study, adopted the Nevius principles, and from there the policy of the Mission in Korea was settled. The principle was unanimously approved and required that every new missionary, upon arrival in Korea, use this principle in his ministry.[52]

In China, Nevius also learned a method used to established national churches. This method consists of missionaries hiring Chinese people to sell Bibles, to evangelize, and to work as missionaries. For Nevius, this method was unsatisfactory, because the nationals were dependent on the missionaries. This system, called "the Old System," involved the use of foreign funds from the beginning to develop native churches. This method resulted in the natives' lack of self-confidence since it inhibited their initiative. Therefore, Nevius adopted a new method, which he called "the New System." This new method applied principles of self-confidence and independence from the beginning.[53]

The "Old System" was described by Charles A. Clark as one that "depends largely upon a paid native agency and strives by the use of foreign funds to foster and stimulate the growth of the native churches in the first stage of their development, and then expects gradually to

---

52   Charles Allen Clark, *The Korean Church and the Nevius Methods* (New York: Fleming H. Revell Company, 1930), 74; Horace G. Underwood, *The Call of Korea* (New York: Fleming H. Revell Company, 1908), 109-10.

53   Keith Eitel, "To Be or Not to Be?: The Indigenous Church Question," in *Missiology: An Introduction to the Foundations, History, and Srategies of World Missions*, ed. John Mark Terry, Ebbie Smith, and Justice Anderson (Nashville: Broadman & Holman, 1998), 308.

discontinue using of such funds."[54] Both methods were used to foster native churches, but the differences were in the use or non-use of foreign funds. The "Old System" used foreign funds to foster native work from the beginning, while the "New System" tried from the beginning to apply a principle of independence.[55]

The arguments for the "Old System" include that this system is the natural one. There is a necessity to get immediate results; so it is necessary to employ natives in the work as soon as possible, while the missionary struggles to study the native language. Another factor is economic—the natives were poor and had to spend more of their time working to get their subsistence; as a result they did not have enough time for personal evangelism.[56]

Some arguments against the "Old System" were that this system harmed the local churches since the chosen worker took away the natural leaders and caused jealousy among others. It was also difficult to distinguish between the true and the false believers because of the element of material gain that came along with belief. It encouraged unscrupulous interest in believers and tended to destroy the spiritual purpose. In addition, this system stopped voluntary, unpaid effort.[57]

The "New System," on the other hand, supported the idea that the new converts should remain in their vocations and jobs. Each newly converted individual was called to evangelize his neighbors and friends without payment, preaching the gospel while living his normal life.[58] This "New System" was later developed and called the Nevius Plan.

---

54 Charles A. Clark, *The Nevius Plan for Mission Work* (Minneapolis: Christian Literature Society, 1937), 24.
55 Ibid, 24-25.
56 Ibid, 25.
57 Charles A. Clark, *The Korea Church and the Nevius Methods* (New York: Fleming H. Revell Company, 1930), 18-19.
58 Ibid, 23.

Charles A. Clark, who studied the Nevius plan in Korea, has summarized this method. "Bible emphasis, personal evangelism through wide itineration, self-propagation, self-government, self-support, strict discipline, cooperation and union, non-use of secular motives such as help in lawsuits, etc., and helpfulness in the economic problems of the people."[59]

Horace Underwood described the Nevius plan in four principles:

> First, to let each man 'Abide in the calling wherein he was found,' teaching that each was to be an individual worker for Christ, and to live Christ in his own neighborhood, supporting himself by his trade. Secondly, to develop Church methods and machinery only so far as the native Church was able to take care of and manage the same. Third, as far as the church itself was able to provide the men and the means, to set aside those who seemed the better qualified, to do evangelistic work among their neighbors. Fourth, to let the natives provide their own church buildings, which were to be native in architecture, and of such style as the local church could afford to put up.[60]

The three elements of the Nevius method developed by Rufus Anderson and Henry Venn (self-support, self-government, and self-propagation) were further developed by Nevius.[61]

Charles Allen Clark summarized the Nevius principles:

1. Missionary personal evangelism through wide itineration.
2. Self-propagation: every believer a teacher of someone, and learner from someone else better fitted; every individual and group seeking

---

59   Clark, *The Nevius Plan for Mission Work*, 240-41.
60   Underwood, *The Call of Korea*, 109-10.
61   Eitel, "To Be or Not to Be?" 306-07.

by the 'layering method' to extend the work. 3. Self-government: every group under its chosen unpaid Leaders; circuits under their own paid Helpers, who will later yield to Pastors; circuit meetings training the people for later district, provincial and national leadership. 4. Self-support: with all chapels provided by the believers; each group, as soon as founded, beginning to pay towards the circuit Helper's salary; even schools to receive but partial subsidy, and that only when being founded; no pastors of single churches provided by foreign funds. 5. Systematic Bible study for every believer under his group Leader and circuit Helper; and of every Leader and Helper in the Bible Classes. 6. Strict discipline enforced by Bible penalties. 7. Co-cooperation and union with other bodies, or at least territorial division. 8. Non-interference in lawsuits or any such matters. 9. General helpfulness where possible in the economic life problems of the people.[62]

One of the critiques of the Nevius plan was that in Shangtun, China, the mission field where Nevius worked for many years, this method did not produce results. Underwood answered this critique by explaining that in Shangtun both methods were in use and clashed. The reason why it was successful in Korea was that this method was applied from the beginning of the mission work.[63] Also, T. Stanley Soltau says the most important element for the growing of the church in Korea was that from the "beginning the responsibility for maintenance and leadership has been with the church."[64] This indigenous principle from the beginning gave the strength and vitality to the Korean church, and this was the foundational element that has allowed the church to grow.

---

62 Clark, *The Korean Church and The Nevius Methods*, 33-34.

63 Horace G. Underwood, "Principles of Self-Support in Korea," *Korea Mission Field* 4, no. 6 (June 1908): 91; cited in Paik, *The History of Protestant Missions in Korea*, 282-83.

64 T. Stanley Soltau, *Missions at the Crossroads: The Indigenous Church–A Solution for the Unfinished Task* (Wheaton, IL: Van Kampen Press, 1954), 10-11.

Problems and Strengths

The Three-Self Formula was a process that Venn and Anderson brought separately. Even though this formula was developed by both missionaries, "historical evidence does not suggest that one depended on the other in arriving at his conclusions."[65] While Anderson proposed a quicker approach in implementing this formula, Venn, on the other hand, was more concerned to give more time to implement it. They were both concerned for the indigenous church, that the natives must become church leaders and implement the Three-Self Formula. They both were struggling to define the principle to apply it in the mission field. They saw self-support of the native leader as the starting point for the new church. Venn was the first to express this idea in a paper. He pointed out that the missionary work is temporary, while the national work is permanent. The ultimate purpose of the mission is to plant a self-supported church so that the missionary can go to other places to do missions. Anderson, however, published a book that expressed this idea more explicitly. In his work *Foreign Missions, Their Relations and Claims*,[66] especially in chapters 4 and 7, he better expressed his ideas and principles.[67]

The key principle of this formula for Venn was the support of the local pastor by their congregations and the church's self-government. From the beginning the mission had to implement the idea of self-support and self-government. As Veen explained: "The Mission is the scaffolding; the Native Church is the edifice. The removal of the scaffolding

---

65 Wilbert R. Shenk, "Rufus Anderson and Henry Venn: A Special Relationship?" *International Bulletin of Missionary Research* 5, no. 4 (October, 1981): 168-69. There are interesting similarities between the two men— regarding birth, the loss of their parents, their leadership of the largest American and European missionary agencies, and the strategies employed in their time.

66 Rufus Anderson, *Foreign Missions: Their Relations and Claims* (New York: Charles Scribner and Company, 1869).

67 Shenk, "Rufus Anderson and Henry Venn," 171. Shenk, *Henry Venn*, 44.

is the proof that the building is completed. You will have achieved the greatest success when you have taught your converts to do without you and can leave them, for fresh inroads into the 'regions beyond.'"[68]

The achievement of this purpose involves several stages, from the establishing of the work of the missionary until the native church has reached the Three-Self Formula. When this happens, then they reach "the euthanasia of the mission," i.e., that the missionary's control is finished and the mission church has become an autonomous missionary church.[69]

The critique of the Three-Self Formula is that that emphasis on the self could make the mission church concentrated on themselves, making the national church the center of all things. It is the danger of human pride, so concentrated in them that they become a self without God and could exist without the need of others. As a consequence of this attitude, the mission church can become isolated, independent and self-sufficient, separate from the body of Christ. The calling of Jesus in the Great Commission is the church as one unity, and this emphasis on the self could make the daughter church separate from the mother church. The church has to be "Christonomous" rather then autonomous, and responsible rather then independent. The center of the church has to be God, and each part of the church has to be responsible for the others in the universal body of Christ.[70]

68   Henry Venn, "Instructions to Missionaries, March 26, CMI, XIV (5), May 1863," *Bibliography of Henry Venn's Printed Writing with Index*, 112"; cited in Shenk, *Henry Venn*, 46.

69   Shenk, *Henry Venn*, 46.

70   Peter Beyerhaus, "The Three Selves Formula", 25-30.

Partnership

Partnership is an important word used in several fields. In education, partnership between teachers and parents is needed for the improvement of the education of the children. Another partnership may be formed when, to pursue the goal of losing some weight, a group of partners begins a dieting program together. Another partnership is in the business field—e.g., airlines have partnerships with hotels and car rental companies. Partnership is a key concept in multinational companies, since fierce competition made these companies looks for partnerships to cut costs and gain consumers. In politics one can see the partnerships that have formed in Europe. Countries that were enemies in the Second World War are unifying to be stronger and to have more relevance in the political struggles of the world. Even in marriage there is partnership, since marriage involves commitment and compromise between two partners. Partnership is everywhere, and everyone is looking for partnership to improve and better fulfill their purpose.[71]

In the mission fields, "partnership" emerged as a missiologically term several years ago. Partnership was always present, since the Bible and the history of Christianity mentioned it, but being mentioned as a missiological term was in some ways recent.[72] In 1988 Maurice Sinclair drew attention to the importance of partnership: "Yes, partnership!

71 Luis Bush and Lorry Lutz, *Partnering in Ministry: The Direction of World Evangelism* (Downers Grove, IL: InterVarsity Press, 1990), 14-19, 44-45.

72 One can see that in the book *Perspectives on the World Christian Movement*, the 1992 edition does not mention about Partnership while the last edition of 1999 has three articles commenting this issue. Stan Guthrie mentioned that in the David Hesselgrave's book *Today's Choices for Tomorrow's Mission* (Grand Rapids: Zondervan, 1988)), the term "partnership" does not appear in the index of the book while some discussion about partnership in missions appears in most of the missiological journals today. See: Stan Guthrie, *Missions in the Third Millennium: 21 Trends for the 21st Century* (Waynesboro, GA: Paternoster Press, 2000), 94

There is nothing more interesting, exasperating, and exciting than partnership."[73] Partnership can be exciting and interesting, but it does not magically produce results, nor is it easy to implement since there are many players in the field and many of them have differences that sometimes are difficult to overcome. However, partnership is imperative in a changing world—necessity makes its application essential.

Definition

In the mission field "partnership" is defined as "a complementary relationship driven by a common purpose and sustained by a willingness to learn and grow together in obedience to God."[74] Another definition from Luis Bush, former president of Partner International, is "an organization of two or more autonomous bodies that have formed a trusting relationship and fulfill agreed upon expectations by sharing complementary strengths and resources, to reach their mutual goal."[75] In this definition one can see the phrases *mutual goal*, since there is some purpose in reaching partnership; *autonomous bodies*—both parts are equal in their relationship and complementary; *sharing complementary strengths and resources*, because each partner has to put in something to reach their goal.

Daniel Rickett, talking in more practical terms, adds that a good partnership requires three preconditions: (1) the partners have to be autonomous. Each one has to have his own identity and condition. (2) Beliefs and values from partners have to be compatible to avoid conflicts and problems in the future or in the purpose to reach their goals. (3) It is necessary for each part to give their strengths and re-

---

73   Maurice Sinclair, *Ripening Harvest, Gathering Storm: What is the Relevance of the Christian Faith in a World Sliding into Crisis?* (London: MARC, 1988), 201.

74   Daniel Rickett, *Building Strategic Relationships: A Practical Guide to Partnering with Non-Western Missions* (Pleasant Hills, CA: Partners International, 2000), 1.

75   Bush and Lutz, *Partnering in Ministry*, 46.

sources to complement each other. A partnership has to be beneficial to each participant.[76]

Historical Background of Missions

According to David Howard, former president of Latin America Mission (LAM), the church is interconnected, everyone is part of the big machine. The church has many things to do in world evangelization. Moreover, the Majority Church is more mature. These indigenous churches are not dependent, and they can stand alone and grow by themselves. This era is a time of interdependence, which means that not one group or nation can do the work alone—everyone is part of the whole, and the church needs to work together as a body and in partnership to fulfill the Great Commission.[77] Warren W. Webster says that the answer "does not lie in the patterns of dependence or independence, but in the recovery of that interdependence of the one spirit that marked the New Testament churches. In this basic spiritual unity and interdependence of the younger and older churches today lies the future of the church mission to the world."[78]

Benefits and Problems

One of the benefits of partnership is to save dollars and effort, to join hands and work together to reach some unreached group with the gospel. According to Lundy, there are several forms of partnership. One he called the "Joint venture between semi-independent partners." Operation Mobilization (OM) is one example. This partnership consists in that each national field of OM is a semi-autonomous entity, joining with OM International and working together. Each part has indepen-

76 Rickett, *Building Strategic Relationships*, 4-5.
77 Howard, "Incarnational Presence," 27-28.
78 Warren W. Webster, "The Nature of the Church and Unity in Mission," in *New Horizons in World Missions*, ed., David J. Hesselgrave (Grand Rapids: Baker Book House, 1979), 247.

dence and autonomy but still works together in partnership. Another partnership is what he called a "joint venture between full partners," in which one organization supplies financial funds for another mission in another country. Examples of this type of partnership include the Tear Fund, Partners International, and Gospel for Asia.[79]

The third type of partnership is what Lundy defined as "vertically integrated networking of independent partners."[80] This is a big effort, involving "various ministries coming together specifically to pray, plan, and work together over the long term for evangelism and the building of a church among a major unreached people group."[81] This effort involves several elements and people working together, using all available sources—such as mass media, Scripture translation, personal witness—with a conscious purpose of reaching this particular group. Phil Butler adds another type of partnership, which he called the "horizontal integrated" partnership. This effort involves, for example, Scripture translation. This work has many elements, however, in contrast to the "vertically integrated" network; this effort is not a complete one, since it does not make a complete effort to reach one particular group.[82]

The last type of partnership consists of independent agencies that form partnerships to work in specific types of ministry. This is similar to the "horizontal integrated" partnership in that different agencies work together informally for necessity. Examples of agencies that use this type of partnership are the Arab World Ministries and Gospel Missionary

---

79   Lundy, *We Are the World*, 161-62.
80   Ibid., 162.
81   Phillip Butler, "Kingdom Partnerships in the '90s: Is There a New Way Forward?" in *Kingdom Partnerships for Synergy in Missions*, ed. William D. Taylor (Pasadena, CA: William Carey Library, 1994), 13.
82   Butler, "Kingdom Partnerships," 13-14.

Union. These ministries work primarily in closed countries where few missionaries are welcome and many enter as "tentmakers."[83]

As in all human effort, partnerships have many problems. Cultural differences are one problem. The cross-cultural enterprise of missions involves differences in language and worldview. What seem to be minor or unimportant can be significant differences in another culture. The Western world is more individualistic, but in most of the majority world countries the community is more important than the one individual. Awareness of those differences can help but sometimes can make matters worse. Another related problem is the lack of clear communication. Who will be responsible for each task, how resources will be distributed, the reports on how the missionary effort is progressing—those are problems that need to be addressed and resolved within in the partnership. Personal conflicts can also make a partnership fade away; love and trust are elements that help to resolve tense situations.[84]

Accountability is another problematic aspect of partnership in that it is easy to understand but difficult to implement. Accountability is universal not only as a Western idea, since all must have some accountability in every relationship. It is also biblical, because God calls for accountability for one's action and choices. Accountability can be broadly defined as "the condition whereby one person is subject to review, examination, and judgment by another person or authority structure concerning his or her motives and actions."[85] To reach the goal of the partnership, each partner has to do his job. So, it is important that partners evaluate each other as well as themselves to know if each one is doing their committed job. Healthy accountability does

---

83 Lundy, *We Are the World*, 163.
84 Butler, "Kingdom Partnerships," 20-24.
85 Alexandre Araujo, "Confidence Factors: Accountability in Christian Partnerships," in *Kingdom Partnerships for Synergy in Missions*, ed. William D. Taylor (Pasadena, CA: William Carey Library, 1994), 120.

not mean control but mutual trust. For those who have the financial resources, it is easy to have control and use money to effect one's will, so there is a need to see that one is equal in the Lord and in the job, that everyone has gifts and weakness.[86]

As in all human enterprise, not everything is perfect, and partnership is not the magic word that resolves all problems. In fact it could cause more problems if it is done unwisely. Bill Taylor summarizes his idea of partnership and the reasons why it does or does not work: (1) most partnerships work when they are built over a long period of time on the strength of trustworthy relationships. (2) Both partners know their cultural differences and each understands the cultural differences of the other. (3) There is a common purpose to reach for each partner. (4) Agreement about accountability and how to handle problems will help to avoid problems. This is one of the critical elements. (5) Dynamic evaluation and ongoing processes are necessary, since factors can change during the partnership alliance.[87] The majority world church calls for partnership,[88] and they are mature and ready to work as partners. They also have strengths and weaknesses, as does the Western church. This is a time to unify as a church of Christ and work together as true partners to reach the unreached.

CONCLUSION

The growth of the church in the majority world is surprising. In 1910 there was a very optimistic spirit that the *evangelization of this generation* was possible. After two world wars, disillusionment appeared in Western

---

86 Araujo, "Confidence Factors," 121-22.
87 Bill Taylor, "Lessons of Partnership," in Ralph D. Winter and Steven C. Hawthorne, eds., *Perspectives on the World Christian Movement: A Reader,* ed. Ralph D. Winter and Steven C. Hawthorne (Pasadena, CA: William Carey Library, 1999), 751-52.
88 Brother Yun and Paul Hattaway, *The Heavenly Man: The Remarkable True Story of Chinese Christian Brother Yun* (Grand Rapids: Monarch Books, 2004), 347.

society. Later on, liberal ideas and tolerance spread into society, so that many thought that the main religion of the Western society would fade away and that Muslims would prevail several years later. However, surprisingly and amazingly this situation did not happen. Christianity had shown its muscles and returned to growth. What will be the future of Christianity? According to some authors, Christianity will prevail over Islam, and Christians will outnumber the Muslims. Because of this growth, Christianity is not merely a Western religion—it has become a global religion. Another consequence of this growth is that the "center of gravity" of Christianity has changed from North-West to South-East. This shift affected the theology that will prevail in the future global Christianity. The liberal and tolerant ideas will switch to a more literal and fundamentalistic view of Christianity in the South.

Three main strategies have been applied in the history of Christianity. In Latin America, the birth of Christianity started with forced conversions. The militant Catholic brought the message of love with sword and ambition. The result was a formidable expansion and conquest. Another important strategy is the Three-Self Formula. This strategy was started independently by two prominent missiologists Henry Venn and Rufus Anderson. Both drew conclusions about, from different sides of the Atlantic Ocean, the need to do self-supporting, self-governing, and self-propagating in the missionary enterprise. This strategy, later developed as the Nevius Plan in Korea, was one of the key elements for the extraordinary expansion of the church in Korea. The right foundational beginning helps to bolster the expansion of the church in Korea.

Partnership is another strategy that has lately been expanding in the mission world. As happens in the business world and in other fields, partnership has taken root in the missionary enterprise. Even though there is an agreement that it is necessary to work in partnerships, the implementation of this strategy is not easy work. However, the growth of the church and the maturity of the majority world church make this strategy imperative. Despite the existing economic and technological differences between both partners, partnership is necessary. The implementation of this strategy is not an easy job. Economic differences, cultural misunderstanding, and lack of accountability and trust can make this enterprise very difficult.

2. SEVEN ESSENTIALS OF MAJORITY WORLD EMERGING MISSION MOVEMENTS

Howard Brant

PREFACE

In July of 1986, I attended the *Second International Conference for Itinerant Evangelists* sponsored by the Billy Graham Evangelistic Association. I had spent the previous 15 years church planting, often on motorcycle, sharing the gospel in village after village in East and West Africa. At Amsterdam, I was looking forward to meeting 10,000 evangelists of like passion who had been doing what I myself was doing. I will never forget walking into Amsterdam's RAI Conference Center. As I looked out on that virtual sea of evangelists, what overpowered me was not their number – but their diversity. They were a mix of brown, black, yellow and yes, only a few Caucasians like me among them. That was my introduction to the new reality of *Kingdom diversity*.

Eighteen years later, in 2004 I was back in Amsterdam. One of the speakers, Bruce Wilkinson,[1] spoke on how our lives should become more focused as we grew older. He specifically stated that when we reach 60 we ought to be focused on our life passion. I prayed, "Lord if you can get me out of administration – I will serve the rest of my days to help these new emerging missions become successful." In 2006 my mission released me to this ministry full time. I became the SIM Champion for New Initiatives in Mission (read "emerging missions").

These past two years, I have witnessed dozens of emerging missions at various levels of development. Some are no longer emerging – they have emerged. My focus, however, has been with the new startups. I have tried to define the essentials of what it takes for an emerging mission to take root and develop as well as what it takes for these individual efforts to turn into emerging mission movements. In this paper, I will define seven of these essentials and make a few observations about each one.

---

1. Called Individuals

God has and will call individuals to bear his Name before the nations of the earth. The Apostle Paul had a very clear call. On the way to Damascus, Jesus told him: *"I have appeared to you to appoint you as a servant and as a witness of what you have seen of me and what I will show you. I will rescue you from your own people and from the Gentiles. I am sending you to them."*[2] From that point on, Paul could introduce himself as, *"Paul… called as an apostle and set apart for the gospel of God."*[3]

---

1   This is the same Bruce Wilkinson who wrote *The Prayer of Jabez.*
2   Acts 26:16-17 This is the only passage in the book of Acts which details the direct call which Paul received in his Damascus Road experience.
3   See Rom. 1:1. Paul introduces himself by mentioning this calling in seven of his thirteen epistles.

About 20 years ago, an Ethiopian bank manager named Yoseph awoke suddenly and said to his wife, "God is calling us to go to Hariana." "Where is that?" she asked. He had no idea. The next day at his bank, Yoseph asked an Indian employee. "Have you ever heard of a place called Hariana?" "Of course," replied the Indian. "That is a state of India with over 30 million people—right around Delhi."

Believing that God had called him to Hariana in India, Yoseph called together six of the local Ethiopian church leaders and asked to be sent off for missionary training. They rightly responded, "God may have spoken to you but He needs to speak to us as well." After months of waiting, he heard nothing. So sure of his calling was he that when his first son was born, he named him "Hariana"—"so that the vision would always be before me." He continued working for another six years until the Lord made it clear that he needed to leave his work and seek ways to get to India. He left his job and acquired a visa for India.

When I met Yoseph about 7 years ago he pled with me to help him get to India. I took him to the national church office, but they insisted that he and his wife go through a four year training course in a theological college. He wept when he heard of the delay. But Yoseph and his wife, Sinidu, took the four year course. When they graduated everything came into place and they set off for India. When they got to Hariana, Yoseph literally got out of the car and kissed the soil. Today he has learned Hindi and is leading Hindus to the Lord – along with his first born son, Hariana—who travels with a father that wants to pass on his legacy—to Hariana.

In contrast to this, I was recently involved in an evaluation of an indigenous mission in West Africa. We soon discovered that the missionaries in this West African mission were discouraged, had a low self image, and were not all that effective. When we asked questions about their selection process, we found that most applied to the church as pastors but when there was no place for them, they were told "to fill out the missions form." If they were found acceptable they were sent a "letter of employment." Most of these new missionaries set off to "work for the church."

"Called" missionaries enter into the Mission of God. Nothing will stop them! They will be the "bulldozers" who are willing to pay the high price of self-sacrifice in order to blaze a trail for the gospel. They will force all the rest of the mechanisms around which emerging missions function to become active. Without them, we cannot expect any real mission movement to begin in a new part of the world. Emerging missions start with "called individuals."

2. VISIONARY LEADERS

While called individuals see God's plan for their own life, visionary leaders comprehend the larger purposes of God for the group of people they represent. James Plueddemann in an upcoming book writes, "*The visionary leader has a mental picture of what God could do in the world. The ultimate purpose of an individual, a church or an organization is to be used of God to bring about His plans for time and eternity.*"[4]

It takes time for this kind of conviction to settle in on a new community of believers in any part of the world. Jesus commissioned the apostles in 33 AD and the Holy Spirit came upon them within a few days. Yet we observe the apostles painfully reluctant to embrace their global responsibility. All through the early years of the church, we find the apostles still in Jerusalem. When Christians scattered after the death of Stephen the apostles stayed in Jerusalem. Even after his experience with Cornelius, Peter and the apostles stayed in Jerusalem. It was only Herod's threat on his life that proved strong enough to dislodge Peter

---

4   James Plueddemann in an upcoming book *Leadership in the Global Church*

to "depart to another place." It is most likely that there was little to no cross cultural mission activity in the early church until the reign of Claudius which began in 41 AD.[5]

Many nations around the world still see themselves as a "harvest field." They do not realize that every nation has the potential to become a "harvest force." This paradigm switch is not simply an academic one. It is a different way of seeing the world and *it completely changes the perspective of both foreign missionaries as well as national indigenous missions.* When visionary leaders in a country realize that they are called to play an important part in evangelizing the world with the gospel, they rise to their highest potential. When foreign missions get the idea that part of their job is not just to plant a church, but even launch whole mission movements, there is a breath of fresh air that sweeps though their organizations.

Latin America: This is exactly what happened between 1983 and 1987 in Latin America when the early founders of COMIBAM came together and realized that Latin America, which had been seen as a mission field for many decades, was ready to become a mission force. Today COMIBAM records show that they have about 12,000 missionaries working cross culturally in Latin America and over 4,000 of them are serving outside of their own country. To my knowledge, they were the first to come up with the metaphor of turning harvest fields into a harvest force, but this idea is catching on all over the world.

Ethiopia: A few years ago, an Ethiopian named Bekele Shanko was sent by Campus Crusade to South Africa. As he prayed and fasted for his own country, God gave him an idea of how he could bring a coordinated strategy and vision to his country. Back in Ethiopia, he gathered the church leaders and asked them, "How would you like to see the church in Ethiopia operating 100 years from now?" Together they envisioned

---

5   See Acts 11:28. Emperor Claudius ruled from 41-54 AD.

the church after 100 years. Then he asked, "Now if we are to achieve that vision, what do we have to do today to make it happen?

The result has been a very aggressive vision in ten different areas. In the "evangelism" track their goal is to see a million discipled believers, and 50,000 Ethiopian missionaries working outside of Ethiopia.[6] This is a visionary leader setting a mission vision before his country.

China: Perhaps one of the best known missionary movements today is the "Back to Jerusalem Movement" in China. This vision came to the attention of the outside world after Luis Bush went into China in 2002 and came out with the report of a prayer meeting where leaders of several denominations embraced the vision of sending 100,000 missionaries from China back to Jerusalem.[7] It later became highly publicized in the writings of Paul Hattaway and David Aikman.[8] The actual vision, however, stated back in 1943 when a Chinese pastor named Pastor Mark Ma received this vision from God – to send missionaries from China all the way back to Jerusalem.[9]

---

6   This information from the unofficial and unpublished minutes of the recent Ethiopian National Evangelism Council..

7   E-mail: A Report from Dr. Luis Bush in China, Wednesday, February 13, 2002 7:54 AM

8   Hattaway wrote *Back to Jerusalem* and then *The Heavenly Man.* David Aikman was the Time correspondent in Beijing for many years and wrote *Jesus in Beijing.* The Back to Jerusalem Movement has been the matter of much debate within the Chinese Diaspora. Some think the story is overblown. All information that we have is that the movement is alive and well. We ware personally acquainted with the one writing the teaching materials for this movement and his report is that there are thousands of training centers (many of them in house churches) preparing missionaries for this movement.

9   In his book, *Back to Jerusalem*, Paul Hattaway records Pastor Mark Ma's dialogue with the Lord.

     Lord: Since the beginning at Pentecost, the Pathway of the gospel has spread… in a westward direction: from Jerusalem to Antioch, to all of Europe, from Europe to America and from America to the East… You may go Westward…preaching the gospel to complete the circle around this dark world."

     Ma: Lord, who are we [Chinese] that we can carry such a great responsibility?

Nigeria: I was recently in Philippines teaching at a school which invites Mainland Chinese for training and sends them back into China. At the lunch hour I found myself beside a very bright young Chinese lady. I asked her if she knew about the Back to Jerusalem Movement. She looked at me like I had just uncovered her deepest secret. She assured me that many in her area of China were very keenly involved.

I told this lady that I had just been working on a project in Nigeria with Timothy Olonade, the head of the Nigerian *Evangelical* Mission Association. Timothy, along with many of the Nigerian mission leaders had heard about the Back to Jerusalem Movement. He and the Nigerian Evangelical Missions Association (NEMA) have a plan to raise up 50,000 Nigerian missionaries and meet up with the Chinese in Jerusalem in 2020 AD. Just as the Chinese have targeted all the countries between China and Jerusalem, so the Nigerians have targeted the countries of North Africa – all the way from Nigeria to Jerusalem. I told the Chinese lady to go back and tell the Chinese that the Nigerians were coming to meet them in Jerusalem. She was so excited!

Lord: I want to manifest My power through those who of themselves have no power.

Ma: That section of territory is under the power of Islam and the Muslims are the hardest of all people to reach with the gospel."

Lord: The most rebellious people are the Israelites, the hardest field of labor is my own people the Jews… Even you Chinese, yourself included, are hard enough, but you have been conquered with the gospel.

Ma: O Lord, if it is not that their hearts are especially hard , why is it that missionaries from Europe and America have established many churches in China but are still unable to open the door to Western Asia?"

Lord: I have kept for you a portion of inheritance, so that when I return you will not remain poor. (Last phrase edited for better understanding).

The next year, 1944 a band of seven set off for a short trip into Western China. By 1946 a mission board had been established and the next year a second group of seven set off and reached as far as Kashgar – the very edge of China just above Pakistan. Those early pioneers never got out of China, but their vision erupted again when one of them was released from prison after 31 years. When he gave his testimony back in Henan province – the vision revived – and the rest is history.

When I got back to my room I ripped off an e-mail to my friend back in Nigeria telling him of this encounter. I suddenly remembered my Ethiopian friend Bekele Shanko. Within minutes my computer was flashing with a message from Bekele – Tell the Chinese and the Nigerians that we Ethiopians are coming too!

Visionary leaders – we need them. Thank God for Pastor Mark of China, Timothy Olonade of Nigeria, and Bekele Shanko of Ethiopia.

---

3. MISSIONAL CHURCHES

What is a missional church? This question is being debated widely in the context of what is called the "emergent church." They define "missional church" as one which is outwardly focused and ministers cross-culturally into the non-Christian world. They usually mean reaching the unchurched in a nearby community. That emphasis is to be highly commended. But we have to recognize that all churches are called upon to be salt and in their own community. If we take their definition, then all evangelism is "missional." There is nothing new or usual about that. In this paper a missional church is one that participates in global missions as well as evangelism in their local community.[10]

Latin America: We have already mentioned the fastest growing emerging mission movements in Latin America under the umbrella of COMIBAM. During the early years of this movement (started in 1987) there was an unusually high attrition rate. Leadership found one of the most significant variables was that missionaries who came from

---

10   I am sometimes accused of focusing too much on distant mission as over against neighborhood or "close proximity" mission. I have no problem with either. What I see however, is that God has a love for the whole world and the job to which Jesus challenged us in the Great Commission looks to all the world as well.

strong sending churches seemed to be able to survive the storms of the mission field, but that who did not were found "weary in the way."

COMIBAM leadership recognized a fundamental mistake had been made. They were going around the local church bodies and sending missionaries without their full involvement and backing. [11] The mission movement was seen as coming out of COMIBAM rather that the local churches. COMIBAM went back and took a hard look at what they were doing, and determined to bring the Latin churches along with them.

Ethiopia: In 1996, my wife and I led a team of 10 Ethiopian missionaries to south India. When we returned to Ethiopia with these 10 Ethiopians selected and salaried by their denomination, we went to their local churches and told how God has used them in that land. The last of the 10 churches we visited was in the area where my own father had first brought the gospel 50 years earlier. The Ethiopian missionary from that area was Subsibe. In his local church we shared how God had used him in India. When I finished, an old man stood up weeping and pointed at me. "Howie," he said, calling me by my nickname, "Fifty years ago your father brought us the gospel; we were little children. We used to look up at him from off the earthen floor where we sat and he used to say to us, "One day, you will send your own missionaries to the ends of the earth to preach the gospel." He continued. "This day, the words of your father have come true and *our* sons have gone to India to preach the gospel." Somehow, many years ago, my father had planted the seeds of a missional church.

What can be done to fire up churches for missions? Detailed research like that of DAWN Ministries in Philippines, Ross Campbell in Ghana, and Dean Carlson in Zambia has done much to motivate those nations

---

11   This from a message by David Ruiz who was the longtime General Secretary of COMIBAM.

to look within themselves. Powerful lectures and messages from African church leaders such as Dr. Panya Baba and Dr. Reuben Ezemadu have done much in Africa to awaken the church to its missional responsibility. Sometimes it is through special conferences where missionaries tell their stories and where the Great Commission is carefully explained. Sometimes, as with Ethiopia, vision trips are helpful. But when people become passionate for God Himself, they start caring about what He cares about. They begin to pray for what God cares about, and as they pray to the "Lord of Harvest" they find themselves looking onto the whitened harvest fields and entering into His work. When revival comes people are filled with His Spirit, which brings holy boldness, enabling them to take the gospel to Jerusalem, Judea, Samaria and the ends of the earth. Great mission movements have been the direct result of revival movements. A revived church, an informed church and a praying church – very quickly becomes a missional church.

---

4. APPROPRIATE TRAINING

If we look at Christian education in the majority world we will quickly find that the Bible schools, theological colleges, and seminaries are largely committed to training Christian workers for work in their own context. Most are heavy in theology and pastoral skills. Few are devoted to giving their students the tools they will need to become cross-cultural workers in distant parts of the earth. This is understandable in an age when denominations are very concerned to provide good theological training for their churches.

We are in no wise decrying theological education! That is extremely important for the emerging mission movement. The theological challenges of Islam, Hinduism and Buddhism are enormous. What we find in short supply, however, is a lack of appropriate training in cross-cultural mission that is really contextualized to the needs of those going out as emerging missionaries. Where cross-cultural mission courses are offered, they are usually reworked lessons from the Western gurus of contextualization.[12] While these pioneers pointed the way to very important (and supra-cultural) principles of contextualization, they were writing from a context that they knew. It was difficult for them to dig down into the kinds of contextual issues that are faced by this new breed of emerging missions.

I recently had opportunity to attend a gathering of Chinese missionaries held in Nairobi, Kenya. The Kenyan speaker was Pastor Oscar Muriu from Nairobi Chapel. This brilliant African statesman gave three lectures to the Chinese on how *not* to do mission.[13] His assumption was that the Diaspora Chinese would be the ones who would have most influence on the new emerging mission movement out of China. Basically his plea to them was, "When you teach the Mainland Chinese how to do missions, please do not make the same mistakes that Western missionaries made when they came to Africa." His lectures were filled with examples of where our Western systems have fallen short of the mark. What he was calling for was a missiology that works in the majority world. What Pastor Oscar was describing is really what the Latin American, Samuel Escobar, has been telling us for a long time. "There is a vast difference between doing 'missions from above' and doing 'missions from below.'"[14]

The emerging missions movement needs specialized training in three areas:

---

12 Rufus Anderson, Rowland Allen, Donald McGavran, Chuck (or Meg) Kraft, Goerge Peters, David Hesselgrave, Paul Heibert, Sherwood Lingenfelter are some of the pioneers of contextualization as we know it in the west.

13 See http://highway-howie.blogspot.com/2008/05/oscar-muriu-lectures.html Oscar Muriu Lectures.

14 Samuel Escobar, "Mission from the Margins to the Margins: Two Case Studies from Latin America" *Missiology* 26:1 (1998), 87–95.

- Solidly biblical[15] but contextually relevant theology.

- Contextualized missiology that works in the majority world.

- Practical skills that the emerging missions movement is going to need to sustain itself financially as well as contribute to the felt needs of the people they serve.

The best example of a school that has reinvented itself on the first two points above is that of the Hindustan Bible Institute in South India. We highly recommend the book coauthored by Robert Gupta and Sherwood Lingenfelter: *Breaking Tradition to Accomplish Vision: Training Leadership for a Church-Planting Movement: A Case Study from India.*[16] One of the remarkable things that Robert (known affectionately as Bobby) Gupta did was to break the link of the Hindustan Bible College with the highly acclaimed degree program at Serampore. By doing so he was free to experiment until he found something that worked in the Indian context. This is the kind of revolution we need in the missiological schools of the majority world.

Training for emerging mission is the wave of the future. It has grown cold in the Western world but it is alive and well and in the majority world nations. It is one place where the affluent West cane come in alongside the emerging missions movement and significantly stand with them. My own sense is that outside financial input is legitimate

---

15 Note we are saying "biblical theology" rather than "systematic theology." In the Western attempt to systematize theology we may well have give some of it our own cultural slant. Dr. Raju Abrams of India gave a series of lectures in Chaing Mai Thailand (2005) on the Gospel of Mark from the point of view of the disadvantaged. When the story was told from the point of view – not of the power brokers – but of the poor, the demonized, and the sick totally different applications emerged that westerners often miss. .

16 Dr. Paul R. Gutpa (goes by Bobby) and Dr. Sherwood Lingenfelter to write *Breaking Tradition to Accomplish Vision,* (Paul R. Gupta and Sherwood G. Lingenfelter, BMH Books, Winona Lake, IN: 2006), www.bmhbooks.com

in such cases.[17] It does *not* create any dependence and is an investment in the lives of future mission leaders. What may be even more important is that we search out (and if possible train) the McGavrans, Heiberts, David Lees, Panya Babas and Samuel Escobars of each and every culture and set them free to theologize and contextualize in their own cultural settings.

5. FLEXIBLE STRUCTURES

As a part of the SIM International administrative team, I was sent to Korea in 1995 to help set up an SIM sending council. I did not have the wisdom or cultural background to do that effectively so I sought out a wise Korean statesman, Dr. Ilsik Choe, who was then the General Secretary of the Korean World Mission Association. He agreed to help me—if I did things his way.

In Korea, Dr. Choe took me to church after church and we met pastors whom he thought would make an effective council. In between each sermon, the pastor takes a 30 minute break, 15 of which could be given to a visitor. As we went in to see the pastor, Dr. Choe would say to me, "Please let me do the talking here; don't say anything." On Monday the routine was similar but different. This involved a breakfast with the pastor we had visited the day before. Again I got my instructions, "Please let me do the talking; do not say anything." We did this with about 15 pastors of major churches.

Now, said Dr. Choe, "We are ready. You must call a meeting for all these pastors. It will be in a hotel and you will be the sponsor, and of course

---

17   In fact we know of no theological or academic institution anywhere in the world which is totally funded from local resources. We are even hearing now of Western institutions looking to the more affluent countries in East Asia for financial assistance for their capital improvement programs.

you will pay the bill!" I handed over the money and the arrangements were set. Most of those whom we had visited showed up. Dr. Choe told me, "Now tonight you will explain what SIM wants to do in Korea."

I gave as clear a presentation as I could. They all looked at me and nodded at one another. By now they knew exactly why I was there and what I was going to say. "Any questions?" asked Choe. "Yes" said one old Korean pastor. He looked at me intently and said, "Do you believe in indigenous churches?" I was a bit taken back as I knew well the origins of the indigenous principles (Korea). I dodged by asking what he meant. He gave the classical expression and I quickly agreed that is what SIM had been doing all over the world. "Now," he went on, "Do you believe in indigenous missions?" Again, I dodged the bullet and asked him what he meant. "We have all kinds of western agencies like yours who come to Korea and ask us to open an office for them. They present their big mission handbook and set it on our table. Inside is a complete list of the way you handle every single problem of issue that comes up. Frankly, we are *not* interested. In Korea we have our own way of doing things. If you allow us to do things 'the Korean way' we are happy to work with you."

This pastor had asked a very significant question. In missions, we believe that every culture should have a contextualized church. Why should the same standard not apply to emerging missions? The penetrating question of this Korean pastor was a "truth moment for me." I replied then as I would today, "I believe in indigenous mission."[18] As I have pondered this over the years now, I am totally convinced that the emerging missions movement *must* have flexible structures which take into account the cultural diversity of a global missions movement.

---

18   The author is well aware of the controversy regarding the term "indigenous" if it is meant to be "self sufficient." In the context of this article "indigenous mission" simply means that the mission is encouraged to function contextually.

I would like to take this one step further. Don Richardson introduced the missiological world to the idea of "redemptive analogies." Richardson himself uncovered one of these in Irian Jaya[19] and told the story well in "Peace Child."[20] I suggest that *just as God has uniquely prepared every people to RECEIVE the Gospel – God has also prepared every people to TAKE the Gospel.* All the dynamics, the structures, the systems etc. are already in every culture, so that when these are redeemed, they enable each culture to make their own *unique* contribution to global missions.

A justification for this theory comes from seeing that God has distributed spiritual gifts throughout His church. If we believe that God gives *all* the gifts needed to bring a church to full maturity, then it follows that every church in every culture of the world has the capacity and gifting needed to become a missionary church. The genetic codes of mission are embedded within the DNA of each church. As a part of that, we suggest that these flexible structures can and will carry the movement forward.

So what we call for here is for each mission, whether in the majority or minority World, to become flexible enough to accommodate ethnic and cultural diversity. This is a great challenge and one that must be taken seriously.

---

19   Called Papua since 2002
20   Don Richardson: *Peace Child,* YWAM Publishing, 2004

6. SUSTAINABLE FINANCES

Creating and maintaining a sustained income stream for emerging missions is probably *the* greatest challenge of the emerging mission movement. Passionate servants of Jesus Christ are called, prepared and ready to go. But the sending capacity to launch these great movements and sustain them over long periods of time is the question of our day.

The prevailing theory is that the more affluent nations need to propel this giant forward with outside funding. In our opinion, unless this paradigm is challenged and changed, at both ends, no long lasting change will result. The West can and should contribute in appropriate ways. But the needed income for the emerging missions movements will only become sustainable as their leaders develop internal systems that generate core funds.

Again we state our thesis. God has created *every* culture to be a missionary sending culture. If that is true then, we believe that God has placed workable systems within each culture that, when redeemed, enable mission to function. Financing God's work is one of those systems. If we tap into these indigenous systems that God has already place in the culture, we will find both the capacity and sustainability that is already there. That is why we hear African leaders all over the continent saying, "Finance is *not* our biggest problem." If all believers gave what they could for missions the windows of heaven would open and the nations of the earth would be blessed.[21]

This leads us to the question of how outside agencies (Western or Eastern) can best serve the emerging mission movement. Our sense is that these indigenous systems for sustainable finance need to be

---

21   Pastor Jose Abias, the General Secretary of the Association of Evangelicals in Angola estimates that if every Christian in Angola gave one US dollar per year, he would have 20 times more than he needs to run a full operation in Angola.

identified and communicated widely in the majority world. We can empower the new missions movement with information about how others are doing it already. When we discover systems that are already working we can offer to enhance those systems. Sometimes there is just some little catalytic action that we can contribute which enables a whole system to work (like maybe teaching book keeping or accounting skills). Or we can ourselves become a part of the indigenous system. If their system is to sell goat skins at Christmas time for missions, I can make an annual contribution to the mission arm of the church at Christmas season. Where ever these systems are found we can blow on the sparks until they ignite into flame.

A second vehicle for creating sustainable income may lie in the development of entrepreneurial skills, or ongoing projects that will generate income for emerging missions. If only a tithe of the money which is given directly from the West went into this kind of capacity development it would have reaped rich rewards by now. When training emerging missionaries, could they also learn skills that would help them to generate income, and maybe provide a service for the communities to which they go? Much more discussion is needed on this point.

Rift Valley Vision—Southern Ethiopia: A new mission society has sprung up in Southern Ethiopia known as Rift Valley Vision. Their goal is to train missionaries, plant churches and see healthy productive communities. Although this mission has only been in existence since 2001 they have already grown to 230 missionary units.[22] According to their own statistics, they have planted 599 churches, preached to 780,000 people, seen 38,680 people respond to the gospel, 71 of whom were Muslim sheiks. Now 40 of these Muslim sheiks have just completed a nine-month course strengthening their faith and teaching them how to do evangelism and cross cultural mission.

---

22 A unit is either a single missionary or a missionary couple.

Besides being the leading interdenominational and indigenous mission of its kind in Ethiopia, RVV is unique in that the first year's operating and salary costs were covered by World Vision Ethiopia. But within that first year, they were able to build the capacity they need to be self-supporting. They found ways of building vision into the existing Christian NGOs in Ethiopia (like World Vision and Prison Fellowship), not to get support from the NGO itself – but rather the Christian workers in the NGO have pledged to support Rift Valley Vision from their (usually significantly higher) salaries. They also found Christian affinity groups like the Ethiopian Christian Pilots Association and challenged them to take on the support of some of their missionaries. They have been able to activate the Ethiopian Diaspora in South Africa and other countries to support their programs. RVV is breaking new ground here and showing the way ahead for new emerging missions.

Bolivia: Christian Rocha is a Bolivian pastor who was assigned to the tiny village of Guyamarine located on a tributary of the Amazon. The congregation was small (about 130 people) and their income was from fishing in their river. Pastor Rocha, however, was determined that he would be faithful to his little flock. From the beginning he taught them to pray specifically every day for seven important items. One of those items was that God would raise up a missionary from their church.

Within a year, Pastor Rocha was in Equatorial Guinea (Africa) assessing the needs. By faith he promised the people in Africa that within a year he would have a missionary from his church ministering among them. He determined that a Bolivian family living in that country would need about $720 per month to survive. The problem was how could his tiny church support such a program?

Back in his church Pastor Rocha had an idea. One Sunday, he divided his congregation into 13 groups. The first group, he called "January." Then "February" etc., one for each month of the year. Group 13 he called "Christmas." Then he told them his plan. Each group would raise the needed $720 salary for their missionary. They were not to worry about any other time of the year – only the month to which they were assigned. Using this creative method, the missionaries from Guyamarine were fully supported each month for many years.

Tent Making: Paul used tentmaking as a way to support his missionary efforts. From our observation of the New Testament, it was only Philippi that ever gave financial gifts to Paul – and then only two or three times. Usually he preached and taught until he ran out of money and then went to tentmaking. This work sustained not only him, but sometimes his team as well. When he received money to operate, he stopped tent making and went back to preaching.

We think that the role of income generation will increase in the future – particularly as it comes to emerging missions. This may come at three levels. First, it might involve building up the capacity of the sending churches to send more missionaries.[23] Second, it might involve helping the receiving church develop its capacity.[24] The area that needs a lot of thoughtful reflection, however, is how new emerging missionaries could be taught skills that would supplement their income. Before we start thinking that this is "ungodly" or "unspiritual" let us remember that such groups as the Moravians, Basel Mission, William Carey and many others worked to provide at least some of their finances. The Moravians sent out teams of people where several of them had income generating trades and supported the Abbot who did the "spiritual"

---

23   By this we definitely do *not* mean to help them write projects to western donors – but rather to help them find ways of using their creativity to find funds for missions.

24   It is not impossible to think that as the missionaries from the poorer South move into the more affluent north, that they could create or find financial resources in the places where they go. I once talked with a Japanese pastor who had the idea of starting a company in Japan and hiring workers from the emerging churches – so that they could send money back to their countries for missions.

work." All these are models that enable missions from all parts of the world to participate in global missions.

---

7. POWERFUL PRAYER MOVEMENTS

When we speak of powerful prayer movements, we cannot help but remember the beginnings of the modern mission era. For the Western world, that started in a place called Herrnhut, Germany, on the estate of Count Zinzendorf. There, in 1727, the Spirit of God descended upon a group which had formerly been in deep disagreement but had just made peace with one another. A prayer meeting started a movement that was to go on for a hundred years. And from that location, and in that spirit, Moravian missionaries set out for all parts of the world. The modern age of missions had begun. Now as we see the rise of emerging missions around the world, that same spirit of fervent prayer for the nations of the world is coming to the forefront again.

The Antioch Mission of Brazil: In the late 1960s, a charismatic revival broke out in the Parana province of Southern Brazil. As a result of this a group of young enthusiastic Brazilians clustered around a leader named Jonathan Ferreira dos Sontos. These zealots preached by day but came together for Bible studies and prayer in the evenings. Soon they felt the need for a school so the students themselves purchased a piece of land, cleared the forest, and built themselves a Bible school. By 1970 there were 100 students in their school. This "student run school" became such a powerful preaching community that a census soon showed that within a 400-kilometer radius of the school, 20% of the population had become evangelical believers.

In 1972 WEC missionaries visited the school and encouraged the leadership to introduce courses on cross-cultural missions. In one of these classes, a student who had shown himself to be more skeptical than the others suddenly broke into tears—asking God to forgive him for not accepting missions as part of God's plan for the churches. "Within seconds the entire class was praying and crying. Other classes heard the prayers and came to join in."[25] One of the students touched in that prayer meeting soon left for Mozambique where he started ministering to drug addicts. When the Marxists imprisoned him, news got back to his school in Brazil. The news so electrified the students there that many were deeply moved to pray every day for their friend, Celsius. Soon God showed them that they were not to just pray for their friend, but for Mozambique, Africa, and the whole world. In one emotional meeting they all joined hands and vowed to give their lives for missions. In this way the Antioch Mission was born in 1975. Since that time the Director of Antioch Mission, Márcia Tostes, reports that 203 missionaries have gone out from that school.

Ethiopia: We have mentioned the 10 Ethiopians who went to India in 1996. One of the young men named Desta (Joy) Langena. In India he was at his station for only a week when he asked the local Indian pastor for a "place to pray." The pastor encouraged him to pray in his room but Desta told the pastor that he needed a quiet place where he could pray aloud. The pastor suggested he pray in the church. Desta's habit, like a number of Ethiopian workers, is to take Friday for prayer and fasting. Early on Friday morning Desta was in the church, pouring out his heart to God. Passersby were amazed to hear an African praying aloud in a language they did not understand. They were sure he was mad.

But week after week Desta kept up his prayer vigil. After about a month, one Indian lady thought to herself, "Why should an African come all the way to our church and pray for us so fervently when we do not pray

---

25 Barbara Helen Burns who has been a professor at this school since 1971 told the story at Iguassu, 1999, *"From Spirituality and Community into Mission: The Antioch Mission Model of Brazil."*

like this ourselves?" She slipped inside the church and knelt beside him for his day of prayer. The idea caught on. Before Desta left that church three months later, he was accompanied by 70 Indians who came out on Fridays and spent the day in prayer and fasting.

When Desta returned to Ethiopia, he sought a place to seek the face of God. Not too far from his home was a mountain called Ambaricho. Desta chose a special day in the Ethiopian religious calendar called *Timket* (Baptism). On that day he climbed the mountain and spent the time alone with the Lord, pouring out his heart for the nations of the world. After he had done this several times, his own teenage daughter asked if she could join him. The next year she brought some of her friends with her, and a collection of money which they had raised for world missions.

Each year the group grew until now, on about January 19th each year, literally thousands of Christians stream out from the valley floor up to the top of Mt. Ambaricho for a day of prayer for the nations. In 2007 I was invited as the guest speaker. They estimated between 25,000 and 30,000 people showed up. It was deeply moving to see thousands of Ethiopians interceding with God and hearing they cry out the names of the nations before God. "Afghanistan….!" Indonesia…! Lebanon…! Morocco…! One and on they went. An old man not far from me fell on his knees and I heard him pray, "Lord I cannot go but help my crops to prosper so that I might send someone."

I spoke that day of another mountain long ago from which our Lord and Savior cried out, "All authority has been given to me…Go therefore and make disciples…." Hundreds of young people stood with their hand in the air: "Lord, Here am I, send me."

The Ambaricho prayer movement has spread into other parts of Ethiopia until now many mountains have been claimed for the Lord.

On "*Timket*" the Ethiopians faithful flock to the mountain tops to pray for world missions. Believers in three adjacent ethnic areas have picked up the vision.[26] Desta reports that in his ethnic area alone "almost all the mountains are being used for prayer movements." He goes on, "My guess is that a minimum of 50 mountains are engaged with prayer movements in Ethiopia. [27] When you add all those who pray in the weekly early morning prayer meetings this is a formidable prayer force. No wonder God is blessing them by sending their people to India, Pakistan and Sudan. We will see much more to come.

South Africa: In July 2000 a South African business man named Graham Power sensed the Lord telling him that Africa was to become a "light to the world." This vision inspired him to call believers together in Cape Town, South Africa for a "Day of Repentance and Prayer." On March 21, 2001, 45,000 people assembled for this amazing event.

The next year (2002) the movement spread to eight other South African cities. Both Trinity Broadcasting Network (TBN) and the God Channel broadcast the event and Christians in homes, businesses, churches and even in prisons joined in the event. By September of that same year, so many people were moved that 220 church and business leaders held a consultation in which they declared a vision for transforming Africa called "Africa for Christ." Their goal was to transform Africa through unity and prayer.

Out of this movement came a proposal to institute a Global Day of Prayer on Pentecost Sunday, May 15, 2005. This focus on Pentecost Sunday was not unlike what the South African, Andrew Murray, had initiated with his Ten Days of Prayer, from the Ascension to Pentecost

---

26 These would include the southern church areas of Woylaita, Gedeo and Sidama. Desta comes from Kembatta where he says almost all the mountains are taken.
27 Desta Langena is doing his Doctoral thesis on this movement at Portland's Western Seminary. The information shared here comes in a personal letter.

(as the early church had done). The goal of this Global Day of Prayer was to have all 56 countries in Africa participating. In actual fact, one estimate is that in that year 22 million people participated across the continent of Africa. Since that time the Global Day of Prayer has become a worldwide phenomenon. Now on Pentecost Sunday around the world, you will find people gathered in these Powerful Prayer Movements.

These are the kinds of Powerful Prayer Movements that challenge the powers of darkness and allow the blessing of God to reign down up on the earth. These are the kinds of Powerful Prayer Movements that take us back to what happened in Herrnhut – and we can be sure that a there will be a huge surge of emerging mission movements around the globe. It has already started.

CONCLUSION

Should the Lord tarry, what will the face of missions look like fifty years from now? My guess is that the issue of Kingdom diversity in mission will be so common that no one will write a paper about it. But for those of us living in the early part of the 21st Century, this is what God is doing in our generation.

A famous Canadian hockey player named Wayne Gretskie was once asked what made him to be such a good player. He responded, "I seem to have this uncanny ability to know where the puck is going…and I get there first." For those who understand what God is doing in our generation, we have the opportunity to get involved. Like the men of Issachar we can "understand our times."[28] Like David we can "serve God in our generation…"[29] May God help us to do so.

---

28 I Chron. 12:32
29 Acts 13:36

3. GLOBAL MISSION PARTNERSHIP: MISSIOLOGICAL REFLECTIONS AFTER TEN YEARS OF EXPERIENCE

Douglas L. Rutt

A PERSONAL JOURNEY

As always, this conference seeks to explore the issues under discussion not only from a formal research perspective, but also from the perspective of practitioners. While I have been teaching missiology at Concordia Theological Seminary, including Missiological Research Design, for several years, what I have to offer on the topic of "majority world missions" is born more out of my experience as a missions executive for Latin America and the Caribbean for our denomination than from any formal research I have conducted on the topic.

In 1970, Dr. Ralph Winter produced an excellent work titled *Twenty-five Unbelievable Years: 1945 to 1969*. He picks up where Kenneth Scott Latourette left off; pointing out several phenomena from those twenty-five years, including the end of political imperialism and the emergence of "national" churches around the world. But especially he explains how the return of veterans from different parts of the world after World War II brought a consciousness of the outside world to the United States, which soon translated into an explosion of Christian mission from North America. He then tries to deal with the way ahead, particularly concentrating on the structure of Christian mission. In his analysis of the pros and cons of what he calls "vertical" and "horizontal" structures, however, he finally concludes—and this is the last sentence of his book:

> One thing seems clear: the fact that in Protestant missions many of the most significant forward steps in both the strategy of support, and the strategy of overseas operations, depend upon a far better understanding than we now have of the "anatomy of the Christian mission."[1]

In other words, who can really understand Christian mission and the way God works?

I would have to say that if those twenty-five years were unbelievable, as equally unbelievable to me are the past twenty-five years since I have been involved in world missions. In 1970 I don't think anyone could have predicted the opening of China and the fall of the Soviet Union. In addition, while Winter did predict the growth of Christianity in what we now call the "majority world," especially Africa, I don't know if any of us were truly aware just how significant that growth would become.

Of course today we have the likes of scholars like Philip Jenkins, who has made it abundantly clear that we are in the midst of a great change in the look and locus of Christianity—what we now know of as the

---

1   Ralph Winter, *Twenty-five Unbelievable Years: 1945-1969* (Pasadena: William Carey Library, 1970), 98.

famous "shift in the center of gravity of Christianity." His books on the topic of what is happening globally[2] have also revealed the great commitment to Scripture and the evangelistic zeal of Christians in the majority world, two factors to which he draws a connection.

Rob Moll has stated that the phenomenon of majority world missions "is forcing scholars and missionaries to create new ways of talking about the global scene."[3] Finding those new ways of talking has been a personal challenge, I will admit.

REFLECTIONS FROM A PRAGMATIC PERSPECTIVE

I would like to talk about what this means from the perspective of our experience with something relatively new. For many of you, this may be nothing new, but for our church body, working in global partnership with our sister churches around the world from what we would call "Confessional Lutheranism," is somewhat new.[4] We talked about it for a while, but never really put it into practice. Now, however, certainly it is becoming more significant for us.

Following are a few examples of what we have done in the past fifteen years or so: We have formed partnerships in mission with our sister

---

2   *The Next Christendom: The Coming of Global Christianity* (Oxford University Press, 2002); The New Faces of Christianity: Believing the Bible in the Global South (Oxford University Press, 2006); and, God's Continent: Christianity, Islam, and Europe's Religious Crisis (Oxford University Press, 2007).

3   Mark Moll, "Mission Incredible," *ChristianityToday.com*, March 2006, http://www.christianitytoday.com/ct/2006/march/16.28.html (accessed April 12, 2008).

4   Dr. Otto Hinze, my predecessor as our mission board's area secretary for Latin America/Caribbean, wrote a Ph.D. dissertation in 1980 en entitled, *Complementarity: A Mature Interrelationship between Partner Churches for Better Effecting God's Mission* (Ph.D. Dissertation, Lutheran School of Theology, Chicago). It would be safe to say that his ideas had little impact until at least fifteen years later.

church in Brazil to carry out mission work in the Dominican Republic, Guatemala, Panama, Venezuela in Latin America, Mozambique in Africa, and Portugal in Europe; we have formed a partnership with our sister church in Nigeria to carry out mission work in Jamaica; we have formed a partnership with our sister church in Argentina, for mission work in Spain; we have formed partnerships with our sister church in Ghana West Africa, to carry out mission work in Benin, Uganda, and in the United States.

These are just a few examples of a new way of working that has come to the fore in the past fifteen years or so, what we have come to call "strategic alliances."

While I wholeheartedly believe that these efforts have been and are a great blessing and are healthy approaches to world mission, they have not been without some serious bumps along the way and raise some concerns for reflection. So what I am offering are simply some areas of concern and reflection from a pragmatic perspective as we embrace what I think can be an enormously healthy movement in world Christianity.

Training of Majority World Missionaries is an Urgent Need

Most of the U.S. career missionaries that we have sent have gone through a great deal of preparation before departing for their field of service. In my own case, I had several months of missions training at the seminary where I learned mission theology, something of cultural anthropology, linguistics, missions history and practice; but also I was assigned the task of doing research projects on the specific history of Guatemala, on the specific culture of Guatemala, the history of the church in Guatemala, the current events important in the life of Guatemala, and, of course, the Spanish language. In addition, I was led through a study of missions from a biblical/theological perspective, so that I could see and understand how what I was doing fit into the *missio Dei*.

What we have seen in our circles is that there is precious little preparation of a missiological nature for those missionaries coming from the majority world. While typically they have a thorough theological education at a residential seminary, most have had almost no orientation in cross-cultural ministry, linguistics, mission strategy, mission history, and theology of missions. The dynamics of how to work together in an international team setting is another area where preparation would be helpful, a topic that I will touch upon under a separate heading.

Too often we have made assumptions about the readiness of a family to live and work in another part of the world that have proved to be false because we assume the cultures are similar. For example, if you send a Brazilian family to work in a place like Panama, you may assume that, since they are Brazilian from Latin America, they will have to cross very little cultural and linguistic distance to minister effectively in Panama, another Latin American country. Our experience has been that in this kind of situation those Brazilians who go to a place like Panama run into the same kinds of misunderstandings in their new home, make the same kinds of inaccurate judgments about the new culture, go through the same culture shock, experience the same loneliness and isolation, often have similar linguistic challenges, and go through the same kinds of trials and tribulations that are a part of becoming enculturated[5] in a new society, just like any of our missionaries from the U.S. In more than one case this has been a part of the reason why some of those

---

5   Wikipedia provides a helpful, succinct, definition of enculturation: "Enculturation is the process whereby an established culture teaches an individual by repetition its accepted norms and values, so that the individual can become an accepted member of the society and find their (sic) suitable role. Most importantly, it establishes a context of boundaries and correctness that dictates what is and is not permissible within that society's framework." "Enculturation," Wikepedia. org, http://en.wikipedia.org/wiki/Enculturation (accessed April 10, 2008).

missionaries have returned to their homelands after only a short while discouraged, disillusioned and embittered.

Perhaps all the training in the world would not have changed the result in some cases; however, I firmly believe that basic training in missiology in all its dimensions would, first, help to make life more satisfying for the missionary and family in the new place, as they would have a clue as to the typical nature of what they are experiencing; second, it would help these missionaries to work more effectively; and third, it would give them a fighting chance at surviving in the new place.

Without a doubt, some are doing much more in this arena, and I applaud the work of organizations such as COMIBAM[6] (Cooperación Misionera Ibero-Americana), COSIM (The Coalition on the Support of Indigenous Ministries)[7] and the Mission Commission of the World Evangelical Alliance,[8] and I am gratified by the impact our programs of missiology and intercultural studies have had around the world, but the need for proper training for front-line missionaries from the majority world is crucial.

Churches in the Majority World Can Improve Their Recruitment Procedures

Of course this is true for all of us, but I have been quite startled by the lack of understanding sometimes on the part of our sister church leaders of what needs to be seriously considered when choosing people for foreign mission service. This is closely related to the issue of missionary pre-field training.

I suppose we have become somewhat "sophisticated" in our procedures for recruitment. First, we look for the kind of person and family we

---

6   www.comibam.org
7   http://cosim.info
8   www.worldevangelicals.org/commissions/mc

feel will make a good missionary family. But as part of the selection process we go through a whole host of testing and evaluation in terms of the individual's flexibility, sensitivity, training, experience, maturity, etc. Then we bring the whole family in for extensive interviews with several people to get a feeling for how the family interacts, what their feelings are about the possible move to a foreign country, and what their suitability is for the situation for which we are considering them. In most cases we consult with the mission field or sister church to which the missionary and family will be going to be sure the field is comfortable with them.

Sometimes I have been shocked by how quickly and even haphazardly missionaries from our sister churches have been chosen. In one case, the church officials simply asked the candidate how his wife felt about possibly going overseas. He was so enthusiastic himself about going that he responded that she was very open and willing to go. In fact, nothing was farther from the truth. I won't go into more detail. Suffice it to say that the results were nothing less than tragic.

There are other situations where the missionaries' personalities simply were not suited for the work to which they were called. Of course we've made those mistakes too.

This situation has improved greatly in recent years, though. For example, the new missionary couple from Nigeria that is working in Jamaica was very carefully screened by several people on both sides of the Atlantic. Most importantly, the people who make up the small Lutheran Church in Jamaica had an opportunity to ask questions and provide input in the selection process. The careful selection process has meant that the missionaries are in a much better position to have a rewarding experience in Jamaica and to be supported and successful in their work. The Jamaican Lutherans have ownership in their new missionary.

Team-Building Must Take Place, Especially in the Cases of a Multi-National Missionary Teams

Our early attempts to form global, strategic alliances by having our U.S. missionaries working side-by-side with majority world missionaries were less than satisfying, to say the least. The reality is that we struggle with missionary-to-missionary tension and conflict even when the people involved come from the same cultural background. When you throw in all the potential cross-cultural faux pas, miscues and misunderstandings, the likelihood of friction and stressed-out relationships is magnified many times over.

Conflicts and ill-will, in our experience, have developed over several factors. One big problem we have experienced is the discrepancy sometime in the level of financial support of the U.S. missionaries compared to the majority world missionaries. Sometimes conflict arises because of the different ways in which the partners look at leadership and strategy. Our U.S. missionaries—no big surprise here—are often thought of as being too impatient and task oriented, and often paternalistic. On the other hand, the U.S. missionaries will complain that the majority world missionaries appear to waste too much time standing around talking, joking and enjoying social time with others, instead of getting the real mission work done.

Misunderstandings regarding expectations have led to at least one majority world missionary calling it quits early and returning home with his whole family. He didn't understand the North American's way of setting goals as something to strive for, but not necessary being the indication of complete success or failure. When about nine months into his first year he realized that he just wasn't going to reach the somewhat ambitious goals that had been set to have so many converts in the new church plant, he decided to return home, rather than face the shame of not having met the goal, which he thought was a hard and fast indicator of his performance. As far as he was concerned, he was going to fail, and therefore it was better to go home now.

These kinds of problems, of course, point out the need for cross-cultural sensitivity and understanding, as well as work on all the other challenges to working as a team. People come at the task at hand from different perspectives, none of which are necessarily wrong. But what is necessary is an understanding of those differences—an understanding of yourself and of the perspectives of your mission partners. Patrick Sookhdeo affirms that "if Christians are to enter into meaningful partnership relationships with each other, then this will involve a whole new way of thinking and behaving. It will demand of us a trust and openness such as we have not previously seen."[9]

Daniel Rickett, in his little book, *Making Your Partnership Work*, makes the point that the need for mutual trust is conditioned by two factors: 1) the degree of interdependence; and 2) the cultural difference between the members of the partnership.[10] This would mean that the fostering and maintenance of mutual trust among inter-cultural mission teams would be of paramount importance, since the members are likely to be interdependent, and the cultural difference may be wide.

As Rickett states, "trust is not something that happens by accident. It is crafted on purpose, with each partner's full awareness of how his or her actions affect the relationship."[11]

---

9   Patrick Sookhdeo, "Cultural Issues in Partnership in Mission, in *Kingdom Partnerships for Synergy in Missions*, ed. William D. Taylor (Pasadena: William Carey Library, 1994), 61.

10   Daniel Rickett, *Making Your Partnership Work* (Enumclaw, WA: Winepress Publishing, 2002), 75-77.

11   *Ibid.* 78.

If trust is a key to the success of partnerships, and it doesn't just happen by accident, then it is something that must be worked towards through intentional team-building.[12]

The most successful missionary endeavors that we have undertaken with our global partners have been when the mission team sent out is homogeneous, that is, when we don't try to put together multi-national teams. That is probably because many, but not all, of the pitfalls of teamwork are avoided thereby. However, I'm not sure that we are truly capitalizing on the strengths that we all can contribute to the extension of God's kingdom if we apply a sort of homogeneous unit principal to our mission teams. We can do better, but we must begin to be intentional about team building and maintenance.

There is a Need for Improved Support Structures

In most cases, missionaries face a whole host of challenges on the mission field. These range from personal issues, like emotional or family struggles, or health problems, to logistical issues such as finding suitable housing, to strategic issues, such as how to develop a plan or direction for what the missionary hopes to accomplish and how he or she is going to get there, to relationship issues with the local Christians, or just the culture in general.

I have seen culture shock impact majority world missionaries just like it can impact U.S. missionaries. One majority world missionary became so depressed that he wouldn't, or couldn't, eat. When I happened to

---

12 Patrick Lencioni has listed five problematic areas in teamwork: 1) Absence of trust, 2) Fear of conflict, 3) Lack of commitment, 4) Avoidance of accountability, and 5) Inattention to results. From Michael Pocock, Gailyn Van Rheenen, and Douglas McConnel, *The Changing Face of World Missions: Engaging Contemporary Issues and Trends* (Grand Rapids: Baker, 2005), 253.

meet up with him on a visit to the country where he was serving, his sending church had no idea about how bad things were getting for him, and they didn't bother much to ask either. Moral support—someone caring, praying for, providing guidance and counsel—is necessary.

Related to the moral support, of course, is the logistical support that can be provided to a missionary, first, as the entire family enters into new territory, and then as they continue to live there. Some major issues are related to questions of health insurance, housing, education for children, food, transportation, what to do in emergencies, not to mention the quagmire of going through the process of obtaining a visa. In one place, the sending church was quick to throw in the towel because a missionary was having trouble getting visas for himself and his family. When I found out about it, I was able to suggest a number of possible approaches to the visa issue, which the sending, majority world church just didn't know about.

But there is even another kind of support that is crucial for success and gratifying mission work, what I call "strategic support." There is nothing worse than being stuck somewhere without any clear direction, no plan, no reasonable goals, no way of knowing how you are doing, and/or no clear expectations. Strategic support is absolutely essential, both for the advancement of the mission, and for the well-being of the missionary.

Part of this is just plain old accountability. Everyone needs to be accountable. While it is true that we are accountable to God, we must also recognize that being accountable to other people is important. Paul even spoke of this when he was talking about how he would handle the offering for the Jerusalem church that he was collecting. He recognized the need to be accountable when he said: "For we are taking pains to do what is right, not only in the eyes of the Lord but also in the eyes of men" (2 Cor. 8:21).

Funding of Majority World Missionaries

A deep concern of mine has to do with the funding support of majority world missions. I will admit that I have been very influenced by people like Glenn Schwarz,[13] who has tried to help mission organizations avoid unhealthy dependencies. I'll admit that I am not quite comfortable with a situation in which majority world missionaries are sent out, often with great fan-fare that the new, young church is now "sending" missionaries too, when all, or almost all, of the funding support is coming from the U.S. This has been the situation in almost every case in our experience.

Roland Allen observed long ago that the importance of the way we handle money cannot be underestimated, saying that it's not the ar-rangements *per se* that are the problem, but "how they affect the minds of the people."[14] My first reaction to what we are doing would be to say, "Paying others to do our work is not partnership in mission!"[15]

There are a host of problems with our current system from my perspec-tive, but time does not permit adequate discussion here. Suffice it to say that this question needs to be addressed seriously. Again, how is this arrangement affecting the minds of the people? My fear is that in many cases, if not most, the "sending church" of our U.S. supported majority world missionaries has little ownership in the work he and his family are doing, nor does it require much accountability.

Maybe it is time, however, to rethink my stance. In the great book, *The Changing Face of World Missions*, the authors include a chapter in the section called "The Strategic Context," whose title is "The Changing

---

13   www.wmausa.org

14   Roland Allen, *Missionary Methods: Saint Paul's or Ours* (Grand Rapids: Eerdmans, 1962), 49.

15   I wrote a paper on this topic entitled: "Hiring National Missionaries: A Good Idea?" You can find it at www.LutheranMissiology.org.

Uses of Money: From Self-Support to International Partnership."[16] After reviewing the major missiologists throughout history on the topic of the "indigenous church," the authors conclude that the self-support mentality "reflects the reality of Western individualistic cultures more than group-oriented cultures of the two-thirds world."[17]

They describe four models for mission: the personal support model, indigenous model, partnership model, and indigenous/partnership model. The latter is the preferred model, in which a church is begun under indigenous principles, but when it grows to maturity, it seeks partnerships with others, presumably wealthy, Western Christians, to then, in turn, carry out world mission.[18]

The world is changing, and globalization is making partnership—strategic alliances—ever more crucial. We see this in business, and we will see more and more of this in missions. Of course we should work together with our fellow-Christian worldwide, but I would only reiterate, let us not naively forget how deeply the financial arrangements can and will "affect the minds of the people."

This Does Not Replace Our Sending

This final point relates closely to the previous one. This is probably not your problem, but in my experience I have a fear that instead of sending our own sons and daughters we are in effect hiring people to

---

16 Michael Pocock, Gailyn Van Rheenen, and Douglas McConnel, "The Changing Uses of Money: From Self-support to International Partnership," in *The Changing Face of World Missions: Engaging Contemporary Issues and Trends* (Grand Rapids: Baker, 2005), 279-297. While I appreciate the authors' discussion of this topic, I do not believe we can in a facile way brush aside the concerns over how the way we handle money "affects the minds of the people" by just saying the issue is simply one of "western individualism."

17 *Ibid.*, 287.

18 *Ibid.*, 292-295.

do it for us. While there are certainly many gifted and capable people from the majority world churches that we can help to mobilize with our financial support, let us remember that Jesus commanded us to go, to send our own, and not just to send money.

In 2001 I wrote a paper directed to our own mission board on the idea of, as I put it, admittedly in a cynical way, "hiring others to do our mission work for us." Let me conclude my comments by quoting from the last paragraph of that paper:

> There may be some ways in which true partnerships can be worked out, and perhaps someday there will be a truly international Lutheran missionary movement, in which all the participants are truly equals, in which manipulation by those who hold the purse strings is not practiced, in which proper accountability systems are able to function, and through which all participating churches are able to realize their potential, rights and privileges of bearing witness to all the world of the power of the gospel. In the meantime, however, it will be exceedingly important to exercise wisdom and caution, lest unwittingly the gospel be compromised, and we think that it is possible to fulfill our responsibility to "go," to be "sent," and to bear witness to "the ends of the earth," by hiring others to do so for us.[19]

CONCLUSION

In spite of what has been said regarding the bumps along the way to global mission partnerships, there really is no doubt as to their value in God's kingdom. My plea is that as we enter into such strategic alliances with fellow Christians from around the world, we do so with our eyes open to both the blessings and to the challenges and issues that such collaboration in the gospel brings.

19   Rutt, 2004.

References

"Enculturation," Wikepedia.org, http://en.wikipedia.org/wiki/Enculturation (accessed April 10, 2008).

Hinze, Otto. *Complementarity: A Mature Interrelationship between Partner Churches for Better Effecting God's Mission*. Ph.D. Dissertation, Lutheran School of Theology, Chicago, 1981.

Jenkins, Philip. *The Next Christendom: The Coming of Global Christianity*. New York: Oxford University Press, 2002.

_____. *The New Faces of Christianity: Believing the Bible in the Global South*. New York: Oxford University Press, 2006.

_____. *God's Continent: Christianity, Islam, and Europe's Religious Crisis*. New York: Oxford University Press, 2007.

Pocock, Michael, Gailyn Van Rheenen and Douglas McConnel. *The Changing Face of World Missions: Engaging Contemporary Issues and Trends*. Grand Rapids: Baker, 2005.

Moll, Mark. "Mission Incredible." *ChristianityToday.com*, (March 2006), http://www.christianitytoday.com/ct/2006/march/16.28.html (accessed April 12, 2008).

Rickett, Daniel. *Making Your Partnership Work*. Enumclaw, WA: Winepress Publishing, 2002.

Rutt, Douglas L. "Hiring National Missionaries: A Good Idea?" 2004. Available at www.LutheranMissiology.org.

Sookhdeo, Patrick. "Cultural Issues in Partnership in Mission." *Kingdom Partnerships for Synergy in Missions*, edited by William D. Taylor. Pasadena: William Carey Library, 1994.

Winter, Ralph. *Twenty-five Unbelievable Years: 1944-1969*. Pasadena: William Carey Library, 1970.

4. IN THROUGH THE BACK DOOR: REACHING THE MAJORITY WORLD IN NORTH AMERICA

J. D. Payne[1]

The region of the world known as North America contains much ethno-linguistic diversity. As the world's third largest continent, North America contains over a half a billion people. Though the United States and Canada are the two most popular countries serving as magnets to draw immigrants from other parts of the world, peoples from across the globe continue to migrate to other North American countries as well.

By far the greatest need for the gospel today extends to those unreached peoples not living in North America. Any cursory examination of the world's unreached peoples reveals that they are concentrated in non-North American contexts. The Church must place a strategic priority

---

1   J. D. Payne is a national missionary with the North American Mission Board and Associate Professor of Church Planting and Evangelism at The Southern Baptist Theological Seminary. He is also the founder of www.northamericanmissions. org, a web-based resource for the multiplication of disciples, leaders, and churches throughout North America.

on evangelism and church planting among such peoples. This paper is not written to diminish such work, but rather to suggest a complimentary approach to reach the majority world. Such a suggestion calls for global-thinking in our strategies.

Global Status of Evangelical Christianity Model

	Status	Description
Last Fronttier	0	No Evangelical Christians or churches. No Access to major evangelical prin, audio, visual, or human resources.
	1	Less than 2% Evangelical. Some evangelical resources available, but no active church planting within past 2 years.
Unreached	2	Less than 2% Evangelical, Initial (localized) church planting within past 2 years.
	3	Less than 2% Evangelical. Widespread church planting within past 2 years.
	4	Greater than or equal to 2% Evangelical.
	5	Greater than of equal to 5% Evangelical.
	6	Greater than or equal to 10% Evangelical.
	7	Unknown.

FIGURE 1. GSEC Model[2]

2   International Mission Board, "Global Status of Evangelical Christianity; March 2008." Taken from http://www.peoplegroups.org/Downloads/2008-03%20 GSEC%20Overview.pdf; Accessed 3/11/08.

Over the years, various color-coded maps have been used to display the percent of evangelicals comprising the nations of the world, with various color shades depicting "reached" and "unreached"[3] areas. Two of the best scales depicting evangelization used today are the Global Status of Evangelical Christianity Model (see Figure 1), developed by Global Research of the International Mission Board and the Joshua Project Progress Scale (see Figure 2).

Both of these resources are great blessings to the Church and should be used in the advancement of the gospel even though Global Research and Joshua Project are quick to note the limitations of these scales and their people group databases.

The purpose of this paper is to make the argument that many of the world's unreached people groups (UPGs) reside in North America, and that the North American Church needs to identify, understand, and develop appropriate global strategies for working with those UPGs to reach the majority world with the Good News of God's love. Guided by the present databases from Global Research and Joshua Project, this paper will note:

- There are numerous UPGs living in North America.

- There are numerous people groups living in North America who, by virtue of their geographical location, have been removed from official UPGs listings.

- There are hundreds of people groups living in North America with an unknown evangelical percentage, especially in Canada and the United States.

---

3   Joshua Project uses "Least reached" and "Unreached" interchangeably to avoid giving a cut-and-dried impression that evangelization is complete. See "From 'On/Off to a Scale,'" in *Missions Frontiers* 26 #6 (November-December, 2004), 9, or on-line at http://www.missionfrontiers.org/2004/06/PDFs/06-13.pdf; Accessed 3/11/08.

• There is a great amount of discrepancy between these two
databases as related to North America.

Stage	Level	Level Description
Unreached /Least- Reached	1.0	Status data unavailable. Located where gospel is not generally available.
	1.1	Very few, if any, known believers. Adherents <=5%
	1.2	Evangelicals > 0.01%, but <=2%. Adherents <=5%.
Formative or Nominal Church	2.0	Status data unavailable. Located where gospel is generally available.
	2.1	Very few, if any, known believers. Adherents >5%
	2.2	Evangelicals > 0.01%, but <=2%. Adherents >5%.
Emerging Church	3.1	Evangelicals >2% but <=5%. Probable group of evangelical fellowships.
	3.2	Evangelicals >5%. Accelerating rate of new fellowships.
Growing Church	4.1	Evangelicals >10% or One evangelical fellowship per 10,000 individuals.
	4.2	Evangelicals >15% or One evangelical fellowship per 5,000 individuals.

FIGURE 2. Joshua Project Progress Scale[4]

---

4   Joshua Project Progress Scale taken from http://www.joshuaproject.net/progress-scale-definition.php; Accessed 3/11/08.

WHERE IS NORTH AMERICA?

Geographers and anthropologists generally note that the southernmost country of North America is Panama; the northernmost country is Canada (Nunavut); the westernmost country is the United States (Aleutian Islands of Alaska); and the easternmost country is Greenland. When these four nations are taken together with Middle America, Caribbean, and a spattering of islands and territories, North America is composed of the following thirty-six lands:

Anguilla
Antigua and Barbuda
Aruba (Netherlands)
Bahamas
Barbados
Belize
Bermuda
British Virgin Islands
Canada
Cayman Islands (UK)
Costa Rica
Cuba
Dominica
Dominican Republic
El Salvador
Greenland (Denmark)
Grenada
Guadeloupe (France)
Guatemala

Haiti
Honduras
Jamaica
Martinique (France)
Mexico
Montserrat (UK)
Netherlands Antilles
Nicaragua
Panama
Puerto Rico
Saint Kitts and Nevis
Saint Lucia
Saint Vincent and the
Grenadines
Trinidad and Tobago
Turks and Caicos Islands
(UK)
United States of America
U.S Virgin Islands

TABLE 1. Countries and Territories of North America

WHY NORTH AMERICA?

When compared to the other continents of the world, North America boasts a very large evangelical population. There is absolutely no doubt that the greatest need for the gospel, new churches, and resources is found outside of North America. However, in the attempt to reach the majority world from solely outside of this continent, I believe the North American Church may be overlooking some significantly strategic matters:

- About the number of UPGs in North America representing the majority world

- About the strategic significance of equipping and partnering with reached majority world peoples to return to their UPGs living outside of North America

- About diminishing the significance of the role of the missionary and E-2 and E-3 forms of church planting in North America.

THE 35,000-FOOT VIEWPOINT

When flying over any given city at 35,000 feet, the observer is able to make out certain details of the city. Industrial parks, wooded areas, major roadways, bodies of water, center city districts, suburbs, and major sports stadiums are noted. However, until the plane descends to a much lower level, all significant details about that city go unnoticed. High altitudes are great for the big picture perspectives, but are of little help in truly understanding what is occurring at the street-level.

It is my fear that the North America Church is dangerously close, if not already there, to making a similar mistake in North America that Ralph Winter spoke against at Lausanne. It was at this global congress on world evangelization, that Winter called the evangelical community to recognize the unreached peoples of the world and the necessity for E-2 and E-3 evangelism and church planting, what he described as "the highest priority." There are striking parallels between his words spoken in 1974 describing the attitudes of the churches toward non-

North American missions and today's attitudes of the North American Church toward her own context. Winter observed:

> On the other hand, many Christians as a result have the impression that the job is now nearly done and that to finish it we need only to forge ahead in local evangelism on the part of the now worldwide church, reaching out wherever it has already been planted. Many Christian organizations, ranging widely from the World Council of Churches to many U.S. denominations, even some evangelical groups, have rushed to the conclusion that we many now abandon traditional missionary strategy and count on local Christians everywhere to finish the job.[5]

At a time when North America is the largest missionary sending continent on the planet (with the United States being the largest sending country), it is my concern that we have failed to recognize the priority of reaching the UPGs here (E-2 and E-3 church planting) and partnering with reached majority world people groups living in North America to return to their unreached peoples living outside of this continent with the hope of Christ.

In March 2008, the Pew Forum on Religion and Public Life released the results of the "U.S. Religious Landscape Survey," noting that evangelicals now comprise 26.3% of the U. S. population.[6] Color-coded evangelization maps rightly designate the United States as over 10% evangelical. However, I fear that the North American Church has become content with the 35,000-foot viewpoint, and is blinded to the street-level

---

5   Ralph Winter, "The Highest Priority: Cross-Cultural Evangelism," in *Let the Earth Hear His Voice: International Congress on World Evangelization Lausanne, Switzerland,* J. D. Douglas, ed., (Minneapolis, MN: World Wide Publications, 1975), 213.
6   The Pew Forum on Religion and Public Life, "U.S. Religious Landscape Survey-2008," 5. For a full report of the study see http://religions.pewforum.org/pdf/report-religious-landscape-study-full.pdf; Accessed 3/11/08.

perspective; we do not understand the peoples living with us, and the necessity of E-2 and E-3 evangelism and church planting.

To be fair, the Church must have the high altitude perspective. The Church must know what is generally occurring within the countries of the world. With over six billion people, the Global Status of Evangelical Christianity scale and the Joshua Project Progress Scale are to be commended for use in Great Commission work. However, just as Global Research and Joshua Project are not content with the 35,000-foot perspective among the majority world nations, thus revealed by them reporting individual people group-level research, the data for North America's people groups must also be as accurate as possible. An examination of the present North American data from both Global Research and Joshua Project is very helpful, but is at times contradictory and inadequate.

UNSEEN NORTH AMERICANS

In his book, *American Mosaic: Church Planting in Ethnic America,* Oscar I. Romo mentioned the "unseen Americans," those people in our midst "who are not identified, since they comprise less than 1 percent of the population in a census tract."[7] Several years earlier, Winter at Lausanne, referred to this problem as McGavran's notion of "people blindness," noting that this Great Commission malady, "seems more prevalent in the U.S. and among U.S. missionaries than anywhere else."[8] It is typically only at a street-level perspective that the Church will see the unseen, recognizing that many of these invisible peoples are UPGs. The need for accurate and reliable data on North American

---

7 Oscar I. Romo, *American Mosaic: Church Planting in Ethnic America* (Nashville, TN: Broadman Press, 1993), 46.

8 Winter, 221.

J. D. Payne

people groups is very significant for multiplying churches throughout *both* North America *and* the rest of the world.

———————

ESEARCH METHODOLOGY

The research supporting this paper draws heavily from two of the best databases on the planet, those of Global Research and Joshua Project. Both of these databases can be accessed on-line through search engines found at www.peoplegroups.org (Global Research) and www. joshuaproject.org (Joshua Project). Such incredible data is a gift to the Church and reflects years of difficult work among the approximately six billion people on the planet. Though this paper will address some of the concerns of these databases when studying North America, they are reflections of outstanding work and provide an outstanding starting point for understanding the peoples of North America.

After searching and gathering people group data for North America, I organized the data according to country and people groups. I was particularly interested in three categories.

First, I extracted and compared the data of the listings of North American UPGs from both Global Research and Joshua Project. When examining the data from Global Research, I looked for those peoples who were assigned an "unreached" status rating of 0-3 (see Figure 1), with all such peoples consisting of an evangelical presence of less than 2%. When examining the Joshua Project data, I extracted all peoples who were assigned an "unreached/least reached" level of 1.0-1.2 (see Figure 2), with all such peoples consisting of an evangelical presence of less than or equal to 2%.

Second, I wanted to know what people groups, simply because of their presence in North America, were removed from the UPG listings and

83*

categorized as "reached". Sifting through 11,571 people groups in the Global Research database, I collected the complete list of people groups, grouped them by "Population Entity Name" and extracted all of those who met the following criteria: 1) had a categorization of a 0-3 status rating in at least one country in the world (including North America); and 2) had a categorization of a 4-6 status rating in at least one North American country/territory.

I was able to gather similar data from Joshua Project with the help of one of their researchers. Following Joshua Project's Progress Scale, I requested data on the people groups who 1) had a categorization of 1.0-1.2 level in at least one country of the world; and 2) had a categorization of 2.0-4.2 in at least one North American country or territory as defined in this paper.[9]

Third, as a result of some preliminary research with the two databases, I quickly noticed that hundreds of North American people groups, especially those listed as "unreached" while living in non-North American countries, are categorized as having an evangelical percentage as "unknown." Global Research assigns such people groups with a status of "7" (see Figure 1) while Joshua Project records them with a progress level of "2.0" (in the reached category, see Figure 2). Because hundreds of people groups were found in the "unknown" evangelical category, especially those located in the United States and Canada, I had to draw attention to what quickly became one of the most important findings in this study.

---

9   It should be noted that Joshua Project categorizes Central American countries with South America and not with North America and the Caribbean. Because of this difference, I had Joshua Project to search for the requested data in North America, Caribbean, and the specific Central American countries that I include as North America (see Table 1).

Unreached People Groups
Living in North America

A comparison of the two databases reveals a significant discrepancy in both the total number of clearly identified UPGs living in North America and their locations. Despite the fact that research of this nature is difficult, findings are always in flux, and some people groups can be identified by more than one name, there is a difference of 127 UPGs, a discrepancy much too large for effective global strategy.

Joshua Project identifies 113 UPGs living in North America.[10] Table 2 shows their numbers according to the geographical area:

---

10 For a listing of these groups, see Appendix 1 in "In Through the Back Door: Reaching the Majority World in North America," J. D. Payne, http://northamericanmissions.org/files/in_through_the_back_door.pdf; Accessed 6/15/09.

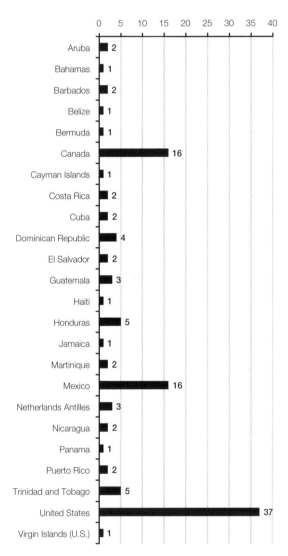

TABLE 2. UPGs in North America, Joshua Project
Global Research identifies 240 UPGs living in North America (see Table 3). [11]

---

11   For a listing of these groups by name and status, see Appendix 2 in "In Through
     the Back Door: Reaching the Majority World in North America," J. D. Payne,

UPGs by Country Global Research, International Mission Board

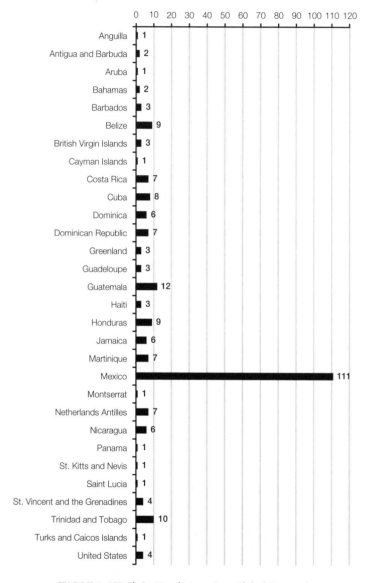

TABLE 3. UPG's in North America, Global Research

http://northamericanmissions.org/files/in_through_the_back_door.pdf; Accessed 6/15/09.

STRATEGIC IMPLICATIONS

Though such conflicting numbers between the two databases must be resolved, the point is that there are a large number of UPGs presently living in North America. *Not only have the nations arrived on this continent, but also some of the most unreached peoples can be found in our backyards.* Again, the North American Church needs to heed the words of Winter spoken in 1974:

Are we in America, for example, prepared for the fact that most non-Christians yet to be won to Christ (even in our country) will not fit readily into the kinds of churches we now have? ... Present-day American Christians can wait forever in their cozy, middle-class pews for the world to come to Christ and join them. But unless they adopt E-2 methods and both *go out after these people and help them found their own churches,* evangelism in America will face, and is already facing, steadily diminishing returns. You may say that there are still plenty of people who don't go to church who are of the same cultural background as those in church. This is true. But there are many, many more people of differing cultural backgrounds who, even if they were to become fervent Christians, would not feel comfortable in existing churches.[12]

Cross-cultural evangelism and church planting *must* become one of the priorities of the Church in North America. The North American Church *must* return to the apostolic nature of the church planter and define church planters more as missionaries and less as pastors. We must also stop conceptualizing church planting *primarily* along ethnic lines. At present, Anglos are to plant Anglo churches; Hispanics are to plant Hispanic churches; Asians are to plant Asian churches; and Africa-Americans are to plant African-American churches. E2 and E3

---

12   Winter, 221, 222.

expressions of church planting must be emphasized among all believers regardless of ethnicity.

According to Joshua Project, some of the highest priority UPGs are residing in North America (see Table 4).

Name	Need	Location	Est. Pop.	Considered Unreached in North America?
Arab, Najdi Bedouin	92	United States	5,200	Yes
Tay, Tai Tho	91	United States	600	No
Arab, Saudi-Najdi	91	United States	5,500	Yes
Arab, Ta'izz-Adeni	90	United States	4,900	Yes
Berber, Arabized	85	United States	23,000	Yes
Parsee	85	Canada	26,000	Yes
Parsee	85	United States	76,000	Yes

TABLE 4. Joshua Project's Highest Need People Groups Living in North America[13]

Also, according to Joshua Project, there are several UPGs with populations of 10,000 or more members residing in North America (see Table 5):

13 According to the Joshua Project web site, "The Priority-Ranking (or Need-Ranking) was developed to identify the people groups that have the greatest spiritual need

People Group Name	Country	Est. Population
Punjabi	Canada	828607
Jew, English Speaking	Canada	303477
Japanese	Canada	61473
Jew, Eastern Yiddish-Speaking	Canada	51789
Hindi	Canada	46753
North African, generic	Canada	41213
Somali	Canada	35165
Bengali	Canada	31073
Parsee	Canada	26080
Jew, Israeli	Canada	17608
Turk	Canada	16707
Khmer	Canada	15722
Indo-Pakistani	Cuba	34402
Pocomam, Southern	Guatemala	40959
Arab, Palestinian	Honduras	54434
Deaf	Honduras	33599
Arab, Syrian	Mexico	422595
Jew	Mexico	39142
Mixteco, Juxtlahuaca Oeste	Mexico	27565
Sarnami Hindi, East Indian	Trinidad and Tobago	523393
Han Chinese, Cantonese	Trinidad and Tobago	20282
Jew	United States	4763719
Khmer, Cambodian	United States	229113

and priority attention. The higher the ranking the greater the need. The maximum score is 100 points." Taken from http://www.joshuaproject.net/faq.php#ranking; Accessed 3/12/08. It should be noted that Global Research reflects different names and populations for these groups.

Bengali	United States	154848
Urdu	United States	151811
Thai, Central	United States	136630
Parsee	United States	76195
Phu Thai	United States	51478
Jew, Bukharic	United States	50797
Kurd, Northern	United States	48579
Pushtun, Northern	United States	47335
Somali	United States	24290
Uzbek, Northern	United States	24290
Berber, Arabized	United States	23319
Sindh	United States	21568
Sinhalese	United States	20798
Jew, Spanish Speaking	United States	14349
Okinawan	United States	12996
Burmese, Myen	United States	10565
Tatar	United States	10160

TABLE 5. UPGs with a Population of 10,000+
Living in North America, Joshua Project

If the missiological community has given priority to such peoples across the globe, then the question should be asked: What is being done to reach and plant churches among these peoples here? Though I do not have any definitive research to support my assumption, my initial reaction is that very little is being done by the North American Church to reach these people in our backyard. Why does the Church travel to the ends of the earth and spend vast amounts of resources to attempt to reach the unreached in dangerous and creative access nations, but yet will not simply walk out her back door to their front doors and love them? Though we absolutely must continue to give, go, and send missionaries to these peoples across the world, even to the dangerous areas, it is both strategically foolish and biblically sinful to neglect those whom the Lord has sent to us. This is not an "either/or" matter; it is a "both/and" matter. What we do "over there" will be more strategic and efficient, and likely more effective, if we include in those strategies what we do "over here." Strategic integration is the key.

NORTH AMERICAN PEOPLE GROUPS WHO HAVE BEEN REMOVED FROM THE UPG LISTINGS

In the course of my research, I began to notice a recurring matter that though possibly missiologically accurate is potentially strategically problematic. In my search of UPGs, I recognized that there were certain UPGs who lost their UPGs status/ranking whenever their populations showed up in North America.[14] Joshua Project has a listing of 189 such people groups and Global Research 133 people groups. For example, according to Joshua Project, the Japanese are designated as a UPG if they are residing in Japan, Italy, Germany, Russia, and several other nations. However, if they are located in the United States, they are no longer considered a UPG (progress ranking of 1.2), but rather a reached people group, with a progress ranking of 3.2 (evangelicals >5% and an accelerating rate of new fellowships. See Table 2).[15]

Most missiologists designate a people a UPG if the evangelical population is 2% or less (for the slight differences between Global Research

---

14   See Appendices 3-4 in "In Through the Back Door: Reaching the Majority World in North America," J. D. Payne, http://northamericanmissions.org/files/in_through_the_back_door.pdf; Accessed 6/15/09.

15   It should be noted that discussion of this shifting in status because of geography has been discussed. Patrick Johnstone discusses elements of this matter and the need for global strategies in the article "Affinity Blocs and People Clusters: An Approach Toward Strategic Insight and Mission Partnership," Mission Frontiers 29 #2 (March-April, 2007): 8-15. For the on-line version, see http://www.missionfrontiers.org/2007/02/PDFs/08-15%20Blocs,%20Clusters,%20Peoples.pdf; Accessed 3/13/08.

and Joshua Project, see Figures 1 and 2). If Joshua Project's data is correct, then missiologically speaking the Japanese living in the United States have an evangelical population that would rightly remove them from the UPG listing. However, if I *only* look at the UPG listing of those residing in North America, seeing a group as "reached" is not likely to cause me to consider asking whether they are "unreached" in other nations.

Joshua Project (and Global Research) is right to remove certain groups based on their geography, but somehow such groups need to be "flagged" to inform researchers and missiologists of their global status. I fear that in light of believing that the people is reached in North America, we will fail to see the *enormous* potential in equipping such people groups to return to their peoples (as missionaries) who remain on the UPGs list.

Depending on the situation, such peoples already will have dual citizen-ship, a working knowledge of their mother tongue, cultural familiarity, and a valid passport to return to their countries. The North American Church faces a wonderful opportunity to enter into partnerships with such peoples who have the potential to travel faster and farther with the gospel doing E-1 church planting, than missionaries who by their nature would be faced with E-2 and E-3 church planting in foreign lands. Again, it is not an "either/or" matter, but rather a "both/and" strategy. E-2 and E-3 church planting are absolutely necessary, but a biblical missiology for the North American Church recognizes the potential at hand and calls us to strategize accordingly. We must live by the the motto of Zinzendorf and Wesley: "The world is our parish."

The X-Factors of the United States and Canada

One of the most surprising observations from my research is the fact that *hundreds* of people groups living in North America, including many who have been clearly identified as UPGs outside of North America, have an evangelical status as "Unknown." *Because of this fact, I believe the actual numbers of UPGs in North America greatly exceed the present numbers of known UPGs as listed by Joshua Project (113 UPGs) and Global Research (240 UPGs).*

Joshua Project records as "unknown" 231 people groups in North America while Global Research lists a much larger number of 794 "unknown" people groups.16 Though the number of groups and their populations differ between Joshua Project and Global Research, one matter is absolutely clear: we are ignorant as to what is going on in our backyards. It is amazing that we can travel across land and sea and develop fairly accurate understandings of the UPGs living in some of the most hostile environments of the world, but we have little understanding of what is going on among the world's peoples in our safe and secure hometowns. What is even more baffling is the fact that the nations listed with the greatest number of people groups with an "unknown" evangelical status are Canada and the United States, two of the most highly studied, developed, churched, educated, and resourced nations in the world.

The cover of the January–February 2008 edition of *Mission Frontiers* declares "God cannot lead you on the basis of information you do not have." Though I do not believe that God's leadership in our lives is limited to our knowledge, there is some truth in this statement. God

---

16   See Appendices 5-6 in "In Through the Back Door: Reaching the Majority World in North America," J. D. Payne, http://northamericanmissions.org/files/in_through_the_back_door.pdf; Accessed 6/15/09.

generally guides His people based on their understandings of reality. For example, Joseph knew that a famine was coming in Egypt so he stockpiled food; Joshua sent spies to scout out the land; Gideon's courage was strengthened when he overheard the interpretation of the Midianite's dream about the barley loaf; and Nehemiah was moved to rebuild the wall based on a report he hear about Jerusalem. Indeed, God has used and uses knowledge about our realities to guide us for His glory. May the North American Church be moved to understand better the peoples living here and be more global in our missional thinking and strategizing.

Conclusion

Not only have the nations of the world come to North America, but also many of those nations are some of the least reached in the entire world. Unfortunately, the North America Church has not taken the time to understand those peoples, evangelize and plant churches among those peoples, and partner with those who are believers to return as missionaries to the UPGs of the world. The time is ripe for the Church to recognize the need and the global missionary potential found among the peoples living in North America. We must continue to send cross-cultural missionaries to the UPGs of the world; this is missions through the front-door. However, we are unwise stewards if we fail to respond to the need in our backyard. It is here we can reach into the majority world by doing E-2 and E-3 evangelism and church planting; this is missions through the back door.

5. KOREAN CHRISTIAN WORLD MISSION: THE MISSIONARY MOVEMENT OF THE KOREAN CHURCH

Timothy Kiho Park

INTRODUCTION

The Korean Church has been a missionary church from the beginning. Since the 1980s, the church experienced a shift from being a "missionary-receiving" church to a "missionary-sending" church. Today, thousands of Korean missionaries are going to the corners of the world, risking their lives for Christ.

The *New York Times* wrote,

"South Korea has rapidly become the world's second largest source of Christian missionaries…it is second only to the United States and ahead of Britain. The Koreans have joined their Western counterparts in more than 160 countries [180 as of February 2006], from the Middle East to Africa, from Central to East Asia. Imbued with the fervor of the born again, they have become known for aggressively going to—and sometimes being expelled from—the hardest-to-evangelize corners of the world."[1]

Christianity Today predicted that the Korean Church will be the number one missionary-sending church sooner or later: "South Korea sends more missionaries than any country but the U.S. And it won't be long before it's number one."[2] The Korea World Missions Association (KWMA) has released recently a statistics of the Korean mission. The number of Korean missionaries as of February 2006 is 14,086 in 180 countries (about 19,000 according to non-official counts).[3] Leaders of the Korean churches and missions made a resolution to send one million tent-making missionaries by 2020 and 100,000 missionaries by 2030.[4] It is a bold faith projection, but not an impossible task.

Many churches around the world have begun to recognize the dynamic emergence of the Korean Church as a missionary church, and it is expected that the Korean Church will play an important and unique role in the missionary movement of the 21st century.

In this analysis, I will briefly overview the missionary movement of the Korean Church, from its beginning to the present, describe the current situation of the Korean mission, assess the strengths and weaknesses of the Korean mission, and make suggestions to the Korean Church for more effective missionary work.

---

1   Norimitsu Onishe, "Korean Missionaries Carrying Word to Hard-to-Sway Places," New York Times, November 1, 2004

2   Rob Moll, "Missions Incredible," *Christianity Today*, February 24, 2006.

3   Sung Sam Kang, "The Statistics of the Korean Church Mission and Future Ministry," Kidok Shinmoon, February 15, 2006.

4   kwma.org.

I. A Brief History of the
Korean Mission

The story of church growth in Korea has been well-known throughout the world for several decades now. However, the missionary movement of the Korean Church did not garner much attention until the beginning of the third new millennium, though the Korean Church had been a missionary church from the time of its organization.

The mission history of the Korean Church can be divided into three periods: 1) mission during Japanese colonial rule (1907–1957); 2) mission after the independence of Korea (1955–1991); and 3) current mission (1980–present). Each period was unique in terms of their characteristics, so let us examine the missionary movement by time frame.

A. Mission During Japanese Colonial
Period (1907–1957)

The Korean church's missionary work outside the Korean peninsular began as early as 1907. That ushered the formation of a self-supporting, self-governing independent Presbytery of the Presbyterian Church in Korea. As the first native Presbytery was constituted, seven men, graduates of the Theological Seminary of Korea (Pyungyang), were ordained to the ministry. Yi Ki Poong, one of the seven, went to Jeju Island as a missionary. George L. Paik wrote:

"Yi Ki Poong, one of the seven ordained ministers, volunteered to go to the Island of Quelpart [Jeju], about sixty miles off the southern coast of the mainland, as the first Protestant missionary of the Korean church. The Presbytery accepted his offer and appointed a missionary committee to administer the undertaking and ordered the whole church to make a special offering to carry on the propagation of the faith"[5]

"From its very organization," Reynolds said, "the Presbytery of Korea unfurled its blue banner to the world as a missionary church."[6] This missionary movement gradually won the support of the believers, and the church sent missionaries to other parts of the world.

In 1909, the Church ordained the second group of ministers. There were nine. The Church sent one of them, Rev. Choi Kwan Heul, as a missionary to Vladivostock, Siberia. In the same year, the presbytery of the church also sent Rev. Han Suk Jin to Korean students in Tokyo, and Pang Hwa Chung to Korean emigrants in California and Mexico.[7]

In 1912, when the General Assembly of the church was organized, the Presbyterian Church in Korea made a resolution to send three ministers to Shantung, China, which was the birth place of Confucius. It was a memorial work for the organization of the General Assembly. The three missionaries went into the field the following year, in 1913. "Again, as an expression of the joy of the Church in the great event, a Thank Offering was taken throughout Korea and the three pastors and their families were sent to open a real Foreign Mission work in the Chinese language for the Chinese in Shantung, China"[8]

The Korean Church sent about eighty missionaries outside the Korean peninsula during the Japanese colonial regime. The church sent missionaries to Jeju Island, Siberia, Japan, California, Mexico, Manchuria,

5   George Lak-Geeon Paik, *The History of Protestant Missions in Korean 1832-1910*. Seoul, Korea: Yunsei University Press. 1929.

6   W.D. Reynolds, "The Presbytery of Korea," *(The) Korea Mission Field*, Vol. III, No. 11, (Ed. by C. C. Vinton and W. G. Cram), Seoul: Evangelical Missions in Korea, 1907.

7   Paik 1929: 390; *Northern Presbyterian Report* for 1910, p. 281).

8   *Korean Mission Field*, Vol. XXX, No. 8, August 1934.

Shantung, Shanghai, Nanking, Peking, Mongolia, etc. Most of her missionaries during the Japanese colonial period were missionaries to Korean immigrants in other countries, but they also engaged in ministries to win the natives to Christ.

The most significant and greatest missionary work of the Korean Church was the mission to Shantung, China. Its significance was in the fact that it was a genuine foreign missionary work. In fact, that was the first Asia mission by Asian people since the days of the Apostles. Interestingly, these missionary works were carried out by despised people who had lost their sovereignty. Denominations played a major role in the missionary movement of the church during Japanese colonial rule.

B. Mission After Independence of Korea (1955–1991)

After the World War II, the political situation in the Far East greatly hindered the missionary movement of the Korean Church. The Communist Revolution in the Mainland China and the Korean War compelled the Church to temporarily suspend her missionary enterprise. Korea restored its sovereignty in 1945 but then suffered the consequences of the Korean War. However, before long, the Korean Church resumed its missionary work. Dr. Samuel I. Kim, a former Korean missionary to Thailand, said:

After the Korean War, the Churches in Korea were looking for new mission fields besides the Red China area. In 1956, the Korean Church began to send two missionary couples to Thailand and [others] to other parts of the world. It was the signal for the missionary advance of the Korean Church for new fields and new era. The burning missionary zeal was rising up from the dedicated Christians in the midst of the ruined streets of the war. Even before they were restored from the destruction of the war and from the poverty, they sent many full-time missionaries to various places such as Thailand, Taiwan, Japan, Vietnam, Hong Kong, Indonesia, Pakistan, Nepal, Ethiopia, Okinawa, Brazil, Mexico, Argentina, Brunei, USA, and so forth. The total number of Korean missionaries overseas are 234 (M2 and M3).[9]

Though Korea restored her sovereignty from Japan in 1945, she underwent the civil war from 1950 to 1953 and was in extremely difficult situation. Hence, the three decades of mission after Korea's independence could be seen as sprouting from a position of weakness. Korean missionaries in this particular period carried out their missionary responsibility without strong political, ecclesiastical, or financial support.

C. Mission in Affluence (1980–Present)

Though the Korean Church has been a missionary church from the beginning of the church, the church has aggressively sent out her missionaries since 1980s and has become one of the major missionary-sending churches. Korean missionary work in the last two decades has been characterized as "mission from affluence." Multiple factors contribute to the phenomenon, including: explosive church growth, marvelous economic growth, continued immigration growth, the nation's diplomacy growth, higher education, and accumulated missionary experience. These factors, and even more, have enhanced the missionary movement of the Korean church in recent years.

---

9   Samuel I. Kim 1976: 124.

II. CURRENT SITUATION OF THE KOREAN MISSION

The Korean Church has emerged as a new missionary force by aggressively launching her missionary enterprise to the world. Most of the Korean Church leaders are aware of their missionary responsibilities to the world. They believe that the Lord is using them for the coming of the kingdom.

A. Current Status of the Korean Mission.

According to the survey conducted recently by the Korea World Missions Association, 14,088 Korean missionaries are working in 180 countries (19,000 missionaries by an unofficial tally). This reveals that an average of 1,317 missionaries increased each year since 1998, but the number sharply increased last year, adding 610 more missionaries.

Increase of Korean Missionaries

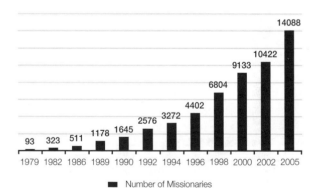

(Source: http://www.krim.org; KWMA 2005:1)

In terms of mission agencies that sent missionaries, denominations sent 6646 missionaries (47.4% of the total missionaries), while missions sent 7366 (52.6% of the total missionaries). Denominations added 702 missionaries while missions added 1151 last year. The numbers of commissioned missionaries by both denominations and missions are almost the same as we consider the fact that about 1,000 missionaries have dual membership.

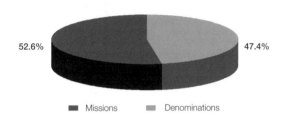

Mission vs. Denominations

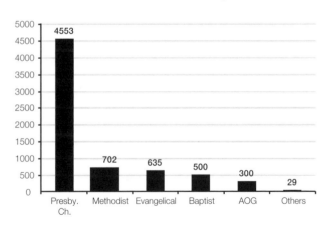

Number of Missionaries Sent by the Global Mission Society

Among the missionary sending agencies, the Global Mission Society has sent the largest number of missionaries (1307), keeping the unbeatable first place for several years. GMS sent 144 more missionaries in 2005 than 2004. Presbyterian Church of Korea (Tonghap) sent 845 missionaries, Korea Methodist Church 702, Korea Baptist Church 500, Presbyterian Church in Korea (R1) 421, Korea Jesus Evangelical Holiness Church 394, Presbyterian Church in Korea (R2) 383, Presbyterian Church in Korea (Daeshin) 318, Korea Assembly of God 284, Presbyterian Church in Korea (Koshin) 273, and Korean Christian Evangelical Holiness Church 241.

Among Denominations

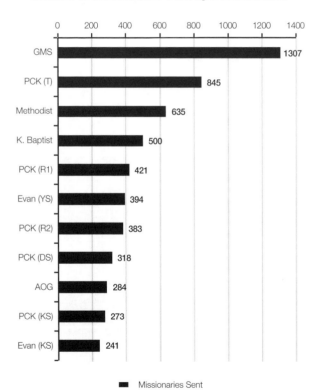

Number of Missionaries Sent by Denomination

Among the missions, University Bible Fellowship has the largest number of missionaries (1267), International University Mission Association (599), Korea Campus Crusade for Christ (397), Youth With A Mission (390), Paul Mission (258), Tyranus Overseas Mission (245), Korea Overseas Frontiers Missions (227), WEC International Mission Korea Center (220), Korea OM Missions (212), and Full Gospel Mission (211) follow GMS.

Number of Missionaries Sent by Missions

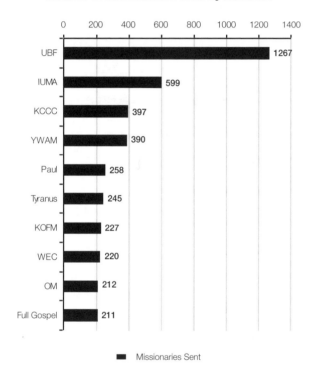

Missionaries Sent

Among Missions

In terms of years of service as missionary, the number of career missionaries who serve more than two years are 12,594 (89.9%), while the number of short-term missionaries 1418 (10.1%). The number of short-term missionaries is increasing gradually. However, the number of career missionaries grows more.

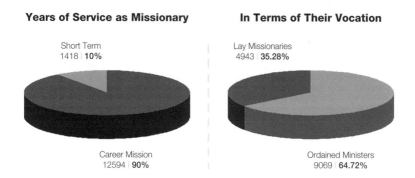

Years of Service as Missionary

Short Term
1418 | 10%

Career Mission
12594 | 90%

In Terms of Their Vocation

Lay Missionaries
4943 | 35.28%

Ordained Ministers
9069 | 64.72%

In terms of their vocation, ordained ministers including their spouses are 9069 (64.7 % of the total number of missionaries), while the number of lay missionaries are 4943 (35.3%). Ordained ministers are still dominant.

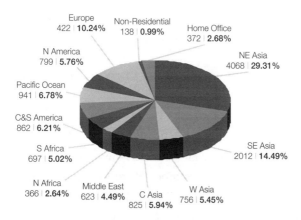

Geographical Proportion of the Korean Missionaries

Europe
422 | 10.24%

Non-Residential
138 | 0.99%

Home Office
372 | 2.68%

N America
799 | 5.76%

NE Asia
4068 | 29.31%

Pacific Ocean
941 | 6.78%

C&S America
862 | 6.21%

S Africa
697 | 5.02%

SE Asia
2012 | 14.49%

N Africa
366 | 2.64%

Middle East
623 | 4.49%

C Asia
825 | 5.94%

W Asia
756 | 5.45%

Geographical proportion of the Korean missionaries shows that 4068 (29.3%) are working in North-East Asia including AX and Japan. 2012 (14.5%) are in South-East Asia,, 756 (5.4%) are in West Asia, 825 95.9%) are in Central Asia, 623 (4.5%) are in the Middle East, 366

(2.6%) are in North Africa, 697 (5%) are in Southern part of Africa, 862 (6.2%) are in Central and South America, 941 (6.8%) are in Pacific Ocean/Oceania, 799 (5.8%) are in North America, 1422 (10.2%) are in Europe, 138 (1.0%) are missionary-at-large, non-residential missionaries, and missionaries in Korea who take care of foreign workers (33 home missionaries increased last year), and 372 (2.7%) are involved in administration at home offices, mobilization, etc. [10]

B. Some Major Changes in the Korean Mission

Major changes in Korean mission have occurred in the last two decades.

1. From Mission to Korean Immigrants to Mission to Unreached Peoples:

Korean mission in the 1970s was mainly targeted toward Korean immigrants in other countries. However, by the end of the 1990s, the majority of Korean missionaries were involved in cross-cultural mission, particularly to unreached people groups.

2. From Western Missions to Korean Native Missions:

Another change is the emergence of Korean native missions. In the past, particularly after the independence of Korea, most of the Korean missionaries belonged to foreign missions. Now, just some of them belong to Western missions. The number of missionaries who work under Korean native missions such as Global Mission Society, Global Partners, UBF, GMF, Paul Mission, Intercorp, etc. is increasing greatly.

---

10   Choong Hun Noh, "2006 Korean Mission Statistics," *Kidok Shinmoon*, January 11, 2006.

3. Symbiotic Relationship Between Denominations and Missions:

Another change in Korean mission today, unlike the ones in the past, is that both denominations and missions are able to maintain a symbiotic relationship. The missionary movement of the Korean Church during Japanese colonial rule and after independence was launched dominantly either by denominations or missions. The missionary movement of the Korean Church today, however, shows that both denominations and missions are working together to send people into the field. One of the characteristics of the Korean mission in the current period is the mission from the position of strengths— hence the term, mission in affluence.

IV. Strengths and Weaknesses of the Korean Mission

The Korean Mission has both strengths and weaknesses. Strengths are: 1) dynamic growth of the church, 2) marvelous economic growth, 3) consistent growth of immigration, 4) diplomatic ties with almost all the nations, 5) zeal for higher education, 6) accumulated mission experiences, and 7) passion and commitment for the cause of the Great Commission.

Weaknesses are: 1) unbalanced mission theology, 2) mono-cultural perspective, 3) lack of understanding of the fields, 4) unwise missionary deployment, 5) inappropriate missionary selection and training, 6) competitive individualism, 7) missionary education and mission administration by non-professionals, 8) lack of cooperation between the sending, receiving, and supporting bodies.

The Korean Church has been faithful to the preaching and teaching the Word of God, but in some aspects has neglected the social responsibilities of the church. Many church leaders have become increasingly church-oriented versus Kingdom-oriented. It is imperative that leaders preach the gospel in word and deed. They should be concerned with the coming of the kingdom of God, not just extension of their churches. Theology produces methodology. The Korean Church needs a balanced mission theology.

The Korean culture is, in essence, mono-cultural. Thus, Korean missionaries in fields often try to impart their culture to the churches they serve. It is important to respect the host cultures and communicate the gospel in a way natives can accept. Unfortunately, some Korean missions and missionaries work without accurate information of the fields and workable strategy.

Also, missionaries have been inappropriately selected, trained, and deployed. Korean missionaries did not learn about the cooperative spirit from their early missionaries. Competition may create a lot of problems in the fields. One of the most serious problems of the Korean missions is lack of cooperation between the sending, receiving and supporting bodies. Local church pastors who do not have proper knowledge and experience are often in a position of control over their missionaries and their ministry.

V. Summary and Conclusion

The bold faith projection of the Korean Church to send one million tent-making missionaries by 2020 and 100,000 missionaries by 2030 will continue to challenge the Korean believers to move on. Despite certain setbacks, especially with the recent Afghanistan kidnapping incident, the Korean Church is expected to play an important and unique role in the missionary movement of the church in the 21st century.

In the light of this overview of Korean missionary movement and assessment of the Korean mission, here are some suggestions to consider as we look to do mission in the twenty-first century:

1 Korean churches and missions need to establish a mission theology that is biblically sound and culturally relevant. The focus must be on the Kingdom of God, not on denomination or mission.

2 Korean churches and missions, as western missionaries in Korea and the early Korean missionaries in Shantung, China, did, need to pursue team ministry with fellow Korean missionaries and partnership ministry with other ethnic churches and mission groups. To evangelize to the growing world population, missionaries should use various methods and working with short-term missionaries, professional missionaries, non-residential missionaries and business missionaries.

3 Korean churches and missions need to avoid paternalism and missionary methods depending on hired workers. This only hinders the indigenization of the gospel and the independent spirit of local churches. Instead, missionaries should develop methods that promote indigenization of the gospel through local churches, as the early foreign missionary to Korea did.

4 Korean churches and missions need to depend on the Holy Spirit and also need to develop missionary methods that will work. In order to do so, mission leaders should conduct in-depth area studies and discern the gifts of their missionaries in order to strategically deploy them.

5 Korean churches and missions should recognize the importance of lay people and help them to maximize their potential.
After all, the gospel was first preached to Korea by laymen.

6 The Korean Church has about 100 years of mission history.
Korean churches and missions need to learn from their past
history and critically evaluate existing methods, so that they
can better carry on their missionary responsibilities in the
twenty-first century.

REFERENCES

Sung Sam Kang, "The Statistics of the Korean Church Mission and Future
Ministry," *Kidok Shinmoon*, February 15, 2006.

Kim, Samuel I. Kim, "Korea," *New Forces in Missions.* ed. by David J. Cho, Seoul:
East-West Center for Missions Research and Development. 1976.

Korea Mission Field, Vol. XXX, No. 8, August 1934.

http://www.krim.org

Rob Moll, "Missions Incredible," *Christianity Today*, February 24, 2006.

Choong Hun Noh, "2006 Korean Mission Statistics," *Kidok Shinmoon*, January
11, 2006.

Norimitsu Onishe, "Korean Missionaries Carrying Word to Hard-to-Sway
Places," *New York Times*, November 1, 2004.

George Lak-Geoon Paik, *The History of Protestant Mission in Korea 1832-1910.*
Seoul, Korea: Yunsei University Press. 1929.

W. D. Reynolds, "The Presbytery of Korea," *(The) Korea Mission Field*, Vol.
III, No. 11, (Ed. by C. C. Vinton and W. G. Cram), Seoul: Evangelical
Missions in Korea. 1907.

APPENDIX

Factors that Contributed to the Korean Mission

Various factors contributed to the missionary movements of the Korean Church: divine factors, human factors, organizational factors and contextual factors.

Divine Factors

The Great Revival Movement

One of the remarkable divine factors that contributed the growth of missions of the Korean Church was revival movements of the Korean Church, particularly the Great Revival Movement occurred in Pyengyang in1907. As a result of the fire of the movement, the Korean Church began expressing her dynamic vigor, not only in local church growth, but also in sending out missionaries to surrounding nations. The manifestations of the power of God and healing of the sick also contributed the growth of missionary work in the Island of Quelpart.

The great revival movement of the Korean Church in 1907 must have its indirect relation with the missionary movement of the Western churches. Since "the early faith of the Korean Protestant Church has its background in the pietism and evangelical faith of the American missionaries" (Min 1972: 126), there must be missionary vision also in the believer's faith. The foreign missionary work of the Korean Church can find its indirect motive in the world missionary movement of the Protestant Church at the end of the 18th century and the beginning of the 19th century (Chung 1973: 25).

It is well known that the fire of the revival movement that arose in England in the 18th century had been fueled by the launching overseas missionary work, and the fire had eventually spread to China and all Asia. In America, the order of the church was established after the Civil War, when the fire of revival began to arise and the churches in America began launching their missionary work outside America. The missionary movement of the American churches became vigorous especially after the American Board of Commissioners for Foreign Mission was organized in 1829.

Because of these factors the worldwide missionary movement of the Christian Church expanded even to Korea. These kinds of revivals occurred and spread also in Korea in 1907 and the Great Revival Movement swept the Korean peninsula. Coincidentally the revival movement in Wales and marvelous revival movement in India occurred in the same period (Min 1972: 209).

Human Factors

Gratitude of the Koreans

Regarding human factors, the Koreans by nature were the people who paid the gratitude they received from others. That sense of gratitude had them carry out their missionary responsibilities. When the Presbyterian Church in Korea set apart one out of seven of its first ordained ministers and sent him to the Island of Quelpart (Cheju) as a missionary, it was to express their joy and gratitude over the founding of the Presbytery in 1907. The sending of three missionary families to Shantung, China, for missionary work was also to express their gratitude to God and to the Western missionaries who brought the gospel of eternal life. In both occasions, the Church collected thank offerings throughout the nation to support their missionaries. In choosing the Shantung area as their mission field from among all the areas of China, they considered that it was the birth place of Confucius. Korean Christians, then, were grateful to the Chinese who passed on to them the great doctrines of Confucius and Mencius that became the foundation and standard of their ethics. The Korean missionaries were so happy that they could pay their debts to the Chinese by bringing the eternal word of God to them.

Extra-ordinary Zeal and Dedication

Korean Christians had extraordinary zeal for missionary work for their own people and the aliens. The most of the early Korean missionaries, if not all, were very dedicated and able men and women. They, under extremely difficult political, social and financial situations, carried out missionary responsibilities in foreign lands. From Rev. Yi Ki Poong, missionary to the Island of Quelpart (Cheju) and the pioneer of the Korean mission, to Rev. Pang Ji Il, who worked in China until he was driven out by the Chinese Communist Government in 1957, all the missionaries sacrificed themselves for the cause of the Kingdom of God. The Korean missionaries, as Asians, could easily adapt to the cultures of their mission field—this was their strength. In the cafe of the missionaries to Shantung, China, their knowledge and writing skills of the Chinese character were greatly used, resulting in a successful mission.

Able Mission Leaders

Today's Korean missionaries find missionary vision mainly through the works of Dr. David J. Cho, Dr. Samuel I. Kim, Dr. John E. Kim and Dr. Joon Gon Kim. Dr. Cho deserves to be called the pioneer of Korean native mission. He, as the founder of Korea International Mission (KIM), Asia Missions Association (AMA), and Third World Missions Association (TWMA), has greatly influenced not only the Korean Church, but the Asian church and Third World churches for missionary movement. Dr. Samuel I. Kim, as a veteran field missionary in the Thailand, challenged Korean Christians to attempt missionary work. Dr. John E. Kim was an OMF missionary to Japan. But, when the Japanese government refused to grant him missionary visa, he could not work as a missionary for the Japanese. He, in the providence of God, taught in the Chong Shin Theological Seminary and imparted to the students the missionary vision and responsibility. Dr. Joon Gon Kim, the Director of the Korean Campus Crusade for Christ, motivated Korean Christians through the mass crusades, like the Explo '74 and the '80 World Evangelization Crusades, to give their lives for world missions. About 100,000 believers who attended the '80 World Evangelization Crusade made commitment to get involved in missionary work either by going themselves or by sending their children to mission fields. He had a plan to send 100,000 young men and women to the world by 1995.

Organizational Factors

Spiritual Awakening and Growth of Korean Church

Today's mission growth of the Korean Church has to do with the explosive growth of the Korean Church. The first Protestant residential missionary came to Korea in 1884. In the next year the first Korean Christian was baptized[11]; in 1887 the first Korean Christian church was organized with seven members (KMF, Vol. VIII, No. 11, November 1912). By the centenary in 1984, there were nearly 30,000 churches (Johnstone 1987: 269). The membership of the Protestant church in Korea grew up to almost 11 million, which is one-fourth of the total population of the nation. The largest denominational churches of the world emerged in Korea: the largest Presbyterian church, the largest Methodist church, and the largest Pentecostal church. The largest evangelistic meeting in Christian history was held in Korea ('73 Billy Graham Crusade) and the largest Christian gathering was held in Korea ('80 World Evangelization Crusade).

In recommending the book, *Korean Church Growth Explosion,* edited by Ro Bong-Rin and Marlin L. Nelson, Thomas Wang described the growth of the Korean church as an explosion. He said, "'Explosion' accurately describes the growth of Korean churches." Billy Graham said, "The growth of the Christian faith in Korea during the past 100 years is one of the most remarkable and inspiring stories in the church's history." And C. Peter Wagner said, "The impressive growth of the Korean church has inspired and encouraged Christians on all six continents."

The Korean missionaries, unlike today's Korean missionaries, worked under the thorough supervision and direction of their home church. They also worked in a close co-operation with fellow missionaries, Western Missions and even

---

11   Some said that when the first missionaries arrived in Seoul in 1885, there were at least 100 Christians who welcomed them. See Samuel I. Kim, "Korea." *New Forces in Missions.* ed. by David J. Cho, Seoul, Korea: East-West Center for Mission Research and Development. p. 127).

with the national church especially in China. The missionaries were sent out as bands of missionaries: missionary, helper, Bible woman and colporteur. Leadership training in the seminary was ministry-oriented; on-the-job training under the senior missionaries were effective enough in raising able workers. The Korean Church had church structures and mission structures from the beginning of its mission. Though the missionary works were carried out mainly by the church structure (modality), mission structure (sodality), like Women's Missionary Society, the Student Missionary Organization, etc., had positively involved in the missionary movement. When the church structure was about to give up the missionary enterprise, the mission structure groups undertook the responsibilities.

Emergence of Native Missions and Association of Missions

Hundreds of native missions emerged and associations of Korean missions such as Korea World Mission Council (KWMC), Korea World Mission Association (KWMA), and World Korean Missionary Fellowship (WKMF) emerged. They facilitated the missionary movement of the Korean Church in the past two decades. Mission Korea has challenged young people to become missionaries.

Contextual Factors

Korean Emigrants to the Main Cities of the World

As contextual factors, the political, social, and economic conditions of the nation caused immigration of the people to surrounding countries, and the Korean Church sent their missionaries to them and the aliens among whom their people lived. Korean emigrants are a potential mission force. A great number of Koreans and national leaders, before and during the Japanese regime, made national exodus to the surrounding nations: Manchuria, Siberia, Shanghai, Peking, Japan, etc.

"Wherever Korean Christians have gone," C.A. Clark said, "their churches have accompanied or followed them for the quickening of the peoples among whom they have come to live. This is true to the North in Manchuria and Siberia, to the South on the Island of Quelpart, to the West in Shantung, China, and to the East in Hawaii, Mexico, on the west coast of America, and among the Korean students in the city of Tokyo" (KMF, Vol. XI., No. 7, July 1915).

C. Peter Wagner called the Koreans a "Church People." Wherever they went they started churches. Wherever the Koreans are, there are also Korean churches. In Southern California alone there are about 1,300 Korean churches. The spirit-filled Korean Christians are spreading into the world with different motives. They not only evangelize their fellow Koreans in other countries but also become missionary forces like the first century Jewish diaspora did. These Korean emigrants and residents, both the permanent residents and temporary residents, in the main cities of the world are the potential missionary forces for the evangelization of the world.

IMC and WCC Missionary Movements and Korean Missions

Dr. David J. Cho, in my interview with him, said that the mission to China had to do with the International Missionary Council held in Edinburgh in 1910 and the mission to Thailand with the WCC missionary movement in terms of their tradition.

Korea Mission Field and the Christian Messenger as Information Distributors

For information distribution, the Korea Mission Field, published in Korea for the Evangelical Missions in Korea for exchange of information among the foreign missionaries in Korea and for mission promotion in their home churches, and the Christian Messenger, which was jointly published in Korean by the Methodists and Presbyterians in Korea, were greatly used by God. These weekly newspapers introduced missionary works of the foreign missionaries and home missionaries to the public. Especially, the Christian Messenger stirred up the missionary spirit among the Korean Church by inserting an article of the missionary David Livingstone consecutively forty-four times for a year from the first edition of the newspaper. Today, there are many Christian newspapers and mission journals that distribute information on missions.

Economic Growth of Korea and Diplomatic
Ties with Almost All the Nations

With its dynamic growth of the church, the economy of Korea has achieved incredible growth during the last decade. The economic growth of the nation and the successful hosting of the XXIVth Olympiad in Seoul in 1988 opened a way for Korea to establish diplomatic ties even with Communist countries like Hungary, Poland, Soviet Union, People's Republic of China, etc.

Why is the Korean church growing so rapidly? Church leaders have analyzed the various factors in the Korean church that have contributed to its explosive growth. Why is the Korean economy growing so incredibly? Economists might have asked this question. But there must be complex factors in the growth of Korean churches and the Korean economy. But if I can list one of the main reasons of the growth of the church and economy in Korea: I firmly believe that it must be a divine will that makes the Korean church a missionary church and Korea a missionary-sending nation.

When I interviewed the Rev. Choi Chan Young, a former Korean missionary to Thailand, he said, "We must understand the unprecedented growth of the Korean church and the marvelous economic growth of Korea in a mission perspective. Even the increase of the Korean emigrants to the main cities of the world must be understood in the same mission perspective" (May 8, 1988). I agree with him and many Korean Christians would also. God has not only grown the Korean Churches and Korean economy, but also has increased the Korean emigrants into the main cities of the world so that they can carry out missionary mandate.

APPENDIX REFERENCES

Cho, David J. (my interview with him in Pasadena. n.d.)

Choi, Chan Young (my interview with him in Los Angeles on May 8, 1988.

Chung, Sung Kyoon. 1973 *A Study of the Overseas Misionary Work of the Korean Church*. M.Div. dissertation, The Presbyterian Theological Seminary. Seoul, Korea.

Clark, Charles Allen. 1915 "Korean Student Work in Tokyo." *The Korea Mission Field*. ed. by Allen F. Decamp, Vol. XI., No. 7, July 1915. Seoul: The Evangelical Missions in Korea.

Johnstone, Patrick 1987 *Operation World*. London: Wec Publications.

Kim, Samuel I. 1973 "Korea." *New Forces in Missions*. ed. by David J. Cho, Seoul, Korea: East-West Center for Mission Research and Development.

Korea Mission Field, Vol. VIII, No. 11, November 1912.

Min, Kyung Bae. 1972 *History of Korean Church*. Seoul The Christian Literature Society of Korea.

6. UNIVERSITY BIBLE FELLOWSHIP: WHAT HAPPENS WHEN MISSIONARIES FROM KOREA DESCEND ON NORTH AMERICAN COLLEGE CAMPUSES?[1]

Joseph L. Schafer[2], Mark Yoon[3] and A. Scott Moreau[4]

South Korea holds a commanding lead in majority world missions (Park, 2002; Johnstone and Mandryk, 2003), with approximately 13,000 long-term missionaries in foreign lands (Moll, 2006). Most of these missionaries serve in Southeast Asia, Africa and former Soviet republics (Moon, 2001). By and large, Korean missions follow the traditional

1   Opinions expressed in this article belong to the authors and do not necessarily reflect the views of any organization or institution to which they belong.
2   Joseph L. Schafer (jls@stat.psu.edu) is Associate Professor of Statistics at The Pennsylvania State University. He has been a member of University Bible Fellowship since 1982.
3   Mark Yoon (markyoon@bu.edu) serves on the senior staff of University Bible Fellowship and is currently pastoring a house church near Boston University.
4   A. Scott Moreau (asmoreau@gmail.com) is Professor of Intercultural Studies and Missions, Wheaton College.

pattern of wealthier nations sending missionaries to less advantaged ones (Ma, 2000). One notable exception, however, has been the work of University Bible Fellowship (UBF). This evangelical student movement has sent more than 1,350 tent-making missionaries to 89 nations, including 670 to North America. For more than three decades, UBF has been evangelizing and discipling students on college campuses across the United States and Canada, experiencing some degree of success as well as generating some controversy. The story of UBF in North America provides an illuminating case study in cross-cultural missions and addresses a question that is rarely asked: In this age of post-Christendom, can majority world missions be used by God to challenge existing ecclesiological models and encourage spiritual renewal in the West?

THE DESCENT BEGINS

In 1974, a handful of UBF missionaries arrived in New York for the purpose of evangelizing American college campuses. At present, over 650 missionaries are living in the United States and Canada, serving in 80 self-supporting local UBF ministries or chapters.

Who were these missionaries, and how did they come to believe that God had called them to evangelize and disciple North American students? UBF was founded in 1961 in Kwangju by Samuel Chang-Woo Lee, a local Presbyterian pastor, and Miss Sarah Barry, a Mississippi-born Presbyterian missionary who had been in South Korea since 1955. The ministry provided Christian outreach and Bible study to students at Chonnam and Chosun Universities. The purpose and activities of UBF were similar to those of Campus Crusade, InterVarsity and Navigators, which were operating in Korea at that time (Lee had previously worked as a translator for Navigators). Unlike those Western-led efforts, however, UBF sought to establish itself as an indigenous movement organized and directed by Korean students. By the mid 1960's, UBF had spread to campuses in Daejun, Daeku and Seoul, and the organization became financially independent of the Korea Mission of the Presbyterian Church. Commentary on UBF's early history and cultural roots has been given by Chung (2003).

From the beginning, UBF members prayed according to Matthew 28:19-20 that God would use them to go and make disciples of all nations. But given the poverty and lack of economic opportunity in South Korea, the notion of sending missionaries to foreign lands seemed unrealistic and counterintuitive. In the post-war period, Koreans had become accustomed to receiving charitable gifts and support from other nations, not to giving. But a breakthrough occurred in 1964, when UBF students pooled their resources to send a missionary to the southern island province of Cheju. This event bolstered the students' faith and challenged their assumption that impoverished Korea could only accept missionaries, not send them.

Distinguishing characteristics of the UBF movement were its missional orientation, heavy emphasis on Bible study, and spirit of sacrificial giving. Poor students worked odd jobs, pawned their personal belongings, and even sold pints of their own blood to support the ministry's efforts in humanitarian relief and evangelism. They did these things by faith, believing that through their sacrifice God's blessings would come to Korea. UBF also fostered long-term commitment and a philosophy of self-support. After graduation, students did not leave UBF to join community churches; many remained active in the ministry as they pursued advanced degrees, served in the military and joined the workforce. UBF began to operate as a church, assuming basic ecclesiological functions including weekly Sunday worship, performing marriages, etc. Many UBF graduates committed themselves to a lifetime of service within the ministry—not as paid staff, but as lay volunteers at high levels of participation. As the Korean economy boomed in the 1980's, many of these graduates went on to become successful professionals in medicine, law, business, education and government. They married other UBF members and pledged to go to foreign countries to evangelize campuses as tentmaking missionaries.

Within twenty years, a Christian movement born in poverty was sending out gospel workers on a scale unimaginable to ministries that followed traditional Western ecclesiological models. By the early 1980's, these maverick evangelists had descended on dozens of North American college campuses, asking students in broken English, "Would you like to study Bible?"

WHY SEND MISSIONARIES TO NORTH AMERICA?

By most objective measures, North America is more Christian than Korea. According to the Association of Religious Data Archives, 41.2% of the inhabitants of South Korea adhered to Christianity in 2005, compared to 76.7% in Canada and 82.0% in the United States. Why would members of UBF, which only a few years earlier had been spawned by the efforts of Christian missionaries from the United States, believe that they had been called by God to carry the gospel back to North America?

One reason was simple obedience to God based on a direct and unequivocal interpretation of Scripture. Matthew 28:19 commanded them to go and make disciples of all nations. In 1970, UBF members identified 145 nations in the world and prayed to send missionaries to each and every one. Emigrating from Korea was not a simple matter, and UBF missionary candidates were willing to go to any nation that would accept them. But they were especially eager to go to the United States, because of America's dominant role on the world stage. As the

Apostle Paul hoped to plant the gospel in Rome (Ac 19:21, Ro 1:15), UBF members prayed to raise disciples in North America, and from there to eventually send missionaries throughout the world. In 1977, cofounders Lee and Barry left Korea to settle in the United States, and the international ministry headquarters were moved to Chicago.

When UBF members arrived in North America, few of the students they met were unchurched. Many had been raised in mainline Protestant and Catholic families and some were still active in their own congregations. The missionaries did not hesitate to ask them to come to UBF as well. What were these missionaries trying to accomplish? They sensed that, although most North American youth were culturally Christian, the students lacked a vital experience of faith and needed to develop a personal relationship with Christ. Rightly or wrongly, UBF missionaries aggressively pursued students of all backgrounds, and in the process raised eyebrows and caused some to take offense.

UBF in North America: The American Perspective

A typical UBF chapter in North America was located near a major college or university and functioned as a hybrid of a student fellowship and a local community church. American students approached by UBF members were invited to "one-to-one Bible study," in which one missionary and one student performed exegesis of passages and chapters from Scripture. Students were also invited to group fellowship meetings, Sunday worship services, and regional or national conferences held approximately twice a year.

Core activities in UBF centered on systematic, textual Bible study. After studying a Bible passage, missionaries and students alike were urged to write personal statements or testimonies about what they learned, including some concrete personal applications, and share them in small or large group meetings. The ministry published Daily Bread, a devotional guide that covered the entire Bible within four years. The practice of Daily Bread involved personal prayer, meditation on a Bible passage, and writing about what they learned along with prayer topics in a personal journal.

Students who became involved in UBF soon discovered that they were being called to discipleship at a high level of commitment comparable to that exhibited by UBF members in Korea. Students were exhorted to study hard and achieve good grades while participating in the ministry. It was assumed that every professing believer would be active in evangelism, witnessing to their friends and leading Bible studies. They were encouraged to develop and use their talents in musical and dramatic performance at services, meetings and conferences. When balancing commitments to jobs, family and friends, they were expected to put God first. Dating was strongly discouraged; those who showed evidence of spiritual growth were expected to eventually marry within the church with the blessing of ministry elders. Discipleship in UBF was life-changing and intense, a radical departure from the freewheeling and individualistic American youth culture.

Why would young Americans take part in such an unusual ministry? Many were looking for something truly different. UBF was unlike anything they had ever seen, and by comparison other churches could seem lukewarm and banal. Members of UBF sensed they were taking part in something exciting and revolutionary. One former student (Schafer, 2007) recalled:

> At a megachurch, my life could have been easier. But I would have missed a great spiritual blessing... Steeped in the values of the American upper-middle class, I did not need a church that would accommodate my easy-going and superficial lifestyle. I needed shep-

herds who would personally challenge me to display real faith and grow in ways that I did not expect.

For others, it was the atmosphere of Christian joy. UBF meetings and services, while lacking in ceremony and traditional liturgical form, were enthusiastic and frequently punctuated by uproarious laughter. The awkwardness of Korean immigrants preaching in English and interacting with the Americans infused the group with infectious humor, a sense of hilarity that was self-deprecating yet reverent. To some Americans, the levity in worship was disconcerting; they simply did not "get it." But others were attracted by this environment, finding it authentic and refreshing.

In other cases, it was the quality and depth of personal relationships. Young people from broken families, societal outcasts, and those with various other problems found that in UBF they were not only accepted but welcomed. Evangelism and discipleship were carried out under a sheep-and-shepherd model. A missionary who invited someone to Bible study also assumed spiritual responsibility for that person, befriending him, praying for him, and discipling him. It was not uncommon for missionaries to invite needy students to live with them, providing a stable environment and refuge from the world where they could grow in their faith. As the missionaries would soon discover, this heavy involvement in the lives of young Americans carried enormous risks. In other cases, growing disciples would become roommates, living together in apartments or rented houses near the local UBF center. Divorce rates in the United States had risen steadily and dramatically from 1960 to 1980. For many children of divorce, UBF became the family they never had.

From a sociological perspective, there are many reasons why young Americans would eschew traditional churches to participate in this unconventional ministry. But one cannot overlook the spiritual dimension. Those who came and remained in UBF were convinced that God had called them to do so. As one young man (Rabchuk, 2007) said:

> I can testify that the Holy Spirit came to me and convinced me that Bible study was what I had been looking for, and was the one way to find true freedom from the trap of sin I had fallen into.

Many Americans testified that they found Christ through this ministry, along with new purpose and direction for their lives.

UBF in North America: The Korean Perspective

Before coming to America, many UBF missionaries enjoyed high levels of prestige based on their university pedigrees. In Korean society, they were counted among the best and the brightest. In the United States and Canada, however, many of these new immigrants took menial jobs to meet their basic living expenses. One man in Washington, DC worked as a cashier in a convenience store. A group of women who arrived in Winnipeg in 1981 operated sewing machines in a clothing factory. Early struggles of UBF missionaries to survive in the American economy were humbling and transformative. They began to identify with Jesus who, being in very nature God, lowered himself to become the essence of a servant (Phil. 2:5-11).

While adjusting to their new occupations and surroundings, UBF missionaries adhered to a rigorous schedule of ministry-related activities. Most were married and had young children. Yet they gathered for early-morning prayer, visited campuses to meet students, and participated in fellowship meetings and worship services without fail. Juggling the demands of full-time work, mission and family physically and psychologically taxing. This lifestyle, though harsh by American standards, was not necessarily extreme for idealistic young adults who came of age in post-war Korea. Seeing themselves as soldiers of Christ on the frontlines of world mission, they spoke of their struggles in military terms and wore sacrifice as a badge of honor. They drew encouragement from passages such as 2 Timothy 2:3-4: "Endure hardship with us like a good soldier of Christ Jesus. No one serving as a soldier gets involved in civilian affairs—he wants to please his commanding officer."

Perhaps the most challenging aspect of missionary life was adjusting to the alien culture. Young Americans of the 1970's and 1980's were not like Koreans; their mannerisms and behavior could seem shocking and outrageous. Koreans were traditional; Americans were nonconformist. To the missionaries' eyes, American teenagers with shaved heads, torn clothes, punk hairstyles, dark makeup and body piercings looked almost deranged, reminding them of the Gerasene demoniac whom Jesus healed in Mark 5:1-20. As cultural outsiders, the missionaries could sense how these young people had been wounded by divorce and influenced by an increasingly secular and permissive culture. They fervently prayed for wayward Americans and called them to a new life of faith and commitment to Christ.

UBF IS A CULT?

Over three decades, UBF in North America experienced steady and moderate growth. Many American students came to study the Bible and participated casually before moving on. Others embraced this unconventional ministry, remained involved after graduation, married within the church, and adopted the values and lifestyle of the missionaries who discipled them. In Korea, UBF has been accepted and commended by other organizations including Korea Campus Crusade for Christ, National Council of Churches in Korea, Christian Council of Korea and Korea Evangelical Fellowship. In North America, however, reactions to UBF were mixed. Some believe it is a work of the Holy Spirit, a fruit of the spiritual revival that swept through Korea. But others have called it a dangerous cult. From time to time, UBF has been denounced by Christian leaders, "exposed" by local media, investigated by cult watchers, even targeted by deprogrammers.

Suspicions about the ministry were fueled by UBF's fierce independence and minimal interaction with other Christian organizations in North America. Until recently, UBF maintained such a low profile that many Christian leaders had never even heard of it. Others had gained their knowledge from second-hand reports and rumors that were largely negative. For example, in June, 2006, *Christianity Today* (*CT*) published a letter by Greg Parsons of the U.S. Center for World Mission. After editing by *CT*, the letter mentioned UBF by name and described it as "a Korean group that almost all Korean missions and church leaders called a cult." When UBF leaders objected to this characterization, Dr. Parsons later acknowledged that his comments were ill-advised. He contacted the magazine editors, who published a correction in August, 2006. Greg Parsons' original letter mentioned a group that some considered a cult, and he noted that the *CT* editors had added the group's name to the letter, University Bible Fellowship (UBF), which he had not intended for them to include. As he noted in his published follow-up letter to *CT*, "While UBF is controversial to some in their approach to campus ministry in the U.S., their doctrinal statements line up with mainstream evangelicalism. After further study, I do not consider them to be a cult" (Parsons 2006).

In the mid-1980's, UBF was targeted by Cult Awareness Network (CAN), a non-Christian organization that acted as a conduit for pro-fessional deprogrammers who kidnapped and detained young people to bring them out of controversial religious groups. CAN maintained files on more than 1,500 organizations, including many well-known evangelical Christian groups (e.g., Jews for Jesus, Promise Keepers,

Campus Crusade). CAN gathered only negative reports and failed to verify the authenticity of the information. In 1996, CAN leaders were found guilty of participation in the kidnapping of a young man and were ordered to pay more that $1 million in damages, after which the organization declared bankruptcy and disbanded. CAN materials about UBF have resurfaced, however, and may still be found on a number of anti-UBF websites.

UBF was denounced as a "fringe church" in the book Churches that Abuse by Ronald M. Enroth (1992). But others have disputed Enroth's conclusions. Dr. Ruth Tucker, a counter-cult researcher, called his analyses "sadly misdirected" and "seriously flawed" (Cornerstone, 1994, 22:41). She wrote:

> The real tragedy of Ron's "research" is that it gives the impression that there is only one model for the contemporary Christian church— that being the fashionable, affluent, suburban church with all its middle-class values.

She argued that Enroth and other counter-cult investigators base their research on narratives of "victims" and unhappy ex-members, with little or no attempt to counterbalance those allegations by careful internal study of the organization. And there is scant recognition of cultural differences and the subjectivity of the investigator's own frame of reference. With this kind of methodology, she argues, it is essentially a foregone conclusion that a potent but unconventional Christian group will be deemed dysfunctional.

Apologetics Index, a popular on-line Christian resource for information about cults, currently describes UBF as a group that professes to be Christian but lies outside orthodox Christianity. However, the editors of this website do not indicate how they believe UBF deviates from orthodoxy or orthopraxy. UBF's Statement of Faith, which is available on its website (http://www.ubf.org), is uncontroversial and agrees closely with the Statement of Faith of Apologetics Index.

CONTROVERSY, CONTEXTUALIZATION AND CULTURE

To properly understand and evaluate the work of UBF, one must acknowledge that there are profound differences in mindset between peoples from the East and the West. Many of the controversies surrounding the ministry can be ascribed to cultural misunderstandings and the unconventional manner in which UBF members contextualized the gospel in North America. In certain respects, missionaries tried to recreate the kind of ministry where they first met Christ. They imported cultural forms which seemed fairly normal in Korea but were alien to Americans.

Korean society is strongly hierarchical. The Korean language contains honorifics (modifications to nouns and verbs) that acknowledge social status, age differences and the nature of the relationship between the speaker and the listener. To ignore these conventions of speech is to invite peril. American English, on the other hand, makes no such distinctions. To establish a more comfortable social environment, UBF missionaries created their own honorifics, carrying into English some polite forms of address that had been developed in Korea. They added titles to each person's name, calling one another "Missionary," "Pastor" or "Doctor." Growing American disciples were called "Shepherd" and "Shepherdess." New members were collectively called "sheep" and individually addressed as "Brother" and "Sister." Some Americans thought this to be unusual, but eventually began to speak in these terms. Others interpreted these titles as degrading (who likes to be called a sheep?). Critics of UBF pointed to these forms of address as evidence that UBF is a cult-like organization with a rigid hierarchy. These Korean-style mannerisms have been slowly disappearing from American UBF, but old habits die slowly.

UBF missionaries were disconcerted by the informal and revealing clothing styles of America. They encouraged young women to dress with modesty and propriety. Young men were urged to shave off facial hair and wear dress shirts and ties to meetings and services. American UBF adopted styles of dress that were commonplace in Korea, but a radical departure from the causal culture of the West.

In general, Koreans also differ from Americans in attitudes toward physical training and discipline. It is a simple fact that Koreans (especially men) value physical training far more than Americans do. South Korea suffered through a painful war and lives under threat of attack by a hostile and militaristic neighbor. All able-bodied Korean men are required to serve in the military. Some of the physical discipline that they experience in the Korean army would shock and dismay a westerner, but Korean men endure it with a sense of honor and pride. On occasion, UBF leaders used physical measures to discipline Korean missionaries and American students (e.g. walking long distances) to help them to learn a "soldier spirit." Some Americans were able to accept his training and benefited from it. But others who were trained in this manner became resentful and critical of the ministry.

Major differences also exist between East and West in the extent to which members of a family, church or community may influence, interfere with or intervene in others' personal lives before it is considered a breach. In a traditional Korean family, it is commonplace for elders to act as matchmakers for young people. In fact, an elder's failure to act when a young person reaches a marriageable age is regarded as neglectful. To court and marry in Korea in the 1970's without the blessing of one's parents and pastor was unthinkable. These cultural attitudes persist in American UBF. In UBF it is assumed that a young disciple will not date until he or she is ready to marry. It is expected that decisions about marriage will be reached after prayerfully seeking God's will along with input and blessing of spiritual elders. The practice, which in UBF has been called "marriage by faith," starkly contrasts with contemporary American attitudes toward dating and marriage which emphasize individual choice.

It would be wrong, however, to assert that UBF's practices regarding marriage are merely an artifact of Eastern culture. The ministry has an explicit and well-developed theology of marriage based on the understanding that God unites men and women for a higher purpose. UBF believes that marriage is not an end in itself, but a blessing to help man and woman carry out their God-given mission. In a commentary on Genesis 2:18-25, cofounder Sarah Barry (1992) wrote:

> God created a woman to help the man fulfill the mission God had given him. She was to be his companion, his friend…. No suitable helper could be found for Adam among animals because the animals could not share man's spiritual life or his mission… The man was not so concerned about his lack of a suitable helper. God was concerned… God was the one who saw man's need and understood it and filled that need in his own way at the right time. God knows us better than we know ourselves, and he is ready to give us the best co-worker, and lead us into the most fruitful life.

Samuel Lee (the former General Director of UBF) and the directors of local chapters were proactive in bringing couples together by introducing eligible singles. In many cases, American disciples gratefully accepted this input. Seventeen years after marrying within UBF, Sharon Schafer (2007) wrote:

Dr. Lee taught the importance of the God-centered "house church" as the building block of society, and as a primary vehicle for world salvation work. He wholeheartedly prayed for young women to marry with this purpose. He took an active role by introducing me to eligible bachelors. For me, it was a welcome relief to stop dating and a great blessing to marry to please God.

The vast majority of marriages within North American UBF have been successful, and divorce is rare. Some have disagreed with the ministry's methods, however, and cite individual examples of failed marriages as evidence that the practice of "marriage by faith" is fundamentally unsound or even heretical.

LEADERSHIP STYLE

Another major reason that UBF was looked upon with suspicion was the controversial leadership style of Samuel Lee. Lee was born in Japan in 1931. After fighting in the Korean War, he was educated at the Presbyterian seminary in Seoul and Chonbuk National University (the latter awarded him an honorary doctorate of letters in 1991). He moved to Chicago in 1977, became an American citizen and led the ministry until his death in 2002.

Lee did not mince words. He spoke freely, passionately and bluntly. He tended to micromanage the ministry and, on occasion, aspects of the personal lives of some UBF members. It would not be an overstatement to say that there was not a single person in UBF who knew him personally and was not offended by him on some occasion. Lee came from a society in which it was quite normal for the patriarch of a family or an organization to exercise a great deal of personal control over corporate affairs. Even by that standard, Lee went further than many Korean managers would go.

Nevertheless, Lee was an exceptional leader whose leadership did not come from any obvious human qualities. He was short and appeared unimpressive. He was not a glib or gifted speaker of English. He was soft-spoken, sometimes awkward, humble and shy. Yet he was respected for showing exceptional discipline in his personal life. He spent a great deal of time in Bible study, prayer, and letter writing.

Lee's leadership style was not conducive to dissent. UBF bylaws created voting members and a Board of Directors, but members of these bodies did not always provide Lee with meaningful direction, because they accepted him as their pastor and spiritual leader. They usually submitted to his wishes and did not feel they had the spiritual authority to challenge his ideas. Dr. Lee could also be sensitive and sometimes interpreted dissent as a personal affront, selfishness or as a general disrespect of authority.

Critics of UBF have claimed that Dr. Lee was cunning and manipulative. But those who knew him found him straightforward and uncomplicated. Lee knew what he believed and said what he thought. After Lee's passing away, his family opened his handwritten prayer journals which no one had ever seen. In these notebooks, he had written certain passages of scripture over and over again. One particular passage to which he often returned was Mark 11:20-25, where Jesus challenged his disciples, "Have faith in God." Throughout Lee's life, he fervently struggled in prayer to believe that God would do the things he had promised. His journals are filled with highly personal prayers for the health and well being of individuals and families in the UBF ministry in Chicago, across America and throughout the world.

UBF Today

After Lee's death, cofounder Sarah Barry assumed the role of General Director and served in that capacity until 2006. The ministry is now directed by Dr. John Jun, who was one of the first Korean students to be evangelized by Lee. Barry and Jun exhibit a less commanding leadership style than Lee, relying more heavily on the input of directors and members of advisory committees. Some UBF chapters are now led by Americans. Other chapters, though still managed by elder Korean missionaries, have Americans placed in key leadership positions. UBF is changing in many respects, but it retains its focus on world mission through campus evangelism. A ministry-wide prayer topic and goal is to send out 100,000 lay missionaries to all nations of the world by 2041.

In recent years, North American UBF has also taken crucial steps to improve its standing and relationships with other parts of the Christian community. In 2004, a group of ex-UBF members and critics petitioned the National Association of Evangelicals (NAE) to revoke UBF's membership in NAE. NAE complied with this request but, upon further investigation, reinstated UBF's membership in 2008. UBF was accredited by the Evangelical Council for Financial Accountability (ECFA) in 2007, and in 2008 received membership in CrossGlobal Link (formerly the Interdenominational Foreign Mission Association). The ministry has also been actively cultivating relationships with American Christian leaders and scholars who are sensitive to issues of contextualization and cross-cultural witness, who can provide guidance, encouragement and prayer support.

Lessons in Humility and Community

Many lessons can be learned from this unusual cross-cultural mission movement which traversed from East to West, against the tide of traditional missions. When members began to arrive in North America, hardly anyone distinguished them from other immigrants who came seeking a better life in a land of opportunity and prosperity. But these people were not ordinary immigrants. They regarded themselves as missionaries, and they fought with intensity to maintain their focus and identity while supporting themselves in a strange land.

For these missionaries, acclimating themselves to North American college campus culture meant doing many things that no one around them was trying to do. They found themselves separated from the Korean ethnic immigrant community. They arranged their careers, families and lifestyle to be more inviting to college students, making incredible personal sacrifices. But the most challenging aspect of these efforts was the inner tension between their new American experience and the thoroughly Korean perspectives and attitudes they carried with them. The clash of cultures was profound. Many years of frustration in building trust with American students passed before the missionaries began to realize that the gospel that they had embraced in Korea came to them woven in their own cultural fabric. Their own faith was contextualized. And now as missionaries, they in turn needed to contextualize the gospel in new terms, in a very different, American culture.

Contextualization meant that they not only had to learn a new culture, but they had to embrace that culture as being as legitimate as their own. It is natural for members of a culture to look down on other cultures and to moralize all differences. It was easy for UBF Korean missionaries to feel culturally and morally superior to their American students, for reasons we have mentioned. But crossing the cultural divide in Christ's name means acknowledging that this is wrong and that steps need to be taken, both personally and organizationally, to overcome it. An important lesson was accepting that there exists no culture with a monopoly on Christian virtue, and that all cultures are both affirmed and challenged by the gospel. At both the sending and receiving end, the gospel comes to all by grace alone.

The experiences of UBF also teach important lessons about Christian community. North American UBF has been ardently independent. Seeing obvious differences between its style of ministry and the work of other Christian organizations, UBF has tended to moralize those differences as well. Members developed an un-Christlike attitude of superiority over other American churches. Scripture confirms that all believers are part of the body of Christ. UBF is a part of that body no more and no less than any other Christian organization. Members of Christ's body need one another, and isolation of any kind, whether intentional or not, eventually becomes unhealthy.

When UBF's practices in North America were scrutinized, its lack of connections to the larger body prevented the organization from addressing criticism in a credible fashion. Lacking fresh input from the outside, the organization had few mechanisms to engage in a healthy process of self-evaluation. Now that UBF has grown, there is an ongoing temptation to believe that it can remain self-sufficient. That illusion must be vigorously opposed. UBF does not need to sacrifice any of its unique character, perspectives and methods that are scripturally sound. But it must acknowledge that it has many things to learn from other parts of the Body of Christ. And it also has many things to teach. Ongoing efforts to improving UBF's connections with the larger Christian community in America and around the world will be essential for organization to realize its long-term prayer topics and goals.

CHALLENGING CULTURE TO
ADVANCE THE GOSPEL

It is an undeniable fact that the universal truths of the gospel will be communicated and expressed differently in different societies and cultures. Some of the difficulties encountered by UBF missionaries can be attributed to their ignorance of America and lack of awareness of how their own understanding of the gospel was shaped by their Korean background. If these missionaries had arrived with better understanding and had been more affirming of American culture and values, then certain conflicts might have been avoided. But would the ministry have been more successful? Not necessarily.

For American youth, joining UBF was challenging and uncomfortable for reasons that we have explained. But for many, this discomfort was spiritually invaluable. In some cases, God used it to reveal how their own westernized, individualized and complacent version of Christianity differed from the gospel set forth in the Bible. To the American students who came to UBF, remained through the years and became committed gospel workers, the alien aspects of UBF were a powerful tool that pried open their spiritual eyes to see God's wider purpose for world salvation. God used an unconventional ministry to communicate his plan of salvation to them in a startling way when conventional North American churches had not.

We are not arguing that North American UBF should retain its Korean character. Nor do we assert that it needs to uncritically embrace more aspects of the American culture. A gospel worker does not need to become American simply because he or she is working in America. Effective cross-cultural ministry does require, however, that missionaries make good choices about which practices they will retain or discard. Good choices don't happen by accident. They must be made consciously, intentionally and prayerfully, based on solid understanding of Scripture and culture.

Contemporary American presentations of the gospel, to the extent that they ignore Christ's missional mandate to go and make disciples of all nations, are deficient. In many respects, North America needs to be evangelized, just as the peoples of less advantaged nations need to be evangelized. Who can evangelize the heartland of North America and awaken the sleeping giant within the American church? Could majority world missions be one of God's instruments to accomplish this task?

For the gospel to reach every society and culture in an increasingly globalized world, it will not be sufficient for rich countries to send missionaries to poor ones. Nor will it be sufficient for majority world countries to send missionaries to poorer or richer places. God's mission may require gospel workers—both tentmaking and professional—to flow from everywhere to everywhere. The concept of missions embedded within UBF resembles this vision. UBF in North America has experienced successes and setbacks, but it has not failed to advance this larger cause.

Scott Moreau's Observations of UBF

I was initially introduced to University Bible Fellowship when I met Dr. Mark Yoon at the Evangelical Missiological Society meeting in 1997 in Orlando, Florida. Being aware of the reality of the Korean mission movement, I realized that this was an opportunity to begin to know one of their organizations. At the time I was unaware of the controversies surrounding UBF. I was also unaware that they were the largest Korean missionary sending agency, and that almost all of their missionaries were self-supporting tentmakers.

Over the next decade Mark and I developed a relationship focused initially on mutual family issues, especially as we shared the concerns, questions, and challenges we faced as fathers. Having lived and served in Africa for a decade prior to coming to Wheaton, I knew what it was like to live in another culture and to start to raise a family there. I anticipated that Mark's children, being bi-culturally born and raised in the United States, might bring challenges about the distinctly Korean values that I saw operating in the organization. Further, as one who trains people how to learn to live in another culture, I wanted to learn what types of adaptation Koreans experienced when they came to live in the United States as long-term missionaries.

At the same time, I was curious to learn more about UBF as an organization. Based on what I knew of Korean churches and the Korean Christian movement in general, I expected to find a strong hierarchical leadership structure, a highly disciplined approach to the Christian life (especially prayer), and a somewhat limited understanding of the role culture plays in the life of the group. I was especially interested to learn how this played out in family relationships when the children of church leaders were raised in a less hierarchical culture. Finally, I was curious to see how UBF worked on university campuses in the United States. David Hesselgrave noted that dynamically growing religious movements tended to be both in and out of the cultures in which they worked (1978). I hoped to observe how this dynamic worked out in the context of UBF.[5]

As I got to know Mark, he also began to share with me that UBF was facing challenges from former members who were angry at the organization and leveling accusations at it and its leadership. At that time, UBF followed a policy of not responding publicly to the accusations. Rather, they chose to trust that God would handle them. This lack

---

5   The focus of the part of this chapter that precedes my observations.

of public response, however, was not helping their reputation as an organization—especially as the use of the Internet made it easier for people who did not like the organization to make their version of UBF readily available to anyone using a search engine. Because of questions as to whether they could continue to operate as they had over the previous several decades—at least in the United States—UBF was in the early stages of discussing whether to modify their policy in some way and respond to the accusations or to simply continue their strategy of pressing on with the ministry while maintaining public silence.

Ultimately I was asked to travel to Korea and address their organization at the annual conference for their missionaries, which I did in the summer of 2006. This gave me the opportunity to learn more about the history and the people who are UBF as well as to introduce them as an organization to issues of contextualization and intercultural communication which would help them understand themselves and better understand the reactions they were facing. The numerous phone calls and warnings I received prior to my trip to Korea also helped me understand how those who felt UBF was a cult perceived my visit, even before they knew what my purpose was.

In the space that follows I will offer a brief explanation of cultural values that help context UBF, followed by some of the observations I shared with them while in Korea, as well as further observations I have made while continuing my relationship with UBF leadership.

Contrasting Values

To help the reader understand the issues involved, however, it is necessary to take a brief detour here to introduce three important sets of contrasting cultural value as they are used in the following discussion.

First, collectivism is an orientation in which a person derives his or her sense of self from the interdependent relationships that characterize life. In Africa one often hears the saying, "We relate, therefore I am." This captures the essence of collectivism, which is that one's relationships determine who one really is. In contrast, individualism is an orientation in which a person derives his or her sense of self from internalized values and independent relationships. The United States has been characterized as the country with the strongest level of individualism (Hofstede and Hofstede 2005, 78). Korea, on the other hand, as with many Asian cultures, is strongly collectivistic. It will be seen below how UBF has carried the Korean value of collectivism into its organizational ethos.

Power distance is the second orientation that plays a role in UBF. Power distance has to do with the extent to which a society values differences in social power. Traditional Korean culture is referred to as a large power distance culture because it values power differentials in individuals, and people seek to maintain these power differentials in their relationships. Subordinates value strong leaders, and leaders value humble and submissive subordinates. In such societies there are clear protocols on how one is to relate to superiors as well as how one relates to subordinates. Often in large power distance societies the leader and a few selected subordinates will have what is characterized as "patron-client" relationships. The patron or leader provides benefits, such as access to resources or information, opportunities for social/political or other advancement, and gifts or other favors. The client brings labor, public allegiance, and support against the patron's enemies. In contrast to Korea, the United States is more of a medium to low power distance culture, in which leaders are expected to operate more like peers and subordinates are allowed more freedom in expressing themselves when they disagree with leaders. While patron-client relationships do exist in American culture, they are more fluid than those seen in Korean culture.

Honor, and its concommitment of face, is the third orientation in which Korea and the United States differ significantly. An honor orientation (Korea) is focused on who you are. It is usually contrasted with a justice orientation (United States), which is focused on what you do. In collective cultures, a person's honor is framed in light of the person's collective group (or reference group). It is the group that gives leaders honor (or face), and the group is responsible for maintaining that honor.

Christians who value honor in this way will tend to search for means to be restored to a pure state through cleansing (Heb. 9:14) and restoration of relationship (John 1:12-13) (Francis 1992). They will unconsciously look for rituals to do this rather than rely on simple declarations of innocence, which are more characteristic of justice orientation. Traditionally in collective honor cultures people who violate taboos or leave the group will be shamed by the group. The purpose of this shaming is not to keep them away but to draw them back into the group.

UBF Organizational Ideas

Every organization has ideas around which it builds its organizational identity. As seen above, UBF conceives of itself as a disciplined, humble, joyful ministry that draws exclusively from the Bible for its values and ministry methods. While the terms are absolutely biblical terms, how they are read, displayed, and valued within the organization will be a blend of biblical teaching and Korean values.

As a collective organization, loyalty to UBF teaching and methods will be considered non-negotiable, especially in the public arena. As a larger power distance organization, displays that are interpreted as demonstrating rebellion, challenging of a leader's face, or in other ways critical will tend to be dealt with quickly and strongly. Further, everyone in the organization will be involved in patron-client types of relationships (e.g., shepherd-sheep) with those above and below them.

One implication is that when the organization deals with disagreement, it will largely be below the surface to external observers. It will stay below the surface until it reaches a stage when it is either resolved or it becomes public. When the latter happens in a collective, it means that things are on the verge of going out of control and that a split is almost inevitable, as the very act of making disagreements public results in such a strong loss of face that only a split can resolve the tension.[6]

It must be kept in mind that UBF is almost exclusively a volunteer organization. Those who "join" UBF are not "employees"; they sign no contracts and make no pledges. Rather, it is through the extended time of intense relationships with their shepherds that they become part of the UBF family. Loosening this collective "family" orientation would threaten the organization's existence, as there are no formal, legal ties keeping it together.

UBF Ministry Methods

While some might mistake UBF's one-on-one discipleship methodology as more individualistic than collective, it can be seen that even this one-on-one approach to ministry is worked out in strongly collective ways. Intense and frequent time spent together, strong encouragement to share at the deepest levels of relationships, the collective discipline of

---

6   In 2001 such a split took place in which Campus Missions International (www. campusmi.org) was formed. While the story is complex, one element is that those who formed CMI made a conscious decision to see themselves as a church rather than just a campus ministry. The subsequent lack of growth of CMI has resulted in leaving UBF members leery about broadening their vision beyond being a campus ministry dedicated to world mission. This continues to play a role in how UBF frames its thinking about its values and vision as an organization.

weekly writing of sogams,[7] and the ideal of developing a patron-client (shepherd-sheep) relationship are all collective traits that are part of UBF ministry. This is all reinforced by the hierarchical vocabulary used throughout the organization.

One area in which the collective orientation is most clearly seen in the way straying members are disciplined. Typically collectivists use shame (including shunning) against those who have strayed. For example, members of UBF seldom say of a person, "He left the ministry." Rather, they usually say, "He ran away." Because the mission is so central to the relationship, once a member "runs away" from mission (or even from God), the relationship ends abruptly. This works well in Korea, where a person's sense of honor and face comes from how their in-group members treat them. They will go to great lengths to be seen as honorable by the members of their in-group, and it is almost unbearable to them to think that they are being rejected or shamed by the collective. In traditional collective societies, they have no where else to turn. Having no group is to lose one's identity. Thus, shame (and shunning) is ultimately not as much about rejection as it is about using rejection to motivate the straying sheep to return to the flock.

In individualistic cultures, however, shame is more often a personal construct framed in light of a person's internal justification of actions. Further, being rejected by one group, a person will simply find a different group to join. Thus, shaming and shunning methods that would be more likely to woo Koreans will have the opposite effect on Americans. Further, Americans who have been thus shamed will be far more likely to become vocal enemies of their former group.

---

7 Translated as "testimony," a *sogam* is a written personal Bible study that involves inductive observations of the text together with personal confession and application. These are read aloud to the shepherd who critiques them.

To the Korean UBF members who do not understand this element of American culture, the level of animosity of their former sheep is confusing and wounding. To Americans, however, it is completely understandable. To complicate matters, from the Korean perspective, those who leave and become critics are no longer part of the group. Therefore, their opinions about UBF carry little weight within the group. It was only when those opinions began to sway groups like CAN and the NAE that the Korean UBF leadership realized that simply ignoring accusations in the United States could result in significantly different—and far more damaging—consequences for the ministry than in Korea.

CONCLUSION

University Bible Fellowship offers a significant case study in understanding issues related to majority world mission agencies and organizations. The reality of the impact of Korean culture and values across UBF and the corresponding issues in relation to contextualization as UBF continues to operate in the United States as well as other non-Asian contexts provides us with perspective and questions that will help sharpen every agency that follows the call of God to minister in settings that differ from the values and culture of the organization. As we continue to see God raise up more and more agencies that are going from everywhere to everywhere, may we recognize that the goal is not to make all of them globalized in some homogenous fashion, but to enable each to make conscious, biblically-informed choices of how best to adapt—or not to adapt—to the varied cultural settings in which they serve Christ.

REFERENCES

Barry, Sarah (1992) *God Planted a Garden*, commentary on Genesis 2:4-25. Online: http://www.sarahbarry.org, accessed October 21, 2008.

Chung, Jun Ki (2003) "The University Bible Fellowship: A Forty-Year Retrospective Evaluation," *Missiology: An International Review* 31 (4): 473-485.

Enroth, Ronald M. (1992) *Churches that Abuse*. Grand Rapids: Zondervan.

Francis, Glen R. 1992. "The Gospel for a Sin/Shame—Based Society." *Taiwan Mission Quarterly* 2:2 (October): 5-16.

Hesselgrave David J., ed. (1978). *Dynamic Religious Movements: Case Studies of Rapidly Growing Religious Movements around the World*. Grand Rapids, Michigan: Baker.

Hofstede, Geert and Get Jan Hofstede. (2005) *Cultures and Organizations: Software of the Mind*. Revised and expanded 2nd edition. New York: McGraw Hill.

Johnstone, Patrick and Jason Mandryk (2003) *Operation World, 21st Century Edition, Updated and Revised*. Milton Keynes, UK: Authentic Media.

Ma, Wonsuk (2000) "Mission: Nine Hurdles for Asian Churches," *Journal of Asian Mission* 2 (1): 103-124.

Moll, Rob (2006) "Missions Incredible." *Christianity Today*, March, 2006.

Moon, Steve S.C. (2001) *The Acts of Koreans: A Research Report on Korean Missionary Movement*. Seoul: The Korea Research Institute for Missions.

Moon, Steve S.C. (2002) *The Status of Missions in Asia: An Overview*. Seoul: The Korea Research Institute for Missions.

Park, Timothy Kiho (2002) "A Survey of the Korean Missionary Movement." *Journal of Asian Mission*, 4 (1): 111-119.

Rabchuk, James (2007) *From a Sensitive Animal to a Ph.D. Shepherd*. Report given at UBF Founder's Day celebration, October 5, 2007, Chicago, IL.

Schafer, Sharon L. (2007) *The Truth Will Set You Free*. Report given at UBF Founder's Day celebration, October 5, 2007, Chicago, IL.

Tucker, Ruth.1994. "" *Cornerstone* 22:41.

7. MAJORITY WORLD HARVEST AMONG TIBETAN BUDDHISTS: HISTORICAL REVIEW, ETHNOGRAPHIC OVERVIEW, AND DYNAMIC DEVELOPMENT

David Oleson and Enoch Wan

INTRODUCTION

Tibetan Buddhism basks in a mystical utopian aura these days. Prior to the Dalai Lama's receiving the Nobel Peace Prize in 1989, Tibetan Buddhism claimed few converts in the West. Most were among the counter-culture folk of the '60's and '70's. The Nobel Peace Prize catapulted the plight of the Tibetans and their pacifist leader's religion to the forefront. The western press's image of a simple burgundy and saffron robed, shaved head Buddhist monk defying the massive hoards of communist Chinese Peoples Liberation Army who had invaded Shangri-la was reminiscent of another religious hero familiar to all, tiny David defying the mammoth Goliath. The Dalai Lama became a folk hero in the West overnight.

The roots of Tibetan Buddhism are far from the near eternal tranquility of Shangri-La as imagined in James Hilton's 1939 novel *Lost Horizon*. Rather, it comes from an occultic mix of animistic and shamanistic practices of the pre-Buddhist inhabitants of the Tibetan plateau, and Indian Tantrism, all of which is blended with Chinese Mahayana Buddhism to form a new esoteric hybrid Buddhism called Tibetan Buddhism.

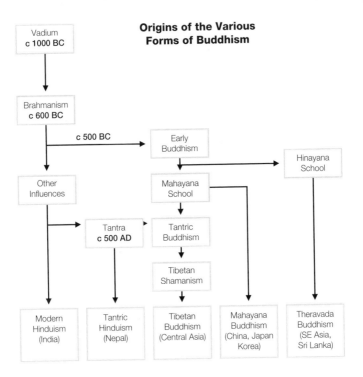

This paper will target the events leading to the current multinational harvest force taking the gospel to Tibetan Buddhists. It places Tibetan Buddhism in the continuum of Buddhist schools and sects and then identifies the major concentrations of Tibetan Buddhist peoples. Because the true nature of Tibetan Buddhism is not revealed in its marketing strategy to the West, the paper will present a brief discussion of tantrism, visualization, mantras and mandalas to give the reader a taste of its occultic underpinnings.

Credit must be given to the hundreds of men and women who paved the way with their blood for today's harvest of Tibetan Buddhists who are turning to Christ. The paper will identify a few of these remarkable saints before it looks at the majority world harvest force that is making great inroads into Tibetan Buddhist lands. The paper will conclude with a few missiological insights and suggest missionary strategies to reach Tibetan Buddhists with the gospel.

What is a Tibetan Buddhist?

Tibetan Buddhism is a branch of Mahayana Buddhism with a heavy influence of Indian Tantrism. It is also known as Vajrayana, Tantrayana, Mantrayana, Lamaism or the Diamond Vehicle. Tantric Hinduism infiltrated Mahayana Buddhism in northern India between the 4th and 6th centuries AD. It is known for its occultic practices and its esoteric teachings[1]. The chart[2] on the right gives a visual schematic of the origins of the various forms of Buddhism. When the Indian Tantric master Padmasambhava was invited to Tibet in the 8th century, he successfully fused his tantric practices with the indigenous shamanistic religion of the region so that the resulting hybrid became a syncretistic amalgamation of the two. Tibetan Buddhism emphasizes yogic meditation, visualization of tantric deities, repetition of mantras, symbolic use of mudras and meditation upon mandalas.

---

1   Tantric teachings first appeared in India in the 4th century. It gained notoriety in the 6th century when it became popular among Hindu ascetics and yogins.
2   M. Tsering, *Jesus in a New Age, Dalai Lama World*, Upper Darby, PA: Interserve/ Tibet Press, 2006, p. 61

Where are the Tibetan Buddhists located?

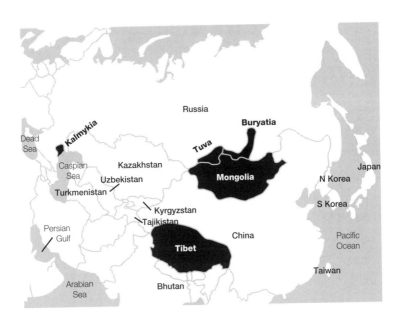

The majority of Tibetan Buddhists live in Central and South Asia. The regional implication in the common name of the religion, Tibetan, is more of a reference to its origin rather than its locus. Figure 1 maps the locations where the religion is considered indigenous. Tibetan Buddhism is also the major religion along the southern border regions of Tibet: Arunachal Pradesh, Sikkim, Northern Nepal and in the eastern region of Jammu Kashmir state of India in Ladakh. Tsering lists forty-six different people groups located in the Russian Federation, Mongolia, China, Nepal, Bhutan and India who "qualify as Tibetan Buddhist" because they "have Tibetan Buddhist shrines, temples, village priests, monks or monasteries."[3]

---

3   M. Tsering, p. 281.

India	85,000
Nepal	14,000
Bhutan	1,600
Switzerland	1,540
Scandinavia	110
Europe (other)	640
USA & Canada	7,000
Japan	60
Taiwan	1,000
Australia & New Zealand	220
Total	**111,170**

TABLE 1. Tibetan Demographic Survey of 1998[1]

Tibetans fled their homeland as a result of Chinese occupation. When the Dalai Lama sought exile in India in 1959, about 100,000 of his countrymen followed. The Indian government settled them in 54 camps throughout the country. The Dalai Lama was given a remote location in the northern state of Himachal Pradesh in the town of Dharamsala. He maintains a "government in exile" although it is not recognized by the Indian officials. The bulk of the exiled Tibetans have stayed in India, Nepal and Bhutan but many have been relocated outside of south Asia. Table 1 is the "official" tally of the Tibetan diaspora but unofficial reports from Tibetans living in North America put their number at 20,000.[4]

---

4   Tsering notes that that unofficial estimates coming from the Tibetan communities in Canada and the USA estimate the true number of Tibetans living in North America between 5000 – 6000 in Canada and over 10,000 legally in the USA with another 3,000 undocumented (p. 265-266).

HISTORICAL DEVELOPMENT OF TIBETAN BUDDHISM

Buddhism entered Tibet in the 7th century from India and China. Tradition says that King Songtsen Gampo (604c.–650), thirty-third king of the Yarlong dynasty, was responsible for the introduction of Buddhism. He added considerable territory to the kingdom, conquering land in China as far as Lake Kokonor (Qinghai Lake). His aggressive expansion of Tibet led to his marrying two Buddhist princesses. To keep the fierce Tibetan warriors at bay the Chinese emperor Taizong (Tang Dynasty 618–907) gave the Tibetan king his daughter, Wencheng. About the same time the king of Nepal gave his daughter, Bhrikuti, to Songtsen Gampo. These two princesses brought Buddhism and their idols. There is little evidence that their husband converted to Buddhism.[5]

Buddhism was not widely accepted until the Indian tantric masters Santaraksita and Padmasambhava were invited to Tibet by King Trisong Detsen in the 8th century. They confronted the leaders of Bön, the indigenous religion. The exploits of Padmasambhava fill Tibetan folklore. Legends claim he had no earthly parents but was birthed from a blossoming lotus as a fully enlightened being with the stature of an 8 year old. When he came to Tibet, he defeated the Bön priests with his occultic powers and converted the Bön gods to Buddhism. Each god was given a menial task as a protector of some aspect of Buddhism. Padmasambhava established the first Buddhist monastery, Samye, in 776. He is considered the founder of the Nyingma lineage, the oldest sect in Tibetan Buddhism.

Buddhism continued to grow under the patronage of the Yarlong kings and among the nobility class but was also the source of much

---

5   John Powers, *Introduction to Tibetan Buddhism*, Ithaca, NY: Snow Lion, 1995, p. 127

discontent because of the lack of attention the leaders were giving to other affairs of state. The kings conducted aggressive translation programs to get Buddhist scriptures in the Tibetan language. The state treasury was emptied to build Buddhist temples and monasteries. In 838 the king was assassinated by two of his ministers and an antagonist to Buddhism, Lang Darma, ascended to power. Darma reigned only four years but wreaked havoc on the Buddhist institutions and foreign cultural programs. He too, was assassinated but the damage was done. The Yarlong dynasty did not survive nor did Tibet's empire, which at its peak stretched from Kashgar in the west to Chang'an (now called Xian), the capital of the Tang Dynasty (618–907) in the east. In the north the Tibetans extended their rule as far as Mongolia and south into Bengal.

Buddhism languished from a lack of support in Tibet until about 1000 AD. At the invitation of the king-turned-monk of the Guge kingdom in western Tibet, Atisa, a renowned tantric scholar and abbot of the most famous Buddhist school, Nalanda University, came to Tibet to revive the religion. This is called the "second dissemination of Buddhism" in Tibet. Atisa had much prestige in Tibet because of his fame in India. He wrote a sutra especially for Tibetans which integrated the Mahayana teachings with Tantrism. Atisa's Tibetan disciple, Dromdon, established the Kadampa school of Tibetan Buddhism. Buddhism never again languished in the country.

With the loss of the powerful leadership of the Yarlong kings, Tibet was at the mercy of its neighbors. Lamas replaced kings and religious orders replaced armies. Lamas conquered lands by converting their leaders to Buddhism. A successor to Genghis Khan, Godan Khan was converted to Tibetan Buddhism in 1240 by Sakya Pandita, leader of the indigenous Sakya school of Tibetan Buddhism. The patron-priest relationship between the Mongols and the Sakya lamas established the supremacy of the lamas in Tibet that remained until the Chinese invasion in 1950.

Over the next three centuries the total power of the religious sects led to their corruption. A young reformer, Tsong Khapa (1357–1419), tried to reverse the apostasy. His efforts resulted in a new powerful sect, the Gelugpa. At first the Gelugpa monks were apolitical but their evangelistic zeal led them to reestablish the patron-priest relationship with the Mongols in 1578. Altan Khan gave the leader of the Gelugpa, Sonam Gyasto, the title "Ta le," or "Ocean" because he was an "Ocean of Wisdom." The title was later posthumously bestowed on Sonam Gyatso's teacher and his teacher's teacher. Thus Sonam Gyatso was the third Dalai Lama. Gyatso became the secular leader of Tibet because he had the armies of the Khan backing him. The Dalai Lama is also considered an incarnation of Avalokitesavara, the god of compassion.

Basic Elements of Tibetan Buddhism

The mixing of Mahayana, Tantrism and the shamanism of the pre-Buddhist religion formed a unique brew of Buddhism. It is occultic in nature and heavily relies on ritual and symbolism.

Tantrism

The Indian tantric form of Buddhism brought to Tibet by Padmasambhava was notorious for its occultic practices and its esoteric teachings. Tantric Buddhism reached its zenith in India in the 8th century during the time of Padmasambhava. New scriptures called Tantras were added to the Mahayana canon.[6] These new sutras claimed

---

6   One major difference between Theravada and Mahayana Buddhism is the canon. Theravada limits their scriptures to the Tripitika whereas the Mahayana have

to be the words of Buddha that were passed secretly from teacher to disciple for nearly 1,500 years. The Tantras describe elaborate rituals and meditation techniques. Some of the more distinctive practices prescribed in the Tantras include visualization techniques and the use of mandalas, mantras, and mudras.

Visualization

All schools of Buddhism practice meditation. For Tibetans meditation is more than quiet contemplation. It involves the use of body positions, speech and the mind in a unified effort to control and focus thought. They call it "one-pointedness" of mind. Most unique to the Tibetan form is using this focused concentration to conjure tantric deities during meditation.

The iconography of Tibetan Buddhism plays an important role in the quest for enlightenment. *Tangkas,* a highly stylistic Tibetan Buddhist art form drawn on cloth and bordered in brocade, are among the most common icons used to represent the ethereal universes of the tantric deities called *yidams.*[7] *Thangkas* have a meditation deity painted on the fabric with intricate details in the background. During meditation the tantric practitioner tries to "enter" the universe of the *yidam* represented in the painting. The objective is for the practitioner to become one with the *yidam.*

A *yidam* is essential to tantric practice. One of the first duties of a new initiate's lama is to assign a *yidam* to the novice. The *yidam* is matched with the initiate's temperament. If the novice is strong willed, the lama

added hundreds of sutras.

7   John Blofeld in *The Tantric Mysticism of Tibet,* states that the Tibetan concept of *yidam* is borrowed from the Hindu concept of *Istadeva,* a Sanskrit word meaning "the indwelling deity." An *Istadeva* is an actual being for the Hindus. In tantric Buddhism however, the *yidam* is merely an emanation of one's own mind (176).

may assign him to worship of Yamantaka, the prince of hell, a hideous blue monster who has the head of a bull and is always depicted as dancing upon the corpses of his victims. But, if the novice is emotionally moved by beautiful women, the lama may assign a female *yidam* such as the Green Tara. The goal is for the adept to use his desires—physical, romantic, or sexual—to merge his total being with the *yidam* to become one in essence. Eliade exclaims that this is not a mere mental task but rather, "it is experiencing 'truth.'"[8] The *yidam* is a very real being to the practitioner.

Mandala

A mandala is a geometrical design that depicts a Buddha land or possibly "the enlightened vision of a Buddha."[9] "Buddha land" refers to a heaven-like realm governed by a Buddha. In Mahayana there are many Buddhas so there are many Buddha lands where the faithful followers of a particular Buddha may be reborn. The most notable example of a Buddha land is the "Pure Land" of Amitabha. It is a place where there is no suffering thus, an almost Nirvana-like existence. The denizens of the Buddha land are there until they perfect their practice and achieve total enlightenment.

The mandala is used in tantrism as an object of meditation much like the *thangka*. The practitioner intently concentrates upon the mandala as if it were a maze through which he needs to find a path to the center where the tantric deity resides. Entry into the mandala is guarded by protector spirits. These protector spirits are gods of a lower class. It is commonly believed that they are the gods converted from Bön who

---

8   Mircea Eliade, *Shamanism: Archaic Techniques of Ecstasy*, Princeton, NJ: Princeton University Press, p. 208.
9   "Mandala" Wikipedia. Online 9 Nov 2005 <http://en.wikipedia.org/wiki/Mandala>.

were given the mundane task of safeguarding the initiatory phase of mandala meditation.[10]

Tibetan monks are known for their painstaking labors of spending weeks detailing intricate sand mandalas and then in a few seconds destroying their work. They do this to illustrate the fundamental tenet of Buddhism that nothing is permanent. As they make the sand mandalas, the monks chant mantras to invoke the deities. Once they sense the tantric deities inhabit the mandala, it is destroyed. The sand is swept or dumped into a waterway so the deities of the mandala can spread throughout the land.

Mantras

The Tantras contain magic formulas that are used to entice the deities. The formulas include hand gestures (mudras) and secret words and phrases called mantras. These have special powers and must be performed or said in a precise manner. When the Tantras were translated from Sanskrit to Tibetan, the mantras were not written in Tibetan script because the mantra would lose its power. The power of the mantra is released when it is said precisely or when it is written. John Powers calls matras "short prayers that are thought to subtly alter one's mind and make a connection with a particular buddha or enlightened being."[11]

Each deity has his own mantra. The most common one among Tibetans is that to Avalokitesvara (Tib. *Chenrezig;* Chinese *Kuan Yin*), the god of compassion, "*Om mani padme hum.*" Literally it is translated "Oh jewel of the lotus flower." Books have been written trying to decipher what that means. In final analysis the translation or meaning is not

---

10 Giusepee Tucci. *The Religions of Tibet.* Translated by Geoffrey Samuel. Berkeley: University of California Press, 1980 p.164.
11 Powers, 13-14

important. Magic is released through the sound of the syllables. Mantras are spiritual conduits that instill one-pointed concentration in the devotee. It focuses on the speech aspect as well as the mind.

Mantra recitation (or writing) is said to be altruistic, that is, it is done for the benefit of all sentient beings. In reality however, most Tibetans repeat the mantra as a talisman to enhance their luck, accumulate wealth, avoid danger, or possibly for the destruction of their enemies. For much the same reason students are told to repeat the mantra associated with the Buddha of Wisdom and a sick person repeatedly recites the mantra of the Healing Buddha.

Mudras

Mudras are symbolic gestures made with the hands and fingers. In this use of the word they constitute a sign language that invokes the force of the tantric deity associated with that mudra. Each *yidam* has a mudra. In Tibetan iconography the mudra is often the only thing that distinguishes between the different *yidam*. The adept uses the mudra during meditation as an element of focus to obtain one-pointed mindedness. The mudra also has a magical quality too. The powers of the *yidam* are released when the practitioner uses the mudra.

The word mudra originates from the name of a seed that was claimed to have aphrodisiac properties.[12] With the advent of esoteric Tantrism, the word mudra became a reference for the tantric master's consort. Eventually the word evolved into its present meaning, that of a hand position. Sexual connotations are still present in the use of the word. Ritual sex is practiced in Highest Yoga Tantra although it is cloaked in a veil of secrecy. The women participants are warned that they will be reincarnated in the lowest hells or suffer sudden death with a low

---

12   Tucci, Ch. 2 note 1 p. 258.

rebirth if they break the vow of secrecy.[13] Philosophically the practice is rationalized as a demonstration of non-duality. It is an ideal union of "skillful means" (the male aspect) with "profound cognition" (the female aspect). High levels of tantric practice, such as the ritual sex, are not for everyone. Only those who have received initiation in Highest Yoga Tantra can engage in ritual sex.

CHRISTIAN MISSIONARY HISTORY AMONG TIBETAN BUDDHISTS

Tibetan Buddhists have been extremely resistant to the gospel. No doubt the occultic nature of the religion creates a stronghold for the enemy of God. This portion of the paper will briefly review some of the efforts to reach Tibetan Buddhist.

Nestorians

The first substantiated encounter Tibetan Buddhists had with Christianity came from the Nestorians via the Silk Road during the Tang Dynasty. A stele in the Tang capital city of Chang An (Xian), memorializes the official recognition of Christianity by the emperor in the year 635. It also confirms the existence of Nestorian Christian populations in several cities in northern China including Kashgar and Dunhuang both cities that Tibet controlled at times during the Tang Dynasty.

---

13 See June Campell, *Traveller in Space: In Search of Female Identity in Tibetan Buddhism*, NY: George Braziller, 1996 for a testimony of one western woman who broke the code of silence. Another account of the secrecy is found in Victor and Victoria Trimondi, "The Tantric Female Sacrifice" *The Shadow of the Dalai Lama*, Accessed Online 30 Oct 2005 <http://www.american-buddha.com/female.sac.htm>.

There is no evidence that many Tibetans became Christians but a prominent Mongol tribe did convert in the 11th century.[14] The Keraits were early followers of Genghis Khan, many of whom married into the Khan's family. This gave Christianity special status within the empire. Later when Marco Polo's uncles met Kublai Khan in 1266, he asked them to bring a hundred teachers of (Roman Catholic) Christianity who could prove Christianity's superiority over all other religions. If they could do this, Kublai Khan said he would become a Christian as would all of his subjects.[15] Two responded but turned back because of the difficulties encountered in the long journey to Chang An. With no challenger to the Buddhists, Kublai Khan turned his religious attention to Tibetan Buddhism, which provided him with many lamas who firmly established Tibetan Buddhism in the Khan's homeland.

Roman Catholics

The next recorded contact Tibetans had with Christianity came from the Jesuits who had established mission outreaches in India and China. The first western Christian missionary to settle on the Tibetan plateau was Antonio de Andrade in 1624. Andrade was well received by the king of Guge in the Ngari region in western Tibet. The king welcomed instruction in Christianity from the Jesuit. He even laid the cornerstone for the first Christian church the following year. But, Tibet was undergoing an internal power struggle between the lamas and the king, which led to Andrade's withdrawal from the country in 1630. The opposition won. The Catholics tried to reestablish their work but had little success until another Jesuit, Ippolito Desideri arrived in Lhasa in 1716. Desideri was a gifted linguist and scholar. Over the next six years he mastered classical Tibetan, the debating style of the monks,

---

14   Hugh Kemp, *Steppe by Step*, London: Monarch Books, 2000, p. 52

15   Tsering, p. 109. Tsering mentions in a footnote that Sir Henry Yule in *The Book of Ser Marco Polo* claims this request is extant in the French archives, but other sources doubt its existence.

and wrote five theological texts in formal Tibetan religious style while living with the monks at Sera Monastery. Tsering attributes Desideri's "medieval Scholastic theology which tried to justify the Christian faith using philosophical methods … similar to those used by Tibetan monks in their debates" as reason for his success.[16] Tragically Rome for political reasons replaced the Jesuits and Desideri in 1721 with Capuchin fathers. The Capuchins had some success but they lacked the finesse and charisma of Desideri. They built a church in Lhasa in 1726 complete with a bronze bell from Rome. By 1742 they had 27 baptized converts and 60 inquirers. Plans to baptize 12 more converts led to the destruction of the church, flogging of the converts and the expulsion of the Capuchins by angered Buddhist monks. Tsering points out that both Andrade and Desideri were treated well and had official permission to evangelize but the Buddhist establishment rebelled when people started converting to Christianity.[17]

Protestants

With the expulsion of the Capuchins and the destruction of the church in Lhasa, Tibet withdrew into itself and forbade further missionary endeavors. A few protestant Christian missionaries wrote about their travels through Tibet over the next 150 years but no significant evangelization took place within the heartland. William Carey generated the initial interest among Protestants for the Tibetan people. After visiting Bhutan Carey led an effort that resulted in publishing a Tibetan-English dictionary in 1826. As a result of Carey's letters about Tibetan Buddhism, the London Missionary Society (LMS) sent three missionaries to the Buryat Mongols in 1817. Their mission ended in 1840 when they were expelled by the Tsar. In 1870 the LMS sent two more to Mongolia. Twelve years of work in Mongolia led to one convert. When these missionaries went into Buryatia, they found no trace of

16   Tsering p. 113
17   Tsering p. 115

the earlier LMS work. But, the dedication of these LMS missionaries inspired others to join their efforts.

The most successful Protestant missionaries were the Moravians. Their initial work (1853) was in Ladakh, an ethnic Tibetan region of India that borders western Tibet. The work was tedious. Few Tibetans converted. Tsering claims the church had only 140 members by 1950.[18] Presently there are about 250 Tibetan Moravians in Ladakh.[19]

A major contribution of the Moravians was their scholarship. Heinrich Jaeschke was the most notable of the missionaries at this time. Jaeschke was a gifted linguist. Among his contributions was the first scripture portions translated into Tibetan. One of the first Moravian converts, Yoseb Gergen, spent his whole life completing this work.[20] The initial challenge the Moravians faced was identifying a Christian vocabulary for the Tibetan language which had no words to convey Christian concepts such as God, sin, and repentance. This led Jaeschke to the compile a Tibetan-German dictionary (1881). That dictionary, now translated into English, is still used by Tibetan language learners.[21]

Because of Tibet's remote location surrounded by the world's tallest mountains, missionary efforts to reach the Tibetans are canalized through three avenues of approach: northward from the Indian subcontinent, eastward from Yunnan and Sichuan Provinces and southward from Qinghai and Gansu. The ultimate goal of most mission groups was establishing a church in Lhasa. No one accomplished that after the Capuchins left. Tibet's policy of isolation kept almost all foreigners

---

18 Tsering p. 121
19 Christina Stoltz, *Opposition to Evangelism in India, China, and Tibet*, Master of Arts Degree Thesis, Florida State University, 2007.
20 Allan Maberly, *God spoke Tibetan*, Orange, CA: Evangel Bible Translators, 1971, tells the story of Gergen and others who struggled to complete and preserve the work against strong opposition. The Bible was first printed in 1948.
21 Heinrich Jaeschke, *A Tibetan English Dictionary*, London: 1881.

away, especially the missionaries. Miss Annie Taylor of China Inland Mission (CIM) was possibly the earliest protestant missionary to attempt this, 1892–1893. The harrowing report of her herculean effort was reported in CIM's *China's Million* magazine in December 1893.[22] She got within "3 days from Lhasa" but was turned back. That she was a woman saved her life. Because of the Tibetans' xenophobia, it is doubtful any western missionaries even visited the city until the early 1980s. One possible exception might be Victor Plymire. Plymire, an Assemblies of God missionary, lived in the Xining, north of Tibet in Qinghai province. David Plymire writes in the biography of his father that he may have visited the city in 1927.[23] Others who attempted to reach the heartland of Tibet from the same direction paid the supreme sacrifice in their attempt. Petras and Dr. Susie Rijnhart, Disciples of Christ missionaries, tried to establish a medical mission in Lhasa in 1898. Their infant son died on the approach and Petras was later killed by bandits. Susie was abandoned by her Tibetan guides and travelled by herself on foot hundreds of miles across Tibet back to her starting point in China.[24]

CIM led the way in establishing mission stations along the border areas between Tibet and China. Hudson Taylor's original vision in founding CIM was to place missionaries in the unreached inland provinces of China including Tibet. James Cameron, who established the first mission station in Sichuan in 1877, made treks into the Kham regions of northern Tibet. George Parker along with his Chinese wife operated out of Lanzhou in Gansu in the early 1880's.[25] Parker's work

22 China's Millions, December 1893. Available at http://www.omf.org/
    omf/us/resources__1/omf_archives/china_inland_mission_stories/a_lady_s_ad-
    ventures_in_tibet
23 David Plymire, *High Adventure in Tibet.* Springfield, MO: Gospel Publishing
    House, 1959, p. 120.
24 Susie Rijnhart, *With Tibetans in Tent and Temple,* NY: F. H. Revell, 1901
25 Valerie Griffiths, *Not Less Than Everything,* Grand Rapids: Monarch Books, 2004.
    Parker's marriage to a Chinese teenager was very controversial. Minnie however,

as a colporteur was a typical strategy used by the early missionaries in these areas.

Robert Ekvall, a second generation Tibetan missionary, also approached the Tibetans from the north. Ekvall was born in China. His parents were with the Christian Missionary Alliance (CMA) the first from their board to establish a work on the Tibetan borders. Robert, who grew up speaking Mandarin and Tibetan (Amdo dialect), became a CMA missionary to the Tibetans in 1923. He wrote extensive anthropological works on Tibet life, especially the nomads. Ekvall's works include fourteen books, thirty-two articles, and eight unpublished manuscripts.[26]

Others attempting to reach Tibetans living in the eastern part of Tibet came from Yunnan and Sichuan. Two who have written about their experiences are Dr. Albert Shelton and Geoffrey Bull. Shelton's twenty years as a medical missionary is chronicled in *Pioneer in Tibet: The Life and Perils of Dr. Albert Shelton* by Douglas Wissing. Wissing says less than ten people converted to Christianity during Shelton's years of ministry. Shelton, like Petrus Rijnhart, was killed by bandits in 1922.

Geoffrey Bull's tenure in Tibet was much shorter. He arrived in China in 1947 and the Tibetan border in late 1948 to work among the Kham people. In October 1950 he was arrested by the Chinese communists and spent three years and two months in captivity. Bull tells his story in *When Iron Gates Yield*.[27]

There are many more saints of Tibetan ministry who were martyrs in their attempt to reach the Tibetans or who gave the prime years of

---

played a vital role in Parker's ministry and was a valuable asset in CIM's total missionary effort in western China.

26   Musashi Tachikawa, Shoun Hino and Toshihiro Wada, *Three Mountains and Seven Rivers*, New Delhi: Motilal Banarshidass Publications, 2004, p. 621

27   Geoffrey Bull, *When Iron Gates Yield*, Chicago: Moody Press, n.d.

their lives in the work. The constraints of this paper do not allow their stories to be told. But without exception, those who labored among the Tibetan Buddhists prior to 1980 "planted the seed" and "watered it" at great cost for those who would later bring in the harvest. God makes the seed grow until they are fruit bearing. Let's now turn our attention to the harvest, especially that of missionaries from the "majority world."

Dynamic Developments

When the communist takeover of China in 1949 and the subsequent occupation of Tibet in 1950 occurred, all western missionary activity ceased inside the regions. The persecution of all religious groups inside Tibet and China from that time until now is notorious. But, as is the case throughout history, the church seems to grow the fastest under oppression.

Chinese Missionaries

The Chinese church is a potent missionary force for evangelization of Tibetan Buddhists. It has shown interest in cross-cultural missions since before the communist takeover. Phyllis Thompson, a missionary, wrote in a newsletter in 1949:

> The thing that has impressed me most has been the strange, unaccountable urge of a number of different Chinese groups of Christians to press forward in faith, taking the gospel towards the West. I know of at least five different groups, quite unconnected with each other, who have left their homes in east China and gone forth, leaving practically everything behind, to the West…It seems like a movement of the Spirit which is irresistible. The striking thing is that they are disconnected and in most cases know nothing about each other.

Yet all are convinced that the Lord is sending them to the western borders to preach the gospel.[28]

Hattaway details the persecution these Chinese missionaries suffered at the hands of the communists for the cause of the gospel.[29] A few survived the many years of slave labor and repeated beatings while in prison with their faith intact.

After the Cultural Revolution subsided in1976 there was a rekindling of that missionary vision by the underground church to reach the minorities of China as well as the Buddhist and Muslim populations south and west of China. This zeal for evangelism was dubbed the "Back to Jerusalem" (BTJ) movement. When the survivors heard of the desire of the younger generation, great plans were laid for evangelizing the lost. They set a goal of sending 100,000 missionaries westward along a route that eventually led back to Jerusalem from whence the gospel originated.[30] Paul Hattaway, who voices to the western church the strategy of three prominent house church network leaders involved in this movement, says, "The Holy Spirit has already called certain church networks to focus on specific areas ... one has many missionary families already working in Tibetan areas. It will be natural for them to lead the thrust into the Tibetan Buddhist world."[31] Lambert says the vision spread across all of China from rural farmers to wealthy urban business men with contacts around the world. He reports that he is aware of one Three-Self church that shares the BTJ vision.[32]

---

28 Tony Lambert, "Back to Jerusalem" OMF Global Chinese Ministries Newsletter, April 2004. Available at http://omf.org/omf/us/resources__1/newsletters/global_chinese_ministries/gcm_newsletter_2001_2006/gcm_april_2004 Accessed 3/15/08.

29 Paul Hattaway, *Back to Jerusalem*, Waynesboro, GA: Gabriel Resources, 2003, p 8ff

30 A history of the "Back to Jerusalem" movement is found at their website: http://www.backtojerusalem.com/

31 Hattaway, (2003), p. 81

32 Lambert

On one hand these Chinese families are best suited to take the gospel to Tibet. They have no visa problems, can travel and live in Tibet very economically while supporting themselves with a small business. But the other hand holds great challenges. The history of conflict between China and Tibet with China forcibly occupying the region has alienated a majority of the Tibetans. Chinese were singled out as targets for the wrath of the Tibetans in the recent riots across the Tibetan Autonomous Region.[33] That animosity is further strengthened by the perceived interference the Chinese government is making into the deep levels of the religion. China's abduction of the Dalai Lama's choice of the reincarnated Panchen Lama, Gedhun Choekyi Nyima, in 1995 and the subsequent appointment of their selection is a case in point. Added to that are standing orders to arrest anyone in the Tibet Autonomous Region who has in his/her possession a picture of the Dalai Lama. Recently the government announcement that all *tulkus* (reincarnated holy men) must obtain government approval before they can reincarnate.[34] Because of these interferences, many Tibetans hold a deep hatred towards Chinese people. But again, Christianity has exploded under severe persecution from the government. The Chinese missionaries to the Tibetans are well acquainted with persecution. It may be that through their persevering love for the Tibetans in the face of persecution, the Tibetans will see God's love in these self-sacrificing missionaries and a thriving church will be born.

Other challenges confronting the Chinese house church missionaries are lack of basic theological and cross-cultural training, and an operational funding system. Additionally, they are oblivious to the attitudes

---

33 For example see *Wall Street Journal*, March 25, 2008 p. A10, "Chinese Dismayed by Tales of Tibet Violence" which describes the fire bombing on a Chinese clothing vendor's shop. Accessible online at http://online.wsj.com/public/article/SB120638214966859837-ZxbZXP0r40ZsH_raRzdxl47q7SA_20080423.html?mod=tff_main_tff_top

34 See "China tells living buddhas to obtain permission before they reincarnate" at http://www.timesonline.co.uk/tol/news/world/article2194682.ece

held by other peoples towards the Chinese and their government. The only news and information the average Chinese receives is filtered by the government to present what it wants the people to hear. Thus, the Chinese house church missionary does not know that Tibetans dislike them. Another fear shared by both the visionaries in China as well as western missiologists is the sudden infusion of large amounts of western funds. This adds further challenges of accountability and questions of motivation.

Some house church networks are exploring the challenges of doing cross cultural missionary work. They have sent members into the targeted lands to investigate the possibility. The results are mixed. Some realize the complications are too great so are not proceeding while other groups see the complexity as a challenge of their faith and thus are pushing forward.[35]

The western missionary can help the BTJ movement by offering encouragement, education and hospitality to their Chinese counterparts. Encourage them to exercise their faith but at the same time be sure they are aware of the challenges they will face. Basic theological training should continue to be an emphasis of the western mission boards. There are many innovative ways to do this with the technology that is widely available—online Bible schools, websites, mp3 files, DVD, radio and more. Finally, western missionaries who are co-located with incoming Chinese missionaries need to establish (albeit clandestine in some areas) a collegial relationship with their fellow gospel workers.

South Asian Missionaries

One exciting outpouring of God's Spirit in the world today is in Nepal. This little Hindu Kingdom was closed to evangelism until 1990. Missionary work was done from the border regions much like

---

35   Lambert

it was done around Tibet. But, when the door opened and a degree of religious freedom was allowed, the true extent of the church became visible. On Easter Sunday 2003 more than 10,000 Nepali Christians from all over the country paraded in the streets of Kathmandu.[36] This has significance for Tibetan Buddhist ministry. Five percent of the population is Tibetan Buddhist. These are the Himalayan mountain peoples who are racially Tibetan and speak languages closely related to Tibetan. As happened in China, the burgeoning Christian church in Nepal received visions about sharing the gospel with their Buddhist countrymen. The result is that Nepali evangelists have established growing churches among the Tamang, Lhomi, and Sherpa peoples. Some accounts of supernatural conversions are unprecedented but the resulting dedication to the Lordship of Christ makes them undeniably valid.[37] The author recently received a report that nearly 100,000 formerly Tibetan Buddhists Tamang have come to the Lord Jesus Christ for refuge![38]

Nepali Christians are the primary evangelists in Bhutan also. Until Monday, March 24, 2008 Bhutan was a Tibetan Buddhist Kingdom where the lamas were second in power only behind the king. On that day the nation peacefully held its first election for a full democratic society at the insistence of the king who gave up most of his authority. The lamas were forbidden to run for office. The implications of this for the budding Christian population are tremendous. Most authorities expect the country will open its borders in their attempt to modernize the nation. Along with that will be an influx of Christian evangelists, probably Nepali. About one third of the 600,000 population of Bhutan

---

36 This was reported to the author by a participant and planner of the event, the Nepali leader of Campus Crusade for Christ, a few months after it occurred.

37 See "The Name above All: The Testimony of Gyalsang Tamang--Nepal" in Paul Hattaway's *Peoples of the Buddhist World*, Pasadena: William Cary, 2004, p. 49

38 Dr. David Beine reported this in a written response to the author after reviewing a draft of this paper. Dr. Beine works with SIL in Nepal.

are Nepali. The young Christian church in Bhutan today has 4500 Christians of which 3000 are Nepali and 1500 Bhutanese.

There is an increasing interest in Tibetan Buddhist ministry in the Indian Churches too. The growing missionary zeal of the Mezzos and Nagas of Mizoram and Nagaland in Eastern India are potentially the most promising source for evangelists to Tibetans. Each of these people groups are nearly 90% Christian. They are of the same racial (Mongol) and linguist (Tibeto-Burman) background as the Tibetans. *Christianity Today* reported an emerging vision "to send 10,000 missionaries from Nagaland to the world"[39] As the decades of civil unrest are subsiding, the Naga church is reinvigorated. They have already placed missionaries in Arunachal Pradesh and Sikkim. Indians are the most likely evangelists to the Tibetan refugee camps as well. Though they are technically not allowed inside the camps unless specifically invited, Indian evangelists and Christian businessmen have made friends and have business dealings with Tibetans in many of the camps. The interest has been high enough in the churches that the author has been invited to teach a class at South Asia Bible College in Bangalore on ministry to Tibetan Buddhists for those who feel called to ministry among the Tibetans.

Mongolian Missionaries

Western missionaries were admitted to Mongolia shortly after the demise of the Soviet Union in 1990. Mongolians with social needs were the first to respond. In the Assemblies of God it was the deaf who came to Christ in Ulan Bator. Those addicted to drugs and alcohol responded to other mission groups. The moving of God's Spirit has reached all levels of the society, both rural and urban and into the government.

---

39 Manpreet Singh, "The Soul Hunters of Central Asia," *Christianity Today*, Feb. 2006, Vol. 50, No. 2. Available online at http://www.christianitytoday.com/ct/2006/february/38.51.html Accessed April 2, 2008

There are now around 31,000 Christians in Mongolia.[40] That figure is amazing considering Christianity went from nearly no believers to 31,000 in 10 – 12 years!

The same desire to reach their lost neighbors is sweeping over the Mongolian church as is happening in China and Nepal. The Mongolian church is sending missionaries to other Tibetan Buddhist groups—the Buryats, Tuvans and to Tibetan people in China including the Tibetan Autonomous Region. Mongolian Christians are reported venturing as far as India to witness of the Good News they have found.[41]

Networking Partnerships

The effort to evangelize Tibetan Buddhists is a multinational operation. An organized networking partnership of evangelical mission groups and individuals is leading the way.[42] The network focuses solely on the Tibetan Buddhist world by training new workers, developing contextualized evangelism tools and garnering prayer. It holds two annual training sessions for new workers. One is for those working inside China and the other is for those working among Tibetans in southern and Southeast Asia. At the 2007 meetings at least fourteen nationalities were represented.[43] Similar training sessions are taught in Nepali for the non English speaking Nepalese evangelists as well as in Mongolia and other locations worldwide. The training introduces the new missionary to the rudiments of Tibetan Buddhism and the

---

40 Hattaway, (2004), p. 179.
41 Reported to the author in a phone conversation with M. Tsering, March 21, 2008. Tsering is undoubtedly the most respected and qualified authority on the state of Christianity in the Tibetan Buddhist world.
42 Specific details including the name of the networking organization is withheld for security reasons.
43 Participants have come from Korea, China, Singapore, Malaysia, Indonesia, India, Nepal, Germany, United States, Canada, Norway, Denmark, Sweden, Switzerland and Russia.

contextualized evangelistic tools available, and helps them develop a Christian vocabulary in the various Tibetan dialects.

One of the first projects initiated by this networking organization was a thirty minute daily radio broadcast in Tibetan. The operation was turned over to Tibetan and Indian leadership soon after it was started in 1990. This ministry, called Gaweylon, which means Good News, now has a discipleship center for Tibetans who respond to the radio broadcasts and weekly broadcasts into Bhutan in Sharchop and Dzongkha. They have a 24-hour web radio station with all their programming available in mp3 format.[44]

Another cooperative project organized by the network was forming a multinational team to complete the Tibetan Old Testament and retranslate the New Testament. That Bible was completed and printed by the United Bible Society in the 1990's. An example of the contextualized evangelistic tools coordinated by the network is the 2007 release of the Hope video/DVD. The Hope video dipicts a traditional Tibetan storyteller who finds Christ and has a set of *tangkas* (a traditional Tibetan Buddhist art form) made so he can continue his profession as a traveling storyteller but now teaching the story of the Bible.

Other important functions of the networking organization include a clearing house for Christian materials on Tibetan Buddhism in the various languages, a lending library of books and videos related to Tibet and sponsorship of new initiatives in evangelism and worship. An ethnomusicologist in conjunction with the network has produced a contextually appropriate Tibetan hymnology, Christian songs in traditional Tibetan melodies. Undoubtedly the most important cooperative work of the organization is the garnering of prayer for the Tibetan Buddhist world. The network publishes a quarterly prayer guide which

---

44   http://www.gaweylon.com

it mails to hundreds of intercessors. It also has been a participant in the "billion hours of prayer" effort for the Buddhist world.

Missiological Insights and Application

We are riding the front edge of a great wave of the Spirit of God flooding the Tibetan Buddhist world. God's multinational force of messengers is sweeping into areas where the gospel has been forbidden. We are seeing the walls of resistance washed away in Mongolia and Nepal. The great Chinese church is mobilizing their best workers for the unevangelized mission fields to their west and south. The Nepali and Mezzo church are taking the gospel to Tibetan Buddhists in their respective countries. So, how can the western church assist this fledgling majority world harvest force?

1. Help majority harvesters establish contextualized churches. There is no conventional church in Tibet. The harvesters are organizing the church and giving it structure. The churches being established in these unevangelized regions must be identified with their culture. Minority world harvesters must work together with majority world harvesters to help each other see their own ethnocentricities. The church in Tibet must be neither Chinese nor Indian. It must be Tibetan.

2. Partnership in evangelization. Western missionaries must welcome and work in harmony with majority world harvesters. It is vital that a unified front is established. The huge economic difference between the two is a major barrier. Western missionaries must use and/or release their purse in a way that promotes partnership, not paternalism. This may mean the western missionary needs to adapt an incarnational life style.

3. Use a charismatic approach to ministry. Missionaries must be charismatic, that is, charismatic in the sense of relational charisma and charismatic in the sense of expecting the Holy Spirit to affirm His word by signs and wonders. It is not necessary to convince a Tibetan Buddhist of the reality of the spirit world. The supernatural is an accepted fact and spirit possession is admired as a good thing! Ecstatic prophecy is accepted and believed because of the many oracles and shamans. The distinction between the Almighty God and the demonic impersonators must be made clear. The missionary to Tibetan Buddhists must fearlessly confront and expose the satanic powers holding Tibetan Buddhist hostage.

4. Demonstrate God's concern for the mundane matters of life. Because of the occultic, shamanistic nature of Tibetan Buddhism, the Christian missionary needs to have a response for everyday problems. This can be done by praying specifically and expectantly for God to provide miraculously the needs of the people. Pray not only for the sick people but also for their sick animals. Tell the stories of how Jesus provided for the everyday needs of the people—feeding them, saving the face of the bridegroom at his wedding feast, providing money to pay their taxes, calming the storm, compassion for the one caught in act of adultery, healing the sick and raising the dead.

5. Use rituals and symbols. There is a trend in western evangelicalism to trivialize religious rituals and secularize the symbols of Christianity. In Tibetan Buddhism however, the symbols not only bring a remembrance to the practitioner but they also contain power within themselves. Christian missionaries need to expect demonstrations of the Spirit upon administration of the sacraments. Whether it is the descending of the Spirit at baptism or the cleansing power of blood of Christ celebrated at the Eucharist, these rituals need to be celebrated with great anticipation of God's confirmation of His supremacy.

Majority world harvest among Tibetan Buddhist is a reality. Many Mongols, Tuvans, Buryats, Lhomi, Tamang, Sherpa, and Ladhaki have begun their journey to Christ and have churches established on their soil, but the heartland of Tibetan Buddhism has not yielded to the advancing gospel. There is no doubt that these brothers and sisters in Christ will share the joy they have found with their near neighbors in Tibet. Prayer, perseverance and persistence will result in a great harvest. "I will build my church and the gates of Hades will not overcome it" said the Lord (Mt 16:19b).

8. STAKES OF MISSION ENGAGEMENT: REFLECTION ON REMODELING MISSION IN THE CENTRAL AFRICAN REGION

Fohle Lygunda li-M[1]

There are many things in life that will capture your eye, but very few will capture your heart. These are the ones to pursue. These are the ones worth keeping. —*Unknown author*

1   Fohle is from the Democratic Republic of Congo. After having served with Congo Evangelical Covenant Church for fourteen years as pastor in three local churches, seminary teacher, administrator and mission director, he was set apart in 2003 to start the *Centre Missionnaire au Coeur d'Afrique* (Mission Center in the Heart of Africa—www.cemica.org). He also serves as visiting lecturer on mission and leadership in two interdenominational universities in Congo, Centre Universitaire de Missiologie in Kinshasa, and Université Shalom in Bunia. He contributes to the French version of the *Dictionary of African Christian Biography* (www.dacb.org), and is writing a Doctor of Ministry dissertation at Beeson International Center of Asbury Theological Seminary, Wilmore, Kentucky, USA. He wants to produce a practical model of training leaders for mission-minded churches that restore, transform and multiply. He is married and has five growing children, two sons (22, 20) and three daughters (17, 15, 14), living in Kinshasa, the capital city of the Democratic Republic of Congo.

The hardest job kids face today is learning good manners without seeing any. —*Fred Astaire*

THE OVERALL VISION OF THE HARVEST IN TODAY'S AFRICA

The Edinburgh conference in 1910 had a view of Africa as mainly Muslim in the north, pagan in its great central areas (where Christianity and Islam were seen to be in competition for the souls of animists) and Christian in the southern tip. John R. Mott, the chairman of the conference, observed that "if things continue as they are tending Africa may become a Mohammedan continent."[2]

Mott's concern still is real in many Central African countries. Islam has become so influential that churches see themselves losing some of their members, mostly young people who long for jobs and scholarships, women who get married to Muslims, and key political leaders because of their search for power and money. The concept and practice of interfaith dialogue has become a challenge in troublesome Central Africa. Christian churches then experience the paradox of claiming the expansion of the gospel and starving for peace and unity of humankind.

In much literature today, the challenge of Islam and the struggle to reach out to Islam-related groups has been pointed out. Some people understand the harvest in Africa mostly in term of Islam. However, today's African harvest is more than that.

---

2   Cited by Timothy Yates, *Christian Mission in the Twentieth Century.* (London: Cambridge University Press, 1996).

As I was reading assigned books in my doctoral studies, I discovered Lee Strobel's categories of populations of America. According to his findings, four groups compose American population: churched Christians, churched non-Christians, unchurched Christians, and unchurched non-Christians.[3]

FIGURE 1. *Population groups in most cities*

Reflecting on the current reality of the harvest in Africa, I came up with a chart that highlights how Africa is ablaze today with a great harvest. The chart highlights the rapid advance of Islam and the increasing growth of converts to non-Christian (African and Asian) religions.

FIGURE 2. *The real harvest components in today's Africa*

Compared with Strobel's categories, these findings show that the harvest in Africa is composed of three groups: unchurched non-Christians,

---

3   Lee Strobel, *Inside the Mind of Unchurched Harry and Mary* (Grand Rapids: Zondervan, 1993), p.162-163.

churched non-Christians, and unchurched Christians. Although we don't have any official statistics now, Fig. 2 shows that the harvest is available within the church (among churched non-Christians) and outside of the church (among unchurched Christians and unchurched non-Christians).

As part of our ministry, we conducted a survey in the city of Bumba, the Democratic Republic of Congo (D.R. Congo) from November to December 2005. We wanted to quantify the unchurched people living in this city and discover how we could help pastors minister to them in a meaningful way. Our students were trained to collect data from the mayor of the city and from church leaders. We wanted to know how many people belonged to one or another church. Out of a population of 215,949, only 28,954 were identified as regular members of Christian churches. That number would decrease if we had limited the survey only to "Evangelical churches" or to "baptized Christians." This surprising finding helped us to cast the vision of reaching out to 186,995 unchurched people through a training seminar we envisioned a few months later.

From 2 to 8 April 2006, we launched a six-day leadership training seminar for church leaders from different denominations in the city of Bumba. "How to Reach Unchurched People in our Area" was the theme of the seminar. Participants came mostly from African initiated churches. They actually had not had the chance to attend Bible schools or seminaries. At the conclusion of the seminar, we initiated an open-air prayer concert that attracted many people who did not attend the pastors' seminar. The concert was so attractive that people kept coming—even those far from Bumba. The common expectation was that Jesus was among us to restore any person who could surrender to him his problem. Indeed, there was healing, reconciliation, repentance, conversion, etc.

These meetings surprisingly resulted in the birth of what we used to call "Restoration Fellowship" with reference to Christ's mission description reported by Luke (Luke 4:18-20). In Bumba, the echo spread from one family to another, from one neighborhood to another, from one mouth to another. This echoes what George Hunter calls catalytic church growth, a conversion movement that drives populations when they see impossible and hopeless people finally surrendering their lives to Jesus.[4]

That was the birth of our first "Restoration Missionary Church" (RMC) which did not hesitate to describe its mission statement: "We [members of the RMC] exist as church to **restore** people in their relationship with God, with themselves, and with others; to help people participate in the **transformation** of their communities through a living activity that longs for excellence; and to **multiply** the impact of the church within and outside of our local congregation." Restoration, transformation, and multiplication are core values of the RMC, our "first fruit" in planting mission-minded churches in an African context. Three months later, six more local congregations were planted in five different cities directly or indirectly by the participants in the prayer concert.[5]

Now, the questions are, "What are actually the groups of the harvest that must catch our attention for our mission engagement in today's Africa?" and "Who can be missionaries among the people who compose these groups?" Most often, for one reason or another, Western mission societies do not have this "holistic" picture. In their counterpart, African churches seem not to be proactive in addressing these questions

---

4   George Hunter III, "New Ways of Thinking About Church Growth," in Maxie Dunnam and Steve G. W. Moore, eds, *A Thoughtful Faith: Cultivating Thinking Theologically* (Franklin, TN: Eds. Providence House Publishers, 2005), p.28.

5   Today, in February 2008, the Restoration Missionary Church is a denomination of twenty-seven local congregations with about twenty-nine pastors and 4,000 members.

even though they have potential resources to start small, go deep, and think big.

Referring to Mott's vision in 1910, the reality today is that the Democratic Republic of Congo and its neighboring countries represent the sensitive heart of Africa, a strategic region to win or to lose for the Kingdom of God. Unfortunately, while international policies and community understand this reality, Christian churches seem to minimize, if not ignore, it. Most church members are similar to the kids in the Fred Astaire quotation at the beginning of this paper. The hardest job most church members in Africa face today is hearing good things about cross-cultural mission without seeing any!

That is why, after having served with Congo Evangelical Covenant Church for fourteen years as pastor in three local churches, seminary teacher, administrator and mission director, I asked the church board to set me apart in 2003 for a new ministry, the *Centre Missionnaire au Coeur d'Afrique* (Mission Center in the Heart of Africa). Many things in my life have captured my eyes, but mission engagement in the African context captured my heart, and I decided to pursue it.

CEMICA Exists to Meet the Need of the Harvest in Africa

The *Centre Missionnaire au Coeur d'Afrique* (CEMICA) exists to mobilize churches for cross-cultural mission, to train church members—pastors and laypeople—and to send out African missionaries. This three-fold objective comes from our vision to get African churches involved in mission, not only in intracultural mission and in transcultural mission, but also in cross-cultural mission.[6] Not only among one unreached group,

---

6   I am referring to Ralph Winter who discussed the issue of understanding missiology in its three dimensions: intracultural missiology, transcultural missiology

but also among what we call "unchurched people" (Islam, members of other Eastern religions, African traditional religious, unchurched Christians and churched non-Christians). Our strategy is a process that starts in the Democratic Republic of Congo, going through the nine neighboring countries (French, English and Portuguese speaking countries), and then to other parts of the continent and the world.

On-Going Activities

Since 2003, our activities correspond to the three-fold objective of mobilizing, training, and sending out.

Mobilizing Activities

Every year, we hold mission-leadership seminars (teaching for 3 days), conferences (teaching and consulting for 3 days), and forums (consulting for one day). We focus our speech on mission (What is it? How to do it? What are the challenges? What are the opportunities?), and on leadership (What kind of leaders do African churches need? How to become a leader who restores, transforms, and multiplies?). We hold these gatherings in several cities, sometime at the national level, other times at a local level. We welcome pastors and laypeople from all denominations without discrimination of denominationalism, tribalism or political parties.

Training Activities

We have several training programs. Since 2003, we have trained about 800 pastors from 75 denominations in the Democratic Republic of Congo and the Central African Republic.

and cross-cultural missiology.

Pastor training schools: We have a three-year program in one city (Bumba) for all denominations, a two-year program in three cities (Bangui, Buta and Kinshasa) for all denominations, and nine-month distance training specifically for CEMICA's pastors. We focus on planting and leading a mission-minded local church in a context of brokenness.

Barnabas Training Center (BTC): We just started last year (2007) in Kisangani and Kinshasa a five-month training program that we call Barnabas Training Center, designed for pastors and laypeople. We try to help people become a "Barnabas" of our time. Leaders take courses on personal leadership development, professional development, community development, and Christian ethics. We use training material published in French by Global University, Springfield, Missouri, USA. Most of our students are professional (pastors, business people, political leaders, university professors and students). Through BTC, they are mentored to raise resources (human and material) for mission (cf. Acts 4:36, 37; 9:26,27).

International School of Mission and Leadership (KISML): This nine-month program began in September 2008 to meet an urgent need in Congo. There has been a tremendous interest in learning English as a second language in Congo. While some people learn English in preparation for their international ministries and business, some others learn English as a requirement for their doctoral or overseas studies; still others learn English for their own knowledge. Most of these learners are influential young and adult Christians –pastors and laypeople. Many have been looking for opportunities to enhance their English skills through biblical and managerial studies, taking advantage of both their language improvement and their faith empowerment. Our vision is to use English to mentor African English speakers (clergy and laity) in Christian mission and leadership development studies so that they may impact their immediate professional communities and get involved in holistic ministries, even worldwide.

Sending Activities

Our first step in sending out missionaries relates to the mission-minded church planting movement. Our slogan is *Sauvé Pour Sauver* (Saved To Save). We want people to get saved in order to save others. We send out our graduates to minister to **unchurched** people. This particular emphasis is not a common evangelistic language in Africa where everybody knows the "un-reached" concept. We have discovered that churched people represent only one-third of the population in most cities. Therefore, unchurched people become a challenge for Christianity in Africa. While unchurched people are generally non-Christians, we have found from our survey that, for various reasons, many influential Christians become more and more unchurched. In 2006, we planted one mission-minded local church in Bumba. It has now about 600 members. In March 2007, we reported 7 churches. And today there are 27 churches in 6 provinces of Congo.

The next step in our sending activities will consist of commissioning missionaries for holistic ministries (education, health care, agriculture, fishing, women's schools, and job creation through small business) where we have already planted churches. In planting Restoration Missionary Churches, we believe that God's plan is to save each human being entirely, his body, his mind, and his spirit. This reality shows how the gospel is really "Good News" to our people who live in extreme poverty.

Our next step consists also in sending out missionaries to nine neighboring countries with the same vision of providing the whole salvation to the whole human being. That is why the International School of Mission and Leadership (KISML) is a strategic training program for us.

How CEMICA is Organized
and How It Operates

Since 2003, we have been working hard to establish the ministry from bottom (grassroot) to top, instead of establishing a bureaucratic system from top to bottom as most churches and organizations do. We try to make sure that in the local setting, there is a facilitator, a local pastor, who helps people to catch the vision of *Sauvé Pour Sauver*. We believe that CEMICA is not just a bureaucratic organization, but a community of mission-minded Christians who act as a team to accomplish the three-fold objective of mobilizing, training, and sending out. We work in three countries, and in each country we have a national director who works with a small team of 3 to 5 volunteers.

We had a plan of developing the administrative system slowly, step by step:

Step 1: (2003–2006) National staff of 2 full-time CEMICA members (1 executive director and 1 secretary-accountant) and 4 local training centers (each center having 3 full-time members from other denominations—1 school director, 1 accountant, 1 secretary— and 4 part time teachers who come from other denominations).

Step 2: (2006–2007) National staff of 3 full-time CEMICA members (1 executive director, 1 accountant, 1 administrative secretary) and Restoration Missionary Churches working as a *group* within a district. We hold an annual meeting (general assembly) at the national level, and in each local center for strategic planning and accountability purpose.

Step 3: (2008) National enlarged staff (1 executive director, 1 finance-administrative coordinator, 1 coordinator for mobilization, 1 coordinator for training and 1 coordinator for mission) and local churches working as a *team* within a province. We hold an annual meeting (general assembly) at the national level and in each local center for strategic planning and accountability purpose.

Step 4: (2009) National executive committee and provincial executive committees working as a team. According to our Constitution and Bylaw, accountability is assured at each level.

CEMICA is legally registered by the Ministry of Justice as a non-profit Christian ministry. While interdenominational through its effort of mobilization and training (serving all denominations), CEMICA belongs to the non-denominational group.

How CEMICA Relates to Other Missions and Church Bodies

The relationship between CEMICA and other denominations is to be understood through the lens of the current picture of Protestant churches in D.R. Congo. The Protestant realm is divided into several sub-groups:

- The Church of Christ in Congo (*Eglise du Christ au Congo, ECC*) is composed of sixty-two Western-related denominations (mainline churches) and some new denominations resulting from a division within mainline churches. ECC became the second most influential Christian federation during Mobutu's regime. Some think that this was due to the fact that the then-president of the ECC, Mgr Bokeleale, was from the same province as President Mobutu. Lands and some other privileges were given to the church. Today, ECC has the same reputation for having been headed by Mgr Marini, a senator who belongs to President Kabila's political party. In partnership with Western churches, denominations of the ECC have initiated many biblical and pastoral training schools. The ECC owns a university with several tracks, including theology and missiology without a specific class on leadership. In general, students of theology and missiology must belong to one of the mainline denominations.

- The Revival Church in Congo (*Eglise de Réveil au Congo, ERC*), the fast growing branch, is composed mainly of African Pentecostal Initiated Churches. Most of their pastors are bi-vocational, without any formal theological training. Just recently some leaders have been enrolled in new modular-training systems mostly led by American non-denominational Pentecostal ministries. A leader is not replaced unless he passes away. In this case either one of his children or his wife takes the command of the church. In some cases, a church splits after the death of the former pastor.

- CEMICA belongs to a third group, the Non-Denominational Churches, which share a similar ethos and characteristics with the Revival Church in Congo, except that they don't adhere to their organizational structure of having a general bishop who acts mostly as an ECC bishop. This third group, however, has a national board with a president who acts as a coordinator, giving freedom to each denomination to organize the administration of its churches according to its vision. Some of them result from division from one of the above bodies. *Others, including CEMICA, emerge from a church planting movement inspired by mission desire. The Restoration Missionary Church, which is the third objective of CEMICA, comes from the effort of sending out African missionaries.*

- Non-aligned churches (independent churches) are those which, for one reason or another, have not made a decision to adhere to any of the above corpuses. Non-aligned churches do share a similar ethos and characteristics in the organization of the church with the three above bodies, but they prefer to act independently.

- Interdenominational ministries are serving churches in several ways regardless their corpus. A few of them are Campus Crusade, Scripture League, and many others initiated by Africans. *Through our ministry of mobilization and training, CEMICA is also to be listed in this category.*

The Christian church in Congo faces several challenges; a few of them that are more sensitive to CEMICA's vision being the following:

- The unity of the body of Christ and the mission of the church in a post-war context where the majority of people are hopeless;

- Holistic ministries that are carried out by the local church as its Kingdom business;

- The raising and development of a servant leadership for church health and church growth, so that the Christian congregations become really "impacting churches."

OBSTICLES FACING CEMICA

We face two major obstacles. The first is the economic instability of the country, which prevents us from getting financial resources locally to mobilize, to train, and to send out missionaries as we should. My colleagues and I work as volunteers without regular and consistent financial support.

The second obstacle is the syndrome of "ism" (denominationalism, clericalism, tribalism, nationalism, paternalism, afropessimism)—the idea that "because everything is bad in Africa we cannot try!" That prevents some churches from benefiting from our effort of mobilizing and training. In the beginning it was not easy to get people from other denominations to attend our seminars and schools. We praise God that he has allowed us to overcome this obstacle.

FUNDING FOR MISSIONS AND MISSIONARIES

Our fund raising effort doesn't meet the real needs of the ministry in regard to our two-fold areas. In the first area, we seek support for mobilization (seminars, conferences and forums) and for training (schools) activities. Due to economical instability, we think that as members of the body of Christ, churches in America, Europe and Asia could provide financial and material support. If our people are not mobilized and trained, they will not be able to get involved in cross-cultural ministry. Some American-based organizations and churches have provided one-time financial support for our pastor training schools (2003–2006). When we express our gratefulness to them, we also continue to encourage them that the need for mobilizing and training still is enormous.

Fohle Lygunda li-M

In the second area, we seek support also for sending out missionaries. As part of the body of Christ, we are not ashamed to ask brothers and sisters from other parts of the world to help our native missionaries who are serving God with so much sacrifice and many financial struggles. Our 29 pastors (actually missionaries) have planted 27 churches within two years (April 2006–January 2008) without regular financial support. They live in a paradox of having passion for mission and being unable to send their children to school in a context where parents have to pay for their children's education.

SOME CHALLENGES AND OPPORTUNITIES IN MISSION ENGAGEMENTS IN AFRICA

Challenges Related to the "Unreached" People

Africa is ablaze today with a great harvest, characterized by the rapid advance of Islam and by the increasing growth of converts to non-Christian (African and Asian) religions. Unfortunately, most of our African churches seem to be less active in taking appropriate actions to address these challenges.

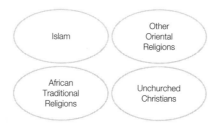

Some missiological questions for fruitful mission in an African context today must be addressed:

- Who are the groups circled above and what is their worldview when they live in an African context?

- What are they doing in order to bring answers to African daily and eternal questions?

- What do they consider as *Good News* or *salvation* that they offer to Africans?

- How should we, as missionaries, demonstrate our *Christian* Good News or salvation?

The challenge of reconciliation and peacemaking: The unrest that characterizes most countries due to civil war and tribal conflicts has revealed the weak side of church members who were implicated in animosity in many areas. Some Christians have betrayed even their coreligionists within the same denomination because of their ethnic group or political adherence. Lay people and clergy are killed because other "Christians" betray them. The church must begin its involved in reconciliation and peacemaking by looking within itself. It must help its members identify ways of ending violence. Six questions for addressing the issue of violence prevention can be addressed: Who is hurt by guns? Who uses guns? How much gun violence is there? What kinds of guns are used most often? Where do people get guns? Who makes money from guns? Because most of the combatants claim to be Christians, one of the significant approaches is to promote and practice tolerance in each local community.

The challenge of evil powers: According to the testimonies, it becomes obvious that those who commit violence are not led by principles of love, forgiveness, or the other fruits of the Holy Spirit (cp. Gal. 5:22). The powers of evil are seen through the actions described in countries in conflict. Therefore, people need to be liberated from these destructive powers. The church must demonstrate that Christ is concerned about the enslavement of humankind. His mission is to free human beings from the power of darkness. This is how we can understand the theology of liberation today in Central Africa: liberation from anger, from killing, from exploitation, from conflicts, and so on.

The challenge of the Kingdom life: Violence in most countries will not come to an end if the reign of God is still being denied in speech and deed in daily life. The message of the Kingdom of God means that by faith in Christ, we become members of a new family, citizens of a new party. Kinship and denominationalism no longer determine our worldview as members of a temporal society. The message of love and forgiveness has to be a leitmotiv for the new family of Christians, who have become children of the Kingdom of God, light of the world and salt of the earth.

The challenge of holistic ministries: The nature of the mission of the church in regard to human needs becomes a preoccupation. Western missionaries spent a great deal of time and energy serving as medical practitioners. In some cases, because of their specialization, they did not really spend much time curing the souls of their patients. Due to the current context of poverty in most countries caused by civil wars, bad governance, and diseases, the passion for holistic ministries has been, since the 1990s, both a challenge and an opportunity for many Christian churches. Serving a people confronted by diseases such as malaria, typhoid, leprosy, and HIV/AIDS has challenged most churches to develop medical programs as a part of Christian ministry. They set up healthcare centers, while also spending time curing the souls of their patients through chaplaincy and healing ministries. This makes a tremendous impact since the spiritual health and physical health are intimately connected for many Africans.

The challenge of education and literacy: Churches are more and more aware of the strategic responsibility of impacting people through the ministry of education and literacy. Western missionaries stressed literacy and education from the very beginning of their work in Africa. One of the first tasks for missionaries in a new mission field was to translate the Bible into the language of the people among whom they lived. Converts had to learn to read so they could read the words of God. The work of translation tremendously shaped many cultures, codified languages, and enabled cultures to write down and preserve elements of their oral history and literature. Literacy also gave individual Christians great power in the new colonial world. Mission schooling was probably the second most important source of Christian converts in Africa. Today, Christian churches in Central Africa are called to use the power of education to save the entire man by using the opportunity of technology and social sciences.

The challenge of mission as a double movement of "going out" and "attracting in": Experience has shown that because of violence, people can find safety only by hiding far away—in the jungle or in other countries. Unfortunately, there they experience an incredible time of extreme poverty or of rejection by inhabitants of the new milieu. The church must move to meet people where they live—both victims and perpetrators—and to serve as magnets to attract people to Christ by living as light and salt in the world. The church must get actively involved in centrifugal and centripetal ministry.

Challenges for Effective Ownership of Mission Engagement by Africans

Without effective ownership of mission engagement by African Christians, the theory that Africa represents a force for world missions will stay a pious vow! There are challenges in getting African Christians in the game:

The challenge of mobilization: Why should we mobilize? Because most of the people used to think that mission is matter of white and wealthy people of the West. Our citizens need to catch the vision (John 4 :35, Matt. 9:37,38). That is why mission seminars, conferences and workshops for all churches are needed.

The challenge of training: Why should we train? Because "God's people die by ignorance," and most of our people need more than preaching. They need to be trained (not just to be taught) how to get involved with strong commitment in God's mission. All church members (not just pastors) need this training to make the local church responsible in mission movement (Acts 13:1-5; Matt. 28:20). Again, we need to help people understand that training is more than teaching or communicating theoretical knowledge. Talking about mission training, we should transfer competencies as we develop and equip students for mission.

The challenge of sending out: Why should we send? Because most of our churches are not ready to move beyond their geographical and denominational barriers even though many Christians seem to be ready to get involved in cross-cultural ministry. Why can not we help those people to move with God? (John 20:21; Luke 4:42, 43; Matt 28:19). So we should feel more like "facilitators" than as "mission statesmen."

Mission Opportunities in Today's Central African Region

Mission engagement in Congo or in other regions of Africa is not a dream; it can be done! There are some opportunities today:

The opportunity of mission-minded churches: Both Western-related churches and African initiated churches must become aware of the mission task. The remainder of the story of Protestant missionaries is really the story of an enormous number of denominational missions and interdenominational agencies often characterized by a bad experience of competition, divisions, conflicts, and paternalism. The traditional leading role of ecumenicalism and evangelicalism has just enlarged the vacuum. The social rejection and the material advantage that result from adherence to one or another of these two movements have called to a new way of partnership in the harvest. That is why local forms of associations have been attempted from one country to another or from one city to another. It has been clear that engagement in mission is at stake. The Movement of African National Initiatives (MANI) has been instrumental for the missionary spirit that tends to break down some barriers among churches in today's context. Church leaders from all over the continent are annually challenged by the urgency and the unfinished task of bringing the light and the power of the gospel beyond their own countries. Mission-minded leaders are needed in order to achieve this unchangeable Great Commission.

The opportunity of mission in the marketplace: In today's context, political and business affairs long for a transforming ministry of the church. One of the struggles that has punctuated the Christian life has been the relationship with political regimes, mostly, in context of bad governance, dictatorship, and civil war. Western missions have been pictured sometimes as either "lieutenant" or "opponent" of colonial powers and then of African leaders. What should be the mission of the church in a complex world where spiritual and temporal worlds are cohabiting? Many churches today have been involved in secular leadership ministry using training strategies from Hagaï Institute, International Leadership Institute, etc. Some churches encourage their key lay members to impact secular institutions and other marketplace areas by incorporating. Unfortunately, this role has been tricky in many countries. Corruption and bad governance have been practiced by the so-called Christians supposed to be the light of the world and the salt of the earth. Voices cry out for transformational leadership within and outside of the church.

The opportunity of media ministries: The strategic role of media is popularly recognized. Radio stations and television represent a power in communicating the gospel in order to reach unreached people. In many Central African countries, this opportunity has been mostly exploited by African Initiated Churches rather than by Western-related churches. Except for the negative side of an occasional bad use of radio and television, churches in Central Africa must take advantage of new communication technologies to impact the world.

The opportunity of worship in an African style: The last, not the least, opportunity deals with the liturgical expression of the faith in an African cultural setting. The African church has inherited a Western form of worship with the risk of seeing African form as evil and non evangelical. More recently, though, and mostly with the emergence of African Initiated Churches, Christian musicology with African folk styles has proved to be one of the channels to spread the doctrines and the praxis of the church in a powerful way. Miracles have been witnessed even within the Western-related churches while people gather and worship God in African manner. Christian singers rise up from almost all local churches, and this proliferation becomes a power of connexion for many churches which could not get along except for their emerging worship bands. The Christian musicology with African folk styles penetrates any barriers. Many lives are reached and transformed by the power of the gospel that is communicated through songs. Worship ministry within Christianity is a strategic opportunity for the spread of the Kingdom of God.

CONCLUSION

More could be said about other missiological insights and for the overall picture of the Christianity in Central African region. As Patrick Johnstone has successfully demonstrated in his *The Church Is Bigger than You Think*, these insights should relate to geographical, people, urban, social and spiritual challenges.[7] Our prayer is that some of the insights discussed above will help give an overview of the most significant trends and opportunities for doing mission in the context of Central Africa today.

With CEMICA, there are many specific opportunities:

- Opportunity of working in partnership with churches within and outside of Africa (necessity of maintaining the concept of Christ's body)

- Opportunity of reaching out to the *unchurched*

- Opportunity of mobilizing church members (clergy and laypeople)

- Opportunity of using communication tools (computer, phone, etc.) to reach out to educated people who become more and more unchurched people.

- Opportunity of using English as a Second Language to minister to opinion leaders and educated people who have a great interest in learning English for their international business, profession and personal studies.

- Opportunity of empowering our mission and leadership schools at the undergraduate level.

---

7   Patrick Johnstone, *The Church is Bigger Than You Think*. Pasadena: William Carey Library, 1998.

I am not sharing this vision as a person who has already completed the race, but as someone who is working to make it a reality. I welcome your critique, input, and help. I am 20% of the way through developing mobilization and training materials. I need help to design the restoration, transformation and multiplication components. I need mentors and all kinds of other supports…because the harvest is plentiful in Africa, but there are few mission-minded churched people!

9. THE UNIQUENESS OF AFRICAN INITIATED CHURCHES: A CAMEROONIAN VIEW

Andre Talla

INTRODUCTION

A friend at the U.S. Center for World Missions asked me about what had led to different kinds of African churches. My tentative reply was this: the great desire for spirituality on the part of Africans, and their frustration in helplessly watching the decline of what I call the mission churches. This combination of desire and frustration prompted some courageous pioneers to start what is today called the African Indigenous Churches movement (I prefer the label African Initiated Churches).

In view of the tremendous vitality in the AIC movement, with its record of successful outreach and evangelism, to discuss mission strategy in Africa without looking upon these churches as a major force would be an unfortunate mistake. In this paper, I will argue that various religious idioms enable African men and women to respond to, to place their hope in, and to identify with the AIC. These idioms are: the prophetic ministry; praying expecting healing and miracles; the deliverance ministry; and the emphasis on sanctification and holiness. I am not saying that these were not taught in the mission churches, but they never became part of the daily life of Christians.

> *The African Initiated Churches are Christian bodies in Africa that were instituted as a result of African initiative, rather than on the initiative of a foreign missionary organization.*

By the year 1960, the mission churches had become social clubs. Masses were still said in Latin, a language very strange to Africans. The role of leaders of mission churches in helping the colonialist master in crushing the national movement for independence was not understood. African Christians were appalled because, after they confessed their sin to church leaders, they would be denounced to the police. There also was the fact that many mission church leaders were members of secret cults, like the Yoruba Ogboni, described by Peter Morton Williams, in a paper titled "The Yoruba Ogboni cult in Oyo":

> …as a typical secret society, with features that seem diacritical for secret societies as a type of association: It has secret knowledge by virtue of which its members claim mystical power, and hence secular power and privilege with regard to non members. To qualify for membership some sort of achievement is necessary. It has the right to impose sanctions over those who reveal its secret to others.

The stage was set for a great revival by the Holy Spirit, who used this means to evangelize the continent and bring his redeemed people back home.

A new dynamic of strongly evangelical,
third-wave Pentecostalism has emerged
over the past 30 years.

In Central, East and West Africa, up till 1970, very few Africans knew they could start a church. It was their view that a white man had to do that. Unlike in South Africa, where some frustrated ordained leaders left the mainline denominations to start their own churches and communities, elsewhere lay African Christians pioneered the AIC. Cameroon was an exception, where the Full Gospel Mission was started by a German missionary, the Rev. Knoor Weener. Seventy percent of AIC leaders in Cameroon today are former members of this independent evangelical church. The real mystery here is, how could people who came out from traditional evangelical churches become Pentecostal? I would like to insist here that this was not the work of men and women, but of the Holy Spirit. How could people who have never been exposed to prophetic, healing, miracle and deliverance ministries perform them so well?

THE CHARACTERISTICS OF AFRICAN INITIATED CHURCHES

These churches are strong on the scripture and outreach, expectant of miracles, fervent and courageous against the powers of darkness.

Prophetic Ministry

A prophecy is defined as a "miracle of knowledge, a declaration or description or representation of something future, beyond the power of human sagacity to foresee, discern, or conjecture" (the online Easton Bible Dictionary). To put it plainly, I believe a prophet always points to someone or something in the future, projecting a vision of the future, and never speaks of himself.

On this point, we have to make a distinction among the AIC, because there are three radically different kinds of churches. The first identify themselves as Bible believers or fundamentalists; their belief is that the preaching of the Bible alone is prophecy. The leaders point people to Christ and his kingdom, but if there is a revelation from God that comes to one member in the form of a dream or vision, he or she should present it to the leaders, who will scrutinize it in the light of Scripture. If it appears useful, a leader will then take upon himself the responsibility of declaring the prophecy to the assembly, without mentioning through whom it was received. This brings humility to the person who received it and discipline in the church.

The second group is comprised of churches in West and Central Africa who base their doctrine of prophecy on the Old Testament; therefore, each church has a permanent prophet who tells members and others what will happen to them and their family. Many unbelievers and so-called Christians consult this man before taking any major decisions. One must distinguish carefully a prophet from a seer by determining who is predicting the future using a means other than the Holy Spirit. Many times, these "prophets" are just charlatans, even though church-based. The ritual one goes through to become a seer is not a secret to anyone in Africa. It is a demonic, traditional practice against which I have no problem in declaring unbiblical; the Bible tell us that such should not even be mentioned among us.

The final group of churches consists of those who were once called Bible believers or fundamentalists, but who have decided to follow the prosperity doctrine picked up from some teachers from the USA and Europe. These prophets move around telling their members how the Lord told them there are 10 people in the assembly who will give them

$100 (which many times does not come to pass), or how our giving will place us in a better position to receive from God.

These three groups are all AIC, and practice the gift of prophecy, but never come together for fellowship.

Praying expecting healing and miracles

Is there a great difference between the gift of healing and miracles? A miracle can be defined as "an occurrence at once above nature and above man. It shows the intervention of a power that is not limited by the laws either of matter or of mind, a power interrupting the fixed laws which govern their movements, a supernatural power" (the on-line Easton Bible Dictionary). The gift of healing will be considered, therefore, to be the miracle of restoring health to the body.

The first question we will ask ourselves is: Do miracles exist today? My reply is yes, but we are inundated with a lot of fake miracles just for the sake of making leaders famous or their ministry credible. It is common in Africa today to hear believers speaking of a man of God who is not anointed, because he has never performed a miracle. We also hear disturbing news items of miracles reported by the media that are seriously questionable.

I personally know of a case in Nigeria of someone who claims to have been resurrected from the dead, although there is no documentation for this. The man seems to be trying just to be famous; he calls for churches to raise funds on his behalf and buy the books in which he tells his story, The website of an organization here in USA carries the photo of this man and his story. I asked a member of that organization, a friend of mine, about the connection. He told me the story is used purely to attract people to the site, to get them interested in the ministry.

I realize that there are many cases of healing in Africa and in the West that are questionable. I personally was part of a great crusade were some people were declared healed, but two days latter I saw them with the same infirmity. When asked what is happening, the reply was: "It's gone, even if I am still feeling the pain and see it physically." I remembered that is what the preacher told them after the prayer. Did Jesus do the same? He asked the lame to jump and he did, and the whole community agreed he was normal once again.

Why does God perform miracles? When Jesus walks on the water or the ax head swims at the command of the prophet, it simply illustrates the grand truth that there is an infinite personal will, separate from and superior to all else, directing and controlling all physical causes. The universe is not under the exclusive control of physical forces, although God ordinarily effects his purpose through the agency of second causes, but he has the power also of effecting his purpose immediately, of invading the fixed order, and thus of working miracles. He performs them to convince the world that he has exclusive control over physical forces, and not for fame for the human agent. We should remember when Jesus was asked, in Matthew 4, to turn stone into bread, or to jump from a tower without being harmed, he rejected the possibility, because he was not interested in becoming famous in that way.

Deliverance ministry

We can compare the condition of African people at the beginning of the AIC movement with the coming of our Lord Jesus Christ to Israel 2000 years ago. Many people knew God, but were wallowing helplessly under satanic harassment. We at AIC view prayer as a gift and a privilege. The gift is offered to all and all may become the wielders of great power in prayer. However, the fact remains that the average believer seldom exercises the power of prayer. We do well to learn from the Holy Spirit the art of welfare prayer. I sincerely believe the present temperature of the prayer life of many Christians needs to rise if they expect serious breakthroughs.

Dr. D. K. Olukoya, in his book entitled *Prayer Rain*, gave the vibrant testimony of the pioneer of the first indigenous church in Nigeria. Brother J.A. and his team of aggressive prayer warriors figuratively entered a forbidden forest, filled with silent demons who demanded worship. They found people paralyzed by deeply rooted, anti-gospel activities, sometimes beginning from the highest places. But they emptied hospitals by the healing power of the Lord Jesus Christ, rendering witchdoctors jobless. And they started the first indigenous Holy Ghost filled church in Nigeria. So far—and we stand to be corrected—none has equaled, let alone surpassed, this humble brother in the field of aggressive evangelism in Nigeria.

Indigenization of Pentecost, however, did not mean returning to African religion. It simply means that African Christians, through the power of the Holy Spirit, could absorb the mode of African religion into their practice of Christianity, singing and preaching in the languages of the people, and using other acceptable cultural behavior.

Emphasis on sanctification and holiness

Let me put it right that the sanctification expression among AIC churches is mostly positional, knowing that perfect sanctification is not attainable in this life. We need to draw a line between the wrong attitude of the leaders of mission churches, who were willing to be involved with witchdoctors in the celebration of funerals, or in accepting polygamous men as elders in the churches, or by becoming members of secret cults. We quickly recognized these as incorrect, spiritually deadening practices that we wanted to avoid.

I have read in some quarters that AIC leaders have been seen as drawing upon African religious tradition in a direct way, and I think this is misleading. We stand against the negative part of our tradition in all forms; we even go so far as not celebrating Christmas, even though it's a great festival here in the West. We consider sanctification as a separation unto God for His use, and we preach this strongly.

SPECIAL STRENGTHS DISPLAYED BY AIC

The AIC is the fastest growing group in Africa. AIC churches were often mislabeled; at the beginning of the movement they were equated with Jehovah Witnesses, because they were going door to door, actually in competition with the tenacious members of that sect. Our intent was, as quickly as possible, to take advantage of the desire of people to study the Bible and to learn more concerning the scriptures. That is why we all have a Bible study session one evening during the week.

Evangelism is our strength. A good member is asked to invite neighbors into his home and speak about his faith. We also organize evangelistic meetings, where preaching is like in the New Testament. We ask followers to make a public declaration of their faith. Those who accept Christ are called "born again believers," unlike mission churches where all are simply Christians. The standard of living of the born again Christian is very high: he is not allowed to drink, fornicate, and attend traditional funerals and dances. Today, the society has started accepting this new brand of Christian; it is common today to hear someone say, "My friend is a born again." This means he cannot go with me to beer parlors or funeral ceremonies. Today, we have dignitaries who are born again; I even heard of a king who recently became born again.

Someone said, "As Christianity is moving south, we are experiencing the renewal of a non-western religion." Was that to be considered a prophecy or a fact? I think that anyone who knows Africa will confirm that great revival is taking place over there. I got a letter from a key leader pleading with me to come and start a simple school in his state for the training of church workers. He said he had assembled 15 people and many were still asking for the commencement date. Many countries in Africa need pastoral training centers. And after the training where are these leaders going? Into the field to preach the

word, as they are trained to do. We understand the urgency of our task, to get there before Islam comes, or any other wrong religion. When one is thirsty, he is tempted to drink even polluted water. We have some wrong religions coming to Africa today, like the Moon sect, who offer free resources, and we need to move fast.

WEAKNESSES

In a recently circulated paper, Ralph Winter argues that:

> The Student Volunteer Movement, in which John Mott was a leader, is noted for the number of universities that it established around the world. The missionaries who went to China made sure there was a university in every province of China. However, in later years Evangelicals, who had never been to college, went out across the world and established Bible Schools, Bible Institutes or theological schools that either replaced or ignored the university tradition. In the last 50 years the majority of American mission agencies have not founded a single university.

I can see the AIC churches going down the same road, as there is not a single University training leaders from this movement in French speaking countries, and this is a great handicap. Not only can our relatively untrained leaders be easily carried by any wind, they absorb all doctrine coming their way. They have an inferiority complex every time they meet with missionaries from the West, who many times are less qualified than they think, but Africans will give them respect. But it's not too late; we can still fill this gap and meet the need.

Dr. Winter has also talked about the blunder of preaching only "Salvation in Heaven," not "Kingdom on Earth." The mainline churches came with hospitals, clinics, schools, vocational training, and agricultural development. The AIC churches are not looking in this direction, not even to meet those needy that government have abandoned, as in the case of education. Many private schools have come out and offered some good stuff, but I wish AIC churches could see the great opportunity here. Many of the so-called Catholics and Protestants in Africa today are helping schools sponsored by mainline churches to have landed property and other privileges. We understand that they all attended that mission school, and even if they do not go to church today, they still identify themselves as Christians due to their early training in these centers.

The AIC could derive the money from these institutions they desperately need to preach the gospel; this could help to transform the society before taking them to Heaven.

CHALLENGES AHEAD

Contextualized training for Christian workers.

I believe today we should be concerned with how the AIC leaders can develop leadership qualities in order to prepare the next generation to perpetuate the God-given vision of turning Africa to Christ.

Dale Kietzman, in his paper on "Effective Cross Cultural Leadership Development," quoted Carter McNamara as saying, "Very simply put, leading is establishing direction and influencing others to follow that direction." Our leaders have done the essential, which is to establish the direction and influence others to follow, but how can they keep this flame alive after they are gone? The biggest issue to me is: How can they be so vulnerable that the prosperity doctrine from the West has moved nearly half of the pioneers to abandon their first love, the sound teaching of scripture? What will be the fate of the movement in the next century?

Dale Kietzman, continuing in the same article, said, "If leadership involves 'influencing others,' then cultural factors are definitely involved." This coordinates with the concept that training for leadership is a process that is dictated by one's own culture. How does this relate to AIC leaders? Today, there is a great need for contextualized training and useful theological colleges available to the AIC in Africa. I can assure you that many AIC leaders see this as urgent and imperative.

What does this burgeoning AIC need most, if not an African curriculum adapted to their culture, which will address their problems and blend the church and culture, instead of destroying culture? The curriculum must give value to the culture while keeping the purity of the faith.

Contextually suitable Christian practice in non-Christian contexts.

Sony Okosun, a Nigerian musician, sang a decade ago, saying: "Africa belong to African and America belong to American." He was saying aloud what many were thinking but had not voiced; we firmly believe in the end of colonialism even if we are fully aware of the presence of neo-colonialism.

When Europeans left Africa and handed over the reins to Africans, our leaders started running the affairs in our own ways, using what the European left behind; I mean things like laws (we still use French law in all French countries) and technique of administrative organizations and economics. We interpret these things, taking into consideration our culture. This is exactly what happened when the AIC churches started—we did not write a new Bible; we use the same Bible but make our own interpretation, according to our custom and values. Matthew 5:13 says, "Ye are the salt of the earth: but if the salt have lost his savor, wherewith shall it be salted? It is thenceforth good for nothing, but to be cast out, and to be trodden under foot of men."

Sustainable development (income generation) to produce self-sustaining and reproducing churches.

In Africa, it is easier said than done to know how to act in response to the great food shortages, poor health, and stagnant economy. These seem to be part of normal life and appear to be symptoms of more serious attitudinal problems—of fatalism, inferiority, dependency and lack of cooperation. The physical situation is complicated by a lack of natural resources in some countries, and a general lack of know-how, capital and initiative on the local and national level to deal with the problems facing Africa.

The real challenge and hope of helping Africa, in the long run, is to foster cooperation, feelings of self worth, and the realization that they can improve their own quality of life. To achieve this, we need to work with the AIC churches,

My PhD dissertation will explore the theme of "The Effect of Simultaneous Community Development and Church Planting," This is based on a preliminary thesis that community development is of definite benefit in planting and growing churches if the development is a product of community participation, and specifically involves church members in a leadership role, thus placing the growing congregation as active participants in the development of the community. Furthermore, this offers a hope for funding the new church plant.

To put these ideas into action, we have started, with the help of some donors in California, the first AIC training center in Central and West Africa called Africa Academy of Christian Leadership, a four-year college offering a Bachelors in International Development. Currently we have 140 students registered, but we are expecting 200 in the new school year. We will also offer a subsidized MA program in 12 different locations in three countries, Cameroon, Nigeria and Burkina Faso. We have a number of community development projects going on in Cameroon and believe many will follow us in this direction

During the last two decades, we have trained more than 600 pastors, some of whom are now working in 38 African countries, Brazil, China and Indonesia. As a vital part of fulfillment of the great commission in Cameroon and Africa, our burden is to see the Lord of the Harvest call, equip, and send out anointed individuals or teams into the fields that are ripe for harvest in each of our country's 250 counties. Workers would need to be gifted and trained in evangelism and church planting. All team members also will be trained in developing a micro-business to support the financial need of their ministry. As evangelism precedes church planting, and recognizing the linguistic diversity of Cameroon, and its orality issues, each worker or team will be equipped with a hand crank player, with recordings in the heart languages of people, and with a bicycle for getting from village to village.

The fulfilling of the vision will be carried out in close partnership with local churches and kindred ministries who will help resource the work of each team, including start up funds for a micro-business project.

We have 250 evangelists, trained and ready to be deployed in villages. We have also identified 48 unreached people groups in the regions of Cameroon, Chad, Central Africa Republic and Northern Nigeria. We are willing to send our evangelists into those villages but we are hindered by lack of resources. In our case, it is not that the laborers are few, but the costs of sending them are beyond the capability of our churches.

CONCLUSION

So at long last we have come to the African Initiative Churches, which took advantage of the failure of mainline mission Christianity to adapt to the whole teaching of the counsel of God: spiritual healing, deliverance from spirit possession, and the preoccupation with witchcraft. But "took advantage of" is the wrong expression; it should be better said that the pioneers of this vast movement responded to those unfilled needs, and were striving to make African Christianity deeper and more effective.

We at AIC have made mistakes, which may be the reason the mission churches labeled us "traditional religion" churches. This has made it difficult for us to receive any support from the West, who trust what their missionaries told them about this great movement. It also has made it difficult for AIC pastors to attend the seminaries sponsored by the mission churches. I can understand the frustration of the missionaries, but this does not explain why they should destroy the characters of the men and women who are used by the Holy Spirit to lead this movement. We need to remember the counsel of Gamaliel in Acts 5:38-39: "And now I say unto you, Refrain from these men, and let them alone: for if this counsel or this work be of men, it will come to naught. But if it be of God, ye cannot overthrow it; lest haply ye be found even to fight against God."

I believe our leaders urgently need to get a contextualized theological training and a solid training in international and community development. The challenge in the years ahead for the AIC churches may be how to convince African churches that our battle is development, and our strategies are education and evangelism.

10. COMIBAM: CALLING LATIN AMERICANS TO THE GLOBAL CHALLENGE

Julio Guarneri

INTRODUCTION

"From mission field to mission force" is the phrase that the Latin American missions leader Luis Bush[1] pronounced at the missions congress in Sao Paulo, Brazil, in 1987.[2] This would become the rallying metaphor and the slogan for what is now COMIBAM International.[3] COMIBAM International is an acronym for *Cooperación Misionera Ibero-Americana* (Ibero-American Missionary Cooperation). It is a missionary network that attempts to connect evangelicals in Latin America and the Iberian Peninsula (Spain and Portugal). At its inception in 1987, it was estimated that 1,600 missionaries were sent from

---

1   For a biographical summary of Luis Bush, refer to Appendix A of this paper.
2   David Ruiz, "COMIBAM as a Process Leading to a Congress," (accessed on 11 November, 2007; available from http://www.comibam.org/docs/COMIBAM_process.pdf; Internet).
3   "¿Qué Es Comibam?" (accessed on 11 November, 2007; available from http://www.comibam.org/queescomi.htm; Internet).

Ibero-América by 70 agencies.[4] By 2006, COMIBAM leaders reported that 10,000 missionaries from the same part of the world were on an international assignment sent by approximately 400 organizations.[5] Though no one would claim that this ±600% increase in sending force should all be credited directly to COMIBAM, these statistics suggest a strong movement in the direction suggested at the first congress in 1987. The significance of COMIBAM as an organization and the context in which it emerged will be explored in this paper.

Relevance of Study of COMIBAM International

There are several reasons for a study of COMIBAM International and the context in which it emerged. COMIBAM as an organization and as a movement is significant not only to the Latin American church but to the entire global church. Bob Garrett, missions professor at Dallas Baptist University and former missionary to Argentina, considers COMIBAM the "coming of age of the Latin American church."[6] The intentional missionary work[7] in Latin America carried out by missionaries from Europe and North America in the 19th and 20th centuries has matured into a missionary sending base to the rest of the world.[8] As

---

4   Ibid.

5   Carlos Scott and Jesús Londoño. "Where Is COMIBAM International Heading? Strategic Focal Points," (Accessed 11 November, 2007; available from http://www. comibam.org/docs/whereiscomibamheading.pdf; Internet).

6   Interview with Bob Garrett on 3-24-08.

7   Justice C. Anderson in *An Evangelical Saga: Baptists and Their Precursors in Latin America* (Xulon Press, 2005) presents the history of Protestant missions in Latin America beginning with what he calls "providential precursors." These Protestant immigrants begin arriving in Latin America in the early 16th century. However, the intentional efforts to bring the Protestant faith, in either its mainline or more evangelical form, by fostering an indigenous church, became more evident shortly after the start of the modern missionary movement.

8   Assuming that the stages of development in the mission field from birth to maturity are (1) the arrival of foreign missionaries; (2) the nationalization of the work; (3) the growth in numbers and the influence of the national work on the rest of society; (4) the sending of missionaries and workers from the mission field to

such COMIBAM can be seen as a case study of the historical, leadership, theoretical and organizational factors present in a mission field that has reached missionary maturity.

Furthermore, the study of COMIBAM International is relevant because of the changing role of the Latin American church in the global scene. In the midst of the global changes at the arrival of the new millennium, the Spanish-speaking world plays a prominent role. Much has been written about the growth of Christianity in the global south and its relationship to the church in the rest of the world.[9] For instance, Justice Anderson states that by 2050 only about one-fifth of the world's three billion Christians will be non-Hispanic whites.[10] Samuel Escobar notes that, more specifically, evangelicals in Latin America numbered approximately 170 thousand in 1916 and estimated that by 2000 there

other mission fields. On a similar vein, Timothy Yates, in his Preface to *Christian Mission in the Twentieth Century* (Cambridge University Press, 1994), refers to Herny Venn's "euthanasia of the mission," whereby the indigenous church stands free of missionary dominance, xi.

9   Philip Jenkins, *The Next Christendom: The Coming of Global Christianity* (Oxford: Oxford University Press, 2002), 2-3. It is surprising that although Jenkins presents a strong case for the importance of the church in Latin America, in his more recent work, *The New Faces of Christianity* (Oxford: Oxford University Press, 2006), he relegates the discussion of Latin America to a brief overview; Samuel Escobar, *Tiempo de Misión: América Latina y la Misión Cristiana Hoy* (Time for Mission: Latin America and the Christian Mission of Today) (Bogota, Colombia: Clara Ediciones, 1999), 15; *The New Global Mission: The Gospel from Everywhere to Everyone* (Downers Grove, Illinois: Intervarsity Press, 2003), 15. Escobar points to Walbert Bühlman, Andrew Walls and Leslie Newbigin who identified these trends before Jenkins; James Leo Garrett, Jr., "Foreword," in *An Evangelical Saga: Baptist and Their Precursors in Latin America*, Justice C. Anderson (Xulon Press, 2005), xiii; Thomas Friedman, *The World Is Flat: A Brief History of the Twenty-First Century* (New York: Farrar, Straus and Giroux, 2006), 393; Justo Gonzalez, "The Challenge of Transitions," in The Latino Church: Converting Challenges to Opportunities, 2007 Rollins Lectures at the Baptist University of the Americas, San Antonio, Texas, 6.

10   Justice Anderson, An Evangelical Saga: Baptist and Their Precursors in Latin America, (Xulon Press, 2005), xix.

would be more than 50 million.[11] David Ruiz has listed some of the missionary realities for the global church. Among them, he mentioned: (1) 69% of Christians in the world live in the southern hemisphere; (2) the rapid growth of the evangelical church in Latin America; (3) and the migration from Latin America.[12] These demographic shifts in the global church call for the serious consideration of movements such as COMIBAM. How does it exemplify trends in strategy, leadership and cooperation for the global church in the 21st century? How does it model Missions from the Majority WORLD?

In addition to COMIBAM's significance to the Latin American church and to the global church in general, this study is also relevant to the Hispanic church in the United States. The Hispanic population in the United States is in a state of growth. Daniel Sanchez reports that between 1970 and 2005 the Hispanic population in the U.S. grew by 33.1 million and that by 2050 there will be 102.6 million Hispanics living in the U.S.[13] The potential for an explosive growth of the Hispanic evangelical church in the U.S. is present. Additionally, the migration of

Latinos into and from the United States necessitates a study of the Latino Church's present involvement in the global mission.[14]

---

11 Escobar, *Tiempo de Misión: América Latina y la Misión Cristiana Hoy*, 38. For a biographical summary of Samuel Escobar, refer to Appendix A of this paper.

12 David Ruiz, "Identidad, Visión y Proyección del Movimiento Misionero Iberoamericano," (Madrid, Spain: Cumbre de Liderazgo, November, 2002), (Accessed on 11 November, 2007; available from http://www.comibam.org/ponencias/cumpliespa/identidad.htm; Internet).

13 Daniel Sanchez, *Hispanic Realities Impacting America: Implications for Evangelism and Missions,* (Fort Worth: Church Starting Network, 2006), 3. One of the ten demographic realities which Sanchez discusses in his book is that, Hispanics are showing more receptivity to the Evangelical message than ever before in the history of the U.S (p. 35).

14 Diana Barrera, "Hispanics Involved in Missions," in *Hispanic Realities Impacting America: Implications for Evangelism and Missions,* ed., Daniel Sanchez (Fort Worth: Church Starting Network, 2006), 203.

Thesis

The thesis of this paper is that COMIBAM International was formed as a result of visionary indigenous leadership in a twentieth century context of ecumenism, missionary fervor, and critical changes in the Latin American landscape. The combination of these two constructs, namely, leadership and context, have given COMIBAM International the impetus of a movement. Factors such as the spirit of cooperation, missionary fervor, an indigenous theology and missiology, and cross-cultural leadership have contributed to it. This is a case study of the right leadership in the right context producing a missions network which in effect has become a missions-sending movement.

Definition of Terms

Several terms and concepts used in this paper may be open to various interpretations. These terms include church, cross-cultural missionary, evangelical, Hispanic, Ibero-America, integral mission, global church, Latin American, Latino, mission(s), missionaries, and visionary leadership. These terms need some definition or explanation as to their use in this paper. Some terms are used according to their definition by COMIBAM International. Please refer to the glossary in the appendices of this paper for these definitions and explanations.

THE HISTORICAL CONTEXT OF COMIBAM INTERNATIONAL

Mark Noll organizes his brief overview of the history of Christianity around "turning points."[15] He lists the Edinburg Missionary Conference

---

15 Mark Noll, *Turning Points: Decisive Moment in the History of Christianity*, (Grand Rapids: Baker Academics, 2000), 12.

in 1910 as the turning point of the 20[16] century.[16] The formation of COMIBAM International at the end of the same century is in some ways a ripple effect of the Edinburg Conference.[17] The impact of the Edinburg conference in this regard was neither intentional nor altogether positive. The rise of COMIBAM International was the result of visionary leadership in the midst of a series of events and movements in Latin America.[18] Some of these events and leaders served as precursors that set the stage for the emergence of movements like COMIBAM. Others had a more direct influence on its formation. A brief treatment of each is presented below.

Revolution and Demographics

The socio-cultural precursors to the formation of COMIBAM International included the rise and decline of multiple revolutionary movements and radical political changes in Latin America, the maturing stages of Liberation Theologies and the reactions to it, the growth of the evangelical church in Latin America and the migration of Latin Americans to other parts of the world.[19] These realities were accompanied by evangelical theological and missiological reflection, by Ecumenical Protestantism, and Evangelicalism.

---

16 Noll, 269.
17 Ruiz, "Cambios Paradigmáticos en el Liderazgo Global de las Misiones," (San Salvador: II Asamblea Internacional, November 2003) (Accessed on 11 November, 2007; available from http://www.comibam.org/ponencias/IIAsamblea/CPEE.htm; Internet).
18 Ruiz, "COMIBAM as a Process Leading to a Congress."
19 Ruiz, "Tendencias de la Iglesia y sus Implicaciones en el Movimiento Misionero Iberoamericano : Amenazas y Desafíos," (Madrid, Spain: Cumbre de Liderazgo, Noviembre, 2002) (Accessed on 11 November, 2007; available from http://www.comibam.org/ponencias/cumpliespa/tendencias.htm; Internet); Dafne Sabanes Plou, "Ecumenical History of Latin America" (from "A History of the Ecumenical Movement," 2004, WCC Publications) (Accessed on 28 September 2007; available from http://overcomingviolence.org/en/new-and-events/archive/past-annual-foci/2006-latin-america.html; Internet); Padilla, "The Evangelical Church in the Latin American Context;" Escobar, *Tiempo de Misión*, 19.

COMIBAM's first Congress took place in 1987. During this time many changes were taking place: the globalization phenomenon, the invention and wide-spread use of the internet, the accessibility of travel by air, and e-commerce.[20] In Latin America, in particular, demographic explosion, migration, and the growth of Protestantism, Roman Catholicism and Pentecostalism were also present realities. Indeed the new millennium arrived in a new world which makes possible an unprecedented advance in the missionary force.[21]

Ecumenism and Missionary Fervor

COMIBAM emerged at the turn of the twenty-first century as an indigenous interdenominational network concerned with world missions from Latin America. Its cooperative spirit, missionary fervor and indigenous autonomy were elements that developed throughout the entire twentieth century. The ecumenical missionary fervor was fueled by several key events and key leaders.

The Edinburgh Missionary Conference in 1910, the Panama Missionary Conference in 1916, the Berlin World Congress on Evangelism in 1966, and the International Congress on World Evangelization at Lausanne in 1974 stand as the backdrop for the formation of COMIBAM. The Edinburgh Missionary Conference was convened by John R. Mott[22] in an attempt for the international church to strategically complete the Great Commission.[23] This conference is significant for two reasons. It ignited the ecumenical movement, resulting in subsequent conferences and organizations such as the World Council of Churches (WCC), the

20 Jonathan Lewis, "El Perfil del Misionero Frente un Mundo Turbulento," (San Salvador: II Asamblea Internacional, November 2003) (Accessed on 11 November, 2007; available from http://www.comibam.org/ponencias/IIAsamblea/EPM.htm; Internet); Tinsley.
21 Escobar, Tiempo de Misión.
22 For a biographical summary of John R. Mott, refer to Appendix A of this paper.
23 Escobar, *The New Global Mission: The Gospel from Everywhere to Everyone,* 51; Ruiz, "Cambios Paradigmáticos en el Liderazgo Global de las Misiones."

Conference of Latin American Evangelicals (CELA), and Church and Society in Latin America (ISAL).[24] Ironically, the idea of evangelizing Latin America was dismissed by the Conference. Surprised by the Edinburgh Conference's neglect of Latin America and concerned for its evangelization, John R. Mott, in cooperation with Robert Speer and Samuel Guy Inman,

Ruiz, "Cambios Paradigmáticos en el Liderazgo Global de las Misiones."organized the Panama Missionary Conference in 1916.[25] This was the first organized effort across denominational lines to consider the evangelization of Latin America.[26] A result of this emphasis was the organization of the Latin American Evangelical Conference (CELA) which would meet in 1949, 1961 and 1969.[27] It was sponsored by the World Council of Churches and associated with the mainline ecumenical movement.[28]

Evangelicalism and Reaction to Mainline Ecumenism

After World War II, the missionary advance from Europe and the U.S. to Latin America would include a new element, namely that of the independent evangelical missionaries.[29] This development mirrored the growth of evangelicalism in the United States. The Billy Graham Evangelistic Association, the publication of the *Christianity Today* magazine, and the establishment of conservative evangelical seminaries were all contributing factors.[30] It was in this context that the BGEA, prompted by *Christianity Today's* editor, Carl F. H. Henry, held

---

24 [25]Escobar, *Es Tiempo de Misión*, 50; Plou, 1.
25 Ruiz, "Cambios Paradigmáticos en el Liderazgo Global de las Misiones;" Escobar, *La Fe Evangélica y las Teologías de la Liberación*, 50.
26 Plou, 1.
27 Escobar, 49.
28 Plou, 1.
29 Escobar, 53-54.
30 Ruiz.

the Berlin World Congress on Evangelism in 1966.[31] This conference marked a shift in the direction of missionary conferences. In contrast to the previous ecumenical conferences related to the WCC, the Berlin Congress resulted in the involvement of the more conservative evangelical churches around the world for evangelization. The concept of cooperation across denominational lines for the sake of evangelism (rather than for the sake of organic unity), would eventually become part of the fabric of these evangelical churches.

The International Congress for World Evangelization at Lausanne in 1974 was the fruit of the Berlin Congress. Convened by Billy Graham and drawing approximately 4,000 people from around the world, the Lausanne Congress produced important documents, marked significant shifts in world evangelization, and launched a movement. Two of the most significant documents were the Lausanne Covenant, which listed the necessity and the goals of world evangelization,[32] and the "A Call to Radical Discipleship," which demanded a greater emphasis on addressing the social needs of those who would be evangelized.[33] This emphasis on a more holistic gospel witness was supported by leaders such as Samuel Escobar, Rene Padilla and John Stott.[34] The theme of the second International Congress for World Evangelization that met in

---

31 Ralph D. Winter, "The Story of a Movement," in *Thy Kingdom Come* (Korea, 1995).
32 "The Lausanne Covenant," (The Lausanne Committee for World Evangelization, 16-25 July, 1974) (accessed on 28 September, 2007; available from http://www.lausanne.org/lausanne-1974/lausanne-1974.html; Internet).
33 "Lausanne 1974: Historical Background," (The Lausanne Committee for World Evangelization, 1974) (accessed on 28 September, 2007; available from http://www.lausanne.org; Internet).
34 Escobar presented a paper in a plenary session entitled, "Evangelism and Man's Search for Freedom, Justice and Fulfillment," where he argued that biblical and effective evangelism must be accompanied by social action. He was one of the leading editors of "A Call to Radical Discipleship." (Anthony C. Smith, "The Essentials of Missiology from the Evangelical Perspective of the Fraternidad Teológica Latinoamericana." Ph. D. diss., Southern Baptist Theological Seminary, 1983, 306). René Padilla introduced the concept of "misión integral" (holistic mission). (Escobar, *The New Global Mission,* 59). For a biographical summary of Padilla, refer to Appendix A of this paper. John Stott was supportive of these concepts.

Manila (1989), namely, "Calling the Whole Church to Take the Whole Gospel to the Whole World," demonstrated that this emphasis had become a part of the movement.[35] Another highly significant outcome of Lausanne was the shift in missionary focus, proposed by missions thinker Ralph Winters, to people groups rather than to countries.[36] A series of congresses and consultations have continued to meet over the years as a result of Lausanne.[37] The global evangelism fervor, the spirit of cooperation across denominations, and the emphasis on people groups and on a holistic gospel was now owned by evangelicals from all over the world.[38]

In addition to the contributions of thinkers and leaders such as John R. Mott, John Stott, Ralph Winter, Samuel Escobar and Rene Padilla, another very important contributor to Latin American missiological thought was John Mackay. Mackay, who was a Scottish missionary to Latin America at the beginning of the 20th century, wrote *The Other Spanish Christ* from Mexico City in 1933.[39] Through it he challenged the Christology introduced to Latin America by the Spanish Conquistadores in the 16th century and how it developed in the new land.[40] This invitation to new missionary fervor through the development of a more complete Christology and his idea of theology "on the road" were very influential on Latin American thinkers.[41]

---

35   "The Manila Manifesto," (Lausanne II: International Congress on World Evangelization, Manila Philippines, July, 1989) (accessed on 28 September, 2007; available from www.lausanne.org; Internet).

36   Winter.

37   see http://www.lausanne.org/gatherings.html.

38   As these similar themes has been part of the fabric of mainline Protestants during the beginning of the Ecumenical movement, now the more conservative and more independent evangelicals were also owning them with some differences in approach.

39   John A. Mackay, *The Other Spanish Christ: A Study in the Spiritual History of Spain and South America* (New York: The Macmillan Company, 1933).

40   Escobar, *La Fe Evangélica y las Teologías de la Liberación*, 53-54; *De la Misión a la Teología*, (Buenos Aires: Cairos Ediciones, 1998), 18-19, 45.

41   Escobar, La Fe Evangélica y las Teologías de la Liberación, 86; Yates, 91.

Direct Influences

The Edinburg, Panama, Berlin and Lausanne Conferences, along with the contributions of John Mott, John Mackay, John Stott, Samuel Escobar and Rene Padilla, stand as a general backdrop to the eventual formation of COMIBAM International. The spirit of cooperation, the missionary fervor and the concern for a contextualized missiology were all themes extended from these events and leaders. Nevertheless, the organizations and events that had a more direct influence on its establishment were the Latin American Theological Fraternity (FTL), CLADE, CONELA and the AD2000 movement. These will be treated briefly in the section below.

The significance of CLADE[42] for the Latin American missions movement was its appeal to the more conservative segment of the evangelical community and the theological controversies that eventually resulted in the development of an indigenous missiology. In a similar shift from Protestant Ecumenism to Evangelical Cross-Denominational Cooperation, the Latin American Congress for Evangelization (CLADE) was formed as an alternative to CELA.[43] As the Berlin Congress was

---

42   For a reference of which movements did these conferences and organizations relate to, see the List of Abbreviations and Acronyms in Appendix C of this paper.

43   Ruiz, "COMIBAM as a Process Leading to a Congress." For a reference of which movements did these conferences and organizations relate to, see the List of Abbreviations and Acronyms in Appendix C of this paper. One of the factors that distanced some evangelicals from CELA was the direction of its ISAL element. Shortly after its second conference in 1961, CELA established ISAL (Church and Society in Latin America) in 1962. (Escobar, *La Fe Evangélica y las Teologías de la Liberación*, 57; Plou, 2) Initially this was a think tank made up of protestant theologians such as Julio de Santa Ana and Julio Barrerio of Uruguay, Jose Míguez-Bonino of Argentina, and Rubem Alves of Brazil. (Padilla, "Evangelical Theology in the Latin American Context.") Its intent was to address the social needs in Latin America as part of the church's evangelistic strategy. Liberation theologies developed as part of these conversations in Latin America (Plou, 3). Eventually liberation theology became more associated with Roman Catholic theologians. ISAL eventually became an instrument of the Revolution and distanced itself from the churches. It is noteworthy that these various think tanks possessed so much

an evangelical alternative to the WCC-related missionary conferences, CLADE was convened in 1969 in Bogotá.[44] CLADE attempted to combine the interest in the evangelization of Latin America with the concern for social action as part of the church's mission discussed at the Berlin Conference.[45] However, some of the Latin American Evangelical leaders felt like CLADE I had too much influence from North American fundamentalism and saw the need to develop a more indigenous theology and missiology.[46]

The perceived need to develop a more indigenous missiology resulted in the formation of the Latin American Theological Fraternity (FTL).[47] The imminent dangers for the advance of the integral mission in Latin America were double. On the one side, identification with liberation theology and liberalism posed the threat of alienating the more conservative portion of evangelical leaders and participants. On the other extreme, a wholesale adoption of North American fundamentalism, which was too individualistic and did not give proper attention to the social concerns, and/or a product-oriented church growth missiology were also undesired by Latin American leaders.[48] A holistic gospel based on biblical authority did not necessarily fit the existing Protestant Anglo-Saxon categories of "liberal" and "conservative."[49] In 1970 at Cochamba, Bolivia, during the first CLADE consultation, these Latin American leaders drafted the Cochamba statement and the guidelines that essentially constituted the formation of the Latin American

---

international diversity. This demonstrates the willingness with which theologians and Christian worked together during these decades.

44 Escobar, 59.
45 Ibid., 209-210; Plou, 6.
46 Plou, 6.
47 Escobar, *La Fe Evangélica y las Teologías de la Liberación,* 81; J. Daniel Salinas, "Evangelical Theological Production in Hispanic Latin American between 1969 and 1979 (A Reception History)," Ph. D., diss., Trinity International University, 2005, 68ff.; Plou, 6.
48 Escobar, 81; Plou, 6.
49 Ibid., 57.

Theological Fraternity.[50] The formation of the FTL shortly after CLADE I insured an indigenous agenda and leadership for CLADE II.[51] The leaders' discernment and ability to do this successfully in a brief period of time proved to be critical. CLADE I and the formation of the FTL took place between the Berlin Conference and the Lausanne Congress on World Evangelization. By, 1974, the year of Lausanne's Congress, the FTL had formulated and articulated its theological and missiological positions. The FTL was an attempt by Latin American leaders such as Samuel Escobar, Rene Padilla, Orlando Costas, Emilio Nuñez, Peter Savage, Andrew Kirk and others for a theological reflection which would be conservative, evangelistic and holistic in its missiology.[52] The FTL was a product of missiological concern, namely the need to advance a holistic mission in Latin America. Thus, the theological developments of the FTL were missiological and its theological method was one of *"el camino"*[53] rather than a systematic theology. The FTL perceived itself to be in living in a *"kairos"* moment of history and their swift actions demonstrated such a conviction. Indigenous theological reflection and a sense of the changing times would be characteristic of the FTL and, later, of COMIBAM International. Furthermore, the resulting missiological theology produced by the FTL would influence the Latin American missions movement.

Theological reflection, the continued concern for the evangelization of the world, and cross-denominational collaboration led the participants of CLADE, and the Luis Palau Evangelistic Association and the World Evangelical Fellowship (WEF), to convoke a Confraternity

---

50 Escobar, *Tiempo de Misión,* 53; Salinas, 94ff.; Terrell F. Coy, "Incarnation and the Kingdom of God: The Political Ideologies of Orlando Costas, C. René Padillas and Samuel Escobar," Ph. D., diss., Southwestern Baptist Theological Seminary, 1999, 54-55.

51 Plou, 7.

52 Smith, 301-303; Escobar, *La Fe Evangélica y las Teologías de la Liberación,* 214.

53 Theology "on the road," a term coined by missionary John Mackay that would influence some of the leaders in the FTL.

of Evangelicals in Latin America (CONELA) in 1982 in Panama.[54] CONELA called for a meeting of leaders in 1984 at Mexico City in order to discuss the organization of an international congress that would promote the missionary vision in Latin America.[55] The initiative of CONELA marked a shift in the thinking and activity of Latin American evangelicals in regard to missions advance.[56] Though missionaries had been sent from Latin America to other parts of the world since the beginning of the twentieth century, the focus on evangelizing the world as a cooperative effort from the Latin American Evangelical church was new. The next time a congress like this would meet would be in Sao Paulo in 1987 and would be called *Cooperación Misionera Ibero-Americana* (COMIBAM).[57] The vision of a Latin America evolving from mission field to mission force came to fruition.

What Samuel Escobar, Rene Padilla, Orlando Costas, Emilio Nuñez, Peter Savage, and Andrew Kirk were to Latin American indigenous missiological thinking, Luis Bush was to missiological action on a large scale across Latin America.[58] Bush was a prominent leader of COMIBAM 87 and founding president of COMIBAM International. During his tenure, he directed Partners International, which associated approximately 70 indigenous ministries in 50 countries. He was also the catalytic leader who launched the AD2000 movement.[59] Inspired by John Mott's vision a century earlier and encouraged by the global efforts for world evangelization, Bush cast the vision of accomplishing the task of world evangelization by the year 2000.[60] Though this specific objective was not reached, the AD2000 movement made several

---

54 Ruiz, "COMIBAM as a Process Leading to a Congress."
55 "¿Qué Es COMIBAM?"
56 Escobar, *Tiempo de Misión*, 49.
57 Ruiz.
58 Refer to Appendix A of this paper.
59 Ruiz, "Cambios Paradigmáticos para el Liderazgo de la Misión Global."
60 Luis Bush, "Catalysts of World Evangelization," (Ph. D., diss., Fuller Theological Seminary, School of World Missions, 2002, *Dissertation Abstracts International*, *63/04*, 1402), 54-55.

contributions to the cause of world evangelization. The most notable of these are: (1) the conceptualization of the idea of the 10/40 window; and (2) a number of established networks that would seek to collaborate at a grander scale.[61]

COMIBAM INTERNATIONAL AS A MISSIONS NETWORK

Decades of missionary and evangelistic fervor, a spirit of international cooperation among evangelicals, an indigenous missiology for Latin America, and visionary leadership resulted in a historical missionary congress and the launching of a movement.

COMIBAM 87

In 1987, over 3,000 evangelicals from churches in Latin America, Spain, and Portugal met in Sao Paulo, Brazil, to consider cooperating together for the advancement of world missions. For many evangelicals this was a turning point in the history of the Latin American church. It cast the vision of a united evangelical people in Latin America becoming a world mission force. Whether the event created this vision or whether the vision created the event might be debated. When seen in the context of twentieth century ecumenism, missionary fervor, collaboration, the growth of the church in Latin America, and the development of indigenous leadership and reflection, it is more plausible to understand this congress as the product of an incipient vision. The Sao Paulo congress would spread that vision across Ibero-America.

---

61   Escobar; Ruiz.

COMIBAM 87 was a congress, but it would be more than an event. It resulted in the organization of COMIBAM International, a missionary network. COMIBAM leaders would be committed to a network model for organization in contrast to hierarchical models. Though the establishing of networks for the accomplishment of organizational objectives is very common in the 21ˢᵗ century,[62] COMIBAM leaders were pioneers in this trend. Referring to structure and networking for world mission, Yong Chen Fah states, "Networking is one of the keys to coping with globalization in the modern world."[63] The fluidity of a network structure is perhaps one of the contributing factors for the effectiveness of COMIBAM International. Though it is not flawless, it minimizes some of the bureaucratic and hierarchical issues of mission boards and denominational agencies while maintaining shared leadership. While the network has a vision casting and a catalytic function, the energy, direction and resources come from the grassroots level. It is also an attractive model to evangelicals who place much value on the autonomy of the local church or of their particular denomination. This kind of visionary leadership has poised the organization for effectiveness in the twenty-first century. The organizational components of COMIBAM are discussed below.

---

62 Friedman suggests that this may be a result of the internet. Some recent examples of networks that have been formed as an alternative to a mission board or a denominational office are Worldconnex (a missions network organized by the Baptist General Convention of Texas that seeks to cooperate with Baptists and other groups in order to help the church send its people as missionaries www.worldconnex.org) and TarrantNet (a network of pastors and churches in the Tarrant County area across denominational and ethnic lines in order to encourage the "city church" to transform its city; www.tarrantnet.org). Both of these have been formed in Texas.

63 Yong Chen Fah, "Stewardship, Partnership, Structure and Networking for World Mission," (*Transformation, 21:* January 2004), 33.

Mission and Vision

COMIBAM International has articulated its mission and vision. Its vision is stated as, "to see the Ibero-American church as a missionary force."[64] The statement fails to describe what that means or what it looks like. Ecclesiologically, it assumes that there is one Ibero-American church. The strength of the statement is its clarity about the church in Spain, Portugal and Latin America becoming a mission-sending base. COMIBAM's mission statement, "to help the church in Ibero-America transform itself in a missionary people, able to take the gospel of Jesus Christ to all nations,"[65] seems to describe the vision statement. It is bold in nature and noble in intent, yet difficult to assess. Lastly, COMIBAM states that their rationale for existence is "to glorify God, strengthening the national missionary movements through the provision of the necessary services so that local churches can fulfill the Great Commission."[66] This statement reads like a strategic plan. Its strength is its focus on the national movements and on the local church. It respects local church autonomy and indigenous leadership in each country.

One of the ways in which COMIBAM tracks its success is by reporting the number of missionaries sent internationally from Latin America. In 1987, it was estimated that 1,600 workers were sent by 70 agencies.[67] By 2006, COMIBAM leaders reported that 10,000 missionaries were on an international assignment sent by approximately 400 organizations.[68] Though some room needs to be given for the interpretation of the missionary and sending terminology and for the direct influence of COMIBAM for these numbers, the ±600%

64 "¿Qué Es COMIBAM?"
65 "¿Qué Es COMIBAM?"
66 Ibid.
67 Ibid.
68 Carlos Scott and Jesus Londoño. "Where Is COMIBAM International Heading? Strategic Focal Points," (Accessed 11 November, 2007; available from http://www.comibam.org/docs/whereiscomibamheading.pdf; Internet).

increase in sending force is admirable. Is COMIBAM the catalyst of a missionary movement in Ibero-America or is it the expression of numerous grassroots movements throughout Latin America and the Iberian Peninsula? Most likely it is both. COMIBAM has likely provided momentum, serious reflection on missiological thinking and praxis, and a rallying sense of unity and destiny. The numerous grassroots movements were not created by COMIBAM but COMIBAM has helped to fan the flame.

Structure and Leadership

COMIBAM was organized as a network and its structure has evolved according to needs and strategy. Bertil Ekstrom, who acted as president during COMIBAM's second congress in 1997, led the administrative reorganization of the network with the intent of avoiding authoritarian leadership and maintaining connection with other mission movements.[69] This sustained concern for the potential of autocratic or charismatic leadership is addressed by organizers in relation to COMIBAM and to local churches.[70]

COMIBAM International is a network of networks. It is dependent on national missionary "movements" or initiatives of each country in Ibero-America. In each country, three kinds of networks are identified: (1) the churches and pastors network; (2) the missionary training centers network; (3) the sending structures network. In the first network, all churches having an intentional missions program in their agenda are included. In the second network are included any seminaries or training centers offering missionary training that includes cross-cultural courses. The third network includes interdenominational agencies, denominational boards and missions departments and other such

69   Ruiz.
70   Carlos Scott, "Manual del Congreso," (Granada, Spain: III Congreso Iberoamericano, 13-17 November, 2006) (Accessed on 11 November, 2007; available from http://www.comibam.org/docs/manual_es.pdf; Internet).

organizations. This comprehensive approach takes into consideration the three elements involved in sending and sustaining a missionary force. It provides a multi-faceted database. Additionally, with these three types of networks in each country, COMIBAM International encourages networks along similar lines on an international scale.[71] Eventually, the leadership of COMIBAM deemed necessary the subdivision of the international work into eight regions in order to facilitate the work and to bring the network closer to each of the participating countries. They are the Iberian Peninsula, the Caribbean, Brazil, the Southern Cone, the Andes, Central America, Mexico, and Hispanics in the U.S.[72] This organization, which is from-the-bottom-up and is pervasively inclusive of diverse denominations, types of organisms and various countries, is unique and particularly relevant for the current global situation. It also demonstrates that even when the intention of leaders is to keep an organization flat and simple, sometimes practicality calls for a more complex organization.

The Executive Board of COMIBAM International consists of its president, the eight regional representatives, and the Executive Director. The current president is Carlos Scott and the Executive Director is Jesus Londoño.[73] Ruben Suarez serves as the Chief Financial Officer.

The Executive Committee consists of the Executive Director and the department and program leaders.[74] This dual organization of execu-

---

71 "¿Qué Es COMIBAM?"
72 Ibid.
73 The current regional representatives are Daniel Bianchi (South Cone), Alfonso Medina (Iberian Peninsula), Jason Carlisle (North America), Ruben Suarez (Caribbean), Luis Marti (Central America), Victor Ibagon (Andes), Jose Luis Ramirez (Mexico) and Marcos Agripino (Brazil).
74 Currently these leaders are Ted Limpic (Information and Research Department), Ruben Suarez (Department of Development), Federico Bertuzzi (Publications Department), Omar Gava (Training Centers Network), Cristian Castro (Sending Structures Network), Edgardo Surenian (Churches and Pastors Network & Intercession Program), Moises Lopez (Reach a People Group Program), Carlos

tive board and executive committee assures participation from all the geographical segments and the assignment of organizational tasks for the accomplishment of the objectives.

In keeping with its mission and the nature of networks, COMIBAM International's strategy consists of strengthening national missionary movements and the local church as a mission force by focusing on five areas: (1) Strengthening of national and regional missionary movements; (2) Focus on unreached people groups; (3) Ibero-American missiology; (4) Leadership development; and (5) Global cooperation and connections. Its programs and departments are organized around this strategy.[75] Although some of these may need further explanation, this strategy is clear and comprehensive.

Progress of Mission

The sheer numerical strength of the missionary force being sent from Ibero-America is noteworthy. In addition to a ±600% increase in less than twenty years in number of missionaries and sending organizations, other informative statistics are published by COMIBAM International (See Appendix B). COMIBAM reports the number of cross-cultural missionary organizations in Ibero-America as of 2006 to be 641. These are subdivided into international agencies, international agencies with Ibero-American leadership, Ibero-American agencies, Ibero-American agencies with foreign leadership, denominational boards, local churches, inter-church initiatives and missionary training centers.

It is noteworthy that the highest percentage (24%) consists of Ibero-American agencies, which signals the progress toward a truly indigenous missionary movement. The number of cross-cultural missionaries

España (Missionary Holistic Care), Jose de Dios (Strategic Alliances and Missionary Cooperation Program), and Francisco Linares (Linguistic Training Program).
75   "¿Qué Es COMIBAM?"

reported in the same year is 9,265. These are further subdivided into furlough, active on the field, years of experience, marital status, denominational affiliation, and continent/region of service. In each category the highest numbers are, active on the field (94%), over 3 years of experience (61%), married (75%), Pentecostal (36%), and South America (35%). According to this, the typical cross-cultural missionary from Ibero-America is active on the field, has more than 3 years of experience and is married. His denominational affiliation may most likely be Pentecostal (36%), Interdenominational (30%) or Traditional (24%). His country/region of service may most likely be South America (35%), Europe (17%), or Mexico and Central America (12%). It should also be noted that while 57% of these missionaries serve within Ibero-America, 51% do so out of Latin America. This means that while a majority of Ibero-American missionaries serve Latin America, Spain, Portugal and Hispanics in the U.S., a simple majority has left Latin America for another region. This marks significant progress in the challenging task of world evangelization from Ibero-America. Perhaps one of the areas of greatest challenge is the percentage of Ibero-American missionaries serving in the 10/40 window (16%). Since this area of the world has been a concern from the inception of COMIBAM, a strategic plan to encourage more missionaries from Ibero-America to this region is needed.

Another of COMIBAM International's strengths is its willingness to openly and critically evaluate its work. COMIBAM's lean organization in terms of staff allows for a more objective opportunity to evaluate its work. Additionally, the openness to have other groups such as FTL and CLADE speak to it, increases this objectivity. On their tenth anniversary, COMIBAM celebrated its Second Ibero-American Missions Congress in Acapulco, Mexico. Its purpose would be to evaluate the achievement of the movement in its ten years of organized history and to "project a new vision for the future."[76] A similar process would be put in place at the third congress in 2006 in Granada, Spain. The very fact that it convened in Spain was an affirmation of the previous (1997) congress's intention to make the emphasis in the Iberian Peninsula more prominent.[77] At events like CLADE IV (2000, Quito) leaders speak to COMIBAM issues. Conversely COMIBAM leaders speak to CLADE participants.[78] This open dialogue is conducive to improved efficiency in the missionary task.

The various conferences, congresses and consultations that relate to COMIBAM are more than just gatherings to hear information and inspiration. Each event has a particular focus item which is addressed in papers and speeches and from which feedback is sought.[79] As a result of presentations, recommendations are made by presenters and evaluators. These recommendations inform the churches and participating organizations, but they also impact the network's strategy.

Missiology

Escobar suggests that Latin American missiology should be developed critically, systematically, biblically, and experientially.[80] COMIBAM's missiology is not necessarily systematic since it is derived from presentations and papers by diverse individuals. Nevertheless it is consistent in the treatment of particular themes. The general missiology of COMIBAM is evident in its mission, vision, rationale for existence and strategy discussed previously. In a more elaborate sense, COMIBAM's missiology is in continuous development and is expressed in the form of

---

76   Ruiz, "COMIBAM as a Process Leading to a Congress."

77   Ruiz, "Manual del Congreso," 19.

78   "Conclusiones: Consideraciones Bíblicas," (Quito, Ecuador: CLADE IV, Octubre, 2000) (Accessed on 11 November, 2007; available from http://www.comibam.org/ponencias/CladeIV/index.htm; Internet).

79   Refer to the "Timeline of COMIBAM Congresses and other meetings" in Appendix D of this paper for a list of the meetings and their particular emphases.

80   Escobar, Tiempo de Misión, 31.

papers and speeches at several of its consultations or those of CLADE. Several examples are mentioned below. At CLADE IV (2000, Quito), Tito Paredes of the FTL offered missiological conclusions on cross-cultural missions based on a study of the New Testament. They deal with the necessity of the whole church in the whole world taking the gospel to all peoples, the necessity of eliminating ethnocentrism, and the attitude of love and service in cross-cultural missions.[81] Another example is the missionary models discussed by COMIBAM's Bertuzzi. He categorizes these models as follows:

"Anglo Franchise Model." Where the Anglo organization opens a branch that is a reflection of its nature and work in its original context.

"Participative Model." Where the Anglo organization establishes itself in the mission field by offering to partner with locals.

"Servant Model." Where the Anglo organization comes to the mission field with a servant attitude and responds to the leadership of Latin American pastors and leaders.[82]

Bertuzzi offers the third model as the most appropriate for Ibero-America where an indigenous church growing into a mission force is present. One may ask how these models will be applied as Ibero-Americans carry out their mission in other places. Another example is David Ruiz' articulation of a missions movement that is church-driven, where the role of the visionary pastor is critical (at COMIBAM's International Assembly on November 2002 in Madrid).[83] At the same

---

81   Tito Paredes, "Las Bases Neotestamentarias de la Misión Transcultural," (Quito, Ecuador: CLADE IV, October 2000) (Accessed on 11 November, 2007; available from http://www.comibam.org/ponencias/CladeIV/ponencia5.htm; Internet).

82   Federico Bertuzzi, "Internacionalización o Anglonización de la Misión," (Quito, Ecuador: CLADE IV, Octubre, 2000) (Accessed on 11 November, 2007; available from http://www.comibam.org/ponencias/CladeIV/ponencia6.htm; Internet).

83   Ruiz, "Iglesias Fuertes, Pastores con Visión," (Madrid, Spain: Cumbre deLiderazgo, November, 2002) (Accessed on 11 November, 2007; available from

event, Ruiz presented characteristics of Latin American religiosity and builds on Orlando Costas' work about the nature of the church to propose an evangelical church typology for Latin America.[84] At COMIBAM's Second International Assembly in 2003, San Salvador, Jesus Londoño, COMIBAM's executive director, proposed the following regarding the missiological outlook of the Ibero-American context: (1) a new reading of the present world through the lens of evangelical and spiritual experience; (2) a shifting from an anthropocentric theology of the church to a more theocentric; (3) the unity of missiology throughout the other branches of systematic theology; (4) an applied missiology from the field; and (5) a Christological missiology.[85] On the negative side, a general disdain for the "theology of results," "management evangelism," "homogeneous units," "church growth" and "evangelical zionism" is shared by some writers and leaders of the FTL and COMIBAM movements.[86] Though this missiology in evolution seems fragmented, there are certain unifying themes. They may be expressed in the following way: (1) the importance of contextualization of the mission; (2) its dependence on the Scriptures; (3) a willingness to suffer and some avoidance of a results-driven approach; (4) a Christological emphasis; (5) the necessity of cooperation; (6) a missiology developed in the praxis; (7) the empowerment of indigenous movements; and (8) leadership models that serve the existing church and which are neither autocratic nor paternalistic. As suggested above, this is indeed not a systematic missiology but one that is constantly under development.

---

http://www.comibam.org/ponencias/lima/ponencia3.htm; Internet).

84 Ruiz, "Tendencias de la Iglesia y sus Implicaciones en el Movimiento MisioneroIberoamericano : Amenazas y Desafíos," (Madrid, Spain: Cumbre de Liderazgo, Noviembre, 2002) (Accessed on 11 November, 2007; available from http://www.comibam.org/ponencias/cumpliespa/tendencias.htm; Internet).

85 Jesus Londoño, "Cambios Teológicos en la Fuerza Misionera," (San Salvador: II Asamblea Internacional, November 2003) (Accessed on 11 November, 2007; available from http://www.comibam.org/ponencias/IIAsamblea/CTEFM.htm; Internet).

86 Peralta, "Manual del Congreso," 24-26; Escobar, *Tiempo de Misión*, 29; *The New Global Mission*, 59-50.

It is also evident that COMIBAM's missiology has been influenced by conservative evangelicalism and by a concern for a holistic gospel that ministers to social and spiritual needs.

CONCLUSION

COMIBAM International is a missions network that emerged as the result of missionary fervor, a spirit of cooperation, an indigenous missiology, and visionary leadership. It is significant to the story of missionary work in Latin America and the Iberian Peninsula. As such it is a sure sign of maturity for the Latin American church. It is also significant to the global church because of the increased importance of Christianity's shift to the southern hemisphere. COMIBAM can serve as a case study of an effective organization doing global Missions from the Majority WORLD. If the emergence of COMIBAM is significant, its progress and effectiveness is much more so. In addition to the numerical advances, COMIBAM can be considered successful by its sustained and focused work throughout its twenty years of existence. It has stayed the course. It has not grown stale or become institutionalized. Instead it has evaluated, evolved, and improved its strategy. In many ways COMIBAM is indebted to other movements and organizations such as the Ecumenical Missionary Movement, the FTL, CLADE, Lausanne, CONELA and the AD2000 movement. It inherited from them a spirit of cooperation, a global missions outlook, and indigenous missiological reflection. In some ways, COMIBAM has made significant contributions to some of these movements. COMIBAM has taken the baton for the holistic evangelization of the world and crossed the twenty-first century line with vigor and optimism.

Those who are concerned with participating as leaders in the mission of the global church can learn important lessons from COMIBAM's history and organization. Though no human can create the kind of sociological, ecclesiological, and missiological events that preceded the formation of COMIBAM, visionary leaders learn to discern the *kairos* and seize the opportunities it brings. These kinds of leaders must exercise reflection of their context, missiology and the global shifts that take place. What are the current social, economic and ecclesial realities that can contribute to effective missionary work as we conclude the first decade of the 21st century?

Though no single individual can take credit for a movement, individual leaders who collaborate with others and who maintain a sustained vision can contribute greatly to its success. A more in-depth study of leaders who were precursors to COMIBAM and of current COMIBAM leaders may be informative for leaders who seek to relate cross-culturally to the global church of the 21st century. Cooperation, diversity, contextualization, scholarly reflection, clear vision and organizational alignment are good ingredients for contemporary leadership in the global church. Leaders who have cross-cultural skills and the ability to create and work through networks are valuable for the advancement of the church's mission.

Appendix A: Biographical Summaries

Luis Bush was born in Argentina, grew up in Brazil, and attended college and seminary in the United States. He pastored Iglesia Nazaret in San Salvador for seven years, leading it to grow, start new churches and support numerous international missionaries. Bush served as director of COMIBAM International during its initial years beginning in 1987, as CEO to Partners International from 1986 to 1992 and as director of the AD2000 & Beyond Movement from 1989 to 2001. Luis coined the term "the 10/40 window" to refer to the region of the world with the least exposure to Christianity. He completed his Ph.D. in Intercultural Studies at Fuller School of World Mission in 2003. ("AD2000 and Beyond: A Church for Every People and the Gospel for Every Person by AD 2000; Luis Bush: Biographical Information Sheet." Accessed on 25 March 2008; available from http://www.ad2000.org/staff/luis.htm; Internet).

Samuel Escobar: Born in Peru, he was ordained as a Baptist pastor and obtained his Ph.D. from Complutense University in Madrid. He was a founder and president of the Latin American Theological Fraternity (FTL), served on staff with the International Fellowship of Evangelical Students in Latin America for 26 years, served as president of the United Bible Societies, and served as the General Director of Intervarsity Christian Fellowship in Canada for three years. A prolific writer, he currently teaches at Baptist Seminaries in Madrid and Pennsylvania. ("Samuel Escobar, Urbana Speaker: Peruvian Missiologist and Missionary to the US and Spain." Accessed on 26 March 2008; available from http://www.urbana.org/u2003.speakers,samuel.cfm; Internet).

John R. Mott: Born in 1865 in New York, he was a Methodist layman who was a leader in the Student Volunteer Movement for Foreign Missions, in the YMCA, the International Missionary Council and the World's Students Christian Federation. Mott traveled much around the world and served President Wilson in various diplomatic assignments. He received the Noble Peace Prize in 1946. ("John R. Mott: The Noble Peace Prize 1946; Biography." Accessed on 25 March 2008; available from http://nobelprize.org/nobel_prizes/peace/laureates/1946/mott-bio.html; Internet).

Rene Padilla: A Baptist who has worked with evangelicals across denominational lines, e is one of the founding members of the Latin American Theological Fraternity. He is a graduate of Wheaton College and obtained his Ph.D. from the University of Manchester under F.F. Bruce. He has been the editor of *Iglesia y Misión* and a prolific writer and speaker on Latin American missiology. ("Baptists in Latin America and Their Theological Contributions." Accessed on 26 March 2008; available from http://www.encycolpedia.com/doc/1G1-94160932.html; Internet).

Appendix B: Missionary Organiziations in Ibero-America[87]

Cross-cultural Missionary Organizations	Total: 641	
International agencies	67	10%
International agencies with Ibero-American leadership	111	17%
Ibero-American agencies	156	24%
Ibero-American agencies with foreign leadership	18	03%
Denominational boards	111	17%
Local churches	111	17%
Inter-church initatives	23	04%
Missionary training centers	42	07%

Cross-cultural Missionaries	Total: 9265	
Furlough	517	06%
Active on the field	8748	94%

Years of Experience		
Over 3 years	5313	61%
Between 1 & 3 years	2567	29%
Less than 1 year	868	10%

Marital Status		
Married	6595	75%
Single Males	978	11%
Single Females	1175	13%

Denominational Affiliation		
Interdenominational	2622	30%
Traditional	2085	24%
Pentecostal	3140	36%
No Data Available	759	09%
Independent	142	02%

Continent/Region of Service		
Asia	566	06%
Africa	861	10%
North America	812	09%

87 "Organizaciones Misioneras Argentina [Resumen Numérico: 2006]," (in *Catálogo deOrganizaciones Misioneras Ibero-Americanas* (2006)) (accessed on 11 November, 2007; available from http://www.comibam.org/catalogo2006/esp/consulta-2006/arg/_resum.htm; Internet).

Mexico & Central America	1028	12%
South America	3092	35%
Caribbean	204	02%
Oceania	28	00%
Europe	1495	17%
Middle East	475	05%
Eurasia	120	01%
Itinerant	67	01%

Distribution in Relation to Ibero-America

Within Ibero-America	4976	57%
Out of Ibero-America	3772	43%

Distribution in Relation to Latin America

Within Latin America	4263	49%
Out of Latin America	4485	51%

Distribution in Relation to the 10/40 Window

Within the 10/40 Window	1440	16%
Out of the 10/40 Window	7308	84%

Administrative and Support Personnel Back Home   Total: 1611

Appendix C: List of Abbreviations and Acronyms

BGEA   Billy Graham Evangelistic Association

CELA   Conferencia Evangélica Latinoamericana (Latin American Evangelical Conference; related to the WCC; see below)

CLADE   Congreso Latinoamericano de Evangelización (Latin American Congress for Evangelization; related to the BGEA)

COMIBAM   Congreso Misionero Ibero-Americano (Ibero-American Missionary Congress)

CONELA   Confraternidad Evangélica Latinoamericana
             (Latinamerican Evangelical Fellowship)

FTL   Fraternidad Teológica Latinoamericana
             (Latin American Theological Fraternity)

ICOWE   International Congress On World Evangelization at
             Lausanne, Switzerland (Sponsored by the BGEA)

ISAL   Iglesia y Sociedad en América Latina (Church & Society in
             Latin America; related to CELA and the WCC)

LMC   Life and Mission of the Church Commission
             (related to the FTL)

WCC   World Council of Churches (Mainline Protestant
             Ecumenical organization)

WEF   World Evangelical Fellowship (Conservative Evangelical
             organization)

Appendix D: 20th Century Conferences Leading to COMIBAM

Ecumenical Missionary Movement (Berlin, WCC, CELA & ISAL)

1910   The Edinburgh Missionary Congress, Edinburgh, Scotland

1916   Congreso de Acción Cristiana en América Latina, Panama
             City, Panama

1949   CELA I, Buenos Aires, Argentina (WCC)

1961   CELA II, Lima, Peru (WCC)

| 1962 | Establishment of ISAL by the WCC, Sao Paulo, Brazil |

Evangelicalism

1966	Congress for World Evangelization, Berlin, Germany (BGEA)
1969	CELA III, Buenos Aires, Argentina (WCC)
1969	CLADE I, Bogotá, Colombia (BGEA)
1970	CLADE's First International Consultation and formation of the FTL,

Cochabamba, Bolivia

1973	Workshop on Evangelicals and Social Concern, Chicago, USA
1974	International Congress On World Evangelization, Lausanne, Switzerland (BGEA)
1976	Congreso Misionero de Curitiba

QUITO I: Church-Mission Consultation, Quito, Ecuador

1978	Consultation on "Gospel and Culture" of the ICOWE, Williowbank, Bermuda
1982	CONELA, Panama City (BGEA, WEF and Luis Palau Evangelistic Association)
1987	Congreso Misionero Ibero-Americano (COMIBAM), Sao Paulo, Brazil

Timeline of COMIBAM Congresses and other meetings

1987	I Congreso Misionero Ibero-Americano (COMIBAM), Brazil
1991	Consultation on Missionary Training, Guatemala
1992	Consultation on Adoption of People Groups, Costa Rica
1994	Consultation on Church-Agency Sending, Panama
1997	II Congreso Misionero Ibero-Americano, Mexico
2000	I International Assembly (consolidation of regions, networks; transfer of leadership), Peru
2002	I Leadership Summit (Strengthening national/regional leadership), Spain
2003	II International Assembly, El Salvador
2005	II Leadership Summit (New Missionary Strategies Project), Spain
2006	III Congreso Misionero Ibero-Americano & III International Assembly, Spain

Appendix E: Glossary

Church. The term church is used in several ways throughout this paper. It includes the sense of a local church as a body of believers who gather for worship and service. When capitalized, the term may indicate a particular denomination such as the Roman Catholic Church or the Presbyterian Church. Often it refers to the grouping of a particular segment of Christianity, although not a formal organism, such as the evangelical church, the Latin American church, or the Pentecostal church, and it may include local churches, individuals and para-church organizations within that segment. In this last sense, it usually infers that this segment of Christianity crosses denominational boundaries. COMIBAM uses the term in the singular to refer to both the expression of the body of Christ in a global sense and to local congregations. ("Definiciones e Información Adicional," in *Catálogo de Organizaciones Misioneras (2006)*, (accessed 11 November, 2007; available from http://www.comibam.org/catalogo2006/Misc/def_es.htm; Internet).

Cross-cultural missionary. According to COMIBAM, this is the individual who crosses a language or cultural barrier in order to fulfill the Great Commission. COMIBAM includes in this group those who go to another country of the same language and similar culture but have crossed national geopolitical barriers. ("Definiciones e Información Adicional." See also definition of "missionary" below).

Evangelical. This term is used here to refer to the element of Protestant Christianity that emphasizes biblical authority, salvation by faith in Christ alone, personal conversion, and the mandate to evangelize the world. Although these emphases may cut across the three larger branches of the church present in Latin America: Roman Catholic, Protestant and Pentecostal, it is most often associated with Free Churches.

Hispanic. This is the term used to refer to individuals who live in the United States of America and who either come from Latin America or whose ancestors came from Latin America. It often includes those whose ancestors lived in regions of the Southwest United States which formerly belonged to Mexico. COMIBAM limits this term to U.S. citizens whose mother tongue is either Spanish or Portuguese. ("Definiciones e Información Adicional"). This usage of the term is peculiar. It leaves out millions of Hispanics who are resident aliens or undocumented immigrants. (Gonzalez, "The Challenge of Transitions," 2). It also leaves out those who by ethnicity are Hispanics but whose mother tongue is English. I propose the following alternative definition, "an individual living in the United States whose ethnic or linguistic heritage can be traced to either Spain or Latin America."

Ibero-America. A conglomerate of countries that share affinity either because of language or ethnicity, consisting of South America, Central America, Mexico, the Caribbean, Hispanics in the United States and Canada, Spain and Portugal. This seems to be used by COMIBAM because of its ability to include the Iberian Peninsula and Latin America in one word. Leaders from these various regions of the world collaborated together in theological reflection and world evangelization strategies before the formation of COMIBAM. (Rene Padilla, "Evangelical Theology in a Latin American Context," (accessed on 28 September, 2007; available from http://integral-mission.org/PDF_files/ Evangelical_Theology_in_LA_context.pdf; Internet).

Integral Mission ("Misión Integral"). This term coined by Rene Padilla refers to the church's mission of evangelizing the world by taking a careful reading of the cultural context in which mission is done and by participating in social action (ie: addressing poverty and social injustice). (Padilla, "What Is Integral Mission?" in *Integral Mission Newsletter*, (10 March 2006, accessed on 27 September, 2007; available from http://www.integral-mission.org/PDF_files/ Rene-What_is_integral_mission.pdf; Internet).

International / Global Church. This term is used to refer to the expression of Christianity around the world. Though it may be used to speak of demographic realities of an otherwise unconnected church, it is more often used to refer to an awareness or an activity that connects Christianity internationally. The term also often assumes a spiritual or missional connection across denominational lines, though it is not to be confused with classic ecumenism. Justice Anderson refers to the global church as the church of the third millennium. (Anderson, 585: In the first millennium, the Eastern church was the leader and it was associated with "Christendom;" In the second millennium, the Western church was the leader and was associated with "World Christianity;" In the third millennium, the Southern church will be the leader and it will be associated with "Global Christianity").

Latin American. For the purposes of this paper, this term is used to refer to people who either live or come from countries in South America, Central America, Mexico and the Caribbean. It includes Brazil because of its affinity in geography, Latin-based language and culture with South America.

Latino. This is a more inclusive term used to refer to both Latin Americans and Hispanics. Consequently, it is sometimes used interchangeably with either of these two terms.

Mission(s). In this paper this term is generally used to refer to the church's activity in the world as it accomplishes the purposes of God. It includes world evangelization, sending missionaries to other countries, and to social action in the community. It often relates the mission of the church to *missio dei* (the mission of God). The term in the singular ("mission") is often used by missiologists to refer to all that the church does while the plural ("missions") may refer to all human activities where the church projects a gospel witness beyond itself to a lost world. ([26]R. Porter, "Global Mission and Local Church" *Global Connections Occasional Paper,* (25: 2007), 2; B. Knell, "Who Owns Mission?" *Global Connections Occasional Paper,* (24: 2006), 1; Bob Garrett's note on student's paper, (March 2008).

Missionaries. Though some missiological trends use this term for all who cross some boundary and share the gospel with unbelievers, COMIBAM limits this term to long-term vocational missionaries for the purposes of research and statistics. ("Definiciones e Información Adicional"). While the inclusion of non-professional missionaries and short-term assignments must be part of a twenty-first century strategy for world evangelization, ([28]Escobar, *Tiempo de Misión,* 47), it makes sense that for the purposes of reporting missionary sending statistics, COMIBAM apply this term in its stricter sense. It is less cumbersome in the process of gathering data and it allows for a consistent tracking of the categories. However, some provision needs to be made to track the explosion of those who serve in one through three years terms and those who do projects ranging from one week to one semester, and those whose job-related migration allows them to be virtual missionaries even if they have not been sent by a church or agency. The initial definition of this term by COMIBAM in 1986 is the following, "A missionary is a disciple called by God and sent by Him through the local church, crossing geographical and/ or cultural barriers, in order to communicate the whole gospel either for the establishment of the church or for its holistic growth." (Ruiz, "La Singularidad de Nuestra Misión Transcultural," (Quito, Ecuador: CLADE IV, October 2000) (Accessed on 11 November, 2007; available from http://www.comibam.org/ponencias/CladeIV/ponencia4.htm; Internet).

Visionary Leadership. Visionary leadership has been described in various ways. For the purposes of this paper, visionary leadership is leadership that assesses accurately its present context and is able to lead change that meets the objectives of a group in a way that impacts the future positively.

BIBLIOGRAPHY

"AD2000 and Beyond: A Church for Every People and the Gospel for Every Person by AD 2000; Luis Bush: Biographical Information Sheet." Accessed on 25 March 2008; available from http://www.ad2000.org/staff/luis.htm; Internet.

Anderson, Justice C. *An Evangelical Saga: Baptist and Their Precursors in Latin America.* Xulon Press, 2005.

"Baptists in Latin America and Their Theological Contributions." Accessed on 26 March 2008; available from http://www.encycolpedia.com/doc/1G1-94160932.html; Internet).

Bertuzzi, *Federico A. Internacionalización o Anglonización de la Misión.* Quito,

Ecuador: CLADE IV, Octubre, 2000. Accessed on 11 November, 2007; available from http://www.comibam.org/ponencias/CladeIV/ponencia6.htm; Internet.

Bibliografía Misionera. Accessed on 11 November, 2007; available from www.comibam.org/docs/bibliografia.pdf; Internet.

Bosch, David J. *Transforming Mission: Paradigm Shifts in Theology of Mission.* Maryknoll, New York: Orbis Books, 1991.

Bravo, Jorge C. "La Misión Integral de la Iglesia." 2000-2007, accessed on 28 September, 2007; available from http://www.angelfire.com/pe/jorgebravo/mision.html; Internet.

Catálogo de las Organizaciones Misioneras de Argentina (2006). Accessed on`11 November, 2007; available from http://www.comibam.org/catalogo2006/index.htm; Internet.

Conclusiones: Consideraciones Bíblicas. Quito, Ecuador: CLADE IV, Octubre, 2000.

Accessed on 11 November, 2007; available from http://www.comibam.org/ponencias/CladeIV/index.htm; Internet.

Davies, Pablo. *Las Bases Bíblicas Veterotestamentarias de la Misión Transcultural:*

Misión Integral y Misión Profética. Quito Ecuador: CLADE IV, October 2000. Accessed on 11 November, 2007; available from http://www.combiam.org/ponencias/CladeIV/ponencia1.htm; Internet."Definiciones e Información Adicional." In *Catálogo de Organizaciones Misioneras (2006)*, accessed 11 November, 2007; available from http://www.comibam.org/catalogo2006/Misc/def_es.htm; Internet.

"Departamento de Investigación." Accessed on 13 November, 2007; available from http://www.comibam.org/depart/investigacion/indice.htm; Internet.

"Departamento de Publicaciones." Accessed on 13 November, 2007; available from http://www.comibam.org/depart/public/objectivos.htm; Internet.

"Directorio de COMIBAM." Accessed on 11 November, 2007; available from http://www.comibam.org/equipo.htm; Internet.

Escobar, Samuel. *De la Misión a la Teología*. Buenos Aires: Kairos Ediciones, 1998.

_____. *La Fe Evangélica y las Teologías de la Liberación*. El Paso, TX: Casa Bautista de Publicaciones, 1987.

_____. "Protestantismo Latinoamericano en el Contexto de una Iglesia Global." In Revista electrónica *Espacio de Diálogo*, (Fraternidad Teológica Latinoamericana), 2 (Abril:2005), accessed on 28 September, 2007; available from http://www.cenpromex.org.mx/revista_ftl/ftl/textos/samuel_escobar.html; Internet.

_____. *The New Global Mission: The Gospel from Everywhere to Everyone.* Downers Grove, Illinois: Intervarsity Press, 2003.

_____. *Tiempo de Misión: América Latina y la Misión Cristiana Hoy.* Colombia: Clara Ediciones, 1999.

"Etnia a Etnia…Esta Generación." Accessed on 11 November, 2007; available from http://www.comibam.org/docs/etniaaetnia_boletindeprens_1.pdf; Internet.

Friedman, Thomas L. *The World Is Flat: A Brief History of the Twenty-First Century.* New York: Farrar, Straus and Giroux, 2006.

Gava, Omar. "Consulta de Capacitación Región México (COMIMEX—COMIBAM Internacional)." México: 3-6 July, 2007. Accessed on 11 November, 2007; available from http://www.comibam.org/docs/rcc_consulta_mexico.pdf; Internet.

_____. "Proyecto (Red de Centros de Capacitacion)." February, 2005. Accessed on 11 November, 2007; available from http://www.comibam.org/docs/rcc_description.pdf; Internet.

General Report of the III Ibero-American Missions Congress. Granada, Spain, 13-17 November, 2006. Accessed on 11 November 2007; available from http://www.comibam.org/docs/reporte_comibamIII_es.pdf; Internet.

Gonzalez, J. (2007, March). The challenge to the church at large. In The Latino church: Converting challenges to opportunities. 2007 Rollins Lectures at the Baptist University of the Americas, San Antonio, Texas.

Guder, Darrel L. *Missional Church: A Vision for the Sending of the Church in North America.* Grand Rapids: William B. Eerdmans Publishing Company, 1998.

Informe. Santiago del Estero: Encuentro de la Mesa Coordinadora y Colaboradores 2005, 1 September, 2005. Accessed on 13 November, 2007; available from http://www.comibam.org/docs/rcc_encuentro_st_esteros.pdf; Internet.

"John R. Mott: The Noble Peace Prize 1946; Biography." Accessed on 25 March 2008; available from http://nobelprize.org/nobel_prizes/peace/laureates/1946/mott-bio.html; Internet).

Lausanne 1974: Historical Background. The Lausanne Committee for World Evangelization, 1974, accessed on 28 September, 2007; available from http://www.lausanne.org; Internet.

Lausanne Occasional Paper 2. "The Willowbank Report: Consultation on Gospel andCulture." Lausanne Committee for World Evangelization, 1978, accessed on 28 September, 2007; available from http://www.lausanne.org; Internet.

Lausanne Occasional Paper 21. "Evangelism and Social Responsibility: An Evangelical Commitment." A Joint Publication of the Lausanne Committee for World Evangelization and the World Evangelical Fellowship, 1982, accessed on 28 September, 2007; available from http://www.lausanne.org; Internet.

Lewis, Jonathan. *El Perfil del Misionero Frente un Mundo Turbulento.* San Salvador: II Asamblea Internacional, November 2003. Accessed on 11 November, 2007; available from http://www.comibam.org/ponencias/IIAsamblea/EPM.htm; Internet.

Londoño, Jesús. *Cambios Teológicos en la Fuerza Misionera.* San Salvador: II Asamblea Internacional, November 2003. Accessed on 11 November, 2007; available from http://www.comibam.org/ponencias/IIAsamblea/CTEFM.htm; Internet.

_____. *La Misión de Cristo: Modelo del Pasado, Presente y Futuro.* Madrid, Spain: Cumbre de Liderazgo, November 2002. Accessed on 11 November, 2007; available from http://www.comibam.org/ponencias/cumpliespa/Palabra.htm; Internet.

Los Evangélicos y los Misioneros Ibero-Americanos. Accessed on 13 November, 2007; available from http://www.comibam.org/Estadisworld01/Ibero-America.htm; Internet.

Manual del Congreso. Granada, Spain: III Congreso Ibero-Americano, 13-17 November, 2006. Accessed on 11 November, 2007; available from http://www.comibam.org/docs/manual_es.pdf; Internet.

Matamoros, Allan. *Misioneros Latinos, ¿Quiénes Son? / ¿Dónde Están?* Lima, Peru: Asamblea Internacional de COMIBAM, Noviembre, 2000. Accessed on 11 November, 2007; available from http://www.comibam.org/ponencias/lima/ponencia1.htm; Internet.

Noll, Mark A. *Turning Points: Decisive Moment in the History of Christianity.* Grand Rapids: Baker Academics, 2000.

Jenkins, Philip. *The Next Christendom: The Coming of Global Christianity.* New York: Oxford University Press, 2002.

"Organizaciones Misioneras Argentina [Resumen Numérico: 1996]," in *Catálogo de Organizaciones Misioneras Ibero-Americanas (2006)*, accessed on 11 November, 2007; available from http://www.comibam.org/catalogo2006/esp/consulta-1996/arg/_resum.htm; Internet.

"Organizaciones Misioneras Argentina [Resumen Numérico: 2006]," in *Catálogo de Organizaciones Misioneras Ibero-Americanas (2006)*, accessed on 11 November, 2007; available from http://www.comibam.org/catalogo2006/esp/consulta-2006/arg/_resum.htm; Internet.

"Organizaciones Misioneras de Iberoamérica (2006)," in *Catálogo de Organizaciones Misioneras Ibero-Americanas (2006)*, accessed on 11 November, 2007; available from http://www.comibam.org/catalogo2006/Esp/consulta-2006/Ibe/_agencias.htm; Internet.

Padilla, C. René. "Evangelical Theology in a Latin American Context," accessed on 28 September, 2007; available from http://integral-mission.org/PDF_files/Evangelical_Theology_in_LA_context.pdf; Internet.

_____. "What Is Integral Mission?" In *Integral Mission Newsletter*, 10 March 2006, accessed on 27 September, 2007; available from http://www.integral-mission.org/PDF_files/Rene-What_is_integral_mission.pdf; Internet.

"Países Donde Misioneros Ibero-Americanos Están Trabajando (2006)," in *Catálogo de Organizaciones Misioneras Ibero-Americanas (2006)*, accessed on 11 November, 2007; available from http://www.combiam.org/catalogo2006/Esp/consulta-2006/Ibe/_Campos_res.htm; Internet.

Paredes, Tito. *Las Bases Neotestamentarias de la Misión Transcultural*. Quito, Ecuador: CLADE IV, October 2000. Accessed on 11 November, 2007; available from http://www.comibam.org/ponencias/CladeIV/ponencia5.htm; Internet.

Plou, Dafne Sabanes. "Ecumenical History of Latin America" (from "A History of the Ecumenical Movement," 2004, WCC Publications), accessed on 28 September 2007; available from http://overcomingviolence.org/en/new-and-events/archive/past-annual-foci/2006-latin-america.html; Internet.

"¿Qué Es Comibam?" accessed on 11 November, 2007; available from http://www.comibam.org/queescomi.htm; Internet.

Rodríguez, Jaime & Omar Gava. *Rumbo a la Excelencia en la Capacitación Misionera*. Guatemala: Consulta de Centros de Capacitación Misionera de Centro América (COMCA), 26 September, 2005. Accessed on 11 November, 2007; available from http://www.comibam.org/docs/rcc_consulta_centroamerica.pdf; Internet.

Ruiz, David D. *Cambios Paradigmáticos en el Liderazgo Global de las Misiones.* San Salvador: II Asamblea Internacional, November 2003. Accessed on 11 November, 2007; available from http://www.comibam.org/ponencias/IIAsamblea/CPEE.htm; Internet.

_____. "COMIBAM as a Process Leading to a Congress." Accessed on 11 November, 2007; available from http://www.comibam.org/docs/COMIBAM_process.pdf; Internet.

_____. *Identidad, Visión y Proyección del Movimiento Misionero Ibero-Americano.* Madrid, Spain: Cumbre de Liderazgo, November, 2002. Accessed on 11 November, 2007; available from http://www.comibam.org/ponencias/cumpliespa/identidad.htm; Internet.

_____. *Iglesias Fuertes, Pastores con Visión.* Madrid, Spain: Cumbre de Liderazgo, November, 2002. Accessed on 11 November, 2007; available from http://www.comibam.org/ponencias/lima/ponencia3.htm; Internet.

_____. *La Singularidad de Nuestra Misión Transcultural.* Quito, Ecuador: CLADE IV, October 2000. Accessed on 11 November, 2007; available from http://www.comibam.org/ponencias/CladeIV/ponencia4.htm; Internet.

_____. *Tendencias de la Iglesia y sus Implicaciones en el Movimiento Misionero Ibero-Americano : Amenazas y Desafíos.* Madrid, Spain: Cumbre de Liderazgo, Noviembre, 2002. Access on 11 November, 2007; available from http://www.comibam.org/ponencias/cumpliespa/tendencias.htm; Internet.

"Samuel Escobar, Urbana Speaker: Peruvian Missiologist and Missionary to the US and Spain." Accessed on 26 March 2008; available from http://www.urbana.org/u2003.speakers,samuel.cfm; Internet).

Sanchez, Daniel. *Hispanic Realities Impacting America: Implications for Evangelism and Missions.* Fort Worth: Church Starting Network, 1006.

Scott, Carlos. *El Representante Regional y Su Ministerio.* Madrid, Spain: Cumbre de Liderazgo, Noviembre 2002. Accessed on 11 November, 2007; available from http://www.comibam.org/ponencias/cumpliespa/represenregio.htm; Internet.

_____. "Projections and Challenges for the Ibero-American Mission Movement."

Accessed 11 November, 2007; available from http://www.comibam.org/docs/projectionsandchallenges.pdf; Internet.

Scott, Carlos and Jesus Londoño. "Where Is COMIBAM International Heading?

Strategic Focal Points." Accessed 11 November, 2007; available from http://www.comibam.org/docs/whereiscomibamheading.pdf; Internet.

Scott, Lindy. "Bases Bíblicas de la Misión: Perspectivas Latinoamericanas." (Book Review). In *International Bulletin of Missionary Research* (January, 2000): 42-43.

Smith, Anthony Christopher. "The Essentials of Missiology from the Evangelical Perspective of the Fraternidad Teológica Latinoamericana." Ph. D. diss., Southern Baptist Theological Seminary, 1983.

Strengths and Weaknesses of the Ibero-American Missionary. Granada, Spain: III Ibero-American Missions Congress, 13-17, November, 2006. Accessed on 11 November, 2007; available from http://www.comibam.org/docs/reporte_investigacion_en.pdf; Internet.

The Lausanne Covenant. The Lausanne Committee for World Evangelization, 16-25 July, 1974, accessed on 28 September, 2007; available from http://www.lausanne.org/lausanne-1974/lausanne-1974.html; Internet.

The Manila Manifesto. Lausanne II: International Congress on World Evangelization, Manila Philippines, July, 1989, accessed on 28 September, 2007; available from www.lausanne.org; Internet.

Tinsley, William. *Finding God's Vision: Missions and the New Realities.* Rockwall, TX: Veritas Publishing, 2005.

Tostes, Marcia. *Cuidado Pastoral del Misionero.* Lima, Peru: Asamblea Internacional de COMIBAM, Noviembre, 2000. Accessed on 11 November, 2007; available from http://www.comibam.org/ponencias/lima/ponencia6.htm; Internet.

Yates, Timothy. *Christian Mission in the Twentieth Century.* Cambridge University Press, 1994.

11. HISPANIC/LATINO OPPORTUNITIES AND CHALLENGES FOR SHARING THE LOVE OF JESUS WITH MUSLIMS

Sergio A. Ramos

INTRODUCTION

At the end of the 19th century, Latin Americans made a paradigm shift toward a missionary call and their contributions have increased since then.[1] The Hispanic population has extended rapidly around the world, and today more than 10,000 Latinos are serving in cross-cultural missions.[2] The Hispanic[3] culture has been able to relate with

---

1   Daniel Bianchi http://daniel-bianchi.blogspot.com/search?q=latino+america, 1.
2   COMIBAN International http://comibam.org/docs/haciadondevacomibam.pdf, 1.
3   The Federal Interagency Committee on Education defined Hispanic in 1975 as "a person of Mexican, Puerto Rican, Cuban, Central of South American, or other Spanish culture or origin, regardless of race. The terms *Hispanic* and *Latino* will be use interchangeably.

the Muslim world, which gives Latinos a window of opportunity to bring the gospel to Muslims.

Christians have been commanded to "Go and make disciples of all nations, baptizing them in the name of the Father and of the Son and of the Holy Spirit."[4] Missionaries have been challenged in their approach to engage unreached people at home and abroad. Changes in economy, politics and technology have dramatically shrunk the world.[5] Philip Jenkins, in his book *The Next Christendom, The Coming of Global Christianity*, states, "We are currently living through one of the transforming moments in the history of religion worldwide."[6] The present is a time of great population growth and migration in human history.

Today, according to Jenkins, the largest communities of Christians are no longer found in the United States, but in Latin America, Africa and Asia. Considering that the church in the United States has assumed leadership for reaching unreached people groups all around the world, and taking into account that Latinos are the fastest-growing segment of the population in the country, it would be helpful to mobilize Hispanics in global evangelization.[7]

The purpose of this paper is to understand the continued Latin American participation in missions that could serve as a catalyst to share Jesus' love to Muslims. There is a window of opportunity for the Hispanic community, and it presents different challenges.

---

4   Matthew 28:19, TNIV.
5   Thomas L. Friedman *The World Is Flat: A Brief History of The Twenty-First Century* (New York: Farrar, Straus and Giroux, 2005), 461.
6   Philip Jenkins *The Next Christendom: The Coming of Global Christianity* (New York: Oxford University Press, 2002), 3.
7   K.P. Yohannan *Revolution in World Missions* (G.F.A.: a division of Gospel for Asia), 85.

LATINOS IN GLOBAL MISSIONS

Latin Americans have become one of the fastest-growing missionary movements around the world. Among the pioneer denominations of this movement are Baptists, Methodists and Assemblies of God. They have sent Latino missionaries to Africa, Middle East, Europe and other Latin American countries.[8] It is an interesting fact that the missionary thrust to be obedient to the call did not depend on mega churches or economically powerful churches. Small churches are already thinking globally and sending missionaries to other parts of the world, sending their missionaries even when they are just taking their first steps as a church.[9]

Challenges in Latin America are being addressed by several scholars and ministers in the world. Philip Jenkins book, *The New Faces of Christianity: Believing the Bible in the Global South*, emphasizes that the church in the South will take the lead in transforming Christian faith in the world.[10] The *Unión Bautista Latinoamericana* (Baptist Union of Latin America, UBLA) has focused on how to become more effective in reaching South America and sending its own missionaries to reach the Muslim world. [11] Hispanic Christians in both North and South America are becoming the new army to help bring the gospel to some of the most untouched areas of the world.

In the past, two mission models have been used to minister to Latin America. The first is the "cooperation model," which was led by European and North American churches for the purpose of engaging in mission projects outside their own countries, bringing financial

---

8   Samuel Escobar *Changing Tides: Latin America and World Mission Today* (New York: Orbis Books Press, 2002), 153.
9   [9]Ibid., 153.
10   Philip Jenkins. *The New Faces of Christianity: Believing the Bible in the Global South* (New York: Oxford University Press, 2006), 21.
11   Unión Bautista Latinoamericana http://www.ublaonline.org/saladeoracion.htm.

resources to the poorest places in Latin America.[12] This model has helped in discipleship, training and evangelism. However, this model also raised several issues concerning ownership and independence by the host culture.

The second is the "migratory model" of missions. This one can be seen in the early church at Antioch in the New Testament when Christians had to leave their own countries because of persecution and at the same time bring with them their values and Christian message.[13]

> Most of the expansion of Christianity in the centuries before Constantine took place not as a result of the work of people dedicated solely to this task, but thanks to the ongoing witness of hundreds of millions of merchants, slaves, and Christians condemned to exile, who went about giving witness to Jesus Christ wherever life led them, thereby setting up new communities in places where "professional ministries" had not yet arrived.[14]

The paradigm is clear. Cities like Madrid, Spain, have experienced significant migration growth in the last ten years mostly from Latin American countries. Perhaps, this could result in an expansion of Christianity.

LATINOS AND MUSLIMS:
CULTURAL SIMILARITIES

Culture has been identified as one of the main issues impacting effective leadership in cross-cultural ministry. As people relate cross-culturally

---

12   Samuel Escobar. *Changing Tides: Latin America and World Mission Today* (New York: Orbis Books Press, 2002), 162.
13   Ibid., p.163.
14   Ibid., p. 163.

and understand their mutual differences and similarities, a new culture emerges. A challenge is presented when the missionaries expect others to become like themselves.[15] Gonzalez suggests that missionaries must be adept at cultural adaptation and adjustment. At the same time this task is made easier when the characteristicsof the home culture of the missionary and the host culture where he moves are more similar.

Missionary-sending agencies must look at characteristics and similarities when trying to connect a missionary with a host culture. Hispanics are sending their own missionaries into the mission field. The similarities that Latinos share with the Arab culture make their assimilation into the culture much more effective.

In Latin American countries and some places in the United States like Texas and California, there are historic, linguistic, cultural, and architectural connections with Arabs and people who adhere to Islam. Approximately 7,000 words in Spanish are pronounced almost identically in Arabic. Approximately 21,000 words in Spanish have Arabic roots.[16] The words *camisa* (shirt), *azúcar* (sugar), *pantalón* (pants), and *zapatos* (shoes) are examples of words adopted into the Spanish language because of the Arabic influence. These linguistic similarities may have a minimal impact in the Latino ability to share the gospel with a Muslim; however, they provide a relational bridge between the two cultures.

The Moors[17] also left an indelible impression on the architecture of the area. One of the greatest examples of Muslim architecture can be

---

15   Justo L. Gonzalez. *2007 Rollins Lectures* at the Baptist University of the Americas, San Antonio, Texas.

16   *Diccionario Esencial de la Lengua Española*. México, D.F. Editorial Laurosse, 1994.

17   Moors is a term used to refer to the Muslims that invaded Spain.

found in the great mosque in Cordoba, Spain.[18] These influences have become evident in Spanish architecture both in the Iberian Peninsula and Latin America. It can be seen in church buildings, museums and houses. The influence that Islamic culture has exerted on Spain and Latin America is one that can be seen today. Latinos are in the unique position of taking advantage of these similarities to better share the love of Jesus with the Muslims.

Family bonds and the authority of men are vital aspects in Hispanic and Arab cultures. "Arab society [and Hispanic as well] is built around the extended family system. Individuals feel a strong affiliation with all of their relatives—aunts, uncles, cousins—not just with their immediate family." Generally speaking, the Hispanic male is the head of the household and in charge of bringing home the majority of the family income, while the wife is in charge of home maintenance including child rearing.[19] Allah's apostle said, "Surely! Every one of you is a guardian and responsible for his charges: The Imam (Islamic Cleric) of the people is a guardian and is responsible for his subjects; a woman is the guardian of her husband's home and of his children and is responsible for them."[20]

These two cultures are also very relationship oriented. In Hispanic households it is still common for the typical evening meal to act as a time to sit down and discuss the day's events. When a guest is present, it is common to use the time to linger longer. Arabs also use the evening meals as a way to socialize. "By far the most popular form of entertain-

18 Maria Rosa Menocal. *The Ornament of the World* (London, England, 2002), 59.
19 Margaret K. Nydell. *Understanding Arabs: A Guide for Westerners* (Yarmouth, Maine: Intercultural Press, 2002), 91.
19 Marvin Mayers. *A Look at Latin American Lifestyles,* (International Museum of Cultures Publication 2, 1982), 57.
20 Hadith 9.89.252.

ment in the Arab world is conversation. Arabs enjoy long discussions over a meal or while sharing many cups of coffee."[21]

The importance that Hispanics and Arabs place on their relationships with friends and similarities in their family composition allow Hispanics to enter into the Arab culture and relate to it in an effective manner.

A key characteristic for the assimilation of Hispanics into the Arab culture is physical appearance. Hispanics' hair, eyes, and skin tones allow them to blend well within the Muslim culture. According to Jason Carlisle, the International Mission Board Hispanic Mobilization Representative, Hispanic missionaries are oftentimes accepted more quickly because they more often than not physically resemble people from their host culture.[22]

When Latino missionaries arrive in the Muslim world they may already be accustomed to the life in that cultural setting, since their practices from home are so closely similar. They may be better prepared to meet the challenges and opportunities that go along with living in a Muslim culture. These similarities are not to be interpreted as meaning that it is always an easy task for any Hispanic to go and serve successfully in a Muslim world. Federico A. Bertuzzi, in his book *Latinos en el Mundo Islámico* (*Latinos in the Islamic World*), shares a story of a Hispanic family living among Arabs and explains the challenges faced as they try to evangelize in a different culture. It is not about imposing any obtained or learned method but it is about learning and adapting to

---

21 Margaret K. Nydell, *Understanding Arabs: A guide for Westerner,* (Yarmouth, Maine: Intercultural, 2002), 101. Bob Roberts Jr. in his book *Glocalization: How Followers of Jesus Engage a Flat World,* shares about his visit with Arab friends and how he got to know them better during their meal gatherings that lasted several hours.

22 Brittany Jarvis "Missions Leader: 'No Boundaries, No Obstacles' for Hispanics" http://www.sbcbaptistpress.org/bpnew.asp?ID=6662; Internet.

their customs through strong relationships. This will take time and patience.[23]

Missiologists have suggested that the most effective resources for sharing the love of Jesus with Muslims will be the Latino missionaries. There is a sense of urgency in sharing the gospel with the world. The call to missions requires multicultural teams, with Latino Christians as effective participants in reaching the Muslims for Christ.

SHARING JESUS WITH A MUSLIM

God has commanded us to share the Good News with a lost world. "Brothers and sisters, my heart's desire and prayer to God for the Israelites is that they may be saved. For I can testify about them that they are zealous for God, but their zeal is not based on knowledge."[24] The apostle Paul expressed his broken heart for the lost sheep of Israel. The question is: could this yearning also be felt for Muslims?[25] The challenge for all Christians with a passion to share Christ with Muslims is how to effectively communicate the plan of salvation to a group of people that knows about Jesus, but has deep convictions against His divine nature.

Abraham Sarker, a Christian author raised Muslim, shares four areas that were critical to his salvation and what he considers are the answer for other Muslims as well. "Prayer is an essential tool in leading Muslims to Christ, for it is not we who draw them, but the Holy Spirit Himself who draws them to the truth. The importance and power of

23 Federico A. Bertuzzi *Latinos En El Mundo Islamico.* (Miami Florida: Editorial Unilit, 1990), 13.

24 Romans 10: 1-2, TNIV.

25 Abraham Sarker *Understanding My Muslim People* (Newberg, Oregon: Barclay Press, 2004), 231.

prayer cannot be overstated."[26] God communicates in multiple ways. He revealed Himself to Sarker in a dream, directing him to the scriptures where Sarker was able to learn about Jesus and His salvation. Facilitating God's revelation through prayer is a catalyst of salvation for many Muslims.

Secondly, the importance of the individual personal example is vital when trying to reach Muslims. Sarker says, "I cannot express how powerful it is to a Muslim the example of a Christian committed to serving God."[27] The Bible is clear when it commands believers to be the light of the world, so others may see God in and through his children. The word "Muslim" literally means "one who submits to God." Submitting to God should be the focus and goal of every believer, and "not doing so will leave Muslims disinterested and disenchanted," commented Sarker.[28]

The next important factor in sharing Jesus Christ as Savior to Muslims is expressing love. "I can also relate to the effectiveness of Christian love in my own life. Not only did believers share the message of the gospel with me, but their lives as well. It is through this God-given love that we should share the good news of the gospel."[29]

Finally, it is about the importance of communicating the message of the gospel through actions and lifestyle. It is the believer's testimony. "Share with your Muslim friend not only the message of the gospel and how he or she can find assurance of salvation in Christ, but report what God has done personally in your own life."[30]

---

26 Ibid., 232.
27 Abraham Sarker *Understanding My Muslim People* (Newberg, Oregon: Barclay Press, 2004), 234.
28 Ibid., 235.
29 Ibid., 237.
30 Ibid., 238.

The development of relationship between Latinos and Muslims needs a model, the same one Jesus Christ himself established for world evangelism at the very beginning of Christian history.[31] A Guatemalan missionary at a COMIBAM (*Cooperación Misionera Ibero-Americana*) conference used his platform to serve. As an engineer, he had contributed to providing a much needed resource within that country, and he had been commended for his work by the government.[32] The missionary shared how he and his family were able to develop friendships and through this platform, and in time, they had the opportunity to share the gospel with their Muslim friends.

Today ministries like WorldconneX[33] are helping churches and individuals in similar ways as that of the Guatemalan missionary: to get Christian ambassadors connected with the individual unique place in the world where God is at work. With their help, both churches and individuals can discover their distinctive mission calling and then be connected with the right people, the right know-how, and the best resources needed to fulfill their calling. This type of innovative example can be used by Hispanics share a passion for utilizing their gifts and talents to minister to Muslims throughout the world.

The Advance of Islam

The Christian community must understand that Muslims want to share their faith with other people too. Many Muslims have come to the Americas with the purpose of sharing Islam and converting the people.[34] Studies are beginning to show that Islam is one of the fastest-

---

31   Acts 1:8
32   Luis Bush, COMIBAM97: "An assessment of the Lain America Mission Movement," Internet; http://www.ad2000.org/re7121ar6.htm.
33   WorldconneX is a ministry started by the Baptist General Convention of Texas. www.worldconnex.org
34   Wendy Murray Zoba. *Are Christians prepared for Muslims in the Mainstream*, Internet: Christianity Today, April, 3, 2000 vol. 44, Nov. 4.

growing religions in the world. Islam began among the desert tribes of Arabia in A.D. 622, but the religion spread rapidly after its inception. Islamic religion continues to grow in global influence and significance.[35] Patrick Johnstone points out in his book, *The Church Is Bigger than You Think*, that the continuous growth in the global influence of Islam needs to be examined more thoroughly.[36]

Daniel Bianchi explains why Latinos need to be involved in global missions. There is a movement among the Hispanic community and a sense of urgency to partner in order to fulfill the Great Commission. He says Latinos need to be involved in missions, especially to the Muslim community because: (1) The Great Commission is for the whole church and being on mission with God is His purpose, calling and desire. (2) Latinos' willingness to adapt makes them particularly suited for mission settings. You will find Latinos working and thriving in all kinds of contexts, situations and ministries. They are sensitive to cultures and are very good interacting with people and adapting to the country in which they are serving. (3) They are creative and are willing to learn. (4) Latinos understand the spiritual dimension of the work. Latinos are willing to discern and engage in the spiritual warfare. Latino Christians serving in their home countries have often experienced first-hand this type of spiritual resistance. (5) They value relationship and community. (6) They are passionate and willing to go. Coming from countries with no colonial or imperial past history, they are not looked upon with prejudices. (7) They see mission holistically. Bianchi believes that Latino community is committed to pursue the mission field with love and has the willingness to partner with other believers to share the Gospel to Muslim communities around the world.[37]

---

35 Abraham Sarker. *Understanding My Muslim People.* (Newberg, Oregon: Barclay Press, 2004), 33.
36 Johnstone, 111.
37 Daniel Bianchi. *Why Us? Latin's in Global Missions* The Insider issue: #7 November 2007. Internet; www.worldconnex.org.

Overcoming Obstacles

In the western world, Muslims are given freedom to practice their religion and to build their Islamic centers by establishing mosques. However, the same privileges are not given to Christians in most Muslim countries.[38] The Muslim community is making a great effort to reach Americans with the Islam faith, in particular the Hispanic and African-American communities. Islam offers the acceptance that most Hispanics look for, but cannot find in the American society.

> Latinos today find that the Church does not adequately defend the Latino-American struggle for equality. Alienations from the Christian American society and poor social and economic conditions may deter Latinos from Christianity—the religion of establishment that has not met their needs.[39]

The Islamic community has aggressively gathered printed material in Spanish to meet the needs of the Latino community. Several organizations have begun strategic translation of materials. Among them are the *Asociación Latina de Musulmanes en las Américas*, the Latino America Dawa Organization of New York, and *Centro Islámico de Traducción e Información*.[40] This Islamic effort presents a bigger challenge for Hispanic Christians to reach Hispanic Muslims. Latino Muslims are beginning to make an impact in the American culture.

By contrast, Christian materials in Spanish are limited. It may be that some Christian publishers in the United States see little or no financial motivation to produce material for what some still consider a minor-

---

38   William Wagner. *How Islam Plans to Change the World.* (Grand Rapids, MI: Kregel Publications, 2004), 72.

39   Lisa Viscidi *Latino Muslims a Growing Presence in America,* Washington Report on Middle East Affairs, Internet http://ispanicmuslims.com.

40   Nicole Ballivan Los Musulmanes, the Spanish Ummah, Internet: http://hispan-icmuslims.com/articles/spaishummah.html

ity group. Still, there are agencies willing to invest in the kingdom by looking beyond the business aspect of publishing much needed resources. Various Southern Baptist agencies have established Spanish departments to address some of these issues: The International Mission Board, the North American Mission Board, Baptistway Press, LifeWay and *Casa Bautista De Publicaciones,* among others.[41]

There are obstacles when it comes to the evangelization of Muslims. Dr. Bill Wagner provides a helpful list of factors leading to a clear comprehension of the similarities among Christians and Muslims: (1) Both have well-defined philosophies as well as fully thought-out methodologies. (2) Both see their faith as a worldwide faith, although their areas of strength are localized. (3) Both see the source of their communion as issuing from their Holy Book, which gives support to their position. (4) Both have mission organizations that have as their main purpose the furtherance of their faith. (5) Both see conversion to their belief as a positive aspect of their actions. (6) Both see the actions of the other as satanic and have some fear of the other's successes. (7) Both Christianity and Islam are "fractured religions," which have many different expressions and theologies. This plurality carries over to mission and *Da'wah.* (8) Both are aware of the paradigm shift taking place worldwide and feel there is a spiritual vacuum that they can fill. (9) Both see Eastern Europe as fertile fields for expansion. (10) Both extend a call for people to enter into a broad community of believers, Christians into the kingdom of God and Muslims into *ummah.*[42]

---

41 www.hispanos.imb.org; www.nameenenspanol.net; www.lifeway.com; www.bpnews.net.
42 William Wagner *How Islam Plans to Change the World* (Grand Rapids, MI: Kregel Publications, 2004), 45. *Da'wah* = "Call or invitation" summoning others to heed the call of God to Islam; propagation of their faith. *Ummah* = "The community of all those who affirm Islam."

Islamic scholars are taking advantage of America's openness and they are convinced that the time has come for the expansion of Islam. They give three reasons for their assumption:

> (1) More and more people either reject or refuse to believe in God. The world has not found true happiness. Because of this, the world is more receptive than ever before. People still have an emptiness that can only be filled with Islam.

> (2) The world today is rational and open. Once the truth in Islam is heard, all will surely accept it.

> (3) In this age, many people are going back to mankind's true nature. This is at least a right direction on the path of life. People's desire to harmonize nature and mankind with God will actually bring them to Islam.[43]

These reasons are more than just an obstacle to the Latino community. They are indications of urgency.

The key factor is prayer. The need is present and clearer than ever before. History has proven over the years that prayer changes lives. Prayer is essential when sending missionaries overseas. Latino churches need to wake up to the reality that God has chosen them as a people group with a purpose—to share the Good News with the Muslim world.

A prayer strategy starts with mobilizing churches to pray for those individuals whom God will raise from His body (church) to go into missions. "There is nothing better than to give a good foundation to the growing Latino missionary movement." [44]

---

43   Ibid., 46.
44   Federico A. Bertuzzi. *Operación Mundo.* (Bogota, Colombia: Centro e Literatura Cristiana, 1995), 12.

Challenges and Opportunities
for Hispanics

The progress of Islam throughout South America clearly indicates that Latinos have a distinct advantage in ministering in the Arab world. Muslims have already realized that the similarities between the two cultures are the platform for great opportunities of mission work in the Latino community. If the Hispanic community takes action to mobilize their churches to be on mission by preparing and equipping missionaries, and becoming prayer warriors, they can become an unstoppable force in the task of global evangelism.

Latin America has a long history of social issues, corruption, environmental pollution and terrorism.[45] In some cases, it is because of this suffering that the evangelical church has experienced such a substantial growth. For example, El Salvador, a country in Central America, endured a civil war for over 12 years.

> The brutality, the destruction and the floods of refugees unsettled much of the continent. Yet few realize how fast evangelicals multiplied during the desperate years of war. In 1965, Evangelicals were only 2.5% of the population, but by 1990 they had become almost 20%.[46]

Argentina and Britain in 1982 became involved in a war for the control of the *Islas Malvinas*. At the time *Malvinas* was ruled by a dictator named Galtieri, and after the war, it became a democracy and open religious expression was allowed. The results are vital as evangelical

---

45 Kenneth D. MacHarg. *From Rio to the Rio Grande: Challenges and Opportunities in Latin America* (Bogota, Colombia: Global Village Press, 2007), 11.
46 Patrick Johnstone. *The Church is Bigger Than You Think.* (Pasadena, California: Christian Focus Publications, 1998), 119.

Christianity went from 2% to approximately 12% in the years immediately afterward.[47]

Philip Jenkins, in his book *The Next Christendom: The Coming of Global Christianity,* says that Protestantism is on the rise in all of Latin America. Protestants or evangélicos are the strongest in Guatemala and Chile, in each case representing about one-quarter of the whole. Brazil alone has perhaps 20 to 25 million Protestant believers. If it were a separate country, then the most Protestant region of Latin America would be the U.S. territory of Puerto Rico, where the numbers stand at around 35 percent. These proportions are so important because Protestants also tend to be more religiously committed, more likely to be active churchgoers, than most of their nominally Catholic neighbors.[48]

The church in Latin and South America has shared the same experience of the primitive church: power and growth as a result of persecution and struggle. Christians will enter the mission field confidently knowing that persecution and struggle will only translate into power and growth. Interestingly enough, persecution and struggle also becomes a way for Christians to identify with Muslims, a religious group with a similar experience throughout history.

CONCLUSION

Latinos have a tremendous job to fulfill. Hispanic churches have the talent, capacity, knowledge and passion to share the gospel with the Muslim World. The historic and cultural ties of Muslim culture to Latin America and Spain have a strong influence that Latinos can utilize to become one of the driving forces in missions today. Today,

47   Ibid., 120.
48   Philip Jenkins. *The Next Christendom: The Coming of Global Christianity,* (New York: Oxford University press, 2002), 61.

Hispanics are represented by migration on every continent of the world. With most of the world's Christians residing in Latin America and other developing countries, it is easy to see that the next major missionary movement could very well begin in Latin America, if it has not already started.

Muslim and Hispanic commonalities should compel Hispanics to take a leap of faith and embrace this window of opportunity to share Jesus with the Muslim culture. There is no way to tell how long this window will be available.

It must be remembered that Muslims perhaps feel the same concern as Christians about their religion and values. They are working with an agenda to change the world with their convictions and practices. The number of Hispanics converting to Islam is evidence that this is already happening. It is an exciting challenge for the Hispanic community, but at the same time a big responsibility. Hispanics are experiencing global missions and are rising up to be one of the major missionary sending groups. Hispanics understand the vision, which is resulting in mobilization. There is room for other people groups to come on board and become encouragers and supporters, and to find their roles as a part of this missionary movement.

BIBLIOGRAPHY

Bertuzzi, Federico A. *Latinos En El Mundo Islamico.* Miami, Florida: Editorial Unilit, 1990.

_____. *Operación Mundo.* Bogota, Colombia: Centro e Literatura Cristiana, 1995.

Crossley, John. *Explaining The Gospel To Muslims.* London: United Society For Christian Literature Lutterworth Press, 1959.

Diccionario Esencial de la Lengua Española. México, D.F.: Editorial Laurosse, 1994.

Escobar, Samuel. *Changing Tides: Latin American & World Mission Today*. New York: Orbis Books, 2002.

Friedman, Thomas L. *The World Is Flat: A Brief History of The Twenty-First Century*. New York: Farrar, Straus and Giroux, 2005.

Garcia, Ismael. *Dignidad: Ethics Through Hispanic Eyes*. Nashville: Abingdon Press, 1997.

Gonzalez, J. (2007, March). The challenge to the church at large. In The Latino church: Converting challenges to opportunities. 2007 Rollins Lectures at the Baptist University of the Americas, San Antonio, Texas.

Jenkins, Philip. *The New Faces of Christianity: Believing the Bible in the Global South*. Oxford, London: Oxford University Press, 2006.

_____. *The Next Christendom: The Coming of Global Christianity*. Oxford, London: Oxford University Press, 2002.

Johnstone, Patrick. *The Church is Bigger Than You Think*. Pasadena, California: Christian Focus Publications, 1998.

MacHarg, Kenneth D. *From Rio to the Rio Grande: Challenges and Opportunities in Latin America*. Bogota, Colombia: Global Village Press, 2007.

Mayers, Marvin K. *A Look at Latin America Lifestyles*. International Museum of Cultures Publication 2, 1982.

Menocal, Maria Rosa. *Ornament of the World*. Boston: Little Brown and Company, 2002.

Nydell, Margaret K. *Understanding Arabs: A Guide for Westerners*. Yarmouth, Maine: Intercultural Press, 2002.

Sarker, Abraham. *Understanding My Muslim People*. Newberg, Oregon: Barclay Press, 2004.

Spencer, Robert. *Islam Unveiled: Disturbing Questions About The World's Fastest-Growing Faith*. San Francisco: Encounter Books, 2002.

Wagner, William. *How Islam Plans to Change the World*. Grand Rapids: Kregel Publications, 2004.

Yohannan, K.P. *Revolution in World Mission*. G.F.A.: A division of Gospel for Asia Press, 2004.

Zoba, Wendy M. "Are Christians prepared for Muslims in the Mainstream?" Internet: Christianity Today, April, 3, 2000 vol. 44, Nov. 4.

Internet

Alberto Reyes available from http://pandulce.typepad.com/pan_dulce/2007/10/
connecting-wi-1.html, Internet.

Brittany Jarvis "Mission leader: 'no boundaries, no obstacles' for Hispanic"
available from http://www.sbcbaptistpress.org/bpnew.asp?ID=6662;
Internet.

COMIBAM International available from http://www.comibam.org/queescomi.
htm, Internet.

Daniel Bianchi available from http://daniel-bianchi.blogspot.com/
search?q=latino+america, Internet.

Daniel Bianchi "Why Hispanics?" available from http://www.worldconnex.
org, The Insider Issue 7, November 2007, Internet.

Lisa Viscidi "Latino Muslims a Growing Presence in America", Washington
Report on Middle East Affairs, Available from http://ispanicmuslims.
com, Internet.

Luis Bush COMIBAN 97: An assessment of the Latin American Mission
Movement, available from http://www.ad2000.org/re71216.htm,
Internet.

Nicole Ballivan "Los Musulmanes, the Spanish Ummah", Available from http://
hispanicmuslims.con/articles/spaishummah.html, Internet.

Union Bautista Latinoamericana available from http://www.ublaonline.org/
saladeoracion.htm, Internet.

12. MINORITY GROUPS IN CHINA: CAN HAN CHRISTIANS REACH THEM?

Meg Crossman

Note: In an academic setting such as EMS it would be usual to foot-note and document sources. However, due to the sensitive nature of the subject and concern about danger to the workers, sources have been willing to disclose information only with a pledge of anonymity. Almost all the information has come from reliable informants, flu-ent in Mandarin and/or other languages, who have well-established, on-the-ground credentials. They are known and respected by people from the house churches.

EXAMINING THE PROBLEM

Within the borders of the nation of China there are enormous numbers of people belonging to house churches from the Han ethnic majority. There are also within China more than 130 million people belonging to a vast array of groups that represent a myriad of languages and cultures. How can these distinctive groups be reached? Must they be brought to Christ by those outside the country or is there a role for the Han Chinese Christians in winning them to the Lord?

While many people knew that there were ethnic minority groups in Mainland China, it was not until the book *Operation China* was published that the larger picture became clearer. That book awakened the Christian world by profiling nearly 500 distinct people groups. It became apparent that reaching them would be no small undertaking.

Many minorities fear and hate the Han Chinese, in ways analogous to the Native American tribes hating and fearing Europeans during the 18th and 19th centuries. Over the centuries, these tribes and peoples have been forced into the hills and the wild and dangerous border regions. Successive dynasties and rulers of China have pursued and persecuted them. Han Chinese communities have been "imported" to their areas to try to "assimilate" the inhabitants.

With such a history, would it be possible for the Han Chinese church to make any inroads in reaching these distinct peoples?

HISTORY OF THE HAN HOUSE CHURCH MOVEMENT

In the 19th Century, many well-known ministries worked to win Chinese people to Christ. There was definite fruit from this kind of work. The Boxer Rebellion itself (which particularly targeted believers and missionaries) was a testimony to the obvious fruitfulness of their work. The presence of both missionaries and believers was perceived as a threat because of Chinese leaving the "old ways."

In 1949, the Communists prevailed and within a short time, any remaining missionaries were expelled, accused of being spies for foreign powers. All visible expressions of the church were removed. Buildings were turned into gymnasiums, soldiers' barracks, even stables. Bibles were destroyed or confiscated. Publishing houses were closed. Possession of any kind of Christian literature was made illegal.

With all these support systems gone, the world wondered if any expression of the Kingdom of God could survive. Information from inside China was restricted. Yet, all over the world prayer went up for those who would still be faithful to the Lord.

Inside China, tiny fellowships secretly formed, mostly of elderly women. They continued to gather, at great risk to themselves, and pray. This was largely a rural movement. However, living under Communist tyranny left a greater and greater void in people's lives. Slowly, cautiously believers began to share the reality of Jesus with others.

In the 1970's, a new boldness arose. Villagers who had come to know the Lord went to the next village and the next with the Good News, which was at last received as truly good news. Signs and wonders often accompanied the preaching of the word. The Kingdom was extended to many places throughout the Han culture. The explosive and exponential growth of the Chinese church has been well documented, so it need not be re-discussed here.

Communist leaders were threatened by these audacious actions and tried to stamp out the movement wherever they could. They assailed the house church gatherings in every way possible. Many of these believers, especially evangelists and pastors, were imprisoned, tortured and killed, but suffering only settled the determination of the church to stand firm.

Reaching the minorities

The Han church had had a desire to reach minorities as early as the 1920's when the *Back to Jerusalem* movement was only embryonic. Han Christians, who lived near the borders of the minorities, such as those in Yunnan Province, often had some contact with them and attempts were made to reach them. The Back to Jerusalem vision clearly intended that Chinese Christians not only reach other countries, but also reach the *ethne* within their own borders.

In the 1980's, various networks of house churches began to consider how, in a more focused way, they might reach minorities with the gospel. Since the government restricted access to minority areas (probably to limit awareness of how badly they were still being treated), there were many difficulties.

Situation of the Unreached Minorities in China

Some of the situations faced by these ethnic minorities—Yi, Miao, Uygher, Tibetans-—go back thousands of years. Others are more immediate. Early on they were pushed out of their lands into extremely remote and inaccessible areas. Not only did they endure hatred and attack, but in some cases there were actual attempts at genocide: destruction of whole villages, even the most brutal killing of babies and children.

Minorities are not allowed to teach in their own languages. Most have no access to media—newspapers, books, etc.—in their own tongues, if those languages are even written. Many groups are persecuted and despised. Most are very poor and little is done by officials to improve their situation.

In the light of this picture, the question must be, "How will the witness of the Han Christian church be received by the minorities? Will the Han be able to win them?"

CASE STUDIES OF THE HAN CHRISTIAN MOVEMENT AMONG THE MINORITIES

Case Study One

If there was any group that would be resistant to the witness of Han believers, it would be Tibetans. In spite of that, in recent years there has been some progress. Scripture teaches that "Love covers a multitude of sins." When Han Christians come with humility and love to *serve* Tibetans instead of oppressing them, there have been small openings. One evangelist, when he enters a Tibetan village, asks to see the leader. He bows down to the ground, takes the leader's feet in his hands and asks his forgiveness for all the wrongs done by the Chinese against them. In some cases, this makes a way for him to share the gospel and his ministry has produced fruit.

When a Christian operates in such an opposite spirit, something happens. Because this is *so* different from the way they have always been treated, it touches hearts. This makes way for the Spirit of God to move.

Case Study Two

One 40-year-old house church evangelist had been working in Gansu Province with powerful results. He'd seen many Han people come to the Lord but was concerned that there was no response among the Tibetans whom he wanted to reach. He was so discouraged he decided to go home, but he didn't even have enough money for train tickets for his family.

The man complained to God about his situation and wondered if he had missed God's call. Suddenly the Holy Spirit spoke to him and told him to start a business. He had no idea how to do that with almost no money. The Lord showed him that all he needed was to buy a pair of scissors and a stool. He began to cut people's hair. This provided a small income for the evangelist and his family. As he cut their hair, it gave him a natural occasion to speak and share with each of his customers. The evangelist now oversees two small Tibetan house churches as a product of this God-given strategy.

Case Study Three

A small team of Han evangelists wanted to reach a minority group but they didn't have jobs that gave them a reason to be there. This was unusual because everyone else wanted to get out of that impoverished area, but they wanted to get in!

They were forced to go home and obtain credentials in order to secure jobs. A major need was for school teachers. No teachers were interested in living there. The Christians studied for two years to gain the necessary qualifications. The authorities in the minority area were delighted to welcome these new teachers. As a result of the Han Christians' love and dedication, three whole villages are now confessing Christian!

Cast Study Four

Many house church evangelists come from rural farming backgrounds. The Lord showed them how to use what they knew. They decided to use their farming skills. They'd offer to plow people's fields if they could share the gospel. They lived in barns, and took the lowest positions.

In one day, a Christian worker plowed 12 acres in a place where the local people only plowed 3 or 4. The people were so impressed they came to his barn at night. He shared the gospel and most of the people became Christian.

Case Study Five

Especially among Muslims, openness often follows miracles done in the name of Jesus. In one area through prayer a Grandmother, a Uygur Muslim, was raised from the dead at her own funeral. She sat up and began telling everyone to believe in Jesus. It's hard to say "No" to your own grandmother, and many of the family came to the Lord!

Case Study Six

Two teenage Christian girls, 17 and 18 years old, from Anhui province were sent by God to reach a Tibetan Buddhist group in western China. As they tried to preach the gospel, they had boiling water thrown on them. They were forced to stay because they had no money to pay for their return. They were desperate for a place to live and they were very hungry. It was bitterly cold. The girls heard about some caves outside the town which local people considered haunted. This seemed to be their only option. They moved into one and slept there, huddled together for warmth.

When they woke up, they found mushrooms growing at the mouth of the cave. They ate them and went back into the town to share gospel. They were beaten and punished in terrible ways, but they persisted.

For 9 months, the mushrooms continued to sustain the two girls. They fixed them in every imaginable way—boiled, fried, grilled. (They got very tired of eating mushrooms, but they had nothing else.) At last there were one or two breakthroughs in reaching the Buddhists. The hostility had lessened enough for the older girl to get a paying job washing dishes in town. The very day her job began, the mushrooms stopped growing outside the entrance to the cave!

Now about 800 have come to the Lord. They are holding Bible training in the once feared caves and are preparing new believers to reach others.

Case Study Seven

A Han Chinese man whose family had escaped from the mainland spent his life working for Bank of America. Upon retirement, his great desire was to spend his remaining years reaching his people. He worked in Yunan but could not find an entry to any people group until a youth ministry prayed for a tribal leader who was losing his sight. When their chief was healed, most of his people turned to the Lord.

The returned banker began to serve in this people group and his age, among other things, opened doors for him. While there, he met a disabled man who had taught himself to use a computer. The disabled man wanted to help other disabled people to do the same. They needed computer equipment, even if it was older.

The banker went to his church in the States but they turned him down. He went to his former bank and they were ready to help him. Now he can share the gospel delightedly as well as helping those with great needs.

Continuing Work

By one count there are at least 350 evangelists sharing the gospel among a total of 107 different unreached tribes and ethnic groups. The first church ever has been established among the Monpa people, a spiritually-dark Buddhist group living in Tibet and north India. 80 Asian evangelists are working among tribes in the Himalayas (Tibet, Nepal, India and Bhutan), and in the tribal areas of Vietnam. Many of them labor in some of the most isolated areas on earth.

Problems and Progress

The Han have very little specific training as to *how* to reach minorities yet the believers are inventive as well as practical. They saw their lack and now have created training options that prepare their workers to be more effective. Some Muslim background believers have come to give them training on how to reach Muslims. This same style of training occurs when former Buddhist monks from within China offer the house churches the kind of focused training they need.

Generally speaking, most of the workers have *not* learned the languages of the minority groups. Workers stay within the national languages when they come. Once a small group develops, the new leaders from that group can use their own language. Since the Han workers are limited in this way, it often allows the national believers to step into leadership more rapidly.

One house church network spent a large amount of money to send their people to a Minorities Institute to learn minority languages. They found it was basically a waste of money. Now they have discontinued this practice.

In myriad different ways, God has shown the house churches how to reach these ethnic peoples. Still that does not mean that Han workers do not sometimes become discouraged when there is a negligible or slow response. Many have gone home. Others came for a time, left, and then returned. The house churches have seen the whole spectrum of response among their workers, just as the West still does.

Of 400 minority groups who are considered *unreached* in China, an estimated 250 are still without any witness. The work is only starting, but it *is* starting. An exciting development is that house churches are now training minorities to reach other minorities, which might become a most effective approach. Even though it seems slow, there is work being done and there is progress.

Translation Problems

One problem is the translation of the Scriptures. Of the almost 500 ethnic groups in China, only 18 even have an orthography from which to start. Some translation ministries are working on this problem but it is very slow. They must develop a script, teach that to the people, translate the Scriptures, print them and teach the people to read. It a massive project, especially in China where the government is exceedingly hostile to any work of this kind.

There are Scriptures in some languages but most groups are years away from possessing the entire word of God in their mother tongue.

The Jesus Film has been tremendously helpful but it is only available in the languages of the larger groups. In some cases there has been limited access to these languages, even when the film is produced. In certain situations, perhaps only 10% of the group can understand the language in which it is available

The complexity of these situations may be seen in the Yi in southwest China. Among this people there are nearly 100 distinct linguistic groups. The Miao include 60 or 70 distinct language variations. There is good work being done but there is much, much more to do.

Other Contributions

Audio gospel recordings are being used effectively. People truly appreciate hearing anything in their own language! These have been useful and valuable among a variety of language groups, although many need to be updated.

Short wave radio, as well as the larger and more well-known radio ministries, have had great impact. For example, a Tibetan broadcast is generated from India. All of these contributions are making a difference.

Outside Workers

God is calling many of His servants from all over the world reach minorities. He's using outsiders like Brazilians, Costa Ricans, and Guatemalans to mention just a few. They are very tough; they'll walk for miles and live in difficult circumstances without complaint. These brothers and sisters are invaluable!

Contextualization is very central and some are learning important lessons by doing it. The great need is to develop groups who worship and teach in their own language and culture. In some cases the minority groups themselves contextualize once they receive the message. There are mixed reports on this—some good, some unfortunate.

Earthquake Crisis

Han Christians responded immediately to the recent earthquake crisis in Szechuan province—at least 70,000 dead and more than 5 million homeless—as Christian workers poured in from all parts of the nation. They took in the gospel, but they also took in relief supplies of many kinds. Enough suitable housing is not available, and particularly in the mountains, there are real concerns about people surviving the winter. Sometimes this allowed for partnerships between Han Christians and Western believers. One outside believer had established a company within China that made temporary housing. When the earthquake hit, his equipment was ready to go and the church was ready to distribute it.

As so often happens with a major catastrophe, most of the aid goes to the cities, and the villages are left unattended. Many roads (even those which are precipitous) are blocked. Soldiers are guarding them, preventing access. Only the bravest find ways get in to the Qiang and other tribal groups.

For those who do, the Lord has unlocked significant doors for their courageous witness. In some cases, photographs have come out to document whole villages surrendering to the Lord. In other cases, minority groups have been displaced to locations where new contact is possible.

Szechuan's people have gotten somewhat beyond the physical devastation, but the emotional trauma is severe. Many people sit and stare, unable to so much as begin the work of rebuilding. Several towns will never be re-established. By government decree, they will remain as virtual ghost towns, surround by barbed wire. With no jobs, few if any resources, and broken people—the winter season may produce even more destruction and death. The counseling, prayer and love Christians can give are priceless.

Partnerships

How can the West extend their partnerships with the workers in China? As trite as it sounds, the first and most significant contribution will be through serious intercessory prayer. Tibet is one place where prayer and fasting are critical if we are to see significant breakthroughs.

In one case, 50 Han evangelists went in to Tibet. Some were afflicted with peculiar diseases; some had breakdowns; some died. Within a short time, not one was left sharing the gospel. This is one of the most significant areas in which the rest of the world can and must support the work of their brothers and sisters.

Prayers from around the world sustained the believers during the dark days after 1949. Though Chinese did not know about those prayers, the Lord answered them. The same concentrated prayer is needed to continue the work of God in reaching the lesser known people of China.

Resourcing and supporting radio, film, audio, and translation ministries are excellent ways to shore up all the work. Backing and encouraging the Han, as well as others who go to these minorities, will be productive. However, overall the need will always be prayer, prayer, prayer.

Keys for the Han

Where there have been breakthroughs, the keys have been those experienced in great movements down through the centuries: humility, meekness, and the ability to hear God's voice. When believers respond in obedience once they hear His voice, the Lord will be glorified and people will be reached. However unadorned and down-to-earth they may seem, these crucial factors have made Han believers effective. In spite of being simple rural people with little education, they have answered the question, "Yes! Even the Han church is capable of reaching the minorities."

13. CAN EVANGELICALS IMAGINE AN ALTERNATIVE FUTURE? OPPORTUNITIES AND CONSTRAINTS OF AN INDIGENOUS AFRICAN DEVELOPMENT IN THE SHADOW OF THE WEST

Joel Matthews

ABSTRACT

I will argue in this paper that the failure to find solutions to poverty in the underdeveloped world in general, and in Africa in particular, is predicated on hegemonic nature of western success and the failure of the Church, most notably the Evangelical Church, to find solutions that are unique to the social and spiritual context of the poor.

The success of development in the West has been so spectacular that it has been almost impossible for non-western people to imagine an alternative– akin to humming one tune while the radio is playing another. It is even more difficult to imagine an alternative when the spectacularly successful development, which is based on a secular model of human nature and the world, has claimed universality.

I argue that most of the current thinking regarding development planning in the majority world can fit under the philosophical antecedents of two key European Enlightenment thinkers, Voltaire and Rousseau, and this has been the model for evangelical development initiatives originating in the West as well.

The Church as a universal institution is quite possibly the one organization that is able to offer unique solutions, if local churches are able to free themselves from the well-worn path of western development ideology. Exactly how western Christians can facilitate this process is not immediately evident. It does seem clear however that the role of western oriented missions and churches should be one of support rather than implementation as we try to imagine, along with our majority world partners, a better alternative.

Western Universalizing Attempts to Address Global Poverty

This paper will present a convergence of themes that are increasingly important to Christians from developing countries that are seeking to address chronic poverty and underdevelopment while re-making missions according to their understanding of the world. One of the major challenges facing majority world missions today is how to address homegrown poverty in a way that is sustainable, and yet reflects the values and modalities that are true to indigenous ways of thinking[1].

---

1   The term "majority world" is used here as a substitute for other terms such as "third world," "developing nations," "underdeveloped nations," and "non-western

The prominent development economist William Easterly has argued in *The White Man's Burden* (2006) that after expending more than two trillion dollars in the last fifty years, poverty in the developing world has not diminished. In fact, many development critics have argued that interventions have exacerbated poverty in developing economies. For every skeptic like Easterly, there is at least one optimist. One of the most vocal is the prominent economist and author of the U.N. Millennium Development Goals, Jeffrey Sacs, who has argued in *The End of Poverty* (2005), that the West has not spent nearly enough, and if we redouble our efforts, the end of poverty is in our grasp.

These two arguments leave us with only two apparent choices, either to greatly increase aid to underdeveloped economies, or to reduce aid and promote a good business climate by funding entrepreneurial approaches to addressing poverty. While both approaches are good ideas in and of themselves, I don't believe that either addresses the heart of the problem of poverty in the non-western world. These two apparently opposite approaches have one significant thing in common; they are both responses that are driven from the West.

Should Christians simply support secular development initiatives, or does the Church have what it takes to formulate a unique response? How can western mission efforts, particularly those from an evangelical tradition, encourage the Church in Africa to devise an alternate development based on African values?

---

nations"; the rationale being that this designation appears more descriptive and less value laden.

WORLD MISSIONS ADDRESSING
POVERTY

J. S. Mbiti began a philosophically oriented conversation between traditional African thought and Christianity in the 1960's (Mbiti 1969), but
this discussion never gained much of a hearing in evangelical Churches
in Africa. Whereas some secular development thinkers, particularly
those from a Marxian political perspective, have criticized western
models of development, the essentially western nature of development
discussions has yet to be challenged by evangelical Christian missions[2].
This failure has been reflected in majority world mission initiatives that
have essentially followed in the footsteps of the western tradition. This
may have been a non-issue *if* western oriented development initiatives
had worked in the non-western world; but they most emphatically have
not worked, and the poor are now poorer than ever.

Development initiatives come bundled with the history and values of
the western nations from which the concepts originate. Indeed, some
conservative western development analysts have equated current approaches to development so closely with western values that they are
virtually inseparable[3]. Thus it becomes increasingly difficult to imagine
another strategy.

Poverty alleviation is no stranger to Christian missions. Indeed some
of the earliest mission activities have been directed toward this aim. As
ministry to the poor has evolved throughout the generations, western

---

2   Whereas some Catholic groups and liberal mainline protestant denominations
    have criticized the hegemonic nature of North/South power relations, much of
    American evangelicalism has maintained strong connections to conservative
    Republican politics, which has tended to support existing business-oriented
    structures.
3   Fukuyama, F. (1992). *The end of history and the last man,* argued persuasively
    that the western institutions of democratic liberalism will eventually triumph
    throughout the world. This, he claims, must occur because the values associated
    with democratic liberalism are universal.

secular strategies have shifted from direct handouts, to participation, to empowerment[4]. Unfortunately, Christian missions have not been at the forefront of thinking about sustainable poverty alleviation. The one exception is the new field of transformational development.[5]

Most of the contemporary approaches to poverty alleviation found in evangelical missions today see ministry to the poor as an opportunity for the gospel rather than an end in itself. Practically, this has meant that extreme poverty has provided a platform for preaching when accompanied with handouts. This has led many secular agencies to accuse Christian mission agencies of taking advantage of the poverty and vulnerability of the poor in order to convert them[6].

With the undisputed failure of western oriented development initiatives to solve the problems of global poverty and underdevelopment, and the dearth of promising secular approaches, the time is ripe for majority world Christians to make a significant contribution. Unfortunately, re-writing development theory based on an indigenous understanding of the world, the realities of local communities, and the Christian scriptures, does not seem to be happening. This paper is meant to point to the urgency of that endeavor among all Christians, but it is most poignantly directed towards evangelicals who have been notably absent from the discussion.

---

4   For one of the most important discussions outlining the changes in western oriented development see: Chambers, R. (1983). *Rural development: Putting the last first*. Essex: Longman Scientific and Technical.

5   The most comprehensive treatise to date can be found in Myers, B. (1999). *Walking with the Poor: Principles andPpractices of Transformational Development*. Maryknoll: Orbis.

6   Often secular thinkers accuse mission agencies because they are confused or disturbed by the language used by evangelicals. An example can be found in the recent SIM publication. An excellent article discussing AIDS in China is unfortunately entitled "A Disease 'Ready-Made' for the Gospel" (Serving in Mission, Issue # 121, May-August 2008, pg. 12).

I do not want to give the impression that the quest for alternatives is new. In fact, Mahatma Gandhi is probably the first modern leader to refuse the standard technological

package offered by the developed world. Alternative movements have continued with the British economist E.F. Schumacher, the Brazilian educator Paulo Freire, and Julius Nyerere in Africa. As important as these movements were, they were always viewed with suspicion by conservative Christians from the West, especially conservative American evangelicals. Alternatives to western driven modernity, it seems, has largely been the prerogative of Catholics and secular thinkers.

In the next section I will review some of the origins of development thinking that will have to be re-imagined, if majority world thinkers hope to create a unique approach to development more suited to their needs and their contexts.

A HISTORICAL BACKGROUND OF WESTERN DEVELOPMENT

The discovery of "primitive cultures," which came to light during the era of European exploration, provided material from which the cultural evolutionary theory developed during the 18th century Enlightenment. This theory, which placed European culture at the apex of human achievement, attempted to locate every other culture in a continuum on this line, from the most savage (hunters and gatherers), to more highly developed literate cultures such as Chinese, and finally with Western Europe at the apex.

This was the foundational concept of modern development, and the origin of the idea that Europeans could help other cultures move along this single path to human progress. The concept of history as a story of continual progress has been a distinctly western idea.7 Voltaire, one of the most brilliant and courageous of the French Enlightenment thinkers, was also the most arrogant and self-confident. He once said, "Books rule the world, or at least those nations in it which have a written language, the others do not count" (Durant, 1962, p.187). The arrogance of this statement is still reflected in the current swaggering and self-congratulatory tone evidenced by some who believe that the West is a model for the entire world. Voltaire is the father of the rational side of western civilization, claiming that a synthesis of reason and science will create the ideal civilization. This rational side of the West can be seen currently in the physical sciences, neo-classical economics, and the Washington consensus.[8]

An alternate understanding of the West was inspired by Voltaire's nemesis, Jean-Jacque Rousseau, who was credited with inaugurating the 19th century Romantic Movement in Europe. Rousseau believed that true uncorrupted humanity was epitomized by what he called the "noble savage." One of the most influential political works of the era was Rousseau's *The Social Contract*. Rousseau opposed the mainstream Enlightenment philosophers, believed that science was bringing moral ruin on humanity, and that progress itself was an illusion. Rousseau is the most obvious ancestor of the current culture-oriented and environmental approaches that offer the most powerful critique of the Enlightenment-based modernization approach.[9]

---

7   Robert Nisbet argued in *The History of the Idea of Progress* (1980), that the idea of progress originated with the ancient Greeks. The concept of continual development of humanity was passed on through the Roman Empire, the early Church, the Middle Ages, Renaissance, and into modern times.

8   The Washington consensus is the label given for the broad agreement between the trade and foreign aid policies of the World Bank, WTO, IMF, and the U.S. government.

9   Although the culture-centered and environmental movements are distinct, both are suspicious of the western hegemony of the global economy, and both movements share similar sentiments regarding the hazards of excessive modernization.

Ideological Camps of Development

These two approaches to modernity, to some degree, still characterize western self-consciousness today. While this classification does not do justice to all development orientations, I believe that placing development orientation under either Voltaire or Rousseau is helpful because it helps us make ideological and historical connections.

This ideological history is a major reason why development thinking in Africa and the underdeveloped world is so confused. One cannot talk of development without invoking one of its fathers, since development has always been associated with one or the other movement.

Whereas western arrogance is certainly out of vogue in liberal academia, the Enlightenment era confidence in the ability of human reason to solve all problems has remained strong in the physical sciences, neoclassical economics, and statistically-oriented social science. Those with a physical science background have been on a continual search for the right combination of techniques, hybrid plants, and technology that will finally produce the goal of high-output productivity. Development from this perspective is simply the application of technology to the limitations of production. Neoclassical economics, also in line with Enlightenment certainty, offers the business model of development— essentially free market capitalism, privatization of state-run institutions, and the promotion of educational institutions that facilitate a productive industrial society.

The social science side of the story becomes complex at this point because social science tends to accept the mandates of both Voltaire and Rousseau. Social scientists can align themselves with either a mathematical approach to human problems, or with a cultural/moral approach.[10] Robert Chambers, who has attempted to bridge the two ideological camps in a synthesis, famously arrayed physical scientists, whom he termed *positive practitioners,* against culturally-oriented social scientists, whom he termed *negative academics* (1983).[11]

It is interesting to note that in America, the former group tends to be associated with politics of the *right*, and the latter tends to be associated with politics of the *left*.

Economists, who are also social scientists, follow the same pattern of association. Thus, *right wing* economists tend to align themselves with physical sciences, modernization theory, neo-classical economics (Adam Smith), and the objectives of the American State Department (the Washington Consensus). *Left wing* social scientists, including left leaning economists, lean toward Marxian analysis, and tend to decry the negative impact of modernization and western hegemony[12].

The environmental movement, which often sees itself in opposition to modernity, has gained momentum in the last few decades. This movement has a complex past but definitely has roots in the Romantic Movement, especially Rousseau, who believed that man's natural pre-modern condition was superior to that found in industrialized modernity. Environmentally based development does not necessarily have

---

10 By *moral* I am not referring to biblical morality, but to moralistic sentiments that are a common thread of liberal, humanitarian, and environmental movements.

11 By contrasting negative academic with positive practitioner, Chambers intended to communicate that social scientists are often critics of development initiatives that are carried out by the positive practitioners (physical scientists) who tend to believe that science will eventually save the poor. Robert Chambers has argued for the need to integrate physical and social sciences into what he termed *pluralism* (Chambers 1983). This has later has been transformed into Participatory Rural Appraisal (PRA), Participatory Learning and Action (PLA), and various *people-centered* offshoots (Chambers 1997).

12 Note that Rousseau is considered the progenitor of the French and Russian revolutions.

Homo sapiens' interest as the highest good, rather the health of the entire planet is sought.

Universal Secular Development

One of the characteristics of all of these approaches is secularity. The background of secular development, at least in the American version, dates to Jeffersonian era discussions regarding human nature and the aims of political organization. The inbuilt secularity has been a problem for Christian development thinkers from the West and their attempt to design a truly Christian development ideology. Of all Christians, evangelicals seem to have the strongest captivity to the secular Enlightenment ideology of progress.

Another characteristic of all western oriented development is the assumption of universality. This can be recognized in the Universal Declaration of Human Rights.[13] The very term, "universal," assumes that all people everywhere agree with the basic goals and assumptions. Although coerced to sign such declarations, many nations, most notably China and Middle Eastern Islamic countries, have expressed anger at the arrogance of such universal statements. Michael Todaro in his text, *Economic Development* (2000) discusses three universals that "represent common goals of all individuals in all societies" (2000, p. 16). These are sustenance, self-esteem, and freedom. One wonders what this list would look like if it were devised by non-westerners such as Persians, or perhaps Maasai. I dare say it would be different, which is to say that development aspirations are not universal.

One of the ways that western hegemony over development initiatives can be measured is to consider educational programs in developing

13   The Universal Declaration of Human Rights was instituted by the United Nations in 1948. This document enshrines basic western assumptions regarding the rights and nature of man and the limits of government, and is not shared by most non-western nations.

countries. In almost every case, the choice of subject matter and the approach to various branches of knowledge exactly parallels western curricula. In other words, the education that a native of Accra, Ghana, might aspire to obtain is exactly the education that he or she would obtain if she were a native of Huston, Texas. It should not take an anthropologist to recognize that profound differences in the ways that people from other societies think should lead to considerable differences in educational style and objectives. Yet the West still offers *the* model for most of the developing world.

Transformational Development

The perceptive reader will ask where Christian development theory fits within the Voltaire/Rousseau framework. Actually there has never been a uniquely Christian approach, or even a cluster of approaches, that has dealt adequately with the multiple realities and complexities required to develop a theoretical model. The only exception is the recent field of transformational development.[14] Transformational development synthesizes several multi-variant explanations of poverty with story of Christian meaning. The multi-variant explanations are based on Chambers' synthesis, and this synthesis is combined with a distinctively Christian approach to understanding the nature of work.

One distinctive of this approach is the focus on discovering identity and vocation as gifts from God—gifts which, if they are fulfilled, have the potential to create harmony, abundance, and meaning. Placing development within the locus of identity and vocation offers a uniquely Christian approach to development that has tremendous potential to forge an alternative approach to development. However, it is not clear how this approach will be re-formulated, or even rejected, by thinkers from the majority world.

---

14   The most comprehensive discussion of Transformational development to date can be found in Bryant Myers (1999) *Transformational Development*. Maryknol: Orbis.

CURRENT AFRICAN DEVELOPMENT
INITIATIVES

Western development initiatives, both Christian and non-Christian, have been under pressure from indigenous rights groups to curtail activities. The fact that the millions of poor in Africa are in dire need of assistance is not in dispute. The central issue of concern for these rights groups is how to help people in a way that does not trample their values and dignity.

It is always dangerous to characterize diverse and multifaceted movements. Nonetheless, there are certain features that typify much of the indigenous African development initiatives. My fifteen years in West Africa has given me the opportunity to observe first-hand many African development initiatives. All of the indigenous development initiatives that I am familiar with fit the same profile—the NGO (Non

Governmental Organization). Americans, who have lived their entire lives in America, will not be familiar with the term, but the NGO (ONG in the French-speaking world) is a western-based development institution, and it is the bread and butter of development initiatives in the underdeveloped world.[15]

Typical African development initiatives, if I may be permitted to characterize this, are not really indigenous, but are essentially western oriented intervention schemes with the money purse in the hands of local Africans instead of foreign development agencies. No doubt

---

15   There are only two sources of development activity in the developing world—government and non-governmental organizations (NGO). Governmental development programs, both in Africa and in the rest of the developing world, focus on infrastructure (such as roads, power and telephone systems) and public services (such as schools and hospitals). NGO's tend to focus on small-scale local-level development initiatives that require more involvement with community members.

many readers will ask themselves, "Why is this a problem?" My answer is that simply putting the purse strings into the hands of African locals has not altered two salient features of these initiatives: their western orientation, and their failure to achieve anything of lasting value.

Despite the criticism of African indigenous rights groups, African initiatives have followed the same patterns laid down by western developers. Typical African development initiatives are based on neo-classical economics, which is a modification of Adam Smith's classical economic principles originally designed to explain economic relationships in 18th century Europe. The problem with neo-classical economics is not that it does not work, but it only seems to work where conditions are similar to those of Western Europe, and where people aspire to the same ends as Europeans. African economists have failed to develop a theory that explains economic relationships in traditional African society.[16]

In addition, typical African development initiatives follow a path laid down by western economists concerning the nature of the good life, when in fact traditional

Africans define the good life differently.[17] Visit anywhere in Africa where poverty alleviation is being addressed and you will see the same models operating—development projects based on the NGO.[18] Project managers, who are hired by the project and run the day-to-day operations,

---

16 Marxian economic analysis is sometimes evoked here, but Marxian economics overplays the universal struggle between proletariat and bourgeoisie and has not done enough investigating the uniqueness of African societies.
17 *The good life* is a term originating with classical Greek philosophers, and it was used to describe the essentials that make life worth living. Western philosophers have continued to utilize this concept.
18 The common means of addressing poverty in the underdeveloped world is through a development project, which is an institution that is funded by donors (mostly from the West) to carry out development initiatives in poor communities. Professional paid staff runs these projects.

typically identify communities that have a need, such as the need for clean water or for increased agricultural output.

Although not visible on the surface, the imposition of western notions of ideal living on Africans actually begins long before communities are engaged, and this problem exists in the imagination of the project or agency and its staff. The project manager is a representative of the project, which has a particular understanding the best way to live. The project manager, who no doubt resides in an urban area and travels to outlying regions to bring development to rural people, has invariably adopted a western conception of the good life.

What is "development" in the mind of this hypothetical project manager? In short, development is the good life as defined by an urban living associated with all the amenities that are found in the West. This entails a nice house in a suburb, three children, a nice car, a college education, children in private schools, and vacations on the coast. Does this vision of the good life sound familiar? It should. I believe this is what we in the U.S. call "The American Dream." I am not suggesting that there is anything inherently wrong with the American Dream, but it is an *American Dream*, not an African dream. Nonetheless it is *this* dream, and not an African dream that African development initiatives are aiming for.

It is my contention that a major reason why development initiatives have not worked in Africa is because of these universal assumptions regarding the nature of the good life. In fact, it is impossible for a rural peasant to achieve any of the previously mentioned aspects of a modern living, even if they were desired. It is very unfortunate that neither the American/European evangelical Church, which has dominated missions in Africa for the last few centuries, nor the African Church has imagined another future other than the ones that the West inherited from the various arguments of 18th century Enlightenment.

Joel Matthews

The Church as a Universal Institution Addressing Poverty

The question at hand is, with all the history that is built into western development, how will initiatives from the majority world find their own way? I believe this is one of the greatest challenges to addressing the perplexing and persistent nature of poverty and underdevelopment in Africa. My studies in anthropology and international development, coupled with my experience in Africa, give me a nagging suspicion that western oriented development initiatives will never work out in Africa unless the entire continent moves in the direction of complete westernization. Since I do not believe this is the future that most Africans really want, the question remains, how and when will Africans begin to design development strategies based on what it means to be African and Christian?

Unfortunately, the western evangelical Church has not been at the forefront of initiatives to address global poverty. This is particularly distressing since the Christian religion has historically paid special attention to the plight of the poor. This is not the place to discuss reasons why the western evangelical Church has been asleep at the wheel. Jean-Marc Ela, the popular Cameroonian priest and African liberation theologian strongly criticized the Catholic Church for its Western orientation in *African Cry* (1980). Ela accused the European dominated Catholic Church of complacency and outright domination of Africans.[19] In addition, Ela complained that too much of the

---

19 Most of this critique of western oriented development is Marxian in nature. For an important, but virulent critique of western based development see, Escobar, A. (1995). *Encountering Development: The Making and Remaking of the Third World.* Princeton: Princeton University Press. One of the most important early criticisms of the global nature of development is Mander, J. & Goldsmith, E. (1996). *The Case Against the Global Economy and a Turn for the Local,* San Francisco: Sierra Club Books.

liturgy was simply a translation of Roman forms into African language. Whereas church-planting missions, both Catholic and Protestant, have made great strides since Ela's criticisms of the 1980's, church-led development initiatives have not made similar advancements. Ela's criticism of the Catholic Church twenty-five years ago applies to the western evangelical Church's anti-poverty strategies today.

The global Church has an unparalleled opportunity to fight global poverty due to its uniqueness as a universal institution. I am aware that other institutions also make claim to universality, particularly Islam and secular humanism. This is not the place to dispute these alternate claims, other than to state that these other claims are attempts to universalize a culture-specific worldview. Only the global Christian Church, which is a collection of all culture-specific churches around the world, has the potential for a universal perspective that is not based on culture—a perspective that is not uniquely western, or European, or southern, or African[20].

One of the difficulties in harnessing this global or universal Christian perspective is that there is no single institution called the global Church. The *Church*, in this sense, is a spiritual institution that must be brought to life through interdenominational, interracial, and multi-class discussion. To date, it seems that the closest we can come to a universal Christian understanding is through a synthesis of worldwide Catholic, Orthodox, and Protestant denominations. This synthesis occurs in global Church conferences. It is these global conferences, if they are all inclusive, that can give the universal perspective we seek.

---

20 No doubt some readers will find the distinction between universal claims of Islam, secular humanism, and the Christian Church artificial. In fact, Islam is an Arab religion, and all worshippers must learn Arabic and bow toward Mecca. Likewise, secular humanism is a distinctly western ideology concerning the nature of the universe and the place of human beings in the world. The Church, despite attempts by Europeans to dominate for the last five hundred years, is not a western institution.

Universality carries certain obligations and opportunities. As noted earlier, one seemingly intractable problem of western oriented development initiatives is that they are, in fact, western. Western oriented development has achieved great things, such as the Marshal Plan and the rebuilding of Europe after WWII. Yet, however hard we try, western oriented development, even when directed by church and mission, has not been able to achieve the same level of success in Africa. This is where the African Church has tremendous, but untapped potential. Although the western Church has been a dominant global player in the last few centuries, the balance has been shifting to the South, or the majority world. Hopefully this will not result in a simple shift of spiritual hegemony from the North to the South, but rather a more theologically and culturally integrated faith.[21]

Encouraging African Church-Led Development Initiatives

Two questions need to be asked at this point. First, how can the African Church lead development initiatives that simultaneously avoid western assumptions, maintain the dignity of African cultures, and provide a unique and effective solution based on biblical principles? Secondly, what should characterize the relationship between church and mission groups from the West and these majority world initiatives?

Church-based development initiatives in Africa have tended to fit the pattern of reliance on western secular ideology. This is actually a failure of imagination, both for western and African churches. Perceptive

---

21 Paul Hiebert encouraged what he called transcultural or metatheology as a synthesis of multiple local theologies to transcend singular culture-bound theologies such as those found in western seminaries. See his *Anthropological Reflections on Missiological Issues*, (1994) Grand Rapids: Baker Book House.

African leaders have recognized this. Julius Nyerere, social reformer and former president of Tanzania, urged Africans to develop their own potential and not be constrained by precedent or orthodoxies[22] Although Nyerere was not thinking specifically of the Church, the Church is the one institution that should be able to escape the strictures of an inherently materialistic and individualistic worldview.

I am not going to speculate concerning the character of the *African Dream*, if indeed there can be such a thing given the diverse nature of African communities, but I will bet that a central feature will be the essential place of community. Wilbur O'Donovan (2000) presented a side-by-side list of African vs. western cultural traits. It is no surprise that "community orientation" makes the first three out of twenty African cultural traits. Interestingly, it does not rate at all on the western list.

Now we should ask ourselves if the centrality of community sounds familiar. It should. This is a core Christian teaching; albeit one that does not receive much attention in the West. And here is where the African Church can begin to envision something entirely different than the American Dream as the object of Christian development in Africa. In fact, this is where an African contribution to a transcultural theology can help transform western theology—by returning to a biblical view that places a high value on community life in the Church. We should not be surprised if the African Church comes up with a dream of how to live that is much closer to biblical ideals than the American Dream, which has been peddled the world over as the ultimate achievement and destiny of humanity.

The Church has been known for its ministry to the poor for the last two millennia, but that ministry of late (the last few hundred years) has

---

22   Quoted from, Shao, J. *Alleviating Poverty in Africa*, In Belshaw, Calderisi, and Sugden (Eds.). (2001). *Faith in development: Partnership between the World Bank and the Churches of Africa.* Oxford: Regnum Books International.

been almost exclusively western oriented, meaning with the implicit assumption that the future of the poor in underdeveloped nations should look like our present. Melba Maggay (1994) raised these issues by asking the question this way:

> Have we really become one with the people so that we are able to be where they are—seeing problems just the way they see them and confronting them in a way that they would? Are we appropriating their technologies, listening to their solutions, taking their context seriously in an effort to go where they would like to go? (p. 65).

Yet Maggay has only addressed one-half of the problem—the willingness of western missionaries to consider alternate solutions that are not based on the American Dream. The other half of the problem is what to do when people in underdeveloped nations have been so enamored by the achievements of the West that they cannot even imagine an alternate future.

Indigenous African Christian development will have to be based on what is good in African traditions and values. This does not mean that all that is western must be rejected. Tokunboh Adeyemo, general director of the Association of Evangelicals in Africa, believes that the Bible inspired certain western institutions such as open systems of government and free economies, and that these are good for Africa. In addition, Daniel Etounga-Manguelle, regarding his own African culture, says this:

> "Our first objective is to preserve African culture, one of the most, if not the most humanistic culture in existence. But it must be regenerated through a process initiated from the inside that would allow Africans to remain themselves while being of their time. We must

however destroy all that is within us that is opposed to our mastery of our future..." (Harrison & Huntington, 2000, p. 75).

One thing is clear; such initiatives must be lead by African churches and not from the West. The conference organized by the Council of Anglican Provinces of Africa and the World Bank to explore collaboration between faith-based organizations and the bank, held in Nairobi in March 2000, signaled that the time is ripe for African church leaders to lead an African development initiative. Just how the African Church goes about this task is not for western churches or western missions to initiate. I believe that our role should be one of encouragement and support.

WESTERN SUPPORT OF AFRICAN DEVELOPMENT INITIATIVES

Support, in this case, should mean offering resources and encouragement. Even though the essential tasks must be initiated and dominated by African churches, western churches and missions do have a role. We can facilitate the church's evaluation of African cultural ideals through a transcultural understanding of the scriptures. We can offer this help because we have had to do this, and are still doing this, in our own civilizations.

Arriving at a transcultural understanding of the scriptures is more difficult that imagined, and neither African nor western Christians have been eager to relativize their faith by a synthesis with alternate forms of Christianity. It is very likely that the help of foreign missionaries will not be sought or appreciated by the African Church. I believe that this is partly due to the historical domination of Africa by the West, and partly because many African church leaders really do want what the West has. In the latter case, missionaries who wish to facilitate an

African understanding of development may appear to be blocking progress in achieving all that the West has.

Nonetheless, judging culture is one of the universal functions of the Church, along with offering a new synthesis of biblical and cultural values. Western missionaries can also be of assistance because they can warn African church leaders of some of the dangers that come bundled with western cultural values, such as excessive individuality, obsessive activity, and materialism. In this way we can offer assistance where we have experience. Finally, we should seek to understand the meaning of the good life for Africans—the *African Dream* if you will. Who knows, we might get lucky and discover a better way to live ourselves.

References

Belshaw, D., & Sugden, C. (Eds.). (2001). *Faith in Development: Partnership Between the World Bank and the Churches of Africa*. Oxford: Regnum Books International.

Chambers, R. (1983). *Rural development: Putting the Last First*. Essex: Longman Scientific and Technical (1997).

------------. *Whose Reality Counts? Putting the First Last*. London: Intermediate Technology Publications.

Durant, W. (1962). *The Story of Philosophy: The Lives and Opinions of the Greater Philosophers*. New York: Time Incorporated.

Easterly, W. (2006). *The White Man's Burden: Why the West's Efforts to Aid the Rest Have Done So Much Ill and So Little Good*. London: Penguin Press.

Ela, J. (1980) (Trans.1986.) *African Cry*. New York: Maryknoll.

Escobar, A. (1995). *Encountering Development: The Making and Remaking of the Third World*. Princeton: Princeton University Press.

Etounga-Manguelle, D. (2000). *Does Africa Need a Cultural Adjustment Program?* In L. Harrison & S. Huntington (Eds.) (2000), *Culture Matters: How Values Shape Human Progress*, New York: Basic Books.

Fukuyama, F. (1992). *The End of History and the Last Man*, London: Penguin Books.

Harrison, L. & Huntington, S. (Eds.). (2000). *Culture Matters: How Values Shape Human Progress*. New York: Basic Books.

Hiebert, P. (1994). *Anthropological Reflections on Missiological Issues*. Grand Rapids: Baker Book House.

Maggay, M. (1994). *Transforming Society*. Oxford: Regnum.

Mander, J. & Goldsmith, E. (1996). *The Case Against the Global Economy and a Turn for the Local*. San Francisco: Sierra Club Books.

Mbiti, J. (1969). *African Religions and Philosophy*. Nairobi: East African Educational Publishers.

Myers, B. (1999). *Walking With the Poor: Principles and Practices of Transformational Development*. Maryknoll: Orbis.

O'Donovan, W. (2000). *Biblical Christianity in Modern Africa*. Carlisle: Paternoster Press.

Rousseau, J., (1968/1762). (Maurice Cranston, Trans.). *The Social Contract*. New York: Penguin Classics.

Sacs, J. (2005). *The End of Poverty: Economic Possibilities for Our Time*. New York: Penguin Press.

Todaro, M. (2000). *Economic Development* (7th ed). Essex: Addison-Wesley.

14. IN WHAT WAY SHOULD THE MISSION MOVEMENTS OF THE MAJORITY WORLD USE NARRATIVE?

Robert Strauss

It seems everyone everywhere is using story. It is a more effective means of communication. But, we know that the story format alone does not displace a worldview. It alone does not prevent syncretism. It alone does not build a new worldview. Given these realities, in what way should the mission movements of the majority world use narrative?

INDIA – PROMINENT IN THE MAJORITY WORLD MISSION MOVEMENT

For more than a few years the consultants of Worldview Resource Group (WRG) had been praying about working in India, and there we were, teaching three courses to master's level students at the Academy for Church Planting and Leadership (ACPL) in Bangalore. Most of the 26 students were from the states of Nagaland and Manipur; others were from West Bengal, Gujarat, Tamil Nadu, and Karnataka. It was November 2007 and consultants from Worldview Resource Group were at ACPL by the invitation of its Founder and President, Rev. Jayakumar. The three courses WRG facilitated in the ACPL Tribal Track of missionary training focused on: (a) worldview issues in cross-cultural ministry, (b) ethnoreligionists, and (c) narrative as a missiological strategy and methodology.

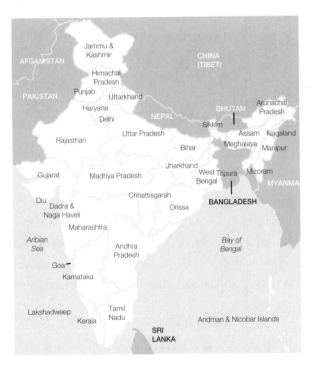

FIGURE 1. Political map of India

India is the 2nd most populous nation on earth with over 1 billion people, originating from more than 400 ethnic groups (Barrett, Kurian, and Johnson, 2001). With an estimated population of 6.5 million people and considered to be the fastest growing city in India due to the IT industry, Bangalore is the capital of the state of Karnataka. Also known as the Garden City, it is home to numerous evangelical institutions and ministries. For example, founded in 1984 by Graham Houghton, the South Asia Institute of Advanced Christian Studies (SAIACS) is a premier institute for higher training in South Asia. Also in Bangalore is the India Evangelical Mission (IEM), now under the leadership of Rev. P. John Wesley, with his wife Mercy. IEM has over 600 missionaries working among the tribal peoples of India and South Asia.

The mission movement in India is well established and capably organized (see details at Barnabas, 2005, pp. 264-290). The India Missions Association (IMA) is a network of over 250 national sending agencies and mission organizations. The India Institute of Missiology (IIM), directed by C. Barnabas and headquartered in Trichy, Tamil Nadu, oversees and accredits approximately 50 Indian missionary training centers. In 2007, the IIM launched a PhD Program to offer post-graduate degrees in missiology to the emerging leaders and trainers in the India mission movement. Currently there are nine scholars enrolled in the PhD Program that is being directed by Siga Arles.

The Academy for Church Planting and Leadership, the 4-year missionary training institution where we taught, is one of the auspicious trainer centers in the IIM network. Without a doubt the mission movement within and from India is prominent in the majority world mission enterprise.

PERVASIVE SYNCRETISM

In the course at ACPL on ethnoreligion [also termed *animism* (Van Rheenen, 1991) or *indigenous spirituality* (Fisher, 2002)], the MA students from Nagaland and Manipur expressed gratefulness that the gospel had come to their region of India through American Baptist missionaries 150 years ago. By some classifications, the northeast states are considered Christian, not Hindu. Yet, the students told many stories of wide-spread syncretism. Eugene Nida wrote, "Syncretism involves an accommodation of content, a synthesis of beliefs, and an amalgamation of world views, in such a way as to provide some common basis for constructing a new system or a new approach" (1990, p. 131; see also Van Rheenen, 1997, p. 173).

A story from the northeast describes a function of the evangelical pastors. If someone is frightened by an unexpected phenomenon, that person's human spirit will leave the body and go to a field adjacent to the village. The person ought to immediately go home and rest because of the imminent threat of physical illness. The pastor is summoned at once. As part of his understood responsibilities, he will go to the field and retrieve the human spirit through an incantation. Carrying the disembodied human spirit on his back, the pastor will make his way to the person's home without stopping or conversing with anyone. Through another incantation he will impart the spirit to the person who then is restored to wholeness and is freed from the threat of illness.

Syncretism is rampant in evangelical churches worldwide (Hesselgrave, 2006, p. 72). This fact is well established and was addressed by the publication of the Evangelical Missiological Society (EMS) in 2006, "Contextualization and Syncretism: Navigating Cultural Currents," edited by Gailyn Van Rheenen. Such stories among Christ followers are common all over the world. In Bolivia an evangelical pastor saw a fox in his bedroom window and knew it was his reincarnated grandfather. In Argentina water bottles are placed at the shrine of the "Difunta Correa" who then in turn will impart good fortune when one is traveling. In Riga, Latvia, a scarf is used to cover the front of one's neck to prevent evil spirits from entering the body. On the island of Java in Indonesia, shamans play the singularly key role in the multi-stage 1000-day migration of the human spirit from earth to heaven after death. This *selamatan* celebration permeates Javanese culture. However, in the evangelical churches, the pastor has replaced the shaman. In the United

States pastors have addressed split-level Christianity (Hiebert, Shaw, & Tienou, 1999) by preaching on "Lordship salvation," while failing to realize that split-level Christianity is a worldview issue of syncretism rather than a topic related to salvation. Paul Hiebert and his colleagues analyze split-level Christianity correctly. "The problem here is not with old religious beliefs, but with the underlying assumptions on which they are built. The gospel must not only change beliefs, but also transform worldviews; otherwise the new beliefs will be reinterpreted in terms of the old worldviews" (p. 378).

Emanuel Gerritt Singgih, Dean of Post-Graduate Studies at Duta Wacana Christian University in Yogyakarta, Indonesia, astutely highlights the power of a worldview when he writes, "In Africa, many Christian leaders and intellectuals suddenly realize that the primal worldviews which they disdainfully termed as 'primitive religions' are not gone at all, but together with Islam are now thriving, i.e., their numbers are increasing rapidly. Many are acknowledging that the grassroots primal worldviews are never put aside" (2000, pp. 361-362). Van Rheenen concurs, "Christian conversion without worldview change in reality is syncretism" (1991, p. 89).

RESPONSIBILITY AND REMEDY

The purpose of this overall chapter is not to illustrate the pervasiveness of syncretism in evangelical Christianity both in the United States and around the world. This has already been established. Rather, my intention is to inquire about a change in strategy. Clearly God has shifted the locus of Christian mission to the South and East (Engel & Dyrness, 2000; Jenkins, 2002, 2006; Neill, 1986; and Walls, 2003). The majority world will lead the mission enterprise into the future and, accordingly, this will call for a change in roles for those of us in the current mission enterprise. What will we do? Should what has been done in the past continue to be done? In David Hesselgrave's challenge to the established mission enterprise, he asked to what degree that enterprise is responsible for the "pervasive syncretism" (2006, p. 72) and in what ways can we help with a remedy? If we do humbly acknowledge our responsibility for a pervasive syncretism, what is our role in examining a more effective strategy in partnership with the majority world mission leaders?

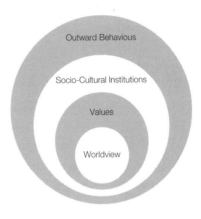

From our weeks of interacting with the Masters-level students from the northeast of India, it was clear that the syncretism in Manipur and Nagaland was closely related to the unbiblical bifurcation of high and low religions. High religions typically answer cosmic questions related to origins, purpose, destiny, ultimate reality, and truth. High religions have written texts and are often institutionalized. In contrast, low religions are concerned with the affairs of daily life, such as the surety of a good crop, reasons for drought, and how to attain good fortune or avoid calamity. The questions are existential rather than cosmic. Without written texts, traditions are passed along through storytelling symbols and repeated rituals (Steffen, 2005, p. 164). Successful living requires rituals that seek to attain and maintain control of gods, spirits, ancestors, and impersonal forces (Hiebert, Shaw, & Tienou, 1999). While high religionists concentrate on truth, low religionists seek power.

It has been the "almost universal tendency" of mission and missionary to present biblical truth as a high religion (Hesselgrave, 2006, p. 76), addressing outward behaviors and socio-cultural institutions (note the worldview model in Figure 2 adapted from Barney, 1973; also see Hesselgrave, 1991).

Furthermore, the presentation has most often been in the form of teaching propositional truth topically. All the while, "the old worldview that influences all else in ways not readily observable is allowed to remain more or less intact. Outer layer change unaccompanied by a corresponding worldview transformation inevitably leads to syncretism" (Hesselgrave, 2006, p. 77).

In the training seminars sponsored by Worldview Resource Group (WRG), attended primarily by mission leaders or trainers, the humble acknowledgement of syncretism is not what other evangelical Christians are doing, but what the participants themselves are practicing on a daily basis. For example, participants at the WRG seminars have told the facilitators that they:

- Sleep with their head facing in the east, the source of good energy; by so doing one will live a long life.

- Sleep with their Bible near their head; if alarmed in the night, they touch the Bible to provide protection from evil spirits; additionally, the power from the Bible will be absorbed while one sleeps.

- Keep a Bible in the home opened to Psalm 91 to protect the household from malevolent spirit beings and impersonal forces.

- Read coffee grounds at the bottom of the coffee cup to predict the future.

- Hang garlic outside the entrance to their homes to ward off the power of the evil eye.

- Believe they have seen tigers turn into men and men into tigers.

- Feel they have seen a woman's hand grow into a tiger's paw.

These simple illustrations of syncretistic beliefs and behavior among evangelicals are not mere cognitive presuppositions that are presumed lightly. These are cultural assumptions that are held with deep emotion (Redfield, 1953, pp. 85-86) and represent an assumed structure of reality (Geertz, 1973, p. 129). Based upon history and memory, these cultural assumptions are part of a whole system of powerful, persuasive, and long-lasting "moods and motivations" (p. 78).

The students from Manipur and Nagaland testified that the Bible and the evangelical church provide the solution to sin and a way to heaven. But, in daily life, the old tribal beliefs and rituals are widely prevalent and zealously practiced. The old forms, functions, and meanings of the low religion have been retained (Kraft, 1999). In essence, the Bible, representing high religion, has been laid over the top of animism, the pragmatic low religion that works in daily life. As such, the animist's basic understanding of the nature of reality is not displaced by the presentation of biblical topics and truths. In actuality, such phenomenological structures and systems indeed cannot be displaced by the traditional presentation of dogma from the high religion. The history of Christian expansion has dramatically shown that syncretism is the assured end result. Hence, tigers are turning into men and men into tigers. A multitude of malicious spirit beings and impersonal forces is the lotus of reality and as such the focus of daily life. God the Creator is not the sovereign LORD. Jesus Christ is not preeminent. Yet, paradoxically, the problem is not doctrinal. "There are within Hinduism large numbers who are the victims of superstition, but even in countries where the higher civilization is said to have displaced the lower, the lower still persists (Radhakrishan, 1988, p. 38).

The insidious influence of worldview systems is not a new concept. We have understood this reality for a long time. Many years ago Bronislaw Malinowski wrote, "Magic and religion are not merely a doctrine or a philosophy, not merely an intellectual body of opinion, but a special mode of behavior, a pragmatic attitude built up of reason, feeling and will alike. It is a module of action as well as a system of belief, and a sociological phenomenon as well as a personal experience" (1925, p. 24). What is emerging as new is an understanding of how to communicate more effectively at a worldview level, even how to address an entire worldview system that is emotionally embraced.

NARRATIVE: A MISSIOLOGICAL STRATEGY AND METHODOLOGY

The entire missionary enterprise, along with most of Western culture, is embracing the effective method of storytelling. Story is the new language of marketing, management, psychology, and education.

The entertainment industry has unmistakably understood the power of story. Last year my wife and I faithfully watched American Idol, USA. One of the contestants was from an evangelical church where my wife's nephew was an associate pastor. We felt an immediate connection with the contestant and the show. Each week we voted repeatedly for Chris on our mobile phones. We were not just watching a show, we were part of it! The lives of the contestants were explored through personal interviews and video clips of their families and homes. Each week was suspenseful; not until the end of the show did the judges, contestants, and viewers know who was voted off and going home and who was staying another week. The show was emotional, exciting, and addictive.

Story involves more than cognitive reasoning; it invokes emotion. It is not just information (Wiggins & McTighe, 1998, p. 143-144). It implants images that are life related. Story mobilizes reason and emotion; therefore it most closely resembles experience (Curtis & Eldridge, 1997, p. 38; note how Laurie Green links "word" and "event," 1999). Story has the ability to make one hopeful, uncomfortable, happy, sad, angry, and empathetic, spanning the entire spectrum of human feeling. Through conflict and mystery, story stirs the imagination, creates curiosity, and fosters hope. A good story has a rhythm of expectation and satisfaction (Egan, 1986, pp. 25-26). Story draws the listeners into the narrative so that they are not just hearing the story or simply observing the plot and action as a distant spectator (Fackre, 1975, p. 59). They are "in the story." Story is not in opposition to propositional truth, but rather story illuminates propositional truth (Miller, 1987, p. 132). Story makes meaning even in the midst of chaotic facts. By weaving together the setting, characters, plot, storyline, ideal/un-ideal arch-types, and foils, story creates a comprehensive whole (Ryken, 2005, pp. 53-89). It is this final characteristic that is the true power of story, that is, "the comprehensive whole."

The optimal insight into the narrative world is to understand the role of narrative in creating the overarching meta-narrative (Wright, 1992, pp. 37-80). We must keep learning, moving beyond simply converting the doctrinal topics from systematic textbooks into story formats. Furthermore, the comprehensive whole of the biblical narrative is markedly more significant than picking the top ten stories from the Old and New Testaments. If one only converts topics to a story format or simply chooses the top stories in the Bible, these well-intended remedies actually fall short. Is it possible that they may be continuations of the same methodologies that historically have caused syncretism (see Peter

Block, 1993, p. 208, regarding culture change)? Neither one addresses an overarching worldview. It is the whole biblical canon as a source of authority and truth in contemporary culture that is important to the cross-cultural worker (Wright, 1997).

Regarding current strategies and methodologies, "we have fragmented the Bible into bits—moral bits, systematic-theology bits, devotional bits, historical-critical bits, narrative bits. When the Bible is broken up in this way there is no comprehensive grand narrative to withstand the power of the comprehensive humanist narrative that shapes our culture" (Goheen, 2005, pp. 5-6). Note carefully Michael Goheen's insight—narrative bits. The objective of storytelling is not merely an adjustment in the *delivery* of curriculum content where hard facts are converted to story. But narrative must involve a patient and careful building of a comprehensive framework that is new and holistic—a worldview framework rooted in the Bible itself. In fact, the whole of the Bible is the comprehensive framework—the overarching meta-narrative. Leland Ryken argues that "the whole story is the meaning" (2005, p. 88).

The Overarching Story – A Missiological Strategy for Majority World Mission Movements?

The history of Christian expansion vividly demonstrates that the gospel is more than creeds, catechisms, and confessions.[1] As rich as these documents are in history and tradition, they are esteemed and

---

1   These documents of endearment include early Christian creeds like the Nicene Creed dated 325 AD. The following represents some of the confessions from the Reformation: Belgic Confession (1561), Heidelberg Catechism (1576), Canons of Dort (1619), and Westminster Confession (1647).

venerable symbols of the high religion of Christianity. But, outside of the narrative format of Scripture, they do not create an overarching story. Yes, hypotheses, assumptions, and presuppositions are embedded in story, but when they are removed from the story context—the teller, hearer, storyworld, and story line—the overarching framework of God's view of reality is diminished. Kevin Bradt (1997) argues that human knowing, thinking, and consciousness are inextricably tied to a mode of communication, namely story. He writes, "Story is not just an art form or literary genre but a way of structuring thought (p. 233). Ken Gnanakan's call to "recover the significance" of the creeds (2004, p. 24) will be answered by "reclaiming story" (Bradt, 1997, p. 88).

> Knowledge that comes in and through the action of storing is mediated as a holographic whole: that is, it is formed by the dynamic interacting of parts together and reveals itself from multiple perspectives and dimensions through multiple modalities simultaneously. Any attempts to isolate, analyze, or separate out any of the individual operations of this contemporaneous contextual event of knowing would destroy the singleness and unity of the experience; it is by its very nature and constitution, intrinsically multimodal and must be grasped as such. (p. 12)

The parts of the biblical story cannot be isolated or separated from the contemporaneous context of the metanarrative if the hearer is to fully understand the meaning of the component parts. In other words, it is imperative that we see the whole of Scripture as a complete system where the whole is greater than the sum of the parts.[2] In systems thinking the parts cannot be understood in isolation from the whole. Rather than fragmentation, in the whole the parts are interrelated and interdependent.

---

2   The whole is greater than the sum of the parts. Water is an illustration. Water (H20) as a whole has the characteristic of wetness. Neither of the separated component parts has such a characteristic.

Furthermore, the story hearer is drawn into the story. Bradt continues that storying demands interactive relationships of personal presence in the here-and-now (1997, p. 233). The bits of systematic theology (Goheen, 2005) can be "unmoored from interests" and disconnected from overarching, pertinent, and real questions (Wiggins & McTighe, 1998, p. 138). The hearer will not interpret the narrative bits through the comprehensive whole of the Bible, but through the existing meta-narrative in which the he already sees himself. He already is "in a story."

BABYLONIAN EMPIRE

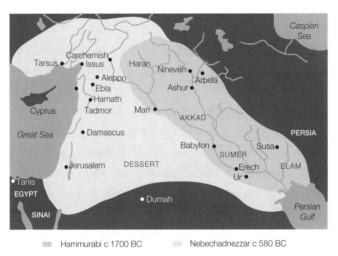

Hammurabi c 1700 BC   Nebechadnezzar c 580 BC

FIGURE 3. The Babylonian Empire of the ANE

Written as a polemic to the cultures of the Ancient Near East (ANE)—cultural cosmologies that were polytheistic, animistic, and holistic at their core (Frankfort, 2000)—the narrative of Genesis begins with God's description of real time/space history. Rather than a linear argument through perhaps a syllogism, God begins the dramatic narrative of Scripture with the story of creation. The uninterrupted storyline continues throughout the Bible building the framework of God's view of reality and, as such, the basis for all meaning. God Himself is the protagonist of the story. In every way and in every place, the Bible is theocentric. God defines origin, purpose, destiny, morality, structures, who is man, what is non-man, boundaries (does a man turn into a tiger and a tiger into a man?), relationships (born out the Triune God Himself), cause and effect, power, and hierarchy.

In the first 11 chapters of Genesis alone, the hearer "sees" the reality of one[3] Sovereign God who is moral and predictable. The gods of the Ancient Near East cosmologies were neither. The storyline introduces: values (God saw that the light was good), designations (he separated light from darkness; "A" is "A" and "A" is not "non-A"), time, space (God called the expanse "sky"), history set in motion (there was evening and there was morning – the second day), ecological systems, God's sovereign control over all His creation, the uniqueness of mankind (created in the image of God), human responsibility in the creation, God's goodness and kindness (the Provider of food, heat, rest, and enjoyment), God as the source of life, the introduction of epistemology, theodicy, the origin of sin[4], the cause of death, delegation, the institution of marriage, the ability to be self-aware, procreation, accountability for sin, a line of people who are God-fearers, man's helplessness in his sin, judgment, covenant relationships, God's faithfulness in remembering mankind, both God's transcendence and immanence, human government, and much more. All this is embedded in the story! The context is real history.

Richard Bauckham writes that a meta-narrative "is an attempt to grasp the meaning and destiny of human history as a whole by telling a single story about it; to encompass, as it were, all the immense diversity of human stories in a single, overall story which integrates them into a single

---

3   Albright writes that Moses "demythologized" religion by eliminating specifically polytheistic elements in the Genesis narrative (1968:184).

4   Man's choice of good and evil is a concept foreign to Islamic theology. Compare Genesis 2:17

meaning…a single story about the whole of human history in order to attribute a single integrated meaning to the whole. It is a totalizing framework, one which tries to subsume everything within its concept of the truth" (1993, pp. 4, 86-87). The overarching story validates or invalidates all other stories (Ward, 2003). Note Donald Carson's application of this critical truth to the use of Scripture. "The Bible as a whole document tells a story, and, properly used, that story can serve as a meta-narrative that shapes our grasp of the entire Christian faith. In my view it is increasingly important to spell this out to Christians and to non-Christians, as part of our proclamation of the gospel. The ignorance of basic Scripture is so disturbing in our day that Christian preaching that does not seek to remedy the lack is simply irresponsible" (1996, p. 84).

Hiebert and his colleagues argue that "ultimately, meaning is to be found in the cosmic story: the 'big' story about the beginning, meaning, and ending of all things" (1999, p. 115). "The good news story of the Bible should be told as a whole" (p. 278). As an illustration of methodology, the authors refer to New Tribes Mission (NTM), an organization that has worked in traditional societies for the past 60 years. From the basic model of NTM's chronological Bible teaching, numerous adaptations have been made.[5]

New Tribes Mission and others strongly emphasize "pre-evangelism," that is, taking the time to build personal relationships in the context of the host society. The implications of establishing trust bonds in deep relationships mean that the storyteller will learn language and understand culture to an effective level of proficiency. A major goal in culture investigation is learning the core worldview assumptions of the

---

5   For the historical foundations of a storied presentation of the Bible, see Tom Steffen and J.O. Terry, "The Sweeping Story of Scripture Taught through Time." Missiology: An International Review. July 2007, 35(3): 315-335.

host society. Thereby, strategic storying targets worldview assumptions. The story objectives are not generic or random; they are purposeful.

Tom Steffen (1997) provides a straightforward overview of the stages in cross-cultural ministry. His reflections are based on his years of cross-cultural ministry in the Philippines among the Ifugao people. In Table 1, I adapt Steffen's stages adjusting some of the terminology found in Steffen's book *Passing the Baton: Church Planting that Empowers.*

Pre-Entry	Research, Training Team formation Strategy of ministry
Pre-Evangelism	Relationships Culture and language acquisition Worldview analysis
Evangelism	Storying Curriculum development
The Developing Church	Contextualization Discipleship Leadership development
The Maturing Church	Transition of roles Multiplication

TABLE 1. The Five-Stage Strategy for Cross-Cultural Ministry

*Steffen's book Passing the Baton has been translated into Spanish by Recursos Estrategicos Globales in Cordoba, Argentina for use by Latino missionaries in the Ibero-America mission movement. Also, an English version of the book is used by the PhD Programme of the India Institute of Missiology.

Table 1 amusingly depicts someone "parachuting in" at the Evangelism stage, bypassing Pre-Entry and Pre-Evangelism. Not only has the Western mission enterprise tended to present biblical truth as a high religion, but regrettably we now tend to bypass crucial stages of the overall strategy of multiplication and thus our tactics foster deadly syncretism. Perhaps based on our Western values, today we stress efficiency, rapid deployment, and a quick Return-On-Investment. If we value story, we must see the inextricable link between story, relationships, and worldview.

What will be passed along to the majority world mission movements from the existing mission enterprise? Will these emerging missiologists use storytelling simply as another way to delivery curriculum, that is, merely a means of communication? After all, storytelling is more effective. Or will the majority world mission movements embrace the true power of narrative? Will its missiologists present the whole biblical story as the meta-narrative of reality, not only to displace the old worldview, but to build a worldview and transform people and communities? Understanding the difference between these questions is critical. The answers to these questions will dramatically impact the unending pervasiveness of syncretism.

References

Albright, William Foxwell, 1968. *Yahweh and the Gods of Canaan: A Historical Analysis of Two Contrasting Faiths.* Garden City, NY: Doubleday.

C. Barnabas, 2005. "Dynamic Expansion of Missionary Movements in India." In *Biblical Theology and Missiological Education in Asia.* Eds. Siga Arles, Ashish Chrispal, & Paul Mohan Ray, 264-290. Bangalore, India: Theological Book Trust.

Barney, G. Linwood, 1973. "The Supracultural and the Cultural: Implications for Frontier Missions." In *The Gospel and Frontier Peoples.* Beaver, R. Pierce (Ed.). Pasadena, CA: William Carey Library.

Barrett, David, George Kurian, and Todd Johnson, 2001. *World Christian Encyclopedia.* Oxford University Press.

Bartholomew, Craig and Michael Goheen, 2004. *The Drama of Scripture.* Grand Rapids, MI: Baker Academic.

Bauckham, Richard, 2004. *Bible and Mission: Christian Witness in a Postmodern World.* Grand Rapids, MI: Baker Academic.

Block, Peter, 1993. *Stewardship: Choosing Service over Self-Interest.* San Francisco: Berrett-Koehler.

Bradt, Kevin, 1997. *Story as a Way of Knowing.* Kansas City, MO: Sheed & Ward.

Carson, Donald 1996 The Gagging of God: Christianity Confronts Pluralism. Grand Rapids, MI: Zondervan.

Curtis, Brent and John Eldredge, 1997. *The Sacred Romance – Drawing Closer to the Heart of God.* Nashville: Thomas Nelson.

Egan, Kieran, 1986. *Teaching as Story-telling.* Chicago: University of Chicago Press.

Engel, James and William Dyrness, 2000. *Changing the Mind of Missions.* Downers Grove, IL: InterVarsity.

Fackre, Gabriel, 1975. *Word in Deed: Theological Themes in Evangelism.* Grand Rapids: Eerdmans.

Fernhout, Henry, 1997. "Christian Schooling: Telling a Worldview Story." In *The Crumbling Walls of Certainty: Toward a Christian Critique of Postmodernity and Education,* Eds. Ian Lambert & Suzanne Mitchell, 75-98. Sydney: The Center for the Study of Australian Christianity.

Fisher, Mary Pat, 2002. *Living Religions,* Fifth Edition. Upper Saddle River, NJ: Prentice-Hall.

Frankfort, Henri, 2000. *Ancient Egyptian Religion: An Interpretation.* Mineola, NY: Dover Publications.

Gnanakan, Ken, 2004. *Responsible Stewardship of God's Creation.* Bangalore, India: Theological Book Trust.

Geertz, Clifford, 1973. *The Interpretation of Cultures.* New York: Basic Books.

Goheen, Michael, 2005. "The Power of the Gospel and the Renewal of Scholarship." Retrieved at http://www.biblicaltheology.ca/blue_files/Inaugural-Goheen.pdf

Green, Laurie, 1999. "Oral Cultures and the World of Words." *Theology* 102:328-335.

Hesselgrave, David 1991 *Communicating Christ Cross-Culturally – An Introduction of Missionary Communication* (2nd Edition). Grand Rapids, MI: Zondervan. 2006

"Syncretism: Mission and Missionary Induced." In *Contextualization and Syncretism*, Ed. Gailen Van Rheenen, 71-98. Pasadena, CA: William Carey Library.

Hiebert, Paul, 1997. "Conversion and Worldview Transformation." *IJFM* 14:83-86.

Hiebert, Paul, Daniel Shaw, and Tite Tienou, 1999. *Understanding Folk Religion*. Grand Rapids, MI: Baker Book House.

Jenkins, Phillip, 2002. *The Next Christendom*. Oxford, UK: Oxford University Press. 2006

The New Faces of Christianity: Believing the Bible in the Global South. Oxford, UK: Oxford University Press.

Kraft, Charles, 1997. *Christianity in Culture* (13th printing). Maryknoll, NY: Orbis Books.

Malinowski, Bronislaw, 1925. *Magic, Science, and Religion* (republished in 1948). Garden City, NY: Doubleday Anchor Books.

Miller, Donald, 1987. *Story and Context: An Introduction to Christian Education*. Nashville: Abingdon Press.

Neill, Stephen, 1986. *A History of Christian Missions*. London: Penguin.

Newbigin, Lesslie, 1989. *The Gospel in a Pluralist Society*. Grand Rapids, MI: Eerdmans.

Nida, Eugene, 1990. *Message and Mission*. Pasadena, CA: William Carey Library.

Radhakrishnan, 1988. *The Hindu View of Life*. London: Unwin Hyman Limited.

Redfield, Robert, 1953. *The Primitive World*. Ithaca, NY: Great Seal Books.

Ryken, Leland, 2005. *Words of Delight*. Grand Rapids, MI: Baker.

Singgih, Emanuel Gerritt, 2000. "Globalization and Contextualization: Toward a New Awareness of One's Own Reality." *Exchange* 29:361-373.

Steffen, Tom, 1997. *Passing the Baton: Church Planting that Empowers*. La Habra, CA: COMD. 1998. "Foundational Roles of Symbol and Narrative in the (Re)construction of Reality and Relationships." *Missiology: An International Review* 26:477-494.

2005. *Reconnecting God's Story to Ministry: Crosscultural Storytelling at Home and Abroad*. Waynesboro, GA: Authentic Media.

Steffen, Tom and J.O. Terry, 2007. "The Sweeping Story of Scripture Taught through Time." *Missiology: An International Review.* July 2007, 35(3): 315-335

Van Rheenen, Gailyn, 1991. *Communicating Christ in Animistic Contexts.* Pasadena, CA: William Carey Library.

1997 "Modern and Postmodern Syncretism in Theology and Missions." In *The Holy Spirit and Mission Dynamics,* Ed. C. Douglas McConnell, 164-207. Pasadena, CA: William Carey Library.

Walls, Andrew, 2003. *The Missionary Movement in Christian History.* Maryknoll, NY: Orbis.

Ward, Glenn, 2003. *Teach Yourself Postmodernism.* Chicago: McGraw-Hill.

Wiggins, Grant and Jay McTighe 1998 Understanding by Design. Alexandria, VA: Association for Supervision and Curriculum Development.

Wright, N.T., 1992. *The New Testament and the People of God.* London: SPCK.

1997. *The Book and the Story.* Retrieved at http://www.biblesociety.org.uk/exploratory/articles/wright97.pdf

15. CALVARY MINISTRIES (CAPRO): A CASE STUDY ON A MODEL OF MAJORITY WORLD INITIATIVES IN CHRISTIAN MISSION

Tesilimi Aderemi (Remi) Lawanson

"The astonishing religious changes of the twentieth century have produced a *post-Christian West and a post-Western Christianity*" (Walls, 2003).

The extent to which the current awakening has occurred without the institutions and structures that defined Western Christendom, including the tradition of scholarship, learning, and cosmopolitanism, is an important feature of World Christianity and its largely hinterland following. In the current resurgence, monasteries, theological schools, and hierarchical agency, for example, have played comparatively little role, nor is there much evidence of state facility, except as a problem and a burden to overcome (Lamin Sanneh, 2008).

When we remember that several missional thinkers and practitioners like J. R. Mott had anticipated that Africa would be taken over by Islam, then the current resurgence of Christianity in Africa is a great surprise and is worth studying. Writing this paper became an interesting venture when it was also remembered that there was widespread speculation among mission theorists and practitioners in the 1970s that the resurgence of Islam would accelerate the decline of Christianity by 2000.

Christianity came to Africa in various organizational expressions of the church such as denominations and mission agencies.[1] Typically these are built around some type of theological tradition and historical polity.[2] Several factors have been adduced as responsible for the phenomenal growth of the church in the majority world in general and Africa in particular. Some trace the growth to the rise of Pentecostalism (Cox, 1995).

A second factor is how this growth took place after colonialism and during the period of national awakening. Perhaps colonialism was an obstacle to the growth of Christianity, Sanneh argues (2003, p. 18). Others, including Sanneh, trace this growth with its expansion to a third factor—the influence of the delayed effect of Bible translation into African languages. A fourth factor little noticed in the statistics is a theological one: Christian expansion was virtually limited to those societies whose people had preserved the indigenous name for God.

I identify with most of these thoughts and much more. Additionally, I trace the expansion of Christianity in the majority world to the good seed planted by pioneer missionaries, who were members of the early missionary movements. Indigenous renewal movements and Christian student missionary movements continue to play strategic part in the resurgence. Emerging today in the majority world are missionary movements generating new initiatives in Christian mission. This paper is an attempt at looking at CAPRO, a member and model of the majority world initiatives in Christian mission (Fuller, 2000, pp. 691-692).

---

1   (Ajayi, 1965, p. 275)
2   (Van Gelder, 2006, pp. 3-4)

Integrating insights from ecclesiology, missiology, metaphorical sociol-ogy, management theory and organizational studies, this paper uses qualitative research methodology to examine the distinctive charac-teristics of these new missionary movements. There are four main arguments that shape this paper. Firstly it argues that the organizations or missionary movements involved in the majority world initiatives in Christian mission have distinctive characteristics that influence their performances in Christian mission. Secondly, this paper posits that, like other missionary movements, they have weaknesses, which need to be addressed. These weaknesses are threatening their continuing impact in Christian mission. Thirdly, it advocates that these movements have some challenges before them that should not be ignored. Finally the paper proposes a missional framework for sustaining a continuing impact of these majority world initiatives in Christian mission.

This paper begins with a historical overview of CAPRO. Each gen-eration and tradition understands the past in terms of its own issues and context. Paradoxically, a misunderstanding of the present is the inevitable consequence of the ignorance of the past (Bloch, 1954, p. 43). Therefore, I will venture to understand the "present" of CAPRO, the organization in this case study, by profiling its past. In doing this, I will also seek to understand the past by the present.

The developmental phase approach will be used, while the elements[3] of an organization, characteristics[4] of an effective organization as well as indicators[5] or measures of organizational effectiveness and biblical

---

3   These include social structure, participants, goals, technology, and environment.

4   These include (i.) organizational goals; (ii.) decision-making; (iii) undistorted communication practice; (iv) effective conflict management; (v) responsiveness to change; (vi) trusting, releasing and empowering members; (vii) seeking member satisfaction; (viii) trusted leadership; (ix) Training; (x) participatory and friendly atmosphere.

5   These are Structure, Process, and Outcome as described in Scott (2003).

metaphorical models will be used as the framework for discussing this organization. CAPRO's emergence from a context of religious plurality makes it a good study for identifying some distinctive characteristics for other missionary movements to embrace in the bid for penetrating the final frontiers of mission.

The impact of Christian mission has been tied with the life and health of the various organizational expressions of the church. Hence the significance of this study in exploring some of the organizational factors that influence the life and health of the various expressions of the church with corresponding influence on their performances in cross-cultural mission.

CALVARY MINISTRIES (CAPRO)

Calvary Ministries (CAPRO) is an indigenous non-denominational mission agency[6] that began in Nigeria in 1975 and currently has missionary work in twenty African nations, two nations each in Europe, the Middle East and North America respectively (Aderonmu, 2006). CAPRO has grown to become one of the largest indigenous mission agencies in Africa. It began with a group of young Nigerian Christians who graduated from some universities in Nigeria and were deployed to do their one-year compulsory national service[7] in Northern Nigeria (Fuller, 2000, p. 692). These young Christians were on national posting to serve in areas related to their professional training, which included engineering, education, and public administration.

---

6   In this paper, "Mission Agencies" refers to non-church Christian mission
     organizations.
7   In 1973, The Federal Government of Nigeria introduced a National Youth Service
     Scheme (NYSC), which made it mandatory for all graduates from universities
     and other institutions of higher learning to serve the nation for one year.

In the course of their service year, these Christians came across huge settlements of people groups with no evidence of ever having heard the gospel of our Lord Jesus Christ preached to them. Most of these people were either Muslims or traditional religionists. The passion to reach these people groups led to the establishment of an informal organization or group called Calvary Productions (Aderonmu, 2003). At the end of their national service, most of these young Christians stayed back in Northern Nigeria because of their desire to reach these Muslims and traditional religionists with the gospel. For the purpose of understanding and subsequent analyses, the CAPRO story will be segmented into phases reflecting some significant encounters, events and people.

Foundational and Pioneering Phase 1975–1988

During this phase, the informal organization, Calvary Production (CAPRO), metamorphosed into a formal organization, Calvary Ministries (CAPRO). It all began when the Calvary Production members attended the first Nigerian National Congress on Evangelization (NCE) held at the University of Ife Ile-Ife in Western State, Nigeria, in August 1975. The NCE was called at the initiative of the Nigerian delegates to the Lausanne I Congress in 1974,[8] as a platform for drawing an action plan for implementing evangelization strategy to reach the then un-reached people groups in Nigeria (Aderonmu, 2003). The Calvary Productions delegates to the NCE discovered at that congress that there was a people group called *Maguzawa* in Northern Nigeria that was yet to be reached with the gospel. The Calvary Production delegates accepted the challenge of taking the gospel to the *Maguzawas*.

---

8   Lausanne 1 was a gathering of about 4000 Christians representing 151 countries in July 1974 in Lausanne, Switzerland for the International Congress on World Evangelization.

On returning back to their base in Northern Nigeria, Calvary Production members agreed to establish a formal organization, called CALVARY MINISTIRES (CAPRO) for the purpose or goal of reaching the *Maguzawas* and other un-reached people groups in Northern Nigeria with the gospel of our Lord Jesus Christ (Olonade, 2004).

During this phase, CAPRO's social structure was fully influenced by its identity with evangelical tenets of faith. The behavioral structure component of its social structure was reflected in a document, called "Guiding Principles" designed by CAPRO's leadership. All CAPRO missionaries, staff and officials were contractually obliged to adhere to the provisions of this document. CAPRO's membership was predominantly filled with volunteers who had commitments and obligations to other organizations. Bayo Famonure, the visionary who initiated the establishment of CAPRO, was the pioneer Executive Secretary to CAPRO (Aderonmu, 2003). During this phase, CAPRO did not have any clearly defined organizational structure.

CAPRO's goals for this phase were as stated above. However, CAPRO has shown through the various changes that took place in its goals from inception until now that the definition of the concept of organizations should not be tied to their goals (Pfeffer, 1997, pp. 7-9). This was because after reaching the *Maguzawas* with the gospel, CAPRO missionaries operated in Niger Republic, a French-speaking country towards North Africa, from 1976 to 1978, then the North Western African country of Gambia in 1979. It was while in Niger Republic and discovering that most of French-speaking West Africa was predominantly Islamic that CAPRO amended its organizational goals to include reaching French-speaking West Africa.

In 1979, Aderonmu, CAPRO's first full-time missionary visited Gambia in response to a news report published about that country in a national newspaper (Olonade, 2004). Gambia was neither French-speaking nor a settlement of the *Maguzawas*. Therefore it took Aderonmu a lot of effort to convince his fellow CAPRO leadership of the need for undertaking a mission work there. While in Gambia, Aderonmu met with officials of the World Evangelism Crusades (WEC), today Worldwide Evangelization for Christ; USA website: http://www.wec-usa. org/ and international: http://wec-int.org/ (WEC). The relationship that emerged from this divine contact led to a partnership between WEC and CAPRO that has been mutually beneficial (Clinton, 1989, p. 260).[9] Some of the benefits are discussed later.

Regarding organizational technology or system, CAPRO adopted discipleship, language learning as well as an incarnational method of ministry. These three became CAPRO's domains of organizational effectiveness. Prior to the contact with WEC, CAPRO mainly engaged in evangelism. However, according to Aderonmu, the partnership with WEC exposed CAPRO gradually to an understanding of the mission concept. WEC also introduced CAPRO to medical mission as another tool for mission. WEC trained a nurse introduced by CAPRO for this purpose.

Training for cross-cultural mission later became CAPRO's main orga-nizational tool for promoting mission as well as for developing mis-sionaries. CAPRO's first School of Mission (SOM), and probably the first in Nigeria, was established in the country's north central city of Zaria in 1980 for the purpose of training its mission volunteers. Later that year, SOM moved a few miles away from Zaria to Kauna, where it operated until 1985 when it relocated to Jos in the Middle Belt area of Nigeria. From this time, cross-cultural mission training became one of CAPRO's domains of organizational effectiveness.

---

9   Clinton defines "Divine Contact" as a person whom God brings in contact with a leader at a crucial moment in a development phase in order to accomplish one or more thing(s) or a related function.

CAPRO operated more like a closed system during this phase with little interface with its environment. This attitude certainly had adverse effects on CAPRO's resource base as well as ministry impact and scope. However, CAPRO developed great depth of spirituality and personal life of sacrifice during this phase, which served as a good foundation for subsequent phases. The national context was influenced by military rule with Islam loosing its dominance. It should also be acknowledged that CAPRO was able to penetrate Northern Nigeria as well as the nations of Niger, Gambia, Guinea and Senegal with the gospel during this phase.

Consolidation and Structuring Phase
1988–1997

This phase began with a leadership succession crisis arising from the first attempt to transition from Famonure's founding executive leadership. Peter Ozodo was eventually elected to take over from Famonure as the executive leader but with Famonure remaining as the chairman. Under Ozodo's leadership, CAPRO was structured after the pattern that CAPRO studied from its partnership with WEC. More volunteers, staff, and missionaries came on board as fulltime members. CAPRO's goals were further refined, reinforced and extended with the support of results from research. During the first phase, WEC had trained CAPRO's Niyi Gbade on mission research in its United Kingdom office.

Research, mercy ministry, health, relief, and rural development were added to CAPRO's organizational technology tools for promoting mission and producing missionaries. Having trained and practiced in the field of human resource management prior to becoming CAPRO's international director, Ozodo initiated a gradual interface between CAPRO and its environment. Thus began CAPRO's gradual transformation from being a closed system to being a natural-open system.

Regarding its context in Nigeria, military rule continued on the national level with some attempts at democratic governance.

During this phase, CAPRO undertook pioneering mission and church planting work in Cote d'Ivoire, Togo, and Benin in West Africa, as well as Botswana, and Malawi in Southern Africa (Aderonmu, 2003). This phase served as a strong launching pad into the expansion phase.

Expansion Phase
1997–2004

Pade Tokun served as CAPRO's international director during this phase. In an interview with CAPRO's first fulltime missionary, Aderonmu and his wife Dupe, in 2003, they described Tokun's tenure as a blend of the restoration of CAPRO's foundational values of incarnational ministry and deep spirituality of the first phase with the good organizational structure and strategy of the second phase. There was resurgence in the number of people participating in CAPRO as volunteers, fulltime staff and missionaries. According to Dupe, CAPRO's human resource strength stood at about four hundred in 2003.

CAPRO's goal was expanded again to include sending missionaries to people groups or nations that the Lord will lead them to (Aderonmu, 2003, p. 3). This was certainly beyond the previous scope in which their goal was to French-speaking West African countries and certainly the original goal of reaching one particular group in Northern Nigeria. Regarding organizational technology, CAPRO expanded its tool options to include prayer mobilization in churches, cross-cultural training, and holistic ministry designed to address the felt-needs of its contexts. Aderonmu became CAPRO's international director in 2005.

CAPRO increasingly became an open system, being receptive to and dependent on flows of personnel, resources, and information from outside the organization. It could be said that CAPRO's relational approaches celebrate process over structure, and becoming over being (Scott, 2003, p. 100). CAPRO is fitting into the descriptions of recent theorists, who see organizations as shifting coalitions (Cyert & March, 1963) or networks (Nohria & Eccles, 1992), as on-going narratives or conversation among participants (Czarniawska, 1997), as a nexus of contracts (Jensen & Meckling, 1976), or as a portfolio of financial assets (Davis, Dickmann, & Tinsley, 1994). I think an organization whose members are so strongly driven by a vision (in this case to reach the unreached with the gospel) will adjust every other organizational aspect to fit and serve that great vision. CAPRO like WEC International has kept that vision alive in its members.

Regarding the context and organizational environment in its home base in Nigeria, this phase witnessed the end of military rule and return to democratic governance as well as privatization of the economy leading to increased demand for accountability. The indirect combined influence of these developments led to CAPRO giving its missionaries more autonomy but with higher accountability expectation.

CAPRO's historical overview (Table 1 sets out the timeline) reflects that it possesses some characteristics of effective organizations such as: healthy communication laterally and vertically; shared value and integrity with leadership strategy to support it; being responsive to change; level of performance goals; adequacy of training; and spreading the control process across various levels of the organization. However, this historical overview exposes the fact that some characteristics of effective organizations are lacking such as member care and decision-making process. This situation has adversely affected the growth and stability of some CAPRO mission field work such as in the French-speaking West African country of Guinea where CAPRO has lost the services of some missionaries.

1975	1988	1997	Present
Foundational and Pioneering Phase	**Consolidation and Structuring Phase**	**Expansion Phase**	
Famonure	Ozodo	Tokun	
Informal Org.: Calvary Productions	Org. Tools: Research, Training, Mercy	Restoration of CAPRO's foundational values of	
Influenced by NCE/ Lausanne 1	Ministry, Health, Relief, Development and	incarnational ministry	
Maguzawa	Human Resource	Org. Tools:	
Formal Org.: Calvary	Management	Prayer, Cross-cultural	
Ministries (CAPRO)	Organizational	Training, Holistic	
Focus/Goal: Islamic	Perspective: Natural-	Ministry	
nations such as Niger	Open System	Africa, Europe and Arab	
Republic	Focus: Malawi, Cote	Countries	
Revised/Additional Goal/	d'Ivoire, Botswana,	Organizational	
Focus: Northern	Malawi, Benin, Togo	Perspective Open	
Nigeria, The Gambia,	Social Structure: Voluntary	System	
Niger Republic, Guinea,	membership with more	Aderonmu	
Senegal and French-	fulltime staff	Church mobiliza-	
speaking countries	Context and Org.	tion through Mission	
Organizational technol-	Environment: Military	Awareness programs	
ogy or tool—Discipl-	rule with attempt on	Social Structure:	
ship, Language learning	democratic rule	Increased Voluntary	
as well as Incarnational	Dominant Ecclesiological	membership with	
method of ministry	Models: Church as	more fulltime staff	
Org. Perspective: Closed	Herald, Servant,	Context and Org. Env:	
System	Institution, Mystical	Return	
Social Structure: Voluntary	Communion and	Dominant Ecclesiological	
membership and mostly	Community of Disciples	Models: Church as	
volunteer staff		Herald, Servant,	
Context and Org.		Mystical Communion	
Environment: Islam		and Community of	
loosing dominance,		Disciples	
Military rule			
Partnership with WEC			
School of Mission			
Dominant			
Ecclesiological Models:			
Church as Herald, and			
Community of Disciples			

TABLE 1. Historical Overview Timeline on the Calavary Ministries (Capro)

It can also be inferred that CAPRO leans toward the use of outcome and processes as indicators or measures of organizational effectiveness. This leaning by CAPRO translates into great cross-cultural mission impact that God has enabled CAPRO to make quantitatively and qualitatively within and outside Africa in the last twenty-years. On the other hand, inadequate attention to the structure indicator also works against the accreditation of CAPRO's programs and training programs by accrediting agencies. Lack of adequate attention to structure is also weakening CAPRO's capacity for better organizational effectiveness in cross-cultural mission.

The next section provides an analysis of CAPRO's organizational performance using biblical models and some organizational perspectives.

USING BIBLICAL MODELS AND SOME ORGANIZATIONAL PERSPECTIVES FOR ANALYZING CAPRO AND ITS PERFORMANCE

The Church as Herald, Servant, Institution, Mystical Communion and Community of Disciples have been the complementary models in all the developmental phases of CAPRO with the Herald model most prevalent. This model-mix, along with other factors, explains the reason behind CAPRO's pace-setting missional impact within and outside Africa, making it one of the largest African initiated non-church mission agencies.

Regarding organizational performance perspectives, the contingency theory approach is the most dominant in CAPRO. As a missional organization that promotes and wants to model indigenization and contextualization in mission, CAPRO's organizational performance has been contingent upon the situation and factors in which it finds itself.

The factors include the environment, goals, technology, and people. CAPRO's performance has been influenced by how far and how well these various elements are aligned.

The population ecology theory is a close second as an organizational performance perspective for CAPRO, which operates with an understanding that organizational forms that have high levels of reliability and accountability are favored by selection processes. The selection process presents organizational forms that are comparatively more suited to the environment or niche within which they are operating as performing better.

The next section employs aspects, questions or tools of missiological analysis to identify some of CAPRO's distinctive characteristics facilitating its effectiveness in cross-cultural mission.

A Missiological Analysis of CAPRO

The convergence of the modern missionary movement with the rise of European empires complicated Christianity's position in colonized societies. Sanneh calls the present resurgence of majority world initiatives in world mission, the "Third Awakening." He also argues that Charismatic Christianity has been the driving engine of this Third Awakening and is largely responsible for the dramatic shift in the religion's center of gravity (2008, p. 275).

The pace of religious expansion in Africa entered its most vigorous phase following the end of colonial and missionary hegemony with the dramatic collapse of postcolonial states fueling the expansion. See Table 2 and Table 3 in Appendix A.

In 1900 the Muslim population of Africa was 34.5 million, compared to roughly 10 million Christians, a ratio of better than 3:1. By 1985

Christians outnumbered Muslims for the first time. Of the continent's total population of 520 million, Christians (including self-styled evangelicals) numbered 271 million, compared to 216 million Muslims. In 2000, the number of Christians in Africa grew to 346 million, with 330 million Muslims concentrated mostly in the Arab-speaking regions of Egypt and North and in West Africa. The projected figure for 2005 was 390 million Christians, with 600 million estimated for 2025. It is a continental shift of historic proportions. (Lamin Sanneh, 2008, p. 275)

In the following section, I will highlight a number of missiological factors demonstrating CAPRO's distinctive characteristics as a part of the majority world initiatives in Christian mission. I will also identify some of the weaknesses that should be addressed. Thereafter, I will give an outline some of the challenges facing CAPRO.

Some Distinctive Characteristics

1. Beyond Career—Calling. CAPRO missionaries and staff treat missionary involvement as a calling and not just a career, employment, job or position.

2. Training Within the Context of Missionary Practice.[10] Training includes formal, informal, and non-formal. CAPRO's School of Mission started in Zaria, later moved to Kauna and then Jos. There are few other mission organizations running training within the context. Training within the context of missionary service facilitates acculturation. Over seven hundred persons from various church and non-church Christian organizations have been trained in CAPRO's School of Mission (Aderonmu 2006).

---

10 Do your best to present yourself to God as one approved, a workman who does not need to be ashamed and who correctly handles the word of truth. 2 Timothy 2:15.

3. Research. CAPRO acquired its initial research skills and insights from relationship and partnership with WEC, whose research department is responsible for the research behind and publication of the much used and well known Operation World.

4. Communication. This is one of CAPRO's flagships endearing it to donors, its members and other publics.

5. Strong Discipleship and Mentoring. CAPRO places emphasis on the discipleship of converts on the mission field as well as the mentoring of mission trainees and leaders of new church plants. CAPRO runs a Discipleship and Mission Exposure Program (DIMEP).

6. Incarnational Lifestyle –CAPRO's "Guiding Principles" document serves as a road map for CAPRO missionaries. This document emphasizes incarnational self-sacrificing life-style. See also CAPRO's Expansion Phase 1997–2004. CAPRO missionaries follow the example of Jesus Christ as articulated in John 1:14.

7. Language Learning. CAPRO employs this age-old mission strategy, which is ignored by several other mission agencies. Language learning has enhanced the effectiveness of CAPRO missionaries cross-culturally especially in Arab nations and French-speaking Sub-Saharan nations.

8. Accountability. I mentioned this in the Expansion Phase. CAPRO's track record in this area of accountability has generated a climate of trust within strengthening internal cohesion. It has also deepened trust with its partners thereby expanding the support base for CAPRO.

9. Openness to Change. This is reflected in the flexibility of the CAPRO leadership to take the gospel to nations outside the region previously defined as their focus. CAPRO was also open to change in other areas as influenced by its partnership with WEC.

10. Leadership Development and Succession. After the crisis generated from the first transition from the pioneer leader to the first successor, CAPRO has enjoyed relatively smooth transitions in subsequent leadership successions.

11. Deep Spiritual Formation. This is foundational to CAPRO, but was de-emphasized during its consolidation phase. New emphasis on deep spiritual formation is furthering CAPRO's growth, which is reflected in its on-going expansion phase.

12. Eschatological Vision. This is central to CAPRO's motivation for mission as disclosed during a focus group research discussion session in 2006.

13. Mission Strategy based on the "people group" concept rather than territorial expansionism. One example is the pioneering outreach to the *Maguzawas.*

14. Holistic perspective on mission developed through relationship with WEC

15. Relationship Building. Puzzled by the scant attention missionaries paid to experience and social relationships, and frustrated by the missionaries' paternal attitude toward them, Africans embarked on an independent course to take the drama of salvation into areas of life and experience where it was eagerly welcomed. Faced with a historic challenge, African leaders made the choice on behalf of their people to reengage the gospel afresh. (Lamin Sanneh, 2008, p. 167)

CAPRO is a typical example of an African mission agency that reengages the gospel afresh through relationship as attested to in a recent interview on its mission work in Mali.

Weaknesses to be Addressed

1. Historical overview exposes the fact that some characteristics of effective organizations are lacking such as member care and decision-making process. This situation has adversely affected the growth and stability of some CAPRO mission field work such as in the French-speaking West African country of Guinea where CAPRO has lost the services of some missionaries.

2. On the other hand, inadequate attention to organizational structure also works against the accreditation of CAPRO's training programs by accrediting agencies. Lack of adequate attention to structure is also weakening CAPRO's capacity for better organizational effectiveness in cross-cultural mission.

3. CAPRO is strong in dispersing disciplers but weak in gathering disciples because of the haste at which leaders of church plants are trained for cross-cultural mission at the expense of good nurturing. This is typical of mission agencies.

4. A mission theology, which presumably assigns church organizations with the role of generating resources (human, financial and material) for cross-cultural mission, while mission agencies like CAPRO are to train and deploy missionaries to identified mission fields. This theology still creates a dichotomy between non-church mission organizations and church-based mission organizations. With this CAPRO is just another example for a new mission agency that employs the old mission agencies' methods. We need new paradigms and approaches from these new Christian mission initiatives from

the majority world countries that fit the environment, resources, people, and visions. This is where CAPRO's close relationship with WEC and learning from it works to CAPRO's disadvantage.

Challenges

1. Tendency to Replication. Though CAPRO's School of Mission includes contextualization in its curriculum, and CAPRO mentors its missionaries regarding giving priority to understanding the host culture, CAPRO missionaries face the challenge of falling into the trap of replicating the "way mission is done by Nigerians."

2. Availability of trainees for cross-cultural mission. Now that churches in Nigeria are increasingly becoming missional, churches are establishing their own schools for training missionaries. This is reducing the number of potential students for CAPRO's School of Mission. Many of the denominational schools of mission are ecclesiocentric, while CAPRO has tried to maintain a Kingdom of God perspective. This challenge is faced even much more by similar organizations in Ghana. Nothing that is interdenominational finds support there easily. The only exception is when there is a strong leader people know and trust.

3. Developing enduring strategic partnership with church organizations. With several church denominations establishing their own schools of mission and sending out their missionaries, CAPRO needs to redefine its mission focus as well as explore meaningful partnership with the churches. Yes, I believe that is one of the keys. These church-based mission schools are mostly very much lacking in CAPRO's greatest strength, cross-cultural training that is really practical and can be used effectively in the field.

Lessons from and to the Western Missionary Movements as well as the Majority World Missionary Movements

Majority world missionary movements have roles to play in sustaining and spreading the current resurgence in Christian mission. They are different from the missionary movements from Western Europe and North America though they have some similarities. Similarities include tendency to replication rather than contextualization. The missionary movements and initiatives from Europe and North America will benefit by picking some insights from the distinctive characteristics of these majority world missionary movements.

Similarly, the majority world mission movements can address some of their weaknesses by learning from their predecessors, the Western Europe and North America missionary movements. Such collaborative and partnership perspectives will facilitate renewal of the Western Europe and North America missionary movements as well as the sustainability and spread of the current resurgence of the majority world initiatives in Christian mission.

Missionary movements from Latin America, Nigeria, Korea, and elsewhere have much to learn from each other including the wisdom of escaping the dependency trap of paternalism. One major insight that the missionary movement from the West can learn from the majority world missionary movement is regarding effective Christian witness and response to religious plurality. The Christian witness and response should not be dependent on or defined by state support and facility with its consequent religious polarization and global political implications. Another will be in the area of integrating faith with life and living without falling into the trap of creating a dichotomy between the spiritual and the sacred.

On the other hand, missionary movements from Latin America, Nigeria, Korea and elsewhere can learn some lessons from the missionary movements from Western Europe and North America in various areas such as in the holistic perspective to mission, member care, paying attention to structure to facilitate accreditation of training programs, decision-making process and eventually organizational effectiveness,

The need for a synthesis of missiological insights from the Western missionary movements and the emerging majority world missionary movements encourages the development of a missiological framework for evaluating and promoting organizational performance in cross-cultural mission. This is discussed in the next section. Considering this framework may help in identifying some insights for sustaining and enhancing the current resurgence in Christian mission.

Proposing A Pilgrim Framework: A Missional Strategy For An Enduring Impact Of Christian Mission

Recent research identifies at least thirteen missional themes for evaluating and enhancing organizational performance in cross-cultural mission. These themes constitute a missional framework, that I will call pilgrim framework, which is proposed here as a missional strategy for an enduring impact of the majority world initiatives in Christian mission (Lawanson, 2007). These themes are discussed in the next section.

1. Contextual Missional Theology. The components of this theme are Crucicentrism, Activism, Biblicism, Conversionism, as well as Contextual and Incarnational components. Theology is needed so that the majority world church and other non-church Christian organizations involved in cross-cultural mission can be who and whose they truly are. Embracing a contextual missional theology will help such Christian organizations see themselves in terms of their calling in the world and participation in God's mission rather than in terms of what they do or what happens within their organizations. However, this should not be misconstrued to promote an ecclesiocentric mission outlook, under which these organizations advance themselves toward other parts of the world. Rather, a contextual misisonal theology spurs a shift to a theocentric vision of the *missio Dei,* wherein the organizations understand themselves as the called and sent people of God.

I agree with Hunsberger's argument that the pressing need of the day is a missional ecclesiology that is biblically originated, practically evident, and contextually potent (2003:110). The four evangelical characteristics presented by Bebbington can also constitute the main distinctive for contextual missional theology (1989, pp. 5-19). These characteristics are Conversionism, Activism, Biblicism and Crucicentrism. Hunsberger describes conversion as the essence of the goal of missions in evangelical understanding of it arguing that churches should become a "converting community"—in other words, one that is not only converting others but also continuing to undergo its own conversion, deeply and daily (2003, pp. 123, 126). It is the participation in the mission of God towards the conversion of others that Bebbington calls activism (1989:10). Biblicism is the devotion to the Bible. Biblical authority is essential to contextual missional theology. CAPRO together with all majority world missions affirms the authority of the Bible in its incorporation statutory documents such as constitutions, trust deeds and others

Understanding one's own culture, becoming effective learners in another cultural context, as well as reflecting on the cultural differences using the perspectives of Scriptures and faith in Jesus Christ will facilitate contextual incarnational mission. Embracing and promoting Conversionsim, Biblicism, Activism, Crucicentrism, Contextual and

Incarnational mission will enhance organizational performance in cross-cultural mission. The basic premise of the missional organization is that mission is not simply one of its programs or functions. It constitutes its very essence or nature (Kirk, 2000, p. 30).

Within the pilgrim framework, the missional model embraced by a mission agency or church organization is shaped by its contextual missional theology, strengthened by trust, refined by periodical evaluation, renewed by continued inspiration, influenced by organizational stability, leadership, membership, performance as well as its accountability structure. This missional model is designed as having "treasures in earthen vessels" (2 Corinthians). That is a biblical illustration of the content of a pilgrim framework. CAPRO's organizational performance was influenced by its missional model.

2. Organizational Trust. Within the pilgrim framework, organizational trust is defined by an inspirational organizational model authenticated or affirmed by organizational evaluation. The majority world initiatives in cross cultural mission thrive in an environment permeated by accountability climate, which encourages members to develop competencies needed to establish and maintain trust as well as credibility with all members. Organizational trust promotes accountability culture, which strengthens people's ability to establish reciprocal, trusting relationships with one another.

3. Organizational Evaluation. This provides guidelines for building organizational capacity for performance. Evaluation promotes partnership as affirmed by CAPRO. Organizational data reveal whether this component is present. Within the pilgrim framework, accountability facilitates evaluation. Accountability is defined by organizational model, thereby establishing the tripartite relationship between these organizational factors.

4. As Pioneering But Not Settling. This pilgrim framework theme
is designed with a perspective of pioneers (Adeyemo, 2001). Therefore
the pilgrim framework will promote breaking new grounds and thereby
facilitating mission and evangelization. This perspective is akin to the
apostolic pattern that Paul modeled. This contrasts the settler mentality, which has stalled several mission efforts. Other relevant scriptures
illustrating this organizational perspective are Deuteronomy 1:6-8;
Joshua 13:1 and Mark 1:38.[11] According to Roland Allen, this lack of
faith leads to or generates fear and distrust of native independence
as well as feeling of indispensability of the missionary (1962, p. 143),
which results in the settler mentality.

5. As Pilgrims Not Tourists. The pilgrim framework generates an
organizational perspective that motivates a Christian organization to
pursue cross-cultural mission with devotion and intentionality of a
long haul rather than the short-term and pleasure perspective found
with tourists and tourism. Tourism is generally transactional with
the tourist sourcing for items to buy from the host community as
souvenirs or for commercial purpose. On the other hand, the pilgrim
framework demands that the missionary operates from a spiritual
approach with a great potential for mutual transformational impact
on the host community and the missionary. This is reflected in the
interview with one of CAPRO's missionaries in South Africa. "Yes.
People know that you are not coming here as a free loader to take
what you can take and go. So there is a synergy and there is a better

---

11 "The LORD our God said to us at Horeb, "You have stayed long at this mountain.
Break camp and advance See, I have given you this land that the LORD swore
he would give to your fathers—to Abraham, Isaac, and Jacob—and to their
descendants after them" Deuteronomy 1:6-8.
"When Joshua was old and well advanced in years, the Lord said to him, "You
are very old, and there are still large areas of land to be taken over" Joshua 13:1.
"Let us go somewhere else—to the nearby villages—so I can preach there also.
That is why I have come" Mark 1:38.

acceptability". This perspective enhances organizational performance (1 Chronicles 29:15; Psalm 84:5). [12]

6. As Witness with Values and Distinctive. C.S Lewis aptly describes this in the book, *The Pilgrim's Guide: C.S. Lewis and the Art of Witness* edited by David Mills (Mills, 1998). A missionary movement operating with the pilgrim framework develops a perspective to bear God's glory, seeing the salvation of human souls as its real business (p. 4). With such perspective, the missionary organization will have a wide historical perspective whose vistas save from local errors (p. 32). This perspective is both Trinitarian (p. 13) and incarnational (p. 60)—affirming and denying the world (p. 225), thereby enabling and positioning organizations that embrace it to impact its world effectively. Responses from three CAPRO officials affirmed this pilgrim framework: "Discipleship lifestyle" (Editor CAPRO's Magazine); "Things like living sacrificial life" (CAPRO's Students Mobilization Coordinator); "Our lifestyle has helped our cross-cultural role" (CAPRO's Mobilization and Media Secretary). A pilgrim perspective derived from an organizational pilgrim framework discourages an organization from relying on pseudo strengths that turn against it.

7. As Exiles. Moving into exiles at different times in its history has contributed to the global spread and growth of the Jewish nation today. I agree with Max I. Dimont cited by Shenk (2004) that

> Had they not been exiled, had they remained in Palestine, they probably would be no more of a cultural force in world history today than the remnants of the Karaites. Today, as once before, we have both an independent State of Israel and the Diaspora. But as in the past, the State of Israel today is a citadel of Judaism, a haven of refuge,

---

12 "We are aliens and strangers in your sight, as were all our forefathers "1 Chronicles 29:15; "Blessed are those whose strength is in you, who have set their hearts on pilgrimage" Psalm 84:5.

the center of Jewish nationalism where dwell only two million of the world's twelve million Jews (1962:417).

Church and non-church Christian organizations need to follow this exilic or pilgrim pattern in order to facilitate continuity in cross-cultural mission and world evangelization. God's pilgrim people need only two things: support for the road, and a destination at the end of it (Power, 1970, p. 28). This exile thematic component is prevalent in the data on CAPRO

8. Centripetal and Centrifugal. Gathering disciples yet dispersing disciplers. I agree with Shenk (2004:7) that there can be no missionary witness without missionary presence. That is the essence of incarnational mission. Indeed, both the Old and New Testaments hold up the image of the pilgrim as the appropriate stance for every missionary—and every Christian—in relation to any culture and its people (Exodus 23:9; 1 Peter 2:11). The centrifugal motion is to be a permanent mark of the church and the church is to keep moving continuously until the gospel has reached every corner of the earth (Shenk 2004:6). The pilgrim framework promotes an organizational model that reflects the centripetal facet of devotion and the centrifugal facet of cross-cultural mission. The research data show that church mission organizations within the emerging majority world mission movement are strong in gathering disciples but weak in dispersing disciplers, while non-church organizations, including CAPRO, are strong in dispersing disciplers but weak in gathering disciples. This observation strengthens the need for closer partnership between church-based and non-church-based Christian mission organizations.

9. As a Movement and Not a Monument. An army succeeds not through trench warfare, but through movement and penetration tactics (Hauerwas & Willimon, 1989, p. 51). The Bible is fundamentally a story of people's journey with God. I have observed that Christian organizations that are not actively involved in cross-cultural mission through moving across culture boundaries and barriers are those that eventually become monumentally bureaucratic. This was one of the negative factors identified as slowing down church-based mission organizations in cross-cultural mission. The church is permanently underway, toward the ends of the world and the end of time (Bosch 1991:374). The presence of this component in the organizational life of church or non-church Christian organization influences its performance in cross-cultural mission. According to Newbigin, "nothing would be more foreign to this conception than a static view of the church" (1953:150-151).

10. As Occupying and Not Just Existing. Luke 19:13. The occupying is done territorially and from one territory to another such that it does not degenerate into settling. Mission organizations that operate with this facet of the pilgrim framework develop a missional perspective that they do not just exist, but they occupy not for any narrow secular nation agenda but for the Kingdom agenda.

11. As Resident Aliens with an Eschatological Vision. Hebrews 11:13-16. Mission organizations operating with the pilgrim framework develop organizational perspective that usually reflects a vision and vitality to confront organizational malaise as well as reclaim or retain the God-given capacity to win and nourish souls. CAPRO includes eschatological reasons as part of the motivation for their participation in cross-cultural mission. This was contained in the responses by CAPRO's Mobilization and Media Secretary to one of the research questions asked recently. Proclaiming its own transience, the church pilgrimages toward God's future (Bosch 1991:374).

12. As Having Values in a 'Devalued' World. The pilgrim framework demands that people in Christian organizations operate with an organizational perspective as a holy nation standing for sharply focused values in a devalued world (Hauerwas & Willimon, 1989). This pilgrim framework promotes organizational accountability "taking pains to do what is right not only in the eyes of the Lord but also in the eyes of men" (2 Corinthians 8:21).

13. Vulnerability and Interdependence. Pilgrims do not choose where to go, rather, where to go is usually a function or determined by the object of the pilgrim's devotion, which in the case of mission is the God of mission because it is His mission (*Missio Dei*). Acts 1:8, Mark 16:15-20, and John 20:21 illustrate this. A missional organization that pursues missionary call and executes missionary projects through the pilgrim framework and with a pilgrim perspective would also recognize that it could not do it alone. It needs to partner and collaborate with the host community, as well as other fellow pilgrims.

In the next section, an evaluation of the pilgrim framework is done both from theological and organizational theory perspectives.

EVALUATING THE PILGRIM FRAMEWORK

From organizational theory perspective, the description of the pilgrim framework demonstrates a consideration for process and outcome organizational performance indicator types.

The pilgrim framework enjoys considerable biblical support, which commends it as a framework for studying and enhancing the organizational life of Church and mission agencies. Derived from the biblical pilgrim metaphor, this perspective gives intimate personal meaning to organizational leadership by connecting with deep human hunger and thirst to know God. The vulnerability component of this framework frees it of any triumphalistic tendency. Pilgrims are both dependent and interdependent.

Operationally, this framework promotes world evangelization and cross-cultural mission, putting particular emphasis on incarnational witness. It operates by matching convictions with commitments characterized by the dialectic of suffering and joy being under the cross yet free.

Theologically, the pilgrim framework looks beyond the Church to the Kingdom, living between the remembrance of history and the hope of the kingdom. The pilgrim perspective lines up with Moltmann's statement that the mission of the church is not to spread the church but to spread the Kingdom (1977, p. 11). However, it reflects the diversity without losing the unity. It promotes both the local and universal influence. It's pioneering distinctive influences any organization that embraces it with both prophetic and apostolic ecclesiological marks. Another area of strength of the pilgrim framework is its insistence on biblical morality (Daniel 7:27; Matt 13:31-34; 1 Peter 2:11).

Strategically, the pilgrim framework has strong visionary components. Pilgrimage is usually not an end in itself but a means to end. Therefore, it can be inferred that a pilgrim framework will fit into highbrow Christology. It also fits into a messianic and relational ecclesiology of Moltmann's doctrine of the church (1977, p. 13).

Like other theological, missiological and organizational models, the pilgrim framework has its limitations, some of which are discussed here. Organizations that operate within the pilgrim framework will have a pilgrim perspective and may therefore develop a tendency toward isolationism and individualism also found in Snyder's interior kingdom model (1991:55). This tendency, which may arise out of over-spiritualization, is counter-system or counterculture and will consequently make the organization weak in contextualization. This is a big negative for the pilgrim perspective, which can probably be rectified through a complementary model that allows contextualization. The pilgrim framework also has a tendency to show little concern for structure and social change.

Summary and Conclusion

Integrating insights from organization theory, sociology, theology, and missiology, this paper has identified the distinctive characteristics of the majority world initiatives in Christian mission, exploring how the new missionary movements differ from the missionary movements from Western Europe and North America. This study also provides a platform for distilling some lessons to be mutually learnt by the various missionary movements, concluding with a proposal on a missional strategy, the pilgrim framework, for an enduring impact in Christian mission.

The proposed pilgrim framework is only one missiological perspective on Christian organizations. Other theological and organizational models, images, and perspectives are needed to remind us that the Church as well as mission agencies are supposed to be organizations established by the Lord and animated by His Spirit.

APPENDIX A

Year	1900	2000	2005 (projected)	2025 (projected)
Africa	8.75 million	346.4 million	389.304 million	600 million
North America	59.57 million	212 million	222 million	250 million
North America and Europe (combined) includes Russia in 1900	427.779 million (82% of the world Christians)	748 million	757.765 million (35% of the world's Christians)	767.9 million
Rest of the World (without N. America & Europe)	93.7 million	1.2 billion	1.378 billion (65% of the world's Christians)	1.85 billion

TABLE 2. The World Christian Resurgence New Center of Gravity

(Adapted from Lamin Sanneh 2008:276)

Year	1900	1985	2000	2025
Population	107.8 million	520 million	784 million	1.3 billion
Muslims	34.5 million	216 million	315 million	519 million
Christians	8.7 million	270.5 million	346.5 million	600 million

TABLE 3. Comparative Resurgence in Africa

(Adapted from Lamin Sanneh 2008:277)

REFERENCES

Aderonmu, A. (2003). *Historical Overview of CAPRO*. In R. Lawanson (Ed.) (pp. Telephone Interview). Pasadena, California and Orlando, Florida.

Aderonmu, A. (2006). Additional Data on CAPRO. In T. A. Lawanson (Ed.) (E-Mail ed.). Pasadena.

Adeyemo, T. (2001). Pioneer versus Settler Mentality: The Challenge before the Church and Mission Agencies in Africa. Unpublished Paper-- An unpublished manuscript presented at the dedication of the Nigeria Office of the Association of Evangelicals in Africa. Lagos, Nigeria. Stewardship and Accountability Commission of the Association of Evangelicals in Africa.

Ajayi, J. F. A. (1965). *Christian Missions in Nigeria 1841-1891: The Making of a New Elite*. Evanston: Northwestern University Press.

Allen, R. (1962). *Missionary Methods: St. Paul's or Ours?* (American Edition ed.). Grand Rapids, MI: Wm. B. Eerdmans Publishing Co.

Bebbington, D. W. (1989). *Evangelicalism in Modern Britain: A History from the 1730s to the 1980s*. London: ROUTLEDGE.

Bloch, M. (1954). *The Historian's Craft*. New York: Vintage Books.

Clinton, J. R. (1989). *Leadership Emergence Theory: A Self-Study Manual for Analyzing the Development of a Christian Leader*. Altadena, CA: Barnabas Resources.

Cox, H. (1995). *Fire From Heaven: The Rise of Pentecostal Spirituality and The Reshaping of Religion in the Twenty-first Century*.

Cyert, R. M., & March, J. G. (1963). *A Behavioral Theory of the Firm*. Upper Saddle River, New Jersey: Prentice Hall.

Czarniawska, B. (1997). *A Narrative Approach To Organizational Studies* (Vol. 43). Thousand Oaks, CA: SAGE Publications.

Davis, G. F., Dickmann, K. A., & Tinsley, C. H. (1994). The Decline and Fall of the Conglomerate Firm in the 1980s: The Deinstitutionalization of an Organizational Form. *American Sociological Review, 59*(59), 547-570.

Fuller, L. (2000). Nigerian Mission Boards and Societies. In A. S. Moreau (Ed.), *Evangelical Dictionary of World Missions* (pp. 1028). Grand Rapids, MI: Baker Books.

Hauerwas, S., & Willimon, W. H. (1989). *Resident Aliens: A Provocative Christian Assessment of Culture and Ministry for People who know that something is wrong*. Nashville, TN: Abingdon Press.

Hunsberger, G. R. (2003). Evangelical Conversion toward a Missional Ecclesiology. In J. John G. Stackhouse (Ed.), *Evangelical Ecclesiology: Reality or Illusion?* (pp. 232). Grand Rapids: Baker Books.

Jensen, M. C., & Meckling, W. H. (1976). Theory of the Firm: Managerial Behavior, Agency Costs, and Ownership Structure. *Journal of Financial Economics, 3*(3), 305-360.

Kirk, J. A. (2000). *What is Mission?: Theological Explorations.* Minneapolis: Fortress Press.

Lawanson, T. A. (2007). *Exploring Organizational Performance: A Case Study of Four Christian Organizations in Nigeria.* Unpublished Dissertation, Fuller Theological Seminary, Pasadena, CA.

Mills, D. (Ed.). (1998). *The Pilgrim's Guide: C.S. Lewis and The Art of Witness.* Grand Rapids, Michigan: William B. Eerdmans Publishing Company.

Moltmann, J. (1977). *The Church in the Power of the Spirit.* London: SCM Press.

Nohria, N., & Eccles, R. G. (Eds.). (1992). *Networks and Organizations: Structure, Form and Action.* Boston: Harvard Business School Press.

Olonade, T. (2004). "New Staff Orientation: CAPRO History." Unpublished manuscript. CAPRO Media and Publications.

Pfeffer, J. (1997). *New Directions for Organization Theory: Problems and Prospects.* New York: Oxford University Press.

Power, J. (1970). *Mission Theology Today.* Dublin Ireland: Gill and MacMillan.

Sanneh, L. (2003). *Whose Religion is Christianity? The Gospel beyond the West.* Grand Rapids, MI: Wm. B. Eerdsmans Publishing Company.

Sanneh, L. (2008). *Disciples of All Nations* (Vol. 1). Oxford, New York: OXFORD UNIVERSITY PRESS.

Scott, W. R. (2003). *Organizations: Rational, Natural, and Open Systems* (Fifth ed.). Upper Saddle River, New Jersey: Prentice Hall.

Shenk, W. R. (2004). Go and Dwell! Jeremiah's Exilic Model of Mission. Unpublished Paper Presented to commemorate 50th Anniversary of Mennonite Ministry in Israel. East Petersburg: Mennonite Church.

Van Gelder, C. (2006). *The Ministry of the Missional Church: A Community Led by the Spirit.*Unpublished manuscript, Grand Rapids, MI.

Walls, A. F. (2003). Commentary. In L. Sanneh (Ed.), *Whose Religion is Christianity? The Gospel Beyond the West.* Grand Rapids, MI: William B. Eerdmans Publishing Company.

16. MIGRANT WORKERS' CHURCHES AS WELCOMING, SENDING AND RECRUITING ENTITIES: A CASE STUDY OF MONGOLIAN MIGRANT WORKERS' CHURCHES IN KOREA

Myunghee Lee

It is not an exaggeration to state that the 21st century is an era of migration and diaspora. A 2005 statistic report claimed that there are 190 million people in the world who live in countriesin which they were not born (Koser 2007). Many of these migrants are temporary migrants, while others are permanent migrants. We can now experience a global village many places in the world where people of various cultures, ethnicities and languages are living together. A 2006 statistic report from the Migration Policy Institute states that Illinois' foreign born population is 1,777,600 out of a total population 12,831,970, representing more than 80 countries. As such globalization and diaspora effects are brought forth, we "face unexpected people at unexpected places" (Cohen 1997, 162). As another example, the long-time homogeneous nation of South Korea now has 2% of its population as foreigners currently and is transforming into a nation with multiple ethnicities, cultures, and languages representing some 40 countries of the world.

South Korea was a labor exporting country just 30 to 40 years ago. However, it has transformed into a labor importing country since the early 1990s. The number of foreign migrant workers in South Korea has been increasing steadily since that time. The number was a mere 50,000 in 1995, but had reached 640,000, representing 40 different countries, by November 2007. Most of these migrant workers are from countries that signed a Memorandum of Understanding (MoU) with South Korea that limits their work contract period to only three to five years. There were 15 countries that signed a MoU with South Korea as of June 2008. The list includes the Philippines, Mongolia, Sri Lanka, Vietnam, Thailand, Indonesia, Uzbekistan, Pakistan, China, Cambodia, Nepal, Bangladesh, Kyrgyzstan, Myanmar and East Timor. There are several points here that Korean Church and mission organizations ought to note. The first is that most of these migrant workers are from countries that present great difficulties for evangelism efforts and living godly lives, including the 15 countries mentioned above. The second is that about 20% of these migrant workers are Muslims. The third is that these workers are replaced about every three years due to the limited contract period (although there are those overstaying in South Korea illegally) with opportunities to evangelize new people every three years. The last is that the average age of the increasing number of industrial trainees is early 20's and early 30's.

The church in Antioch was established as the result of evangelism to the Greeks by the Christians from the Jerusalem church who had dispersed (or migrated) to Antioch due to persecution they faced in Jerusalem (Acts 11:19-20). The Apostle Paul spent his entire Christian life preaching the gospel in many parts of the world as a purpose-driven migrant. Migration and missions kept a close relation in the history of missions since that time. Missionary work and Christian migrants have always gone hand-in-hand, resulting in numerous cases of evangelism, whether voluntary or involuntary. Christian migrants planted the church for themselves wherever they had settled and later also spread the gospel to the people in the midst of whom they lived. From this perspective, migration has been a major "bridge of God" for Christianity's spread in the past and in the present also (Norwood, 1969; Conn, 2000). However, the importance of migration does not apply to just Christian missions, but applies equally to missions efforts of other religions. The Muslim population of the United Kingdom increased from 21,000 in 1951 to 369,000 in 1970 to 1.6 million in 2006, tracking the increase of Muslim immigrants to the United Kingdom. A country that used to send missionaries to Islamic countries now has 3% of its population as Muslims (Hanciles 2008, 122). Hanciles notes, "the link between migration and global religious expansion remains profound and inextricable, and importantly, both phenomena have intensified in recent decades" (2008, 118).

Before the World Wars, international migration was shaped by the needs and purposes of European imperialism. Since it was a period when colonizers migrated to colonized areas, international migration during this period chiefly involved movement from the highly developed, politically powerful nations to areas in the non-Western world. Accordingly, migration in the other direction was an exception during that period (Jongeneel 2003, 30). Since the 1960s, however, a reverse flow of international migration has been taking place—migrant movement has been predominantly from areas with weak economic and political system to the centers of global dominance and advance industrial growth (Hanciles, 122-123). Consequently, migration from non-Western countries to Western countries and migration of South-to-North are on the rise. Although visible political and economical conditions of these migrants may seem weak, the effect of their cultures and religions to hosting nations is not to be ignored. This effect is the same whether the migrants are Christians or people of other religions.

There is "the shift within global Christianity of the concomitant rise of a non-Western missionary movement" (Hanciles, 126) taking place along with the reverse flow of international migration. We can categorize non-Western migrants into two large groups from the mission's perspective. One group is non-Western *Christian* migrants in Western countries that were known as Christian nations as well as currently being called Christian nations. The other group is *non-Christian* migrants in Christian nations or in nations with a strong Christian influence. There are different strategies and results of missions from these two cases. We can find two major types of missions work in "so-called" Western Christian nations by non-Western missionaries. The first type is where evangelical Christian migrants are doing missions in reverse to colonizing nations that brought the gospel to them. People of non-Western Christian missionary groups are convinced of their call to preach the full gospel to secular Europeans, doing the so-called "reverse mission" (Jongeneel 2008, 32). By helping local congregations in their host nation to become spiritually revitalized, Latino Christians in Europe do missionary work among their host Europeans (Palomino 2004, 58). The second type is where these immigrants do missions among their peer immigrants (Jongeneel, 32; Wan 2003). When peer immigrants share the gospel message the acceptance level is much higher. There are numerous cases of many non-Christian immigrants converting to Christian faith through the self-help role of existing ethnic immigrant congregations. The case of Korean-American immigrant churches is a good example of that (Hurh & Kim 1990). Ethnic immigrant Christian congregations provide "a home away from home" to those lonely immigrants going through difficulties of immigrant life which, in turn, bring them to Christian faith as they base their lives centered around these congregations (Kwon 2003; Ebaugh et al 2000, Warner & Wittner 1998).

This is the "go and make disciples" case where missionary Christians emigrated away from their home and preached the gospel to those living in the countries they immigrated to. This trend has been for a couple of decades the most common missions approach called centrifugal approach. The effectiveness of missionary work by Christian immigrants among people in host nation or among other (im)migrants in this 21st century's immigration and diaspora is mentioned in several works (Escobar 2003; Wan 2003; Palomino 2004; Hanciles 2003, 2008).

The latter trend of the reverse flow of international migration that I want to mention contrasts with the first trend. This approach is a centripetal approach where mission-minded Christians in Christian or Christian-influenced nations are receiving non-Christian immigrants with warm hearts and preaching the gospel. Although there are many Christians among international migrants, we cannot ignore the fact that more than half of them are non-Christians. Furthermore, we cannot forget the fact that many of them use their immigrant lives as opportunities to propagate their religions just as immigrant Christians use their immigrant lives as opportunities for missions.

We are at a critical juncture of this international migration era when we either can do God's missions or have non-Christian missions done to us. Immigration could be a threat to Christian missions from one perspective, but could be a great challenge and opportunity from another perspective. For example, a nation with a weak Christian influence could be at risk of being Islamized with a massive Muslim migration into that nation, while the same migration to a nation with world Christians could present a good opportunity to win them to Christ. Risk and opportunity always exist wherever non-Christian migrants migrate. This is the case with many nations along with Europe and the USA. "Contemporary Europe has at least one million Christian migrants. However, it is also clear that the number of the Islamic migrants exceeds that of the Christian migrants" (Jongeneel 2003: 31). The fact that 3% of the UK population is Muslim could be called a product of the international migration phenomenon. The case of South Korea is the same. About 130,000 of the 640,000 migrant workers in South Korea are Muslims. As a reference, Vatican News reported that Islam has become the biggest single religious denomination in the world (Reuters, March 30, 2008).

Churches and Christians of immigrant host nations need to fervently strategize missions work in order for risk and opportunity bearing international migration to be an opportunity rather than a risk from Christian missions perspective.

MISSIONS AMONG MONGOLIAN MIGRANT WORKERS IN KOREA: A CASE STUDY OF MIGRATION AND MISSION

In this section, I would like to examine on-going missions for migrant workers in Korea. The data used in this paper is what I have collected from a five-year study and a three-month field research on the four Mongolian migrant workers' churches in South Korea, with participant observations, 29 interviews with seven Korean ministers and 30 Mongolian migrant workers (16 existing workers in Korea and 14 workers who returned to Mongolia), and the demographic survey data from 158 Mongolian workers of the four churches.

In fact, South Korea is not a Christian country. According to the census done in 2005, 22.8 % of South Koreans are Buddhists; 18.3% are Protestant Christians; and 10.9% are Catholics. However, Korea is ranked second after the US in numbers of overseas missionaries officially sent by mission agencies. South Korea's international missionary force has exploded in numbers from about 100 in 1980 to about 1,645 in 1990, to 8,103 in 2000, to 13,000 in 2006, and to 18,000 in 2008 (Moon 2003, Moll 2006). In addition to sending missionaries overseas to the geographical ends of the earth, South Korean churches put their efforts on missions for migrant workers who came from many countries outside South Korea, the majority of them being non-western and non-Christian migrants who are the cultural-religious ends of the earth within South Korea. There are hundreds of migrant workers' churches in South Korea, although it is impossible to count the exact number. The structure of the migrant workers' churches differs: some have an ethnic structure, and others a multiethnic; some have ethnic leaders, and others foreign leaders. There are many stereotypes even in Mongolian migrant workers' churches, which this paper addresses. Two out of the four research group churches have an ethnic structure, and the other two churches have a multiethnic or international structure. The difference in the two ethnic churches is that one is served by a Mongolian pastor and the other is served by a former Korean missionary to Mongolia. One of the two multiethnic churches is composed of 22 nationalities in similar proportion, and the other one has three nationalities (Mongolian, Chinese and Nepali) and 80% of the congregation is Mongolian.

Migrant workers' churches in South Korea mainly have similar mission statements regardless of the structures and types. "Evangelize the migrant workers first and evangelize people of the nation of their origin through them." The vision statement of 'DIASPORA MOGOLIAN NETWORK' (DMN), for example, is "to build the Kingdom of God through the Mongolian Diaspora." To accomplish the vision, most migrant workers' churches focus on three major ministries: 1) Evangelizing migrant workers, 2) Discipling migrant converts and training leaders among them, and 3) Generating missions among migrant Christians.

Evangelism

Christianity in Mongolia can be summarized briefly: until 1990, Mongolia was one of the most closed countries in the world with no church (Hogan 1999; Johnstone and Mandryk 2001; Rhodes 1996). However, the Mongolian Church expanded rapidly from no recorded Christians on September 23, 1990 to 900 members in 7 to 8 churches by August 1992. This growth continued to 8,000 to 10,000 members in 60 churches and 100 informal worship gatherings by 2000 (Gibbens 1996; Kemp 2000, 496; Johnstone and Mandryk 2001). A more recent estimate reported over 40,000 church members were in 400 churches in Mongolia by 2006 (Kook-Min Ilbo [Seoul], 31 December 2006).

As of August 2007, about 30,000 Mongolian migrant workers, which is a little above 1% of the entire Mongolian population in Mongolia of 2.9 million, are already in South Korea. This number is so noticeable that the South Korean government estimates that "one in two households in the cities has a family member who works Korea" (Han 2006). As the number of Mongolian migrant workers increases, that of Mongolian migrant workers' churches in South Korea also increases. The number of Mongolian migrant workers' churches was 5 to 60 in 2006, and it increased to 80 by the end of 2007 (DMN).

The Mongolian migrant workers' churches in South Korea have demonstrated effectiveness in evangelism in two significant ways. First, evangelism to migrant workers in South Korea is more efficient than evangelism to people living in Mongolia. According to the chief director of DMN, Mongolian migrant workers in South Korea are seven times more likely to become Christians than Mongolians in their home country.

The methods of evangelism vary slightly depending on the structure of the churches. The majority of ethnic churches receive new members through migrant workers seeking people who speak the same language and are of the same ethnic group in churches or following their friends to churches without any particular evangelism effort. Homogeneity in language, culture and ethnicity itself is becoming the contact point of evangelism. On the other hand, multi-ethnic churches let the presence of their churches be known and obtain opportunities for evangelism to migrant workers through regularly scheduled visits to work places of migrant workers as well as providing shelter, medical treatment, job placement assistance or other social services to them. There have been many cases of migrant workers getting to know these churches and listening to the gospel through such social services.

Another significant evangelism method of migrant workers' churches is to preach the gospel to family members of migrant workers. Two methods are used to preach the gospel to family members. First, those ministering to migrant workers in South Korea visit Mongolia once a year for the purpose of evangelism. They gather all family members of church attending migrant workers together in one location then show pictures and video images of their loved ones. Since Mongolians live with extended family members, over ten family members per one migrant worker gather at such occasion. In other words, about 100 people gather for ten migrant workers, and an opportunity opens up to evangelize them. When they feel relieved to see their loved ones living happily even as laborers in a foreign land and to hear that such life is the result of encountering Jesus Christ as their personal savior, most of them accept the gospel. They are introduced to local churches or South Korean missionaries in Mongolia right away. Another approach to family evangelism is to evangelize family members who visit migrant workers in South Korea. Some family members of migrant workers come to Korea to visit their loved ones for two to three months. They attend churches with migrant workers who already attend church during that time. Churches capitalize on this opportunity to evangelize them. There are cases of some family members returning to Mongolia baptized. This method is more prevalent in ethnically homogeneous churches than in multi-ethnic churches. It shows that, for the sake of missions, an ethnic church is providential and more effective than a multi-ethnic church is (Adeney 1984; McGavran 1955; Newbigin 1977).

Discipling and Training Leaders

There are two levels of discipleship training provided for migrant worker churches. The first level is to help new converts among migrants grow spiritually in faith. This training is usually done through small groups and prayer meetings. Some churches use the worship place after Sunday worship to have small groups meet. Some churches have small groups meet one day during the week at a member's home. Small group leaders meet with the senior pastor (usually a South Korean minister) before they lead their small groups. This is a common practice among ethnic churches as well as multi-ethnic churches. Ethnic churches can easily meet in mid-week for a weekly prayer meeting because they share a common language and culture. Multi-ethnic churches conduct worship in English with simultaneous translation (when available) to their own languages. Small groups are usually led by South Korean lay leaders unless there is a leader speaking their own language. This limits mid-week small group meetings in multi-ethnic churches. Multi-ethnic churches, as opposed to ethnic churches, face difficulty in having mid-week small group meetings for this reason. Training each ethnic leadership is a dire issue in multi-ethnic churches.

The second level of discipleship is to develop ethnic leadership through cooperative education program with seminaries. Leadership development by each ethnicity is an absolute necessity in order to properly minister to migrants of various ethnic groups. Missions to migrants in South Korea are especially in need of ethnic leaders who understand their culture and language because of the South Korean labor law that limits their stay to short periods. It is true that ethnic churches need leaders, too. However, multi-ethnic churches are in greater need of leaders. One of my research subject churches is a multi-ethnic church with 22 ethnicities in one church. The church selects potential leaders from each ethnicity to train them with seminary education. Some seminaries provide half of tuition as scholarship to them while the church covers the other half of tuition and living costs. There have been 12 ethnic leaders trained under this program from 2001. Some of them are currently serving as respective ethnic leaders in this church, while some have gone back to their respective countries to work for the gospel. It is noteworthy to see a migrant workers' church acting as the connecting link among migrant workers, South Korean churches and seminaries.

Generating Missions

Three major ministries by migrant workers churches have been considered so far—evangelism, discipleship and training, and reverse send-off with a mission vision. Migrant workers' churches generate missions among migrant believers in South Korea through following ways. First, migrant workers' churches work to inspire migrant workers, who simply left their home to survive economically, to salvation, the biblical view and a vision for the world missions through sermons and education. The first reaction of the migrant workers who became Christians through migrant workers' churches' ministry is to share the joy of salvation with their fellow migrant workers. They also begin to have a vision for world missions. For example, some young migrant workers I interviewed listed their homeland Mongolia, Inner Mongolia (which is located in China and has more Mongolians than Mongolia), China, Russia and North Korea as peoples whom they want to evangelize. In addition, migrant workers' church members adopt needy churches in Mongolia and send monthly financial support to them. Secondly, they obtain mission training through a yearly Vision School sponsored by DMN and exclusively for Mongolian migrant workers. Practical evangelism work accompanies the Vision School curriculum. Additionally, a short term mission team consisting of Mongolians and South Koreans goes to Mongolia each summer. This kind of short term mission trips provides them with opportunities to preach the gospel in their own language and to experience souls returning to the Lord after hearing the gospel. Such experience gives great spiritual growth opportunity to migrant workers preaching the gospel as well as the new converts accepting the good news of the gospel. The transformation of migrant workers from people with zero knowledge of the gospel three to five years ago before coming to South Korea to Christians laboring to spread the gospel throughout the world is taking place through ministries of migrant workers' churches. Thirdly, migrant workers' churches reverse send-off migrant workers returning home after their labor term expires as missionaries to their respective countries. In 2006, I interviewed 14 returned migrant workers who became Christians through ministries of four migrant workers' churches that were in my research target groups. I also visited two local Mongolian churches started by returned migrant workers and one church where a returned migrant worker was ministering. The effect of saved migrant workers who were discipled and trained in South Korea on the evangelization of Mongolia and Mongolian churches was amazing.

In addition, one of the migrant workers' churches selected for this study is participating in a holistic mission where evangelism and community development are done in parallel. As the Korean pastor of one of the four Mongolian churches visited Mongolia, he discovered that a negative trend was continuing in Mongolian migrant workers. He found that returned migrant workers were not investing their hard earned money wisely but wasting it for several years without regular jobs and ending up being migrant workers again. This life pattern made the pastor realize that they could not rebuild their lives in Mongolia by themselves. After returning from Mongolia, he helped them build local churches where they could start and sustain church-based community development programs. After that, the pastor and returned migrant workers started a cattle farm on a large land that Mongolian government gives them the right to use. Local believers grow vegetables and raise cows, pigs and sheep for a business on that land. Their goals were to be self-sufficient with this set-up as well as to help economic development of the local community. This program was well accepted by the community and received a medal of recognition from the head of their state government. The director in charge of community development in this area was a member of a migrant workers' church a few years ago who had returned to Mongolia. She is studying at a seminary in Mongolia and serving at a local church started by existing and returned Mongolian migrant workers in addition to her community development work.

CONCLUSION

In summary, South Korean migrant workers' churches have three characteristics as a mission church. First, they serve as a welcoming mission entity among migrants. Many migrant workers are coming to the Lord as the church accepts them and preaches the gospel to them who came to South Korea on their own. This is a centripetal approach. Second, the churches, as mission entities, disciple and train them while they work in South Korea so that they can be reverse sent-off to their own countries as missionaries. This is a centrifugal approach. As evidenced through examples presented above, migrant workers' churches are performing the double function of welcoming bodies and sending bodies to do effective missions work in multi-faceted ways among migrant workers. Lastly, the churches, as recruiting mission entities, help Christians in Korea see the reality that Korea is becoming a mission field, and challenge them to play their parts of world mission "here" in Korea while overseas missionaries play their parts "over there."

REFERENCES

Adeney, Miriam. 1984. *God's foreign policy: Practical ways to help the world's poor.* Grand Rapids, Michigan: William B. Eerdmans Publishing Company.

Cohen, Robin. 1997. *Global diaspora: An introduction.* Seattle: University of Washington Press.

Conn, Harvie M. 2000. Migration. In *Evangelical dictionary of world missions,* ed.. A. Scott Moreau, 626. Grand Rapids: Baker Books.

Ebaugh, Helen Rose and Janet SAltzman Chafetz, eds. 2000. *Religion and the new immigrants: Contiunities and adaptations in immigrant congregations.* Abridged student edition. Walnut Creek: AltaMira Press.

Escobar, Samuel. 2000. The global scenario at the turn of the century. In *Global Missiology for the 21st Century: The Iguassu Dialogue,* ed. William D. Taylor, 25-46. Grand Rapids: Baker Academic.

Gibbens, John. 1996. The church in Mongolia. In *Church in Asia Today: Challenges & Opportunities,* ed. Saphir Athyal, 78-90. Asian Lausanne Committee for World Evangelization.

Han, Jae-Hyuck. 2006. Today in Mongolia: Everyone can speak a few words of Korean. Office of the President, Republic of Korea (2006-05-05). http://16cwd.pa.go.kr/cwd/en/archive/archive_view.php?meta_id=en_dip-2006&category=166&navi=president&id=923b8c655856408486c7764f

Hanciles, Jehu J. 2003. Migration and mission: Some implications for the twenty-first century church. *International Bulletin of Missionary Research* 27 (October): 146-53.

_____. 2008. Migration and mission: The religious significance of the North-South divide. In *Mission in the 21st century: Exploring the five marks of global mission,* ed. Walls, Andrew and Cathy Ross, 118-129. Maryknoll, New York: Orbis.

Hogan, Brian. 1999. Distant thunder: Mongols follow the Khan of Khans. *In Perspectives on the World Christian Movement. A Reader,* ed. Winter, Ralph D. and Steven C. Hawthorne, 694-698. Pasadena, California: William Carey Library.

Hurh, Won Moo and Kwang Chung Kim. 1990. Religious participation of Korean immigrants in the United States. *The Scientific Study of Religion.* 29, no. 1 (March): 19-34.

Johnstone, Patrick and Jason Mandryk. 2001. Mongolia. *Operation World: 21st Century Edition.* 451-453. Cumbria, UK: Paternoster Lifestyle.

Jongeneel, Jan A. B. 2003. The mission of migrant churches in Europe. *Missiology: An International Review,* 36, No. 1 (January): 29-33.

Kemp, Hugh, P. 2000. *Steppe by Step: Mongolia's Christians from Ancient Roots to Vibrant Young Church*. Monarch Books.

Koser, Khalid. 2007. *Internatioanl Migration: A Very Short Introduction*. New York: Oxford University Press.

Kwon, Okyun. 2003. *Buddhist and Protestant Korean Immigrants: Religious Beliefs and Socioeconomic Aspects of Life*. New York: LFB Scholarly Publishing LLC.

McGavran, Donald Anderson. 1955. *The Bridges of God: A Study in the Strategy of Missions*. New York: Distributed by Friendship Press.

Moll, Rob. 2006. Missions incredible. *Christianity Today* (March 2006): 28-34.

Moon, Steve S. C. 2003. The recent Korean missionary movement: A record of growth, and more growth needed. *International Bulletin of Missionary Research* 27, Vol. 1 (January): 11-17.

Newbigin, Lesslie. 1977. What is "a local church truly united"? *The Ecumenical Review* 29, no.2 (April): 115-128.

Norwood, Frederick A. 1969. *Strangers and Exiles: A History of Religious Refugees*. 2 vols. Nashville & New York. Abingdon Press.

Palomino, Miguel A. 2004. Latino immigration in Europe: Challenge and opportunity for mission. *International Bulletin of Missionary Research*, 28, no. 2 (April), 55-58.

Rhodes, David. 1996. *Cell church or traditional?: Reflections on church growth in Mongolia*. Cambridge: Grove Books Limited.

Wan, Enoch. 2003. Mission among the Chinese Diaspora: A case study of migration and mission. *Missiology: An International Review* 31, no.1 (January): 35-43.

Warner, R. Stephen and Judith G. Wittner, eds. 1998. *Gatherings in Diaspora: Religious Communities and the New Immigration*. Philadelphia: Temple University Press.

17. THE FILIPINO EXPERIENCE IN DIASPORA MISSIONS: A CASE STUDY OF MISSION INITIATIVES FROM THE MAJORITY WORLD CHURCHES

Enoch Wan and Sadiri Joy Tira

INTRODUCTION

This paper about Filipino diaspora in missions is a case study of "Mission Initiatives from the Majority World Churches," which is the theme of EMS for 2008.

This paper is organized in three parts. It begins with a description of the historico-demographic data, followed by the socio-economic context of Filipino diaspora, and concluded with missiological implications deriving from the data.

At the outset, it is necessary to define key terms as follows:

"Diaspora missiology"—In this paper, diaspora is used to refer to "the phenomenon of 'dispersion of any ethnic group'" (Pantoja *et. al.*

2004). "Diaspora in missions" refers to dispersed ethnic groups who are actively engaged or actively involved in fulfilling the Great Commission; regardless of vocation and denominational affiliations of individuals involved (Tira 1998). "Diaspora missiology" is "a missiological study of the phenomena of diaspora groups being scattered geographically and the strategy of gathering for the Kingdom" (Wan 2007).

"The Filipino Experience"—The involvement or participation of diaspora Filipinos in missions. This paper will limit its discussion of the "Filipino experience" to that of Overseas Filipino Workers (OFWs).

"Case study"—A detailed, intensive and in-depth study of a spatial-temporal-specific entity (e.g. a person or group, an institution or phenomenon).

It is assumed that this paper is not primarily about statistics, demographics, economics, labor industry, anthropology, or sociology but about God's mission through the diaspora Filipinos. The purpose is to showcase the Filipino experience within the context of "Mission Initiatives from the Majority World Churches" as featured by papers of EMS 2008 gatherings. The discussion will be delimited to Filipino nationals, specifically Overseas Filipino Workers (OFWs), deployed as seafarers on ocean vessels, and land-based workers in the 10/40 Window.

The Global Context of Recent Phenomena of Diaspora

There have been many diasporas over the centuries; however, the 20th and 21st centuries have been marked by unprecedented movements of people globally. Factors contributing to the phenomenon are: war, natural disasters (e.g. earthquakes, tsunamis, drought, hurricanes, etc.), as well as the breaking-up of states (e.g. the former Yugoslavia, former USSR), demographic changes in aging nations (i.e. declining populations in developed countries forces them to accept more immigrants and workers from the developing countries that are undergoing population increase); urbanization, development, and economic disparities between developing and developed countries coupled with an increasingly mobile labor force. In recent years, there has also been an alarming rise in human trafficking and smuggling operated by international syndicates.

Indeed, international migration is a complex issue that is increasingly changing societies, cultures, and world demography. Undoubtedly, all nations have been affected by mass migration internally. International migration is rapidly changing the demographic distribution globally.[1] In 2005, the International Organization for Migration (IOM)—an inter-governmental organization committed "to promoting humane and orderly migration for the benefit of all"[2]—reported that there were approximately 192 million international migrants.[3] Today, mass migration is one of the dominant forces in the world that is being "watched" not only by government policy makers and social scientists but also by missiologists; so much so that the annual gathering of the American Society of Missiology (AMS) in June 2002 was designated to deal with the topic "Migration Challenge and Avenue for Christian Mission" with the proceedings published in the journal *Missiology*.[4] Furthermore, The Lausanne Committee for World Evangelization (LCWE) included a

---

1   See chart, "Evolution of the Number of International Migrants in the World and Major Areas, and Selected Indicators Regarding the Stock of International Migrants, 1970-2000," in *World Migration: Costs and Benefits of International Migration 2005*. Vol. 3. International Organization for Migration (IMO). (2005). Geneva, Switzerland: International Organization for Migration.
2   Taken from the "About IOM" webpage http://www.iom.int/jahia/Jahia/cache/offonce/pid/2;jsessionid=0A5FBDD6F57A029282028A4464A3ECE8.worker02. Accessed August 8, 2007.
3   IMO, *World Migration* (2005).
4   Muck, Terry C. (Ed.). (2003). *Missiology An International Review: Mission and Migration* 31,1.

track (for the first time)—the DIASPORA PEOPLES—at the Forum 2004 in Pattaya, Thailand, among the many issues in global missions to be tackled. Hence, the diaspora missiology has emerged as a field studying the phenomenon of "diaspora missions."

THE FILIPINO EXPERIENCE: SCATTERED TO GATHER

In recent decades, it has been common knowledge among missiologists that there are mission initiatives from the majority world churches; thus the theme of EMS in 2008. The Filipino experience is one such a case.

People from the Philippines are widely scattered. According to the Population Reference Bureau (PRB),[5] an "estimated 10 percent of the country's population, or nearly 8 million people, are overseas Filipino workers distributed in 182 countries… That is in addition to the estimated 3 million migrants who work illegally abroad."[6] There are now over 11 million Filipinos working outside their homeland. Many of them are found in Creative Access Nations (CANs) and in the "10/40 Window"[7]of the world. According to the Philippine Council of Evangelical Churches, approximately seven percent of the Filipinos working overseas are evangelical Christians[8], and are thus a potential significant force of Kingdom workers. This background information

---

5   PRB informs people from around the world and in the United States about issues
    related to population, health, and the environment.
6   PRB http://www.prb.org/Articles/2003/RapidPopulationGrowthCrowded
    CitiesPresentChallengesinthePhilippines.aspx accessed 09-27-2007.
7   Van Rheenen, Gailyn. (1996). *Communicating Christ in Animistic Contexts.*
    Pasadena, CA: William Carey Library.
8   Rev. Efraim Tendero, Bishop and General Secretary of the Philippine Council of
    Evangelical Churches (PCEC) reported during the FIN Global Consultationin
    Singapore (July 20, 2002) that approximately seven percent of the OFWs living
    outside their homeland are Evangelical Christians.

is essential as to why Filipino is being chosen in this case study of diaspora missiology in action.

1. The Philippines: Geographical Portrait and Historical Sketch

The Philippines is located in the western Pacific, west of Micronesian islands, north of Borneo and south east of China. It has a total land area of 298,170 square kilometers and is composed of 7,100 islands. The islands were first inhabited by "aetas," a small negroid race, and were later followed by Malaysian and Indonesian migrants. As trade developed in the region, Chinese, Indian, and Arab travelers arrived bringing with them a "mix" of culture and religion, including Islam. Hence, Islam had its foothold in southern Philippines prior to the arrival of the Spaniards.

Explorer Ferdinand Magellan landed in Cebu (central Philippine island) "planting the cross" of Roman Catholicism with "the help of the sword" of Spain in 1521. Though the islanders killed Magellan soon after his arrival, his death did not prevent the Spanish from colonizing the islands for over 300 years, and from introducing Catholicism—making the Philippines the first Christian nation of Asia.

Spanish colonization ended in the Philippine Revolution (1896–1898) resulting in the islands' independence on June 12, 1898. However, in the same year the new Republic of the Philippines (the Philippines) fell under American authority as a result of the Spanish-American War and the Treaty of Paris that was signed to end the Spanish-Cuban-American War (1898). A civilian government later replaced American military authorities until the creation of the "ten-year Philippine Commonwealth" in 1935. It must be noted that the Americans brought to the Philippines their own brand of Christianity, which is Protestantism. Providentially, the colonization of the Philippines under Spanish and American rule helped neutralize the advance of Islam in central and northern Philippines.

Though Japanese invasion and occupation of the Philippines during the Second World War interrupted American rule in 1941, the Philippines were recaptured by the United States in 1945. Finally, the American government on July 4, 1946 granted official independence. Since then, the Philippines have suffered under dictatorial regime resulting in a depleted currency, corruption in "high places" and mass poverty of its population.

2. Filipino Diaspora: A Brief Diachronic and Synchronic Reflection

The phenomenon of Filipino diaspora globally has taken place in distinct stages and has accelerated noticeably in the last 150 years. There are records of people from the Philippines traveling during the Spanish era—mostly galleon workers and traders to other ports of the Spanish empire such as Mexico, and wealthy *mestizos* (children as a result of Spanish and native marriages) to Spain and the rest of Europe for education. Large groups of Filipinos leaving the islands for work did not begin until the arrival of the Americans.

The colonial experience of the Philippines with the United States "had a profound impact on Philippine migration."[9] It was during the American colonial period that Filipinos were recruited to migrate to the United States as soldiers in their army, sailors in their navy, workers in their mines, plantations, and factories; and for the children of wealthy Filipinos, as students in their universities.[10] Moreover, Americanization brought the Philippines an education system patterned after the American way, as well as the introduction of American English as a

---

9   Remigio Jr., Amador A. "A Demographic Survey of the Filipino Diaspora," in *Scattered: The Filipino Global Presence*. Luis Pantoja, Sadiri Joy Tira, and Enoch Wan (Eds.). (2004). Manila, Philippines: LifeChange Publishing Inc., p. 6.

10 Remigio, in *Scattered*, p. 27-29, adapting work of Daisy C.S. Catalan (1996).

common language of business and instruction. These American legacies were essential in establishing the Filipinos as important participants in the international labor market, in which English is the current lingua franca and USA-based companies abroad.

In the 1970s, recognizing that their people were assets to the international labor force, the Philippine government formalized an organized system of overseas employment and "started aggressively promot[ing] Filipino skills abroad, particularly in the Middle East" as "a response to the world oil crisis."[11] Demand for Filipino workers increased with changes in the global economy. Pushed out by financial crisis and increasing political instability in the Philippines and pulled by promising jobs in other countries, Filipinos began to leave in massive numbers. By the 1980s what are now referred to as Overseas Filipino Workers (OFWs) were in demand beyond the Middle East and were deployed to most continents.[12]

3. Historico-Demographic Global Distribution of OFWs

Currently, the Philippine Overseas Employment Administration (POEA)[13] reports 8,233,172[14] legal and registered OFWs in 197 countries.[15] Thousands of OFWs leave the Philippines daily. In 2006, new deployments reached a record breaking 1,062,567.[16] The top ten re-

---

11 Baldoz in *Scattered*, p. 39.
12 Remigio in *Scattered*, p. 15-18, citing Rex Varona (February 2001). Excerpted from remarks delivered at the seminar *"On the Philippine Migration Trail: Some Migration and Reproductive Health Aspects."* Bangkok, Thailand.
13 POEA is the government agency responsible for optimizing the benefits of the country's overseas employment program.
14 POEA Philippine Overseas Employment Agency – Department of Labor, Republic of the Philippines, *OFW Global Presence: A Compendium of Overseas Employment Statistics, 2006.* Accessed 15 August 2007, http://www.poea.gov.ph/stats/2006Stats. pdf, p. 51-52.
15 POEA, 2006 Annual Report, p. 8.
16 POEA, *Statistics 2006*, Table 3.

ceiving countries for OFWs in 2006 were (in decreasing order of number of registered OFWs): Saudi Arabia, United Arab Emirates, Hong Kong, Kuwait, Qatar, Taiwan, Singapore, Italy, United Kingdom, and South Korea.[17] They serve their host countries as medical workers, construction workers, performing artists, engineers, teachers, household workers, hotel and restaurant staff, architects, factory workers, and others.[18] Filipino seafarers are also in demand as officers and ship personnel.[19] The top 10 flag registry of deployed seafarers were Panama, Bahamans, Liberia, Marshall Island, Singapore, United Kingdom, Malta, Norway, Cyprus, and the Netherlands. According to Central Bank of the Philippines, OFW remittances to the Philippines reached 12.8 Billion dollars in 2006.[20] For the Philippines, the OFWs are the new "national heroes."[21]

Luis Pantoja Jr., Filipino theologian and senior pastor of one of Metro Manila's largest evangelical churches—Greenhills Christian Fellowship—observes that "on a worldwide scale, royal courts and average households get into disarray because they are dependent on Filipino housekeepers, nannies, and caregivers."[22] This would ring true for the hospitals, offices, ships, airports, and constructions sites around the world that are also dependent on OFWs. Evidently, as the world experiences a "brain gain" because of OFWs, the Philippines has suffered "brain drain" – human resource of massive Filipino leaving the country in droves.

---

17   POEA, *Statistics 2006*, Table 4 and 20.
18   POEA, *Statistics 2006*, Table 17.
19   POEA, *Statistics 2006*, Tables 15 and 16.
20   Central Bank of the Philippines Press Statement, 15 February 2007.
21   President Corazon Aquino first labeled the OFWs the "bagong bayani" or new national heroes for their role in the Philippine economy.
22   Pantoja in *Scattered*, p. 76

4. Religio-Demographic Distribution of OFWs

Despite all the negative aspects surrounding the diaspora of OFWs, their scattering presents an interesting perspective, specifically the Filipino presence in the 10/40 Window.

The Filipino Diaspora's global distribution by major religious blocks is as follows[23]:

- Western World (4 million)
- Buddhist/Hindu World (1.3 million)
- Islamic World (1.7 million)
- Jewish World (30,000)

5. Characteristics of the Filipino

Anthropologists have noted that Filipino culture and language can be described as a fusion of basic Malay traits with foreign influences. Consequently, people in the Philippines are racially and culturally heterogeneous. The Filipinos in diaspora are "natural witnesses of Jesus Christ with great potential for impact wherever they are"[24] due to the following factors: religiously being Catholic, linguistically being English-speaking, socially being friendly, pleasant and adaptable, etc. Due to their history of contrasting cultures and colonization, the Filipinos have been characterized by "The Three 'A's"—adaptable, acceptable, and accessible, as observed[25] by Efraim Tendero, a respected Christian Filipino leader. The Filipinos are known to be culturally adaptable, linguistically flexible, resilient, hospitable, quick to identify

---

23 Estimate of the Filipino International Network (FIN).
24 Dimangondayao in *Scattered*, p. 295
25 ibid.

cross-culturally. They have a happy disposition and are geographically accessible because the government of the Philippines has diplomatic relations with most nations.

SOCIO-ECONOMIC IMPLICATIONS OF FILIPINO DIASPORA

From the phenomenon of Filipino diaspora, several aspects of implications are to be considered (*Lausanne Occasional Paper*, 2005).

1. Economic aspects

Today, there are more than 8 million OFWs deployed in more than 197 countries. As Filipino citizens they are required to send dollar remittances back to the Philippines. According to the Philippine government, OFWs have become the Philippines' major foreign currency earners. In the year 2006 alone, they remitted USD $12.8 billion. Thus, the Philippine president, Gloria Macapagal-Arroyo has hailed OFWs as "the Philippines' modern day heroes."

2. Social aspects

Most of the recent OFW deployments are female (see APPENDIX VII). These women are in the younger age groups (under 35), whereas the male OFWs tend to be in the older age group (35 and above). Many of these female OFWs are employed as medical professionals, domestic workers, caregivers, and entertainers.

A large number of the females have intermarried with locals and has resulted in a surge of *mestizo* children (e.g. Filipino-Japanese, Filipino-Chinese, Filipino-Arab, Filipino-Canadians, Filipino-Italians, etc.). Hence, Filipino blood is now "sprinkled" and "intermingled" across the nations. These OFWs have become an agent of social change in their host nations because they have injected their culture, tradition, and religion into their adoptive communities.

MISSIOLOGICAL IMPLICATIONS FROM THE CASE STUDY OF FILIPINO EXPERIENCE

In the preceding pages of this paper, we have already portrayed the historical, economical, sociological, and demographic dimensions of the Filipino diaspora. Where does it fit into the fulfillment of the Great Commission? What are the threats and opportunities? The Filipino diaspora can now move beyond their obvious concerns (i.e. economic survival) to relate to their host nations and to their own homeland.

Based on the statistic of nearly 8 million OFWs worldwide, 80% are Roman Catholics, 15% are Protestant, and conservative estimates of 7% of these figures are evangelical Christians. With 7% (or 560,000) of the 8 million OFWs being evangelical Christians they become a powerhouse for the cause of world mission.

Wherever there are clusters of Filipino communities, there are also thriving congregations. Today, you will find such congregations in the Canadian prairies, the remote Arctic Circle, the oil fields of the Arabian Peninsula, the urban jungles of Singapore, Hong Kong, Taipei and Tokyo, the islands of the Pacific and in the mega-cities of Europe and North America. There are even fellowship groups on cruise ships and fishing vessels. Since Filipinos are adaptable, acceptable, and accessible, they are now involved in cross-cultural ministries as well. In several cities of the world, including Singapore, Hong Kong, London and Toronto, clusters of Filipino congregations have formed ministerial fellowships for cooperative missions and evangelism initiatives.

Innovative evangelistic strategies include concerts, festivals, literature and video distribution, and compassionate work.

In May 1995, the Filipino International Network (FIN) was launched in response to the need for a coordinated global effort to motivate, equip, and mobilize Christian OFWs to help fulfill the Great Commission. To accomplish this objective, FIN coordinates regional and global strategic consultations for Filipino diaspora leaders: distributing evangelistic tools like the *Jesus Film*, facilitating evangelism and discipleship training seminars, Family Life Conferences to strengthen OFW marriages and to reach the mixed-marriage couples and their families. To undergird all this, FIN gathers Filipino Christian diaspora leaders for Prayer Advance, during which they pray for the Christian witness of diaspora Filipinos both locally and globally.

The effects of Spanish and American colonization in the Philippines are not all negative. Their positive legacy was that they brought Christianity to the Philippines, making it the only Christian nation in Asia. Though their exodus is mainly driven by economics and politics, God's providence and sovereignty has overturned the root cause of the Filipino exodus for His glory. The Filipino diaspora has penetrated the Western world, the Buddhist world, the Islamic world, and the Jewish world.

1. Homeland Connection: Centrifugal and Centripetal Missions

It is a common knowledge that there are more than 3,000 OFWs leaving the country everyday; many of them are bound for CANs. Significant numbers of them are faithful followers of Jesus Christ. "This is not surprising for a number of reasons" says Averell Aragon Professor of Church History at the Alliance Graduate School. He writes:

We live in a country (89 million population) where four million are unemployed and 7.8 million more are underemployed.

Forty percent of the population lives below poverty line (e.g. 2 million families live on less than US$1.00/day).

The average income per capita is only US$1,400. And so because of this grim socio-economic reality, the government through its labor expert program is encouraging its able-bodied and skilled citizens to seek for opportunities to work abroad… In 2006 alone OFWs sent home through commercial banks record US$ 12.8 billion. This accounts for about 10 percent of the country's Gross Domestic Products (GDP). [He goes on:] "Living and working abroad entails personal as well as domestic problems. Many OFWs are often the victims of blatant exploitation and abuse by their recruiters here and employers abroad. Some of them return home physically and psychologically disfigured. To put an end to this problem, representatives of the Association of Southeast Nations (ASEAN) in its 12th Annual Summit held in Cebu City (Philippines) in 2007 signed the ASEAN Declaration for the Protection and Promotion of Rights of Migrant Workers."[26]

Families of OFWs are also suffering at home. Sad and heartbreaking stories are printed in daily newspapers—stories are on the rise of broken marriages, dysfunctional and juvenile delinquent children because of family separations. Consequently, moral instability is increasingly growing and has become a sociological problem and a challenge to the government and the church.

What actions are to be taken by the Philippine Church in light of this situation? Due to the limitation of this paper, we will only highlight a few critical points related to the "Filipino experience."

---

26   Phronesis Vol. 12. No. 2, 2007.

The Philippine Church must intentionally prepare their members for tent-making ministries. It is encouraging to note that the Philippine Missions Association set a goal of 200,000 workers to be deployed by the year 2010 (Lopez in *Scattered: The Global Filipino Presence*). This is a significant number of Kingdom workers to be mobilized. Today, various mission agencies and denominations are conducting tent-making seminars and training "market-place missionaries."

The Central Bank of the Philippines Governor, Armando Tetangco Jr., reported that from January to August 2007 OFW remittances hit US $9.3 billion.[27] It is true that these funds are used to keep the Philippine economy afloat. The point is to show that there are financial resources from the diaspora workers.

Many Filipino Christians working abroad support not only their families but also their home churches. Moreover, in recent years many Filipino diaspora congregations have initiated centripetal missions activities and church planting initiatives in the homeland. The financial contributions of the Filipino diaspora congregation vary from scholarship funds for Bible school students, church planting movements, construction and re-construction of church facilities, and funding of orphanages. Moreover, these diaspora congregations are sending their own short-term mission workers at their own expenses (e.g. medical and dental missions) to conduct holistic missions in disaster-hit areas and with internally displaced communities.

The deployment of Filipino tentmakers particularly to CANs and the Filipino diaspora churches supporting their homeland congregations can be seen as centrifugal and centripetal missions that need to be simultaneously encouraged, affirmed, nurtured and celebrated.

---

27 *Philippine Star* Vol. XXII No. 80 October 16, 2007.

2. Innovative Missions Strategies: Mobilizing the Kingdom's Army and Navy

We have already seen the global dispersion of OFWs both inland and at sea. Filipinos are religious people. Wherever there are Filipinos we find a Roman Catholic or Protestant congregation. We find local churches in the high-rise buildings in Hong Kong and Singapore dominated mostly by Filipino domestic workers. There are fellowship groups among the former prostitutes in Japan. These are women who are now married to Japanese men and have led into the Kingdom their spouses, *mestiso*-children and some of their Japanese in-laws. They are growing in numbers. Every Sunday afternoon, in the central park of Nicosia, Cyprus, we find hundreds of Filipinos turning the park into a meeting point. There we find dozens of bible study and prayer groups meeting in clusters for several hours until sunset. We also find local churches meeting in various places (e.g. government designated worship centers and "underground" places) in the Middle East and North African countries.

We know of a group meeting every Friday in a rented bus. The bus is packed with 50 people; going around the city for two hours. Inside the bus, these Filipino believers with their "local friends" and other expatriate workers worship the Living Jesus Christ who is always present—they sing, they pray, they exhort each other, they receive their tithes and offerings, their leader-pastor preaches, etc. The only thing they don't do inside the bus is water baptism. Three years ago, this group was only meeting in one bus. Today, they have three buses. In a hostile environment these "bus-churches" have to be resourceful for security reasons, but persecution cannot quench their passion for Jesus. Evidently, they are growing!

In recent years there has been an accelerated effort to mobilize Filipino Christian seafarers to reach their co-workers from other countries and many vacationers on board the cruise ships. Martin Otto, a German missions practitioner based in Hamburg, Germany, is intentionally recruiting, training, and mobilizing Filipino seafarers not only to lead Bible studies and facilitate prayer meetings on board the ship, but also to plant "churches on the oceans."[28]

A partnership between FIN, Campus Crusade for Christ, Operation Mobilization, and Seamen's Christian Friend Society has recently been forged to accelerate training of Filipino seafarers to become church planters and pastors of congregations on board the super tankers, con-tainerships, bulk carriers, and cruise ships. Negotiations are underway among partnering organizations to set up a training center in Manila for the future sea-based Kingdom workers.

3. Labor Feminization Impacts Missions

Biblical history and modern history records outstanding women missionaries. Filipino women have a vital role in fulfilling the Great Commission. We refer particularly to the thousands of household maids deployed in high places in the Buddhist, Jewish, and Islamic world. These women enjoy privileged access to the homes of people and families that Western conventional missionaries will never experience. Affluent Arab, Jewish, and Chinese families entrust their children to their Filipino maids. Many of these Filipino nannies and household workers are like the ancient Jochebed who raised Moses to become a national figure in Egypt.

In recent years, some countries have accelerated hiring household workers from India, Thailand, and Indonesia. These workers are hired

---

28 See www.seafarers-ministry.de.

for lower wages than the Filipinos. This current labor trend becomes a missiological issue because workers whose religions are Islam and Buddhism are gradually replacing Filipino Christian women. Philippine labor recruiters believe that Filipino women still have an edge because of their educational background, mastery of the English language, pleasing cultural values and personality traits. However, this labor dominance that they once enjoyed for decades will face competition and will impact missions.

4. Justice and Advocacy Ministry

Aragon notes the suffering of Filipinos who work abroad and the pain of those families left behind in their homeland. Furthermore, he notes that the ASEAN declared to fight for the rights of Migrants Workers. The ASEAN governments need to be commended for their justice and advocacy works. However, the Christian community is specifically exhorted and required to act justly and to love mercy and to walk humbly with God. (Micah 6:8). Both the state and church must develop a strong and efficient mechanism to uphold the rights of the migrant workers. Churches in the diaspora must open their doors as a refuge to the victims of abuse and injustice.

Families of OFWs in the Philippines must be provided with pastoral care. How can Kingdom workers become effective if their own respective loved ones are hurting? This is an urgent need the church in the homeland must address.

5. Missiological Research

The task of mission strategists and missiologists are not only to analyze and describe the phenomenon but also to respond by conducting an ongoing missiological research and formulate a contextual mission strategy. In 2007, the Institute of Diaspora Studies (IDS) was launched in Asia and USA hosted by the Alliance Graduate School in Manila, Philippines and Western Seminary in Portland, Oregon respectively. The "mission" of IDS is to investigate the effective communication of the gospel among the people of diaspora and through their networks to regions beyond. It is a joint effort of researchers and practitioners seeking to understand and minister to the people of diaspora—people dispersed from their original homeland.[29] Filipino missiologists in particular must vigorously engage themselves to research and formulate a distinct Filipino diaspora-missiology in order to accelerate awareness of the unique role of the Filipinos in global missions.

In his recent article in EMS Occasional Bulletin Spring 2007 Issue, Enoch Wan, one of the pioneers in diaspora missiology, describes the distinctive features of "diaspora missiology" from "traditional missiology." In the charts bellow, Wan summarizes the tenets of diaspora missiology. These are helpful guides to [Filipino] missiologists and practitioners to formulate mission strategies.

---

29   See www.globalmissiology.org and www.fin-online.org.

#	Aspects	Traditional Missiology ←→	Diaspora Missiology
1	Focus	Polarized/dichotomized -"great commission" ←→ "great commandment" -saving soul ←→ social Gospel -church planting ←→ Christian charity -paternalism ←→ indigenization	-Holistic Christianity with strong integration of evangelism with Christian charity -contextualization
2	Conceptualization	-territorial: here ←→ there -"local" ←→ "global" -lineal: "sending" ←→ "receiving" -"assimilation" ←→ "amalgamation" -"specialization"	-"deterritorialization"2 -"glocal" (Tira) -"mutuality" & "reciprocity" -"hybridity" -"inter-disciplinary"
3	Perspec-Tive	-geographically divided: foreign mission ←→ local, urban ←→ rural -geo-political boundary: state/nation ←→ state/nation -disciplinary compartmentalization: e.g. theology of missions/strategy of missions	-non-spatial, - "borderless," no boundary to worry, transnational & global -new approach: integrated & Interdisciplinary
4	Paradigm	-OT: missions = gentile-proselyte --- coming -NT: missions = the Great Commission --- going -Modern missions: E-1, E-2, E-3 or M-1, M-2. M-3, etc.	-New reality in the 21st Century – viewing & following God's way of providentially moving people spatially & spiritually. -moving targets & move with the targets

FIGURE 1. *"Traditional missiology" vis-à-vis "diaspora missiology":*

4 elements

#	Aspects	Traditional Missiology ←→ Dispora Missiology	
1	Ministry Pattern	OT: calling of gentile to Jehovah (coming) NT: sending out disciples by Jesus in the four Gospels & by the H.S. in Acts (going) Modern missions: -sending missionary & money -self sufficient of mission entity	-new way of doing Christian missions: "mission at our doorstep" -"ministry without border" -"networking & partnership" for the Kingdom -"borderless church" (Lundy). "liquid church" (Ward) -"church on the oceans" (Otto)
2	Ministry Style	-cultural-linguistic barrier: E-1, E-2, etc. Thus various types: M-1, M-2, etc. -"people group" identity -evangelistic scale: reached →← unreached -"competitive spirit" "self sufficient"	-no barrier to worry -mobile and fluid, -hyphenated identity & ethnicity -no unreached people -"partnership,"3 "networking" & synergy

FIGURE 2. Comparing traditional missiology &
diaspora missiology in ministry

No	Yes
-No visa required	-Yes, door opened
-No closed door	-Yes, people accessible
-No international travel required	-Yes, missions at our doorstep
-No political/legal restrictions	-Yes, ample opportunities
-No dichotomized approach	-Yes, holistic ministries
-No sense of self-sufficiency & unhealthy competition	-Yes, powerful partnership

FIGURE 3. The "yes" and "no" of "Mission at our Doorstep"

Conclusion and Recommendations for Future Study

In this study, the Filipino experience has been described in details to illustrate diaspora in missions. It is a case study of "Mission Initiatives from the Majority World Churches"and was presented at EMS-Northwest to show forth one of the initiatives from the majority world churches, just like the movement of CCCOWE[30] among the Chinese diaspora.[31]

The Filipino experience in diaspora missions also illustrates the providential grace of God in spite of the painful past of colonization of the Philippines by Western powers and sorrowful financial state of contemporary Filipino society. Hence, the sovereignty of God is evidently shown in the scattering of Filipinos globally for a purpose. The Filipino experience is a case study of mission initiatives from the majority world churches. It is diaspora mission in action—those being scattered have become gatherers for the Kingdom in many nations.

The following are recommendations for further study:

Accelerated equipping of tentmakers (land based and sea based OFWs) both for those who are already in the field and for those preparing to leave the country; theological training for those who are leading Filipino diaspora congregations.

Strategic partnership is called for like minded organizations and institutions in the delivery of evangelistic resources (e.g. *Jesus Film*) into

---

30 Chinese Coordination Centre of World Evangelism. For details, see http://www. cccowe.org/eng/content.php?id=9.
31 See Wan, 2007, for details on Chinese diaspora and Christian missions.

the hands of Filipino kingdom workers, particularly those strategically positioned in CANs.

Connect abused and persecuted workers with advocacy and justice organizations in order to safeguard their rights and safety.

Provide pastoral care for the families of OFWs left behind in the homeland.

BIBLIOGRAPHY

Abella, Manolo (1993) "Labor Mobility, Trade and Structural Change: The Philippine experience" in *Asian and Pacific Migration Journal.* Vol.2, No. 3, 249-268.

Agoncillo, Teodoro A. (1990). *History of the Filipino People.* Quezon City: GAROTECH Publishing.

Alburo, Florian (1993) "Remittances, Trade and the Philippine Economy" in *Asian and Pacific Migration Journal.* Vol.2, No. 3, 269-284.

Andres, Thomas D. (1980). *Understanding Values.* Quezon City, Philippines: New Day Publishers.

_____. (1988). *Managing People by Filipino Values.* Quezon City, Philippines: Publishers Press.

Aragon, Averell (Ed.). (2007). *Phronesis: A Journal of Asian Theological Seminary and Alliance Graduate School* Vol. 12, No.2, 2007.

Arcinas, Fe R. (1986). *The Odyssey of the Filipino Migrant Workers to the Gulf Region.* Quezon City, Philippines: University of the Philippines Press.

Ballescas, Maria Rosario, P. (1992) *Filipino Entertainers in Japan: an Introduction.* Quezon City: The Foundation for Nationalist Studies.

Beltran, Ruby P. & Gloria F. Rodriguez, eds. (1996). *Filipino Women Migrant Workers: At the Crossroads and Beyond Beijing.* Quezon City, Philippines: Giraffe Books.

Catholic Institute for International Relations (1987). *The Labor Trade: Filipino Migrant Workers Around the World.* London: Catholic Institute for International Relations.

Central Bank of the Philippines. (15 February 2007). Press Statement. Accessed 2 September 2007. <http://72.14.253.104/search?q=cache:gcX4DnqrCTAJ:www.iro.ph/downloads/pressrelease/021507%2520BSP%2520-%2520OFW%2520Remittances%2520Hit%2520US%2412.8%2520Billion%2520in%25202006,%2520exceeding%2520the%2520forecast%2520by%2520US%240.5%2520Billion.pdf+bangko+sentral+ng+pilipinas+press+statement+%2215+february+2007%22&hl=en&ct=clnk&cd=2&gl=ca>.

Chant, Sylvia & Cathy McIlwaine. (1995). *Women of a Lesser Cost: Female Labor; Foreign Exchange & Philippine Development.* Quezon City, Philippines: Ateneo de Manila University Press.

Chen, Anita Beltran. (1998). *From Sunbelt to Snowbelt: Filipinos in Canada.* Calgary: Canadian Ethnic Studies Association.

Claro, Robert. (2003). *A Higher Purpose: For Your Overseas Job.* Makati City, Philippines: CrossOver Books.

Commission on Filipinos Overseas (COF). (2001). Annual Report 2001. Manila, Philippines: Department of Foreign Affairs.

Constable, Nicole (1997). *Maid to Order in Hong Kong: Stories of Filipina Workers.* Ithaca, New York: Cornell University Press.

Diamond, David (June 2002) "One Nation, Overseas" in *Wired,* Issue 10.06.

Feliciano, Evelyn. (1988) *All Things To All Men: An Introduction to Missions in Filipino Culture.* Quezon City, Philippines: New Day Publishers.

_____. (1990). *Filipino Values and Our Christian Faith.* Manila, Philippines: OMF Literature Inc.

Houston, Tom. (1998, March). Global Clashes, Global Gospel. Unpublished paper presented at the Lausanne International Leaders Conference. Toronto, Canada.

International Organization for Migration. (2005). *World Migration: Costs and Benefits of International Migration 2005.* Vol. 3. Geneva, Switzerland: International Organization for Migration.

-----. (No listed date of last update). International Organization for Migration: The Migration Agency. Accessed 15 August 2007. <http://iom.int/jahia/jsp/index.jsp>

Jocano, F. Landa. (1997*). Filipino Value System: A Cultural Definition.* Metro Manila, Philippines: Punlad.

Johnstone, Patrick and Jason Mandryk. (2001). *Operation World 21st Century Edition*. Giorgia, USA: Paternoster.

Kalaw-Tirol, Lorna, ed. (2000). *From America to Africa: Voices of Filipino Women Overseas*. Makati City, Philippines: FAI Resource Management Inc.

Lausanne Committee for World Evangelization Issue Group No. 26 A and B: Diasporas and International Students. (2005). *Lausanne Occasional Paper 55: The new people next door*. In D. Clayton (Series Ed.), 2004 Forum Occasional Papers, September 29—October 5, 2004. Delhi, India: Horizon Printers and Publishers.

Lee, Samuel. (2006). *Blessed Migrants: God's strategy for global revival*. The Netherlands: Ministry House.

Manzano, Jojo and Joy C. Solina Edtirors. (2007). *Worker to Witness: Becoming an OFW Tentmaker*. Makati, Philippines: Church Strengthening Ministry Inc.

Mercado, Leonardo N. (1975). *Elements of Filipino Theology*. Philippines: Divine Word University Publication.

Muck, Terry C. (Ed.). (2003). Missiology An International Review: *Mission and Migration* 31,1.

Otto, Marvin (2007). *Church on the Oceans: A Missionary Vision for the 21st Century*. Carlisle, California: Piquant Editions.

Paguio, Wilfredo C. (1978). *Filipino Cultural Values for the Apostolate*. Makati, Philippines: St. Paul Publication.

Pantoja, Luis, Sadiri Joy Tira, and Enoch Wan (Eds.). (2004). *Scattered: The Filipino global Presence*. Manila, Philippines: LifeChange Publishing Inc.

Philippine Star. (2007). Philippine Star Vol. XXII No. 80 October 16, 2007.

POEA. Philippine Overseas Employment Agency – Department of Labor, Republic of the Philippines. (August 15, 2007). *OFW Global Presence: A Compendium of Overseas Employment Statistics, 2006*. Accessed 15 August 2007. www.poea.gov.ph/stats/2006Stats.pdf.

Rhodes, Stephen A. (1998). *Where the Nations Meet: The Church in a Multicultural World*. Downers Grove, Illinois: InterVarsity Press.

Schoenberger, Karl (1994), 'Living Off Expatriate Labor", *Los Angeles Times*, August 1, 1994, 1.

San Juan, Jr, E. (1998). *From Exile to Diaspora: Versions of the Filipino Experience in the United States*. Boulder, Colorado: Westview Press.

Seim, Brian (Ed.). (1999). *Canada's New Harvest: Helping Churches Touch Newcomers.* Canada: SIM Canada.

Tano, Roodrigo D. (1981). *Theology in the Philippine Setting.* Quezon City, Philippines: New Day Publishers.

Thomas, T.V. (1998, March). *Mobilizing the Diaspora in Canada for Mission.* Unpublished paper presented at the Lausanne International Leadership Conference hosted by Lausanne Canada at Tyndale College & Seminary, Toronto, Canada.

Tiplady, Richard (Ed.). (2003). *One World or Many?: The Impact of Globalization on Mission.* In Globalization of Mission Series. Pasadena, California: William Carey Library.

Tira, Sadiri Joy. (1998, April). *Scattered With a Divine Purpose: A Theological & Missiological Perspective on the Filipino Diaspora.* Unpublished paper presented at the Asia Pacific Alliance (C&MA) Conference, Taipei, Taiwan.

Torres-D'Mello, Arlene. (2001). *Being Filipino Abroad.* Quezon City, Philippines: Giraffe Books.

Wan, Enoch (Ed.). (1995). *Missions Within Reach: Intercultural Ministries in Canada.* Hong Kong: China Alliance Press.

_____. (Spring 2007). "Diaspora Missiology" in *Occasional Bulletin of EMS* Spring 2007.

Footnotes

1   The Tibetan Government in Exile, "Tibet in Exile at a Glance"; available at http://www.tibet.com/exileglance.html (accessed 1 November 2006). This information is based on the Tibetan Demographic Survey of 1998, conducted by the Planning Council, Dharamsala.

2   "deterritorialization" is the "loss of social and cultural boundaries." (Wan)

3   "Partnership" defined: entities that are separate and autonomous but complementary, sharing with equality and mutuality." (Wan)